Praise for 'SEO

"This Majestic series is always an absolute hit - it sha[res insights from]
experts in the world. SEOin2023 is no different. This [is a must-read for anyone]
in the SEO game!"
BILLIE GEENA HYDE
Learning & Development Manager, SALT Agency

"Everyone is busy these days and prioritisation of what to focus on in SEO can be greatly assisted by the good advice given by the authors in this book."
DAVID IWANOW
Head of Search, Reckitt

"David & Majestic have created a masterpiece with SEOin2023. It's jam-packed with expert practical advice, guidance, and knowledge for all levels of SEO professionals. This is a must-read and will definitely help you to prioritise, plan, and strategise for 2023."
SARAH MCDOWELL
SEO Manager, Captivate

"This might be one of the most comprehensive pieces in SEO today, looking at every aspect of it in detail from high level to the nitty gritty stuff."
ULRIKA VIBERG
Agency Leader and Senior SEO Consultant

"You'll struggle to find a wider range of insightful, practical & thought-provoking tips than this book. Essential reading for any SEO looking to up their game, SEOin2023 has advice from many of the best minds in the industry. Whatever your speciality, you'll find something incredibly helpful here. I know I'll be referencing it for a long time."
CHARLIE WILLIAMS
Consultant, Chopped Digital

"This is a practical collection of advice based on our experience as practitioners, which may benefit other SEOs by helping them to plan for success during 2023 and beyond."
MONTSERRAT CANO
International SEO and Digital Marketing Consultant

"There's no other book that takes so much SEO expertise, from so many experts, and distils it into actionable advice. Whether you're looking for strategy, tactics, or inspiration, this is a must-have."
JONO ALDERSON
Head of SEO, Yoast

"SEO is a massive topic that is changing incredibly fast. It is super difficult to keep up. These yearly books by Majestic and David Bain are brilliant - they are my go-to resource to summarise each year in SEO that allows me to focus better year after year. Genius!"
JASON BARNARD
Founder, Kalicube

"The SEO industry is built on knowledge sharing… and Majestic's annual check-ins with peers and industry thought leaders have become an invaluable way to keep your finger on the pulse of the search marketing world. The huge span of topics included for 2023 just goes to show how much of a varied and rich industry we work in."
JAKE GAUNTLEY
SEO Account Director, Reprise Digital

"The team have done a great job of getting thoughts from every edge of SEO, from a fab panel of experts. Just looking at the contributors you can't fail to see how broad a discipline SEO has become. I'm super excited to read and see what the future holds!"
EILISH HUGHES
SEO & Content Account Director, Mindshare

"This is a powerhouse collection of actionable insights from some of the greats in digital marketing, while also remaining accessible to those who might be first starting their journey. As someone who has to live in multiple online channels, I appreciate the integrated perspective and how much this SEO book is about holistic profit and operational success. A great addition for practitioner, strategist, and owner alike!"
NAVAH HOPKINS
CEO, Navah Hopkins LLC

"If you're new to SEO, you can't find a more comprehensive set of insights into the latest industry trends. If you've been in the industry for a time, you'll know that SEO is constantly evolving. This book is a great way to update your knowledge from leading industry experts."
PAIGE HOBART
SEO Manager, Unily

"The best way to learn SEO is to learn from your peers. What better way to do this than to dive in this book? You'll get direct insights from some of the smartest SEOs in the industry to level-up your game in 2023."
MYRIAM JESSIER
SEO trainer & consultant, PRAGM

"I am loving the fact that SEO is not just an isolated marketing channel but it communicates with other channels, professions, and many stakeholders. Having an understanding of this and helping SEO - or at least the way we make SEO evolve - is crucial. Doesn't communicating with other stakeholders and integrating SEO with other professions such as data science and analytics, UX and web design sound mesmerizing to you, too?"
BEGUM KAYA
Founder & SEO Consultant, BK Solutions

"Whether you've just started out in SEO or been in the industry for a while, SEOin2023 is a great series to educate and stay up to date on the best practices within the industry."
EVA CHENG
Digital PR Consultant, Evolved

"David Bain always creates the most comprehensive and information-rich SEO resource each year! Read this to stay cutting-edge!"

KORAY TUĞBERK GÜBÜR

Holistic SEO & Digital

"Whether you're new to SEO or just wanting to keep up or refresh, this guide is here to take you to 2023 and beyond."

NATALIE ARNEY

Freelance SEO Consultant

"On my desk for 2023 will be SEOin2023! If you need some advice and inspiration, this one is definitely worth your attention. Admired everything from beginning till the very end."

OLESIA KOROBKA

SEO Entrepreneur, Fajela

"SEOin2023 presents a solid guide for what is essential for Search Engine Optimization in the coming year. Presented within are SEO professionals and practitioners who are walking the talk every day and are sharing their experiential knowledge and learned predictions with us all."

BRENDA MALONE

Senior Technical SEO Specialist, NP Digital

"It's often difficult to know where to start, but David Bain has done us all a favour by curating advice from widely respected, leading SEO practitioners and organised them in such a way that you can read chronologically how to think, what to look out for and get an edge on your campaigns for 2023."

NIK RANGER

Senior Technical SEO, Dejan Marketing

"What an amazing and diverse gathering of different opinions and points of view."

FILIPA SERRA GASPAR

SEO Consultant

"This book is definitely one of the highlights of the SEO year. So many inspiring colleagues are sharing their knowledge selflessly and it's worth reading every interview. Thanks for that and thanks to David for his superb way to organize the talks. I enjoyed it."

ANDOR PALAU

International SEO Consultant, AndorPalau.com

"There is no better organizer, crew, and list of professionals than included in this SEO informational masterpiece. If there was anyone who knew how to ask the right questions, it is undoubtedly the master interviewer David Bain with Majestic. I am honored to be a part of it and look forward to sharing my professional SEO knowledge as much as possible with works like this one. I hope to be included in the future! Thanks again for such a fantastic effort for the community!"

JOSEPH KAHN

President and CTO of Hum JAM

"It's not an easy task to keep up to speed with the ever-evolving world of SEO. Thanks to David and Majestic we have an annual guide condensing the knowledge and experience of some of the industry's brightest talents. SEOin2023 is a must-read to stay ahead of the curve."

KERSTIN REICHERT
SEO & Content Lead, Seed Legals

"A must-have collection of advice and techniques used by the best in the industry. This book will help experienced and new SEOs around the world."

LUIS, RODRIGUEZ
Head of SEO, Booking.com

"Thank you to the whole team who made this book possible! It's wonderful to see so many different SEOs sharing their knowledge. I hope it will support and inspire many people in their career paths. I'm happy to be part of a project that contributes to sharing and making our industry a kind place."

ISALINE MUELHAUSER
International SEO consultant, Pilea.ch

"I've really enjoyed sharing tips with David, Majestic, and the readers of SEOin2022 and 2023. David is a lovely interviewer and I was very happy to return for 2 consecutive years. The book and recordings compile so much wisdom from so many experts that it makes me very proud to have been a part of it."

ORIT MUTZNIK
SEO Director, Forbes

"SEO is constantly evolving, as the platforms and user behaviour change. Keeping on top of the techniques that are effective is essential for any digital manager. SEOin2023, is a collection of the tactics and strategies that are being employed across the leading in-house brands globally - as told by the leading practitioners of the discipline."

NICK WILSDON
Founder/CEO, Torque Partnership

"Really pleased to be a part of SEOin2023, it's a great approach of grabbing some of the most important strategies and tactics that are getting actual results."

MARK WILLIAMS-COOK
Director, Candour, and Founder, AlsoAsked

"SEOin2023 is ideal for anyone wanting to apply the principles of SEO to a number of different industries and niches. The interviews are well laid out and show the passion and commitment of David towards the SEO community."

MARCO BONOMO
Global SEO Operations Lead, Philip Morris International

"SEO is above all practice, perseverance, and sharing. With this book, you will expand your vision, leverage the experience of others, and save valuable time."

ANDREA PATERNOSTRO

Publisher and Professor of Digital Marketing

"SEOin2023 is a brilliant project to collect tips from the industry experts who are regularly updating themselves about the ever-changing SEO industry. There can't be a better place to start your SEO strategy for 2023 and beyond, than this."

NITIN MANCHANDA

Founder, Botpresso

"We are in a very exciting time for SEO and digital marketing in general. SEOin2023 is a great way to get insights and trends for what really matters in search."

CRYSTAL CARTER

Head of SEO Communications, Wix

"SEOin2023 is a project that has had a lot of effort put into it. I am happy to take part in this book, where many professional SEOs with different specializations have included their experiences! I would also like to thank David for his professionalism and for giving me this opportunity!"

TEVFIK MERT AZIZOĞLU

Senior Technical SEO, SEO Sherpa

"They really have pulled together a lot of great minds and insights in this book - People who really have their finger on the pulse of modern digital marketing."

CINDY KRUM

CEO & Founder, MobileMoxie

SEOin2023

101 of the world's leading SEOs share their number 1, actionable tip for 2023

DAVID BAIN

Copyright © 2022-2023 Majestic-12 Ltd

All rights reserved.

ISBN: 9798363076367

TO THE SEO AND DIGITAL MARKETING
COMMUNITY –
THANK YOU FOR YOUR CONTINUED SUPPORT

CONTENTS

Foreword		1
Opening thoughts		5
CHAPTER 1	*Key considerations*	9
CHAPTER 2	*Auditing*	41
CHAPTER 3	*Content structure*	75
CHAPTER 4	*Targeting*	113
CHAPTER 5	*Content planning*	149
CHAPTER 6	*Content production*	189
CHAPTER 7	*Guide the bots*	221
CHAPTER 8	*SERP SEO*	249
CHAPTER 9	*User-centricity*	273
CHAPTER 10	*Links*	321
CHAPTER 11	*Local SEO*	349
CHAPTER 12	*Integrate*	365
CHAPTER 13	*Think outside the box*	379
CHAPTER 14	*Analytics & testing*	413
CHAPTER 15	*Evergreen advice*	463
Closing thoughts		497

FOREWORD

Hi! It's a pleasure to introduce SEOin2023. It feels like a lot of time has passed since I put pen to paper to write the introduction for SEOin2022.

If you missed SEOin2022, then I'm sorry! Way back in 2021, David Bain approached us with the concept of Majestic sponsoring a knowledge-sharing exercise where we would interview a number of experts in SEO with the aim of exploring actionable advice for SEO in 2022, and share their interviews and expertise via video, podcast, and the written word. That content is available for free at SEOin2022.com.

If you have read SEOin2022, you will be delighted to know that SEOin2023 is a brand new work. Some of the faces may be familiar, but the content is fresh. David has gone back to the drawing board, with the panel of experts generously giving their time in new interviews for this project.

Once again, we are making the content free, with the book being available for those (like me) who appreciate print on paper.

I'd like to thank David, our team at Majestic who work hard to support this project, and the generous contributors who have kindly shared their time and experience.

Our first venture, SEOin2022, was a learning experience for us. We hope we've taken on board some of the lessons learned to make SEOin2023 a bigger, better experience for 2023. The contributor count has increased – from sixty-six to (just) breaking the century at one-hundred-and-one.

One of the challenges we faced when launching SEOin2022 is one many SaaS founders may identify with – pricing. It can be a challenge to find an appropriate price point on which to place one's product or service. In the end, we opted for a price that sat comfortably amongst its peers. Our decision was, as is much in digital marketing, based on data. However, the choices based on positioning and competitor analysis were a little different to the norm. We were very keen NOT to disrupt the book market. Regardless of the rules set by the publishing platform, we didn't want to upset any authors of other SEO publications by effectively dumping marketing collateral at a price too close to cost. We wanted the print copy to live nicely with its neighbours and to add to the community rather than detract from it.

This brings us to another lesson. Having had very little experience in publishing, it was hard for us to predict sales for the book - a problem made even more complicated by the content being available for free by other means.

This left us with a slight quandary of having an income stream that we didn't wish to be seen to profit from, but with little to indicate the scale of funds that might be realised from it. We knew we wanted to do something with the something that might be raised, but there were a lot of unknowns.

As a result, we earmarked the funds raised from sales of the book (after publishing costs, etc.) in the hope that we could identify a worthwhile cause. As luck would have it, we were approached by Rejoice Ojiaku, Co-Founder & Community Partnership Lead of B-DigitalUK. B-DigitalUK is an online community supporting the Black demographic within Digital Marketing. They share educational content, amplify Black Talent, and offer workshops and events opportunities to their members. We discovered that Rejoice, and her Co-Founder Wilhemina, were seeking to put on their first in-person event and we're delighted to be able to contribute the profits of sales from SEOin2022 towards their event.

This is not our first involvement supporting a community event. For many years now, Majestic has contributed towards the local tech community around its base. We've been involved in events like Hack the Midlands, Student Hackathons and local grassroots tech groups. We don't claim to be perfect. We are, however, working hard to ensure that our business has a healthy relationship with our local community.

Balancing our relationship with the community and our status as a profit-making business presents challenges. It also presents opportunities. It's an approach that's been described to me as "enlighted self-interest". In plain English, it's working with partners to achieve strategic wins. An example of this approach is in our recruitment. We work with local student groups and universities to build relationships with the local student body. We then find ourselves in the position of being able to discuss our career opportunities with, to some extent, a self-qualifying pool of candidates. Our outreach takes the form of sponsoring student events, engaging with student groups and local universities, and performing guest lectures. We steer clear of pushing our program in early contact, instead focusing on each student's needs. From a cynical perspective, it could be suggested that we are applying a blend of the Ansoff Matrix with a content-driven Sales Funnel approach to our outreach. However, to do so would miss the authenticity of our program. Having recognised, and invested in, the strategic value of our program early on, our program is about as self-sustaining as recruitment gets in an SME. Recruits from previous years have gone on to develop and work on various phases of recruitment and outreach. If our placement program has a sales team, it is formed of expert practitioners who have reaped the benefits of the program themselves.

We haven't rested on our laurels. The Princess Royal Training Awards is an annual event run by the respected City and Guilds of London Institute. Her Royal Highness The Princess Royal, Princess Anne supports the awards program which recognises, "employers who have created outstanding training and skills development programmes which have resulted in exceptional benefits." Majestic is pleased to have won an award on two occasions. Firstly, in 2018, in recognition of our innovative approach to working with local universities. More recently, we collected our 2021 award in May 2022. Our award in 2022 was in part a reflection on our work to try to provide a level playing field to applicants seeking work at Majestic. Our team reviewed our interview and selection processes to identify elements which may act as a barrier to recruitment. Subtleties such as gendered language in recruitment adverts were considered, in addition to more significant changes around optimising recruitment processes to minimise the time taken between an application deadline and notification of preferred candidates.

We aren't perfect. We may never be. But we are working hard to achieve our strategic aims for our business and those of our customers and stakeholders. We are a company that is knowledge focused. I wanted to share this part of our story with you to illustrate why the collaborative nature of SEOin2023 is so important to us.

I'd like to thank David Bain, founder of Casting Cred, for working with us again this year to capture a contemporary industry opinion of good practice for SEO. David's experience in podcasting and B2B vlogging has been essential. We wouldn't have a guide without him. I'd like to thank all of our team for supporting this production.

My closing thanks go to you, the reader, and the great many generous contributors who have given their time to share knowledge and help grow the skills of our industry.

I hope you enjoy SEOin2023!

Steve Pitchford
Operations Director
Majestic.com

OPENING THOUGHTS

SEO doesn't change. SEO changes all the time. It's a funny old game!

While it can be argued that the principles of good, solid SEO tend to remain the same - unless you stay on top of the constant flow of evolving algorithm updates, the coding and technical updates required to help search engines quickly and clearly understand what you've published, and the ways in which you can continue to improve on how you serve your users, you're going to find it tougher and tougher to compete with your competitors as time goes by.

It's easy to say glibly "just publish great content" but, unless you surround that great content with best practice in other areas, your chances of success will continue to diminish.

Of course, it's true that if you practiced great SEO in 2022, you won't go too far wrong if you keep on doing the same things in 2023. But, SEO isn't about playing safe. We all know that you can expect a lot more traffic by being in position number one compared with number two, and it's also likely that you have hundreds of competitors in your niche. If you really want to win in this game, you'll want to achieve as many number one rankings as possible. That's not going to be achieved by playing the game how it used to work, no matter how stable and consistent your strategy was.

SEOin2023 is a collection of key areas to contemplate incorporating into your SEO mix over the coming year. However, not every idea in this book is going to be right for you and your business. That's fine - every SEO is dealing with a slightly different situation. Pick the ideas that are right for you in this book, and run with them.

What this book is, and what this book isn't

I also want to say a few words about what this book is, and what this book isn't intended to be. Let's start with what this book isn't. It's not a comprehensive guide to any individual aspect of SEO, and it's not an A-to-Z general guide to doing SEO. There are many different layers to each aspect of SEO, and each conversation that I have had with each of the 101 SEO experts that feature in the book is intended to raise the importance of an individual SEO activity. It's intended to introduce or re-introduce something to your attention and to give you an opportunity to research it further, so that you can decide whether or not to incorporate it into your own SEO strategy. SEOin2023 shares a snapshot of what some of the world's leading SEOs are going to be prioritising over the coming year. It's then over to you to select the topics that you feel to be relevant for your situation, to go and research them in greater depth, and then to decide whether or not to incorporate them in your strategy and, if so, how.

What's included?

What's included in this book? As you know already, SEOin2023 features 101 top SEO experts, all giving their perspective on the key thing that you should be focusing on in 2023. Some tips may be similar, but they all have different perspectives. I've categorised the tips as follows:

CHAPTER 1: Key Considerations – Chapter one intends to provide an overview of what's changed and where SEO is going in general.

CHAPTER 2: Auditing – What drives technical success in 2023 and what you should be looking out for that may harm your technical success.

CHAPTER 3: Content Structure – Why E-A-T is important, and how to structure your content in a way that appeals to people as well as search engines.

CHAPTER 4: Targeting – Why intent matters and how to focus your efforts on reaching the right person at the right time.

CHAPTER 5: Content Planning – The key elements to incorporate as part of a content strategy.

CHAPTER 6: Content Production – What to include in your content specifically, and what type of content works best.

CHAPTER 7: Guide the Bots – How to help Google and other search engines more quickly and more easily understand, and be confident in the meaning of your content.

CHAPTER 8: SERP SEO – Why you need to stay on top of what the SERP looks like for your target queries and how to use the SERP to style your content.

CHAPTER 9: User Centricity – Why focusing on users is important for SEO and how user experience impacts SEO.

CHAPTER 10: Links – What link building looks like in 2023 and how to optimize your internal links.

CHAPTER 11: Local SEO – How Google Business Profile is changing and thoughts around location schema.

CHAPTER 12: Integrate – How you can be more effective at SEO by working more closely with other digital marketing channels.

CHAPTER 13: Think Outside the Box – Opportunities that could radically change the way that you do SEO over the coming year.

CHAPTER 14: Analytics & Testing – What to measure, how to measure it, and how to improve what you do through testing.

CHAPTER 15: Evergreen Advice – Key elements that you shouldn't forget about – and, if all else fails, how to find a new SEO job!

As ever, I'd really appreciate your thoughts as you make your way through the book. Why not share those thoughts as well? Tweet your thoughts to @Majestic, #SEOin2023, and the tip contributor handle to join in the conversation!

Finally, you may be reading SEOin2023 the book, but this content also exists as a podcast and video series. Check that out over at SEOin2023.com.

Until we meet again, happy SEO'ing!

David Bain
Author, *SEOin2023*
Founder, *CastingCred.com*

1 KEY CONSIDERATIONS

Move from SEO'ing for 'information retrieval' to SEO'ing for 'information suggestion' — Martin MacDonald

Martin MacDonald helps SEOs in 2023 to understand how Google is shifting from informational retrieval to informational suggestion, how the game is changing, and why having richer content and good media assets is a must if you want to compete on the SERP of tomorrow.

Martin says: "We're finally reaching the year that Google is moving away from the environment we've had for the last two decades of 10 blue links. They're moving away from being a purely informational retrieval system to an informational suggestion system.

Google Discover has been a thing for the last few years but, increasingly (if you follow Barry Schwartz's updates), we see tests where they're injecting additional panels into the overall search results. This has to be a manoeuvre to try and get back some of the eyeball time that Google has been losing to social media like Facebook and Twitter - and that YouTube is losing to TikTok.

You can expect a much richer content-based front end for search results over the next year. If you aren't ready for this - if you have a website that's entirely based on text, you haven't got good media assets on your website, or you're not using OG definitions for images - then you're going to be losing out.

Unless Google is able to correctly define your content in the Knowledge Panel that's going to become part of the search results, then you're going to lose your CTR. You need to start focusing on things outside of the words that appear on the page and look at the entire multimedia return that each one of your web pages is giving"

What do SEOs need to do differently to adapt to this new world?

"You need to have a clearer understanding. It's not about using marketing personas in the old sense - where we would make up an individual and then target them - you need to think more about marketing personas in the individual sense.

Google has an amazing understanding of the items that a user is interested in once they recognise that individual. If you open a new tab in Chrome now, you get very good and very personalised Discover suggestions, and all of these are entirely unique to the individual. Google has been experimenting with this for over a year now, and it demonstrates that they understand the best results for what people are searching for, but also the items that people are going to be most interested in.

To understand this, look at the entities that individual pages or pieces of content are returning through various APIs. If you assume that Google maintains a table defining the interests of individuals that it recognises in order to build Discover recommendations, you can see how it would be able to associate content with what that content is about and associate what that content is about with whether or not you're going to be interested in it.

In order to have your content surface in that environment (particularly if this way of thinking makes its way through to actual search results), you are going to need a rich level of content to compete.

If you go back 10 or 15 years, we used to get by with two or three sentences of poorly constructed Markov-chained content on a web page. Over time, those requirements have expanded. It became: more text, longer text, more unique text, more readable text, better text, etc. It has become harder and harder as the years have gone by. However, every one of those things was about the text.

Google have the Discover product, they have YouTube, they have user data, and they have people's search queries. What they've never done is tied all of these things together. Now, you can see how they would be able to do that and start taking chunks out of the Facebooks, Twitters, and TikToks of this world.

Ultimately, Google's mission has changed. Back when they formed 20 years ago, they wanted to catalogue and categorise the world's information and make it available to search. I don't think that's their mission statement anymore. I think their mission statement is quite clearly: 'We want to have the most eyeball time and attention focused on us of any company on the internet.' This is the only realistic way that they can leverage their dominance in search to be able to compete in the attention economy, which is something that they've been losing out on to Reddit, Facebook, Twitter, TikTok, et al, for the last couple of years.

When they've tried to compete with these platforms in their own verticals, it's never worked out very well. I can see them developing something that sits in the middle instead, and leveraging their dominance on search by injecting a much richer ecosystem into the search results. That would change Google from the 10 blue links that we think of now into a much more social-media-looking environment, but through the rich content that you're seeing; tailored to what you're searching for, plus what your interests are. That's going to be a fundamental change over the coming years."

How do you define your relevance to an entity?

"It is still about schema and building authority because those things are not going to go away. Schema allows Google to have a much quicker and easier understanding of the content that's on the webpage, and authority is something that's always going to be important from a ranking perspective.

There is more to it now, though. If you pass content through any of the NLP APIs (there's a fantastic tool out there specialising in this right now, but other APIs are available too), what it returns back to you are recognised entities. Those entities are things that it recognises on that page. If you analyse the entities that appear on each one of the pages in a set of search results, you can see what is present on pages 1 through 6 that isn't present on pages 7, 8, or 9.

We conducted some experiments in 2021 and early 2022, where we used this method to plug the gap in the content on a couple of eCommerce sites. We did this by making sure that all of the relevant pages had the information that Google was expecting to see for one of the top results – and our testing was extremely positive. Certain things were highlighted that you simply wouldn't have noticed, had you not been able to accumulate this data for an entire SERP set.

For instance, there was a specific individual that was relevant to the history of a product that was mentioned in the top 3 or 4 results, so we passed this on to the client (a luxury goods eCommerce company). They refactored and rebuilt their content to also include information about the history of that product, and that content enrichment helped improve the overall search rankings. Is that because they included entities that Google was expecting or is it because they had simply enriched their content? Unless you're testing hundreds of thousands of these at a time, it's hard to make a scientific judgement on that.

I can say, from the hundreds that we have done, that it has certainly had a very strong impact. Tracking and understanding this data at scale is also something that I see as being a big competitive advantage in 2023, and moving forward as well."

How do you measure the positive impact of contributing to the enriched SERP more than your competitor?

"It's going to depend on what the actual SERP looks like, and I do have an entirely myopic view because I've spent 20 years looking at 10 blue links on a page (or, increasingly, 7 blue links and 55 ad spots).

I am envisaging the new SERP as roughly 10 information cards, similar to what we see in Discover - and there will be ranking as well. Your inclusion in these cards is either going to be based on having rich media to put in them or you will just have a meta title and meta description in the same way that we do at the moment. If everyone else on the page has a video or images embedded within their listing, then they're going to get the CTR and you're not.

It might simply be that we're going to track this based on overall ranking position but that's, again, my myopic view of having sequential links on a page. We may end up having some kind of tessellation of results instead; there's no way to say what the ultimate UI will be. That UI is fundamentally what's going to drive reporting and the overall targets that we put on it.

If we're still seeing an ordered list, I don't think things will change much, as far as reporting is concerned. However, it's possible that we move away from that model entirely. That would be a very interesting shake-up because it hasn't changed much for two decades now. We're still typing a query into a form on a page, and then getting X number of results back and clicking on one of them. We're overdue a significant technological update to the way that we interact with search."

You've previously mentioned Google's data obfuscation. What do you mean by that and how can SEOs get around it?

"Let's take another trip down memory lane, for those of us that are old enough to remember when Google Analytics actually had keywords in the landing page report. That was fantastic. You could tell which keywords triggered a conversion, but Google took that away a long time ago. Many people working in SEO do not remember, or have no idea, that we used to have access to this data.

They took it away because of 'privacy', yet we still managed to receive it in places like Google Search Console. Fundamentally, that has always been available, and I'll come back to that idea for paid search.

On organic search, the personalised queries that Google is not telling us about are privacy queries - the PII queries. As a ratio, these have been increasing over the last couple of years now. a couple of people have done some work this year into how many queries were reported as specific line items in Google Search Console versus the total amount of organic search traffic that was reported at the site level. They used that to determine how much of the traffic came from keywords that didn't appear in the keyword table.

It's not a perfect approach, because we don't know whether or not there are individual pieces of data or whole keywords that are missing, so it's impossible to make that evaluation. From the data that we can see (I have a tonne of data from enterprise clients as well), that ratio is increasing slowly. I've seen some people claim that 40%+ of the traffic they're aware of is not being reported at a keyword level through Google Search Console. Personally, I've only seen 10-12%, but three years ago I was seeing 2-4%. Even that number has gone up greatly.

It very much depends on the kind of site that you're looking at. If it's the kind of site that has lots of PII data, then it's going to have a much higher share of keywords that it's no longer receiving data on. Either way, it shows the general trajectory that Google Search Console is going in.

This year, Google has also started taking this data away from their paid search advertisers, which is a Rubicon I didn't expect them to cross. I always assumed that, because people are paying for this data, they would have access to it. Google has now managed to obfuscate quite a lot of the keyword reports within AdWords that tell you the specific keywords and broadened phrase-matching that returned the click.

That leaves us in a situation where we're working even more blind on the web than we were before. It becomes incumbent on us to start building our own datasets - and building those as early as possible. A good part of the data that you need to build is from Search Console. The third-party indices that are out there at the moment are all very good at what they do, but they're useless for really telling you every keyword that's important to your site. People need to start cataloguing this today.

There are plenty of tools out there that do it, but start backing up and cataloguing 100% of your Google Search Console data today - if that's the one thing you take away from this. In two, three, or five years, it will be far more important than you would ever imagine it is right now."

What shouldn't SEOs be doing in 2023? What's seductive in terms of time, but ultimately counterproductive?

"I used to do this - we all used to do this - but the algorithm update chasers of the SEO world are akin to the ambulance chasers in the legal world. As an industry, we spend infinitely too much time trying to analyse what happened in the last Google update.

This used to happen once a month, and it was really fun and exciting. It was the 'Google dance'. If you had a good update, it was great because you knew that you were going to keep that number one spot for at least the next three or four weeks before the next update happened. Crucially, that gave us time to try and have a better stab at why things had gone up and gone down.

Now, you can look at directionality, but you cannot look at individual rankings on individual websites to infer any reality – on a single unit basis - about what happened in a search engine update. You just can't do it anymore. There's too much stuff going on simultaneously for you to draw any conclusions that you can learn and work from. If there's one thing that the entire SEO industry needs to stop doing, it's investing so much time, energy, and money into the creation and consumption of content (that fundamentally means nothing) talking about the latest update.

The helpful content update is a great example. We were told a week in advance of it coming out and the entire industry spent the entire week talking about nothing else. Everyone was commentating as to how big it was gonna be - and nothing happened. No one really saw anything. There was a core update 10 days later and everyone suddenly saw big changes. Was it because of the core update? Was it because of the helpful content update? Was it because of something else entirely? There is no way for us to know, and any amount of time that we spend exalting the reasons why something has happened is entirely wasted.

You could have been spending that time doing what will result in better rankings longer-term. From day one, Google has always had the same objective in mind for the search results: to make them better. The answer has always been to make your website better if you want to have more traffic. Make the content better, make it easier for Google to crawl, and make it easier for Google to understand. Those three things encapsulate top-end content production, technical SEO, internal linking, and entities – there are a million things that go into those three little bullet points.

That's what people should be spending time on, not trying to reverse-engineer what happened in the latest Google update. It's tired."

Martin MacDonald is the CEO at MOG Media and you can find him over at mog.media.

Embrace change—Myriam Jessier

Myriam Jessier outlines the importance of navigating rapidly transcending market conditions with a willingness to embrace change and a desire to keep educating yourself and those you work with.

Myriam says: "Things will keep evolving faster and faster in our industry. If you ever feel inadequate, like you can't keep up, remember that we all feel this way from time to time. We shouldn't, but we do, so it's important to remember that you're not alone."

Should we try and stay on top of everything SEO-orientated or is there a better way to approach things?

"It's natural to want to be the best SEO ever. However, in pursuit of this, it's easy to get burnt out. As SEOs we often recommend following the long-tail and finding your niche, but why can't we do this in our industry? If you like something like image SEO, go down the rabbit hole. That doesn't mean you should specialise in something so narrow that you're not able to find a job easily. It simply means that you can add a few things as you go, pile on and build your SEO stack."

Do you need to be more of a generalist when you're working in-house but hone in on something more specific if you branch out independently?

"Absolutely. If you're working in-house you'll already be a niche SEO in a sense because you've specialised in the niche your employer works in. If you're in an agency you'll have lots of generic dealings, but you'll also need to address specific problems that nobody else experiences. In this sense, you could end up becoming a 'clean up on aisle 5' type of SEO. You might also encounter people experiencing technical problems without knowing exactly what needs to be addressed.

You'll have to wear many hats and take on mandates, but you won't have to go after every single eCommerce opportunity. Yes, you can take on some Magento opportunities, but you can choose to specify in a given area - for example, Shopify SEO. That'll be a great way to set yourself apart from SEO agencies. Niching down can be quite smart if you know your market."

Should SEOs be trying to educate themselves about other aspects of digital marketing?

"Definitely. SEO does not operate in a vacuum. It's important to know the context and appreciate that the whole is always bigger than the sum of its parts. Marketing is far bigger than just SEO by itself, CRO, or copy. It's important to educate yourself so you can communicate with the other people you work with. Ensure they understand your priorities and that you can communicate these priorities so that they become their priorities as well.

There's a good chance people won't always take you seriously, but you have to carve out a spot at the decision-making table. This might involve learning some things that aren't shared in SEO tutorials or courses but are instead embracing practical learning in the real world.

Focus on being a human who operates with other human beings: someone who appreciates the importance of communication and understanding. You should do everything within your power to ensure your priorities align with the priorities of the human you're collaborating with. Create an environment where the people you're working with feel comfortable expressing their requirements. You can then clearly communicate the best course of action - for example, your page needing more visibility."

How is being human-centric impacting SEO success?

"The thing about being human-centric is the unpredictability of outcomes. It's a ride that teaches you a lot as you go through life, where the importance of a conversation you've had with someone years ago could resurface at any moment.

In 2023, we need to take time to learn from humans and train the machines, not the other way around. In SEO we tend to think we can beat the machine - we can be smarter - but that's not how any of this works. Being human-centric means consciously correcting algorithm biases instead of reinforcing them. This is a great way to integrate ourselves into marketing and make a huge difference for humans."

What's an example of an algorithm bias?

"Say you type 'Swiss Army' into Google. You'll see a lot of watches but not so many military men. In a location like Switzerland, this search result is biased. Google has learned to show Swiss Army watch models to this demographic. It does this because it deems them to be more interested in watches than military folk.

There is another concern regarding the French language, where describing yourself as a female SEO expert means adding an 'e' to form 'experte'. However, that word has no search volume. You might think about countering this by calling yourself a male expert, but then you would compromise getting hired because you wouldn't have exercised your native tongue properly. To overcome this bias, you could use a middle-ground term like 'epicene' (a gender-neutral way to describe yourself as a specialist). The problem here is that there is lots of search volume for 'specialist' and a very low search volume for 'epicene'. If you type that you're looking for a copy expert using feminine language, Google will show a few female results, but it will assume the most dominant search you want to see is the masculine version.

In this situation, you'd be competing for the top three spots because that's all you're afforded. You'd also be competing with folks that get more visibility than you could ever hope for and all because you have an 'e' at the end of your title. These are the types of biases that, in theory, Google says we adapt ourselves - but in practice, they take some pointing out to correct."

Why does this need to be pointed out? Can't Google use a dictionary to take account of language differences?

"Google explains how that is the theory and that it's working to adjust and show you these results. However, the actual practice often differs from their intentions. Google does understand but it's been biased. It's been autocorrected and not everybody sees this. For example, if you were to have a conversation in Gmail with all ladies you'd be autocorrected to masculine and not exist.

You have to fight against the machine because it's very exhausting to be erased like this. There have been cases where humans have sent very strong messages to the algorithms and influenced the answers to questions. The machine will learn about what people want to know about a given search term, so it's important to focus on correcting inherent biases."

How do you train the machine to understand a result should qualify for the number one position and are there any specific techniques that you could use to train a machine?

"We often experience Google bombings, where lots of people on Reddit send strong messages to ensure every signal sent points to the same thing until search results are impacted.

What can we do, as SEOs, to help provide feedback? We can raise this problem during office hours or we can write about the problem. Our industry is focused on explaining how things work. Google is making a genuine effort to integrate inclusive writing to better understand, for example, specific 'epicene' terms or the fact that more and more women will start using 'experte' and see results.

We can all hope that when people search for the feminine they get the feminine, rather than Google assuming you'd enjoy the male-dominant result more instead.

Would the French language move toward having singular versions of each word in the future?

Inclusive writing is welcomed and encouraged in Quebec but has been banned from French schools because it's been deemed to be an attack on language.

In the UK you have the terms 'actor' and 'actress'. In France, you have specific gender roles for the same job because they're not seen as being as valuable as the male equivalent. The problem is that the machines have learned this from us. We need to consciously correct algorithm biases. When we feed this information - when we use a stock photo of a businesswoman crossing her arms and looking at a laptop - we're sending a message.

As SEOs, we have a small margin of action but, together, the whole is bigger than the sum of its parts. Our conscious efforts as an industry will have an impact."

What shouldn't SEOs be doing in 2023? What's something that's seductive in terms of time but ultimately counterproductive?

"We all fail to prioritise. We get lost. There's so much to know and so much to do, but SEO can often feel like poker. You never know whether you're going to win or how things will pan out. You want to do everything to make sure you're a good student. However, it's easy to get frustrated when your peers and colleagues are not implementing what you asked them to because it's not their priority.

For anyone entering the industry, you shouldn't feel like you need to be the perfect student. You'll be dealing with a website with many moving parts, stakeholders, and people working on it. You are not alone and you are not in a vacuum, so remember to prioritise your time and prioritise your colleague's time."

Myriam Jessier is an SEO Trainer at Pragm and you can find her at pragm.co.

Build quality, trustworthy brands—Izabela Wisniewska

Izabela Wisniewska tells SEOs in 2023 that you shouldn't focus strictly on SEO in isolation, and instead focus on building trustworthy brands and very good websites - and shouting about it.

Izabela says: "My number one tip is that you need to build a quality, trustworthy brand."

How do you build a trustworthy brand?

"I always like to remind people about the basics of SEO like technical or content but once you have done all these, just try to forget you are doing SEO and focus on what your audience needs. In the post-Penguin and post-Panda era of SEO, you should have started moving toward building very good quality content and focus on what you're saying to your audience. Building trustworthy and quality brands means giving your audience what they want to get and promoting it.

For example, when someone is looking for a doctor or financial advisor they don't just go with someone who's put a bunch of stuff that's good for Google on their website. They elect to go with someone trustworthy, recommended, and with great qualifications in those industries."

How does Google determine trust?

"We can't say for sure how they determine trust but we know we have the EAT quality guidelines of expertise, authority, and trustworthiness.

You should get very good at what you do and then shout about your achievements and how good you are. If you've won any awards, or your clients have, then shout about them. If you're very highly educated in your field, shout about that. When you're writing quality content on subjects that are close to your industry, how do people determine that you're trustworthy? They go off recommendations and opinions of others who already know you. It's like the old adage goes which I like to translate into link building: if you hang around with bad people (bad links), regardless of how good you are, people will think that you're not so good. However, if you hang around with good links people are going to think you're as good as them.

Think along these lines when you're trying to build your brand. How can you show people that you're trustworthy? Try to do the same with Google. Show them quality content and how hard you've worked to get to where you are.

Show how educated your employees are. That's what Google wants as well, in the end - they want to show the best of the best. By doing that, people will keep coming back to Google and treat them as the best search engine."

What are some of the better places to shout about your business and build trust?

"It depends on the industry. There was an interesting talk recently at BrightonSEO with an experiment around PR for bike sellers. They went for more relevant placements of PR releases and PR activities rather than generic ones that are just higher Domain Authority or Majestic Trust Flow. They went for more relevant ones.

Think about where your audience is going to hang around and where they would prefer to find information that's relevant and trustworthy. You can't generalise, like back in the day, and assume you can just go for Wikipedia links, for example, because they seem to be the best ones.

Of course go for the general trustworthy ones if you think that's going to help you, however, think before you start going into every possible direction. Where would your audience feel is the best place to find information that's trustworthy?"

Should you just look at where the right people are talking about something in the right way or should you filter the opportunities even further by applying different metrics to those websites and assigning them a quality or trust score?

"In my opinion, it's always best to go for a mixture of those two. Analysing and observing your audience is great. However, we're SEOs and we like technical and metrics, so yes, apply some scores if you like. If you're talking link metrics, then Majestic Trust Flows is great and usually translates into real quality.

It doesn't matter if it's links or content, start by analysing your audience and make sure you show them what they want to see. You should ensure that what you suggest to them is what you're actually doing because that's another thing that you need to be 100% on. We tend to focus so much on ranking that we don't think beyond that. We want to rank but sometimes lose the thought of what's going to happen next. Are you showing the right thing for the right keyword? Is that what they want to see? Are we persuading them enough?

You'll have to think more about overall marketing than just purely SEO rank. You should think about what's going to happen after you get them there and how you're going to persuade them that you belong with the best of the best. That's what we've been missing recently, and that's what you should start focusing on going forward."

Where are the best places to start if you're just trying to establish yourself as an authority and you haven't really done that much in the past?

"Embrace a systematic approach and use trial and error. There are no shortcuts and you won't find any along the way. Follow the quality guidelines - for example, the EAT.

It's not like someone would randomly wake up one day and start a business in XYZ. The same applies to the digital world: you can't just build a website from scratch and start competing. It doesn't happen that way. What usually happens is someone does something within an existing field, starts the education process, and begins the slow grind of building up the business. After enough hard work and time have passed, you can become an expert in your field.

Start by shouting out about what you can offer and start building quality content and great websites. Remember the basics, because if you get them right you'll start to build up your brand's trust and quality. Hard work and persistence pay off, and there's no place you can go to get it. Gaining trustworthiness doesn't happen overnight. In any industry, if you think about building a trustworthy, quality brand, that will rarely happen overnight. You'll have to work for it."

Where do reviews and customer opinions come into this?

"What other people are saying about you is super important as well. This can also contribute to building trust and building the quality of the brand. You can say anything about yourself and you're more than likely going to be talking in a positive light. Your customers are your advocates, so you'll want them to contribute.

By all means shout out about winning, education, and how good your product is - but you'll need encouragement, reviews, and testimonials to make sure prospective customers know they can trust you. Building trust wouldn't work without having quality products/services and the encouragement you gain from the fact that people already use your product. People won't trust you without it."

Is there a best place to try and encourage customers to write reviews?

"Try to think as your audience would think. What are the best places to put reviews? They should be where your audience will trust those reviews the most. Again, it helps to partially forget you're doing SEO.

Your choice of positioning will probably depend on the industry. If you're on the agency side of things, you won't be able to do it yourself - you'll have to work with your client. If you're an in-house SEO, you also won't be able to do it yourself. You'll have to work with the rest of the brand's clients and companies to make everything come together, get the quality across and build trustworthiness. The SEO and marketing teams won't do it themselves; it has to be a joint effort."

Is there any style of content that you prefer nowadays?

"A mixture of all types of content is the best approach in my view but, also research the industry you are in. Think about what would happen in a natural world and do a mixture of things. Some users might prefer podcasts and some might prefer reading blog posts."

Should we be actively encouraging our audiences to view product videos, podcasts, and different types of media other than articles?

"Go for a mixture of things. A mixture of all mediums, or whatever suits the specific thing we're trying to shout about. There might be a message that will be better presented in a podcast or video or you might have something that'll be better in written form. The first place that's easy for people to shout about their achievements is their blog or social media accounts. That's the easiest place to start, and then, if there is a possibility to show somewhere else without it sounding too pushy, you should definitely do this.

Always try to think and say whatever feels natural to your audience, across whatever mediums or channels your audience will best consume content. This will also vary because even if the writing sounds more natural, your audience could well have different opinions. That's why going for a mixture of things is usually the best thing you could do."

What shouldn't SEOs be doing in 2023? What's seductive in terms of time but ultimately counterproductive?

"You shouldn't not follow what I just said. Seriously now, as SEOs, and across the whole marketing industry, we tend to be stuck in our old ways. It's funny because we tend to be stuck yet often forget the basics. We often don't really look into technical aspects or forget to put content out that builds up trust and quality. For example, we push out short blog posts for the sake of it.

We need to try our hardest to not forget the basics and avoid remaining stuck in our old ways. Stop thinking that just because something has always worked it will continue to work going forward.

We should learn these golden rules: Don't forget the basics and don't be afraid to evolve with the times. Think about building up a proper blog or content hub and appreciate the time and effort it takes to build trustworthy brands. Inform your clients that good things come to those who wait. The idea of pushing something out and worrying about it later needs to go away in 2023."

Izabela Wisniewska is Co-Founder and Head of Search Marketing at Creatos Media and you can find her at creatosmedia.co.uk.

Optimise beyond traditional blue-link rankings—Cindy Krum

Cindy Krum believes that SEOs in 2023 need to be looking to optimise beyond normal blue links. The old methods of SEO have become somewhat outdated and simply trying harder and harder to get to page one is not always going to work.

Cindy says: "There are ways to get above big competitors using other sites. For instance: getting things to rank on other sites that have enough SEO value and clout in the algorithm to beat out top competitors. Things like YouTube can displace top competitors and Twitter, Facebook, and LinkedIn can push things down. Getting a Knowledge Graph or Local Pack can count for certain keywords and help you skip the line.

Trying the same strategies of linking, keyword optimisation, countless writing, and semantic SEO can work, but when you go up against huge competitors it's less effective."

Is there less traffic available now through the traditional blue links or is it because there's more competition?

"It's probably a combination of both. Every year the web grows dramatically. New web pages are created, old ones are archived, new people get on the web, new small companies build websites, and the web gets exponentially bigger. There's always new competition emerging and the algorithm tends to favour certain kinds of results, including super high authority sites. This also includes fast and super-dynamic social sites that tend to feature more multi-modal content."

Should you spend a significant amount of time optimising to rank highly in searches from LinkedIn or YouTube? Should people try to obtain rankings within the traditional Google SERP via YouTube?

"Yes. This is a strategy that's been around for a long time. It was originally referred to as Barnacle SEO by Rand Fishkin and it involves getting rankings from sites you don't own. This can be tough in lots of scenarios because it's harder to track and attribute. However, it does work. If you can get something to rank in the top three and get traffic to that thing, then you will see conversion to your site. It might be an extra step but it's better than not being there at all.

Even publishing an amazing blog post might not be enough to displace whoever is ranking there. With the helpful content update, your awesome blog posts will fare better, but when you're a small player up against super high authority sites and super competitive keywords, you have to be scrappy and take non-traditional routes."

Is there still an opportunity to rank on blog posts for long-tail keyword phrases?

"Yes. There's still an opportunity to rank for long-tail keywords. Google still sees new keyword combinations all the time. However, if you're going for things that are closer to the messy middle or the head terms, that's where you're likely to find more of a challenge."

What type of content should you create to match user intent and how do you determine what the user is likely to be looking for? Do you look at the SERP or do you look at YouTube results to try to match or better what already exists for a specific phrase?

"Both. You should look all around to see what's ranking and what Google wants to rank. You should look for what's in the result and look for dramatic changes in ranking signals. If you determine a website is a high authority site but another isn't, what did one do differently to the other? Also, why is that working better, especially if they have high authority sites below them?

Focus on How-To, FAQ, video, written format with images, and rich results that expand Google's new buzzword: 'The Journey.'"

Is there a particular social platform that's best for a particular type of business?

"It depends on where your customers are. You'll want to fish where the fish are. If your customers are all on Reddit, participating there would be good from a marketing perspective. It may not rank, but you should look at where customers are and how you can get things from that platform to rank. If they're not naturally ranking on some queries then move on to a different platform.

You should acknowledge that search occurs outside of Google too. If Reddit is really the place where people are (e.g. you don't see it ranking in search results but you know your people are there) you should make sure you know what's ranking there. We're at a point where search results are packed with really rich engaging content. Simply posting another blog post is not enough."

Do you recommend trying to drive people from those particular platforms back to your website? Would you answer a question on YouTube and then say at the end of a video that you can find a more informative article that people can download directly from your website?

"Yes, and you can even build on that and make the video kind of an entry to a larger, longer journey. You can say that something is just a basic overview of the topic but if you want a more detailed description you can check the link in the description."

How do regular Google algorithm updates impact the SERP? How does that impact what you're advising here?

"As Google gets better and better at understanding the meaning of a query and the meaning of content on a page or website, they are getting better at ranking what users really want. Often, what users really want is not the same as what SEOs want to make.

As a community, we have to do a better job of joining what users want with what we're creating. Users do tend to want these kinds of multimodal multimedia experiences. They want images, videos, diagrams, quick tips, and things like that. TikTok has been getting lots of buzz among younger generations. It is even being used as a search or local search engine to find restaurants and things like that.

This trend is emblematic of the general desire to find quick answers, but also find the answers that are harder to game, are authentically human, and are not specifically written to convince you to buy. No one likes to feel like they're being sold to - it's uncomfortable. Having these multimedia aspects can put a human touch on things and make everything more authentic."

Is there a best place to research what your users are actually looking for? Is it best to have a real live conversation with your users?

"Ideally, conversations with users are great - not only for this but lots of things. You should talk to your customers to learn what their journey has been like. For example: where they started, who they've spoken to, what was persuasive, what was annoying, and how they made their final decision. You can incorporate this insight into SEO rather than this practice of simply representing clever people doing clever things to outrank quickly.

You still have to be clever but you also have to be doing what real companies do. That means creating a good product, supporting the product, having good customer service, etc. You can then think about those things in an SEO context and evolve your collective understanding of what it is to be an SEO.

It's not just about being clever, but also being a good marketer and connecting with users' deeper goals so you can get them to the right answers as quickly as possible. It's more esoteric and less tactical to simply target keywords on the page and use H1 and H2 tags. It's still important to do those things but it's better to do this from a more evolved place."

Does that mean that keywords aren't as important as they used to be?

"In general, keywords are still important, but there is something new happening in search engines.

Let's say a particular search term can be phrased in a few different ways. If Google has decided that these terms are synonyms - or that they understand the bulk of the query but not some parts of it - they can respond with some kind of canonical Knowledge Graph response and satisfy the users.

For example, if you did a long-tail query like 'what is the name of The Cranberries' drummer' (a band that doesn't have a drummer), what would Google rank for that query? They'd rank the Cranberries' Knowledge Graph assuming that you'll look into the band members and see the band doesn't have a drummer. You'd answer your own question. Google couldn't answer it, but they threw a Knowledge Graph on you and that was good enough for users.

In some cases, all Google has to do is get in the ballpark. They would push every website down and still think that the Knowledge Graph is a better answer than your long blog post about why the Cranberries don't have a drummer."

Are big companies better off having multiple websites focusing on distinct niches or should you be driving as much authority to the same domain as possible?

"The latter option is better because resources are almost always part of the decision. It's easier and cheaper to build and maintain one site than it is to build and maintain multiple sites.

If resources are part of the equation and are unlimited, you might lean towards having multiple sites. A multi-site strategy assumes that you can build up those other ones to be super niche specialist sites with really great content. Limited resources can mean you only have so many writers and only so many great pieces of content.

This is not just a question for SEO, but a business question. Looking at the bigger picture is really important."

What shouldn't SEOs be doing in 2023? What's seductive in terms of time, but ultimately counterproductive?

"Spending too much time in analytics believing exactly what tools say about rankings. Avoid looking at a tool and saying, 'Oh, we're position three for this keyword and want to be position two'. Also, avoid not targeting a keyword just because it doesn't get enough search volume.

Deep reliance on tools to push you towards decisions or actions needs to be tempered with real searches. Every tool has its own limitations. If it's giving you a ranking for a country, that ranking might be true as an average or for a particular location, but it won't necessarily be true in other countries. It might not be representative. Even if you have that number you don't really know what it means unless you're looking at what's above that ranking.

You can look at whether there is a featured snippet or Knowledge Graph, but also at how far down the page an item is, or whether it's engaging and interactive. If all you have is a blue link without an image, some star rankings or rich results, you'll be going up against all of these Google things that are more enticing than a simple blue link. It's not just about knowing a number but knowing that number in a larger context. You can then think to yourself, is that going to be enough? If you were searching for that company and this content had no association with it, would you click?

Look at real results and appreciate that Google is mobile-first. We know they're crawling with a mobile crawler and we know more people are searching on mobile rather than desktop in many industries, yet most of the tools still focus on ranking data for desktop. It's therefore important to ask the right questions. Are your users searching on mobile and how much of the data you're looking at in analytics is on mobile? If you're only looking at desktop rankings you might be impacted by the fact that data is mashed together. Using this will not result in a successful campaign or, ultimately, SEO effort.

If it's a Knowledge Graph for you, you'll want to know whether it's there on mobile or not, or whether it's there on desktop and mobile or not. If it's for your competitor or for a general topic, you'll want to know that too. You'll need a realistic idea of what you're up against. For instance, if you see a drop in clicks, can you maintain position? If you were to lose your desktop Knowledge Graph and the website you're tracking maintained position but lost clicks, what happened there? It could either be that the Knowledge Graph came in or the Knowledge Graph went out. When the Knowledge Graph came in and the website lost clicks, did that matter? Not necessarily. However, the benefits of ranking in mobile do trickle across to desktop."

Cindy Krum is the Founder and CEO of MobileMoxie and you can find her over at mobilemoxie.com.

Think sustainably about SEO based on your/your client's website and capabilities— Itamar Blauer

Itamar Blauer stresses the importance of sustainable SEO and looking into the future in 2023. Use common sense and long-term thinking to make the most of what you are capable of and demonstrate your particular expertise.

Itamar says: "Rather than focusing on conventional practices - the ones that you understand and are performing well - you should start thinking about the future.

If you're going to be in business for the next 3-5 years, you need to really focus on what is still going to be applicable. You should work in terms of the way that Google understands, and might possibly understand, your content and SEO as a whole."

What does sustainability mean in practice? Is it to avoid short-term tactics?

"It's a mix of that and just using common sense. The recent Google helpful content update might as well have been called the common sense update. Essentially, Google is starting to talk, and the phrasing of recent updates suggests it's going to be all about proving you're an expert in what you do. If you were to write and try to rank for absolutely everything, common sense would tell you it's very difficult to become an expert in multiple fields.

If you are embracing a jack-of-all-trades approach, it's time to really focus on what your actual niches are and what you specialise in. Then you can double down on all of that to be able to prove you're an expert within that niche."

Would your advice alter depending on the capabilities of your client's website?

"Absolutely. It's not just about the website either - it's about the business too. If you're talking about sustainable SEO, the results you'll get will ensure you're able to rank sustainably throughout the next few years.

You need to think about the business too. Let's say you're working for an eCommerce store and there's a certain amount of products you can have ready to be sold at a certain time. If you act sustainably - you scale up your SEO and bring in more traffic because you're ranking well - do you have the sustainability to sell these products to customers? The last thing you'll want is to have so much demand for your products or services and not be able to fulfil that supply. You might end up getting negative feedback and reviews, so you've got to really think in terms of the more holistic business sense if you're going to be able to scale and rank sustainably."

Just because something has historically driven lots of traffic and sales, that doesn't necessarily mean it's going to be essential in the future.

"Absolutely. It's about understanding your niche and knowing what the industry is like within your area. If you're anticipating certain things to be trendy in the next year or two, you'll need to start thinking about them now.

A massive component of sustainable SEO is being in the know, or being able to predict what's going to be big in the next few years. This is known as 'keyword pioneering'. When you're talking about optimising for content around things that you can predict, you'll essentially be pioneering the sort of keywords you're trying to optimise for, regardless of whether they have any search volume in keyword research tools. You should still be able to understand when you're leading in a field and can anticipate X will be prominent in the next few years. You should always start writing about things in advance.

Sustainable SEO is about being able to identify and predict things and really be a leader within your field. By that time, the stuff you're writing about will become popular and you'll already be dominating in the SERPs because you've got lots of content around it. You should not only identify your experience from the user's perspective but also give Google a better understanding, in terms of how authoritative you are on the topics and areas within your industry."

Is the capability of the client's website also relevant, in terms of being able to publish a certain type of content or be optimised to include different markups that you would want?

"This sort of thing is done on a case-by-case basis, but you want to be able to know that you have the capabilities from the tech side to address any new content you might want to create.

Let's say you're trying to scale up a bunch of content to do with either the markup or any multimedia content you're looking to include, like video. Do you have the right schema to be able to maximise the use of that? Are you hosting it locally on your website? Are you going to have to embed it from another source? These are all important considerations in terms of the capabilities from the tech side on your website. This will be especially important for you to deliver on the things that you are thinking of creating or publishing."

Is there another resource or piece of software you can use to establish which phraseology might be best to incorporate within future content?

"The main thing is trying to be proactive as an SEO. If you're talking to a client you should ensure you're asking the right questions. Are you talking with sales on a regular basis? Do you have some kind of R&D team that can glean insight? You can also go to conferences within that particular industry and ask people about what they think could be the next best thing.

Other than that, it's important to use your own mind. The better you know the industry, the more you can identify issues and implement better alternatives. You can try to create ideas that way or you can work backwards by having some kind of solution."

Are there third-party resources to assist with determining which phrases to use and indicating the likely search volume available?

"It's a bit tricky with third-party sources if you're talking about certain tools. Phrases need to be established and have an established demand for tools to be able to pick them up. If you're assuming there's a term that's not being used at all, you can attend industry meet-ups or conferences that could be helpful.

Apart from talking to people to get an idea, you can use your own thought processes and try to work backwards. Look at what's currently missing and could be better, think about what the solution might be, and then work backwards and see what content you can create about that. This will help you form a cluster around the solutions to this new idea within the industry. It's difficult to use tools for this but the best thing to do is use your brain and other people's campaigns."

How do you build a long-term strategy? How do you achieve this in the long term as part of an incremental approach to achieving your own targets?

"There are two types of things you can do from the content side. If you're experiencing things changing every year, you'll have a couple of options. The first thing you could do is try to lead every year in terms of what's actually happening. For example, let's imagine your niche is in marketing and you're talking about upcoming trends. You would want to create content now (in Summer 2022) because you know that the demand for 2023 will start appearing in August 2022. You need that kind of buffer to be able to build up demand so you're one of the first to show up when people are actually searching for it.

That's not to say you'll be there forever, but you will at least be able to establish some dominance and first-mover advantage. The other thing is around the concept of evergreen content. This allows you to have a wealth of expertise and knowledge in one big content piece that people can return to as a valuable resource. You won't need to change the URL slug of that piece of content and it'll be a great way to demonstrate your expertise.

Evergreen content is great not only from an organic search perspective but as a conversion tactic, in terms of what you're selling or offering. The long-term approach is to think about when things may become popular and then plan several months ahead to brainstorm the content - what you're writing, what you're saying, and who's writing it. You need to get all of that edited and ready, and include any optimisations you want to include.

Timelines are very important when thinking about a sustainable long-term approach. You need to be hitting deadlines if you want to maximise efficiency and effectiveness. This will depend on whether you are correct in your predictions about when certain things are new in your industry and might become popular.

The most important thing is to have a plan. That way, you will avoid missing out and not being as happy as if you had made a plan and everything was structured and executed correctly."

Do you ever have any issues with getting clients on board when targeting effectively zero-volume keywords?

"Education is everything. It's about being on the same wavelength as your clients in terms of why something is important. That'll show you've got their best interests at heart, especially if you communicate the importance of succeeding with something over the next 3-5 years.

Clients will be really appreciative if you're invested in their future, so it's all about how you approach that conversation. Clear, two-way communication is a great way to get them to buy into your idea."

What shouldn't SEOs be doing in 2023? What's seductive in terms of time, but ultimately counterproductive?

"The word that comes to mind is complacency. It's hard to dictate exactly what that might look like, but if you're an SEO and think you can keep doing what you're doing because you've always done things like that, this approach is probably not going to work.

With recent Google updates - whether it's about how Google understands language or the helpful content update - things are always changing. To this day there are still people who believe that spam commenting and posting links on different forums and blogs works.

You don't want to be that complacent person who's stuck in the sand in terms of what has been working well for you over the past few years. That won't necessarily be the case tomorrow. Always think about learning and be willing to adapt in terms of how to do SEO. Otherwise, you'll remain stuck in the past."

Itamar Blauer is a Senior SEO Director at StudioHawk and you can find him over at studiohawk.co.uk.

Cutting through the noise will be your biggest struggle in 2023—David Iwanow

David Iwanow warns SEOs about the volume of noise that you're going to be competing against in 2023 and gives you tips on how to stand out and make yourself heard.

David says: "I think the big issue SEOs are going to face in 2023 is cutting through the noise. Regarding SEO, there's a whole lot of noise out there. You've got paid search, image results, TikTok search, and Amazon search. Yet, for consumers, it's information overload. Now, when you've got billions and billions of results, how can you cut through that noise to reach out to consumers? The big things to focus on are probably where you have the right to play and what you think is achievable. There will potentially be a lot of results around your brand terms or the general industry terms.

Alternatively, you can run a video, however, most people don't have the budget or the resources to produce video content. Therefore, when you're trying to cut through the noise, your best solution is text-based content (which is pretty easy to produce) and image-based content based on existing text. You also have other things, like rich snippets, Local Packs, or reviews.

Google seems to be rolling out a new schema every couple of weeks and then, obviously, there are also Google Ads to consider. Sometimes it makes sense to invest some budget into Google Ads to cut through that noise and validate that those particular terms are things you want to rank for before investing a lot of energy. Generally, the big thing is: how do you stand out from your competitors? You have to be realistic."

What is the best way to determine what you should be focusing your energy on?

"There are a couple of things to do. Firstly, Snippet Digital has built a fantastic keyword tool called Keyword Insights. You can reach out to the Snippet Digital folks to request a free demo; I found it was an amazing and scalable way of classifying intent at a keyword level. Plus, a few third-party tools are out there which also classify keywords into intent funnels like Semrush but don't do it as well. That's one place you want to start.

If you're a transaction website, you want to make sure you're focusing on keywords which are more likely to convert. If you're an informational website, you won't convert by focusing on where or how to buy, and you don't have that functionality. Therefore, you need to consider the keywords, the intent, and whether it matches your website and its purpose."

How do you best determine the intent?

"I like to approach it with manual hard work. You can rely on some tools when you try to do things at scale. Personally, it's the hard work - the classification at an individual keyword level - which is the best way to do it. You just need to be reasonable around this.

If you go to an SEO tool like Semrush (or any of those tools) they give you 5 million possible keywords you could focus on. In contrast, it becomes much more achievable if you use your Google Search Console data and classify your existing search console data into the intent file."

You talked about transactional information. Are there other types of intent that you classify your keywords into?

"There are a few other areas, but you've also got product and brand terms. Typically, if you're a website, you should be able to at least rank for your brand. That is where people sometimes focus on the wrong areas. That is the 'cutting through the noise.'

For example, if you are targeting the term 'Majestic', you're moving from Majestic SEO into Majestic. Now you are competing against Majestic Wines, Majestic apparel, Majestic DJ, etc., and you are fighting with these other brands. You need to at least start by ensuring you have visibility on your brand. Once you've got that visibility, you can start moving towards the category and industry terms like link building or backlink analysis"

You discussed potentially competing with Google paid ads and focusing on brand SEO. Should SEOs be bidding on their own brand?

"It must be done carefully and it depends on how aggressively your competitors are going after your terms. In many situations, it doesn't always make sense. You've likely got larger budgets if you're a big brand or a big company. However, if you're a small retailer or a local tour operator, you may not be able to profitably bid on terms like 'Niagara Falls' or 'big bus tours'.

Therefore, it makes sense to be realistic about what you have available to spend because there's always someone with a bigger budget. For instance, if you're in the travel sector, you're bidding against Expedia and Booking, whose spending pre-COVID was over 10 billion a year on paid traffic. You just don't have the budget to pay the same for retailers, and they will lose money to get that consumer or customer into their store.

You need to consider bidding on brands where it makes sense and not just go crazy and throw all your budget into that.

In the past, I've seen agencies prefer to focus on that because it's easy. There was a business where they spent about 89% of the entire paid budget on brand. When they stopped that, organic traffic increased, strangely, because cannibalisation was happening. Overall, you will get more traffic, but there will be a tipping point where you'll start to achieve cannibalisation."

Should you focus on an individual marketing channel (like Amazon) for each stage of the consumer journey or should you use multiple traffic sources for each query/opportunity?

"It helps to focus on the low-hanging fruit first, which is Google search. Then, you need to chase other opportunities. If you're in the travel space, it may be optimisation within TripAdvisor or memorisation with Google Maps or local listings. It depends on where you are operating with your retail player, which could be Pinterest SEO or Amazon SEO.

You want to focus on Google search because that's where most of the top-of-the-funnel or new-to-category customers come from. Once you get that working, you want to look at your top referral channels or where your top affiliate sales come from.

If it's YouTube, you have to be on YouTube - assuming you'll need more money to be invested in creating some video content. You must ensure that your Google SEO revenue is sufficient to fund some of these other channels. There's no point throwing all your eggs in one basket and hoping Pinterest SEO works for you because that will take a lot more effort than optimising for Google."

How do you cut through the noise and make people aware of what you do through top-of-funnel keyword phrases rather than brand or product phrases, and how do you justify the budget for that?

"For many players, capturing visibility at the top of the funnel is not something you can do in the next 6 to 12 months. Hence, you must be realistic in your timeframes. For products, it should be timed for the next couple of months if you want to focus on it. Then, you start moving into solution-based terms. Consider the Majestic-themed examples given earlier - but more like backlink research.

Then, you go to the next stage of the need-based stuff, where you deal with issues like: How do you understand your competitors? Should you use a competitor's phrase domain authority? That is the top part of the funnel, and you have to work your way up to that.

For seasonal terms, like 'Black Friday 2022' (which is still not for a few months as of this conversation), there are already websites focusing on 'Black Friday 2023'. For these, it can take three to four months to start to get some visibility. According to Forrester research, 30% of US consumers started Christmas shopping in October. Hence, if you have a website with content meant to focus on getting Christmas sales - whether it's selling toys, Christmas cards, etc. - you're already a bit too late to start doing your SEO.

Using tools like Google Trends, you can start to see when there are common seasonal patterns, and you want to get ahead of that. If you plan to switch on your Google Ads in November, many people will have already made their purchases because of global shipping delays, which usually means it may be two or three months before they can get their items.

It also gets very competitive as the months go by. The traffic you could have bought today through Google Ads for 15-20 cents per click will probably double every month until the week before Christmas, and people are desperate for their last-minute sales. Then, they might be paying $5, $10, or $20 per click to capture that traffic.

It's only going to be a handful of competitors - like Amazon, Walmart, or Tesco - who can guarantee that it will be shipped before Christmas. It is thus important to be realistic about it. You also want to ensure you own your product or your geographic space. As you move up in terms of your authority in the space and your content, you can move higher up in the pecking order."

How do you deliver on your content experience and what kind of content is likely to keep people? How do you achieve focus and retention?

"It's ideally about focusing on more of the FAQ types with product usage questions like, 'How do I calculate my Trust Flow?' 'What is the difference between Trust Flow and Citation Flow' 'How to spam or influence Majestic's backlink profile', etc.

Those types of things relate directly to your product but are different parts of the funnel, so you will often find there will be third-party sites. All these various sites are already trying to focus on some of those terms which don't always have high volumes of traffic but can be very engaging for consumers. For example, 'What is the difference between Moz and Majestic?' or 'What is the difference between Ahrefs and Semrush?'

That's where you can start to expand your content topics without going to the very top. If you want to rank for 'backlinks', that's nice, but it's more of a vanity metric. But, in calculating 'backlinks', you are only getting 'backlinks' with 'Majestic'. So, that's where you can touch on the top part of the funnel - although it's much more likely you already have the right to play in that space. Those types of visitors will be more engaged with your brand and hopefully will also lead to conversions.

There could also be new growth areas, like if you are looking for 'SEO metric APIs', 'backlink discovery tools', 'digital maturity models', and others. There's a lot of stuff. An example is 'Majestic', where you have the right to play, and it is possible to capture traffic around those types of terms. Yet currently, no one is playing in that space, outside of SEO bloggers and some of the comparison engines."

What shouldn't SEOs be doing in 2023? What is seductive in terms of time but ultimately counterproductive?

"Getting caught in that SEO bubble. As SEOs, we get curious about stuff, start clicking around and assuming things, and suddenly, we've got 15,000 possible keywords we want to track where it would be better to have 10 great keywords that we can create content around.

Another one is manual reporting. There are still agencies that send an Excel file of the monthly report five or six weeks after the end of the month, and now you can't do anything with them. It's good to also make the report actionable. If you only know general data - like your competitors, a 1% increase in trust flow, Majestic score, etc. - it is still useless without context and since it's calculated every day there will be some fluctuations.

You shouldn't focus on such a small aspect. Instead, you want to look at general trends, like how you are trending over time. We have done this in the past, where we've taken all the data out through the Majestic API, visualised it in Tableau, and started seeing trends. With that, we can say: 'In the next six months, this competitor will have five times the amount of backlinks you have and twice the authority, which means they'll start ranking for your term.'

Hence, you need to make a proactive campaign to look at link reclamation rather than just increases in your Majestic score. It is great, but it's not actionable. Manual reporting needs to be automated, otherwise, it takes too much time. And when the recording is done, it needs to be actionable."

David Iwanow is the Head of Search at Reckitt, and you can find him at reckitt.com.

2 AUDITING

Technical SEO matters—Andy Drinkwater

Andy Drinkwater says that anybody looking to get insight into their website in 2023 should look at some of the more popular issues that arise in technical SEO, and make sure that you are addressing them.

Andy says: "The first and most popular technical SEO issue is getting disallow and noindex the wrong way around when you're trying to get pages deindexed from Google."

What's the difference between disallow and noindex?

"Disallow will prevent Google from ever reaching a particular location on your website (whether that's a file, folder, or image), whereas noindex will prevent any pages from getting indexed in Google's search results.

If you get this the wrong way around and disallow access to a file or location first and then try to noindex it, Google won't be able to reach the file and see the noindex tag.

You have to do this the right way and make sure you put the noindex in first. Make sure that Google has seen this and that the pages have been removed from the results. Then you can go ahead and disallow after that."

What do you mean by the need to devalue pages?

"If anybody searches for their website in Google (searches for the brand name), they'll see the site links which appear underneath the site itself.

Sometimes you'll see pages that are linked when you don't want them to be. This could be an About Us page or a Contact Us page. That's predominantly because of internal linking, which powers the majority of the site search results Google uses.

If you're finding that these pages are turning up and you don't want them to be there, or you're finding it hard getting one page to rank in front of a similar type of page, you might need to devalue those pages.

One of the most popular ways to do this is to look at the internal links to them. That'll probably be the biggest issue with them."

Should you be taking away more authoritative links (the links from your homepage and other significant pages), but keeping links from other pages on your site?

"It all depends on the pages these are linking to. If it is to help devalue a page in the sitelinks, then yes, strong source pages can make a difference."

What does linking to 404 pages mean in practice?

"With most audits, you'll see at least a handful of pages that are linking to 404 pages. This can happen in various ways, but that doesn't mean to say that anyone has been negligent with the site. It might be that you've pushed a product onto a page, and you no longer have that product, so you removed it without doing the other changes in the back end. You can then end up linking to a 404 page.

Google doesn't particularly like that if there are too many. The odd one here and there is fine. Sometimes it can even be that you have external links pointing to web pages that you no longer have on your site.

One of the quickest things you can do is a good old 301 redirect to something similar."

Would it be more valuable to go through these pages and ensure that the links go directly to a page and don't involve redirects?

"Yes, that would be the ideal solution, but it depends on how many you've got. If it's the odd one or two, you can go back and do that, but if you've got thousands coming from all over the place, you might have to create a redirect matrix. It depends if you can do it programmatically.

There are many ways to correct these and avoid this being a huge job, but a crawl will give you an idea of what pages are still live and still being linked to on a site."

Duplicate page titles used to be an issue when CMSs didn't allow you to apply a separate title for each page. Is that still a problem?

"You'd be surprised by how many times you see these sorts of things. With the page titles, it really depends because Google is getting good at understanding more about sites. They are often going to know which pages should be the ones that you want on the site and which you don't.

If you've got too many duplicates, then they'll generally just pick one of those and show that one. Even if the duplicate doesn't need a canonical in place, you'd be surprised by how many of these have duplicate page titles on sites.

If you have too many then it can become a problem. It's fairly straightforward to fix - but that doesn't mean to say that because you've got a duplicate page or a very similar page on a site it doesn't make sense to have it on there.

Sometimes it might be useful for people on the site, but you don't want two similar pages to be indexed. In this case, you could just keep the page live and canonicalize it to the original one too. Try to achieve a best-of-both-worlds approach."

If you've made the mistake of having the same page titles for two different pages with entirely different types of content, does Google now have a better chance of understanding the context of the content on your page?

"Yes. Google has done a lot recently with the rewriting of page titles. This is less of a problem now than it was a few years ago - even twelve months ago. It's not the issue that it used to be, but if you've got a site with thousands of pages on it and you don't manage them correctly, it'll be easy to create a second page that's similar to something that's already on the site.

Keep in mind that, if this does happen, you'll be missing out on the opportunity to say something that you really want to say, and that others are going to listen to. If Google decides they're going to rewrite a duplicate page title for you, you're going to lose out on the option to say what you really mean."

What are Open Site Searches?

"This is where you don't disallow access to searches or search parameters within the site itself. It's very easy to leave that open, and Google will start crawling through the search on your site. This wastes an enormous amount of crawl budget, and different types of searches will give different types of issues.

You'll find that some start appearing in the search results. For example, Google will say it's found 100,000 pages on a site with 3,000 pages. In these sorts of circumstances, the best thing to do is noindex and then disallow, but remember to make sure you get this the right way. Hopefully, that'll prevent any of these issues from being thrown up by Google in future. It is a problem for crawl budget, which is one of the main reasons why it's worth fixing."

What are your general thoughts on auditing? How often should audits be carried out and what are the key things to be looking for on an ongoing basis?

"If you've got a site that's active in terms of development, it's important to keep on top of these things. For some clients, you might need to audit sites monthly to make sure that when changes have been made, they've not thrown up issues – which is something that can happen an awful lot.

If the site is fairly static and doesn't change that much, it might be that you only need to audit it once every six months or so. It's worth keeping in mind that Google performs around 1500 algorithm updates annually. Nobody knows the exact number, but definitely over a thousand.

If they're changing something and you're not necessarily aware of it, you may want to run a fresh audit to make sure that anything current with Google is being picked up as well. There will be plenty of opportunities for people to find these sorts of issues with one of the many tools out there. These can be used interchangeably, and you can use a few of them when auditing because they'll provide different pieces of information."

Do you attempt to define the financial value and ROI of fixing these issues?

"Yes. It's always worthwhile if you can show the benefit of what's being done. This can be built into whatever service you're doing for somebody.

It depends on how often they're making these changes. On smaller sites, you might want to go back over it a few times a year whereas with larger sites that have big development teams, sometimes even a month is too long.

If a change has been proposed, some sites might need to run these through a staging area first. You should be able to crawl this staging area and even perform checks before they go live"

Could you tie it back to something like forecasted ranking improvements?

"It's great to give a forecast on where you expect something to be as a result of doing an audit on a website. Sometimes this can be a little unclear, because it is Google at the end of the day.

We don't always know what's going to happen, but you can always give some sort of indicator regarding what's to be expected when you do an audit. If something new is picked up, what will be the result of that?

It might not always equate to dollar value, but it will equate to what this fix means regarding how the site will perform in Google. That in itself can be interpreted with the natural value."

What shouldn't SEOs be doing in 2023? What's seductive in terms of time, but ultimately counterproductive?

"You shouldn't be ignoring site images. Site images and site speed are always going to be on the tip of Google's tongue. It's about how quick you can make your site - where the quicker it is the better.

One of the quick fixes that anybody can do is to ensure you look for the latest image formats being published on web pages. People ignore this sort of thing, but it's a fairly quick fix - you can use Cloudflare and work through one of their systems. This will simply involve ticking a button and having them deliver a faster image for you. Don't ignore site speed."

Andy Drinkwater is a Freelance SEO Conultant and you can find him at andydrinkwater.com.

Regularly monitor your website—Rebecca Berbel

Rebecca Berbel informs SEOs in 2023 of the importance of regularly monitoring your website and keeping yourself up-to-date on performance so that you can develop a well-informed strategy.

Rebecca says: "You should look at the performance of your website. Monitoring is the key to finding those quick wins to effectively firefight when there's a problem. You can develop a better strategy through data analysis."

What about your website should you monitor?

"This is where we start getting into the 'it depends' territory. It depends on what your website is and its overall purpose. For example, if you have an eCommerce website with lots of variability in product availability, that's something you'd want to monitor. This would be important to ensure you're showing up in search and that people are being directed to the correct pages.

If you're a local shop, you'll want to make sure you're in other places. If you have a really complex tech stack, you might want to monitor page speed and server performance more than other sites would. It'll depend on both the industry you're in and the type of website you have.

However, in every case you should have a daily, monthly, or quarterly overview of what has changed or could change. This will allow you to make incremental improvements rather than waiting for something to blow up."

Does this involve keeping a historical record of what's changed? Is it important to look back and see if there have been any historical issues with the performance of a website?

"Yes. You should also see when there has been a change in rankings. In this case, you might also notice that there's been a change in page speed and how fast your server is responding. This could just be a server change that your IT department implemented that you weren't aware could be a problem.

Catch issues like these early on and resolve issues before they impact the rest of your business performance."

What are some typical areas of performance reduction that you've seen?

"In the past couple of years, there's been a lot about page speed updates. As far as eCommerce is concerned, this is often linked to how Google processes data and what its algorithms search for. Also, how product reviews appear in search and whether or not they're a ranking factor.

There are lots of quality issues today that Google takes into account. These were less important in the past and include things like duplicate content, user experience, and running into lots of missing page errors. The helpful content update hasn't had a huge impact across the board, yet, but it might in the future.

Everything from EAT to basic website health, whether your server is working properly, whether the site provides the content it says it has, or whether or not Google thinks that website should rank. These things are worth keeping an eye on across the board.

There are a couple of sites that do almost daily monitoring. Often, news sites do daily monitoring to see whether a sample of recent articles has registered in search, for example. They can then dig in deeper if there are problems."

What are some typical reasons why 404s happen? How do you decide how to deal with 404s?

"Ending up with a 404 is often due to a link that's directing to an incorrect page. That could be on your site or it could be a link that's published elsewhere. You could just change those links, but if they're published elsewhere there's not a lot you can do.

One of the things you should commonly implement is redirects - to redirect an address to the correct content."

There are plugins on WordPress that automatically 301 404s, is that poor practice?

"Not necessarily. It depends on where you're redirecting them to and what 404s you're redirecting. For example, let's say you've changed the slugs so the address of your WordPress content has a plugin that automatically redirects the old address to the new address of that same content. This would be great practice because then you wouldn't have to do that manually each time. If WordPress sees a 404 and you redirect that to your homepage, this is not necessarily the best way to handle things."

If you've seen a significant decrease or increase in the speed of a web page, what are some typical reasons this could happen?

"It's often due to the technology used to build that page. If you have reworked or used a different plugin to modify how that information is served to the front end - and to the client that's looking at that page - this could cause a huge impact. For example, if you have WordPress set up with lots of Javascript behind it, you might find that optimising your approach can make a huge difference in how much information is transferred to the person looking at the page. This can help to speed that page up.

The advantage here is that you can randomly see a page that's improved in speed or has had an improvement in the traffic to it from search. If you're monitoring regularly you'll observe some opportunities to improve across the board. You can take advantage of small improvements on your site and generalise them for a much bigger effect. A reduction in traffic doesn't necessarily tie back to poor page performance. There could be other reasons why Google decides to reduce your rankings."

What do you track and how do you ensure you're tracking the right things so that when you do have a reduction in the traffic to a particular page you notice it as soon as possible?

"One of the things you can do is break down the website into different parts. A decrease in traffic to a page that isn't essential to your SEO or business strategy will be less significant.

However, if you see a decrease in the sections of the website that are important for SEO, or your business in general, that'll be something you need to look into. Track traffic and position on keywords.

You can group similar keywords - for example, the type of keywords that are important for business, brand keywords and other keywords you're ranking for. This will largely depend on your site and industry. You can also track technical issues, whether that's technical SEO ranging from duplicate content to things like 404s and website health issues. These tend to be server or infrastructure related."

Regarding quick wins, what typical quick wins do many SEOs have an opportunity to gain in 2023?

"It depends. There are lots of possibilities - like looking at a website and realising you have systematic errors. You could make one correction that serves throughout time and the entire website. These are the sorts of things that can make a huge difference in SEO strategy. You must be able to address systematic or immediate issues."

What's an example of a systematic issue?

"Some sites regularly deindex certain pages because, for example, there's a tag that hasn't been removed by the product or tech team. In these cases, every time there's a new release or something is added to the site, someone will need to return and fix the problem. This is an issue that usually comes significantly into play later, when a person goes back to look at a specific page and why they're not getting traffic to it.

It's better to perform constant monitoring so you can identify the pages that have been affected by a release. You can then reveal the reasons behind these types of systematic errors. Rather than constantly going back to fix the same old problems, you'll be better off building an ongoing strategy through the data analysis you're participating in."

How do you build a better strategy through data analysis?

"That's the core of what SEO is about today. There is a lot of data. The more you look at what that data means and the cleaner your view is, the better the tools will be able to find the 'why' and the commonalities between some of the data. Instead of randomly looking at pages and noticing problems, you should regularly look at how that data correlates with other things.

It might be correlated with website updates or technical interventions. With a better view of your data, you can build an effective strategy that's adapted to the website. You can see where the weaknesses and strengths lie. If you have constant performance on, for example, branded keywords, this would be a fantastic approach if you have a strong brand.

The strategy of strengthening the brand and pushing it in certain markets will be different if you do see that strength. If your data doesn't show that type of thing, you'll need to adapt your strategy so it can. You'll then be more able to convince the people you need to work with. If you don't have data to back up a strategic decision, you'll just be working on a small project alone.

However, if you're able to show that something has had a significant impact on business via visibility through the search, this will allow you to push SEO projects to a more strategic level. You can then build those projects in a way that serves the business rather than trying to work against business goals."

Suppose your data analysis identifies consistent performance issues because of technical inefficiencies. How do you quantify the financial impact on the bottom line so you can create a more comprehensive business argument for why that needs to be changed?

"One of the best ways to do this is to look at the time saved. You can easily quantify the time that it takes to correct those issues. The next step would be to look at improvements, especially if it's a recurring issue. You can then make a more reliable benchmark as to what the negative and corrected states are, and also the difference between those. This is a good way to show there is ROI in making a final correction that could otherwise take more time to put into place."

What shouldn't SEOs be doing in 2023? What's seductive in terms of time, but ultimately counterproductive?

"With data analysis, the caution is that there is a lot of information. Too much information can be counterproductive, if you have too much detail or potentially unreliable data. For example, if you have one page that keeps shifting from position 43 to 45 in Semrush on a long-tail keyword that you're not necessarily interested in ranking for. It might even be something contradictory like 'rental for room in july how much does it cost.' This isn't going to be a high-volume search, so it won't be worth tracking or optimising for.

The idea of tracking every single possible data point is counterproductive. Leave those things alone and instead concentrate on areas with a real business impact."

Rebecca Berbel is the Product Marketing Manager at OnCrawl and you can find her at oncrawl.com.

Audit your website frequently during the year—Montserrat Cano

Montserrat Cano believes you should audit your website regularly in 2023 as a way to be more strategic, and gives SEOs guidance on what you should be focusing on during your audits and when you should be doing them.

Montserrat says: "You should audit your technical audience, positioning audience, etc. You should also be monitoring your website, your positioning, what kind of content is being picked up by Google, whether that content is producing results, and whether your competitors are looking for any other type of content that you should be ranking for."

What's the difference between a bigger audit and a smaller audit? What does conducting a bigger audit involve?

"With a bigger audit, you should be looking at technical aspects like technical position. You should make sure all websites are performing correctly and there are no security issues. This might not have as much to do with SEO, but it will affect a website's performance.

Also, look at every single brand's digital PR output. Conduct bigger keyword research and a bigger audit into what they've been doing during the year - in terms of the keywords you should be ranking for that are no longer producing any benefit."

If you work in a large organisation, should you be working in conjunction with your IT department when you audit?

"Definitely. SEO does not benefit from working in isolation, so it's important to do work with other departments. You should be good friends with the experts in your IT department and with the developers who will help you with the more technical aspects.

For example, you can audit the website, assess colours of choice, etc. As you look through, you'll see things that might not be appropriate - like HTML or text that breaks the hat. These are the tips you can give your developers to look into. Perhaps they are not as important as you think they are, or the other way around. This is just a way for you to help them to monitor your website and do their work in general."

From the audits you conduct, what are you finding as quick wins to improve the speed of a site?

"Sometimes images are unnecessarily too big, so why have them in the first place? Compressing images is a great option, however, looking into images of websites after an audit is a project in itself.

Whether it's an eCommerce or SaaS website, most use an incredible volume of images and graphics. These need to be compressed, but this is a big job. That's why it's so important to work with designers and developers who can assist you."

Are CMS systems getting better at automatically compressing the file size of images or is that something that has to be done manually?

"A manual audit is still necessary. There are some very good CMSs, add-ons, and plugins that can help you with your website. However, a manual audit is still better than just having a CMS and using tools. Also, as you start doing the manual audit, you can check whether that's something you should be focusing on.

One of the main benefits of an audit is that you can identify issues that you perhaps didn't know existed or issues that you deprioritized beforehand, like images. It's important to think about your resources and the state of things at a given moment in time. Think about whether you need to look into images or not.

Prioritise properly, because a lot of the SEO things we do need to be prioritised. Let's take Core Web Vitals as an example. When they first came out everyone assumed we needed to look into them, but sometimes looking into Core Web Vitals can break other things. You have to be careful and prioritise accordingly. That's another reason why you have to audit, especially when you've deprioritized something that later becomes a priority. It's important to always be aware of what's happening in the moment and react accordingly."

What is your favourite software for conducting audits?

"Screaming Frog, Sitebulb, Semrush, Majestic, etc. Using a combination of tools is the best approach. With different manual audits, it's more about checking with the tool first and then checking manually to see whether your results are correct. If it's checking properly then it'll be something you need to do."

Regarding Screaming Frog and Sitebulb, what are you looking for specifically from those two tools?

"Screaming Frog is used to perform everyday quick checks. Sitebulb is mostly used when you first come into a project or when you're working on a much bigger one. Both tools are amazing but Sitebulb is a lot more visual, so if you want to do a bigger audit you can save time by looking at the different graphics you find. Screaming Frog is more number-crunching."

How do audits help you to be more strategic and how do you use the data you discover from them?

"It's all about providing search engine algorithms with content that's going to be useful to your target audience. It's about providing content that answers their queries, content that is going to help you convert, that will make you look good from a digital PR perspective, and that will help your brand.

The benefits of doing this are big but they're mostly related to the concept of uncertainty. We're living through uncertain political, economic, and SEO times. Look at the SERPs every day and you'll be able to see the different tests being performed in different markets. You could see something in India but not in Sweden. Sometimes you'll get search results where there's no clickable link.

You need to be prepared for this, and audits can help with anything that might happen - whether that's a URL update or something else. This can help you with uncertainty because all you'll know about are brands, outputs, etc. The next step is to master your audience. How is your audience interacting with your content? Where are they clicking? What kind of formats do they prefer? etc.

We need to master this to avoid being absolutely nothing. Think about the algorithm updates and the weight Google is putting on trust, quality, etc. An audit can help you understand what your current state is so you can prioritise and plan for the year ahead to stand out in the SERPs. For example, are you making the right type of content? And, if keywords are not performing well, is that something you need to improve on?

There might be ongoing projects that can inform you about that. For example, if you're looking into Core Web Vitals as a side project but you audit and realise you are not ranking for a piece of content competitors are ranking for. In this case, you'd need to shift priorities."

What shouldn't SEOs be doing in 2023? What's seductive in terms of time, but ultimately counterproductive?

"Well, people need to be more strategic with content and stop producing more and more content for the sake of producing content. This is completely counterproductive because it doesn't help with your resources. Also, work satisfaction can reduce because you're pressed for time and can't measure the importance of content, how your audience is interacting with it, and whether they're clicking on it or buying something through it. It's important to analyse these things but impossible to do so when content is being published every week.

Be strategic about content and everything else. Identify a type of content that needs to be produced. Think about the resources you'll need to produce it, create a calendar to address the time you'll need to produce it, and think about what keywords need to go in there and your tracking requirements."

Montserrat Cano is a Senior Digital Marketing Consultant based in Madrid, Spain.

Go the extra mile with research, audits, and content creation—Olga Zarr

Olga Zarr believes that SEOs should go the extra mile when conducting website SEO audits and creating content in 2023, and warns you not to rely on just a few tools and tactics.

Olga says: "Always go the extra mile with anything you do in SEO, whether it is keyword research, content creation, content audits, or technical SEO."

How do you go the extra mile on keyword research?

"First, you should treat them as topics, not keywords. Then, when looking for new keywords, don't just rely on one tool, but five or more. You can use standard keyword tools such as Keyword Explorer, Ahrefs, and Semrush, and you can explore Google Autocomplete whenever you have a keyword."

How do you utilise long-tail keyword phrases and questions that don't have much search volume? Do you use a combination of them alongside high search volume phrases?

"In the case of in-depth longer guides, you can usually rely on keywords with high-volume search. Then, for the supporting articles, you can depend on longer-tail keywords that don't have any search volume from the tools.

From experience, even those long-tail zero-volume keywords can bring in significant traffic. Hence, you shouldn't weigh the keyword by what volume it has. Instead, find the ones that you can explore and talk about those topics.

If you create many of those articles about specific long-tail topics, you already have a silo on the site. Usually, the silo works fine and supports those hard, more competitive and difficult keywords."

Why are keywords with allegedly no search volume bringing in a decent amount of traffic? Are platforms like Google and other keyword data providers just not giving us the information?

"Those tools might not have data about those keywords yet. Usually, Google has about 20% of new keywords entered into its search engine every day. Hence, we may not have data about some of those keywords yet.

Sometimes, when a new product comes out, we can immediately know what keywords may be used to search for it. Then, we can decide about those keywords in advance. We might not need that data because there are so many different variations, and you might not want to spend a lot of time analysing keyword volume. Instead, focus on what's ranking at the top and whether you stand a chance of landing there."

Your number two way of going the extra mile was focusing on content creation. What do you mean by this?

"That is slightly connected to keyword research as well. When you create new content, go the extra mile by creating something more in-depth, and don't just summarise what's already in the top 10 results. Rather, create something new, and add your own commentary, unique insights, research results, conclusions, or experience. These are things that will be interesting to people.

Of course, you must keep search intent in mind. You cannot just create something totally different because you will not rank if your content doesn't satisfy the intent. Therefore, spend more time on creating those articles, but do them in a better way."

What about going the extra mile with content audits?

"Don't just rely on the tools to tell you what to do or what issues the site has. You should follow your template and have a list of things you check when you do an audit. Plus, always apply common sense and tap into your SEO experience when doing an audit.

Even though you're supposed to audit the site and find the issues, you may add a "quick wins" section with at least ten things that can be improved easily and bring relatively quick results. Usually, this will make your SEO audit way more powerful. And you will be able to provide results within weeks, months or even years, depending on the case."

Do you have any examples of quick wins that a traditional SEO audit wouldn't necessarily pick up?

"Usually, you can analyse the sites that already rank relatively well and offer further optimisations - for example, through internal linking or on-page optimisation. Check how the site ranks in Google Search Console, Semrush, and all those tools.

Another thing is to check what pages have the best backlinks. On those pages, add internal links to pages which you want to help move higher up. It is not common to do as part of an audit, especially a technical SEO audit, but it could be a bonus."

Coming up with an internal link strategy seems to lie between technical SEO and SEO content strategy. Is internal linking often missed during an audit?

"Practically every site audit always has something to be improved in that regard."

How do you go the extra mile by focusing on technical SEO?

"A good example is JavaScript SEO. Usually, you would simply check the site and do a mobile-friendly test. And in the trials, you see screenshots of the homepage if you have access to the site.

Recently, you can also move things around, scroll a bit, and see more of how the rendered pages look. However, it is recommended to go the extra mile by crawling the site with two crawlers: Screaming Frog and Sitebulb, and executing JavaScript on both. It may be tricky for you to do this manually on a huge site like eCommerce so, if you render JavaScript on all pages, the tool will help you compare the links and identify important content differences. In case of any changes, it will also show you how they can impact your SEO bottom line."

What specifically are you looking for that's different between Screaming Frog and Sitebulb? Is there a potential negative in not knowing which information to trust if you use too many tools?

"Each tool works differently and shows different results. It helps to follow your lead, have a specific checklist, and then analyse the results. That way, it is not the tool telling you what the problem is.

For example, with JavaScript SEO, you check whether canonical links have changed or whether it's the internal linking in navigation. Basically, you already know what you want to check, and then simply use the results provided along with the template and keep updating."

When creating templates for conducting an SEO audit, do you design a bespoke template for each site based on what the issues and outcomes are likely to be?

"You can have a universal template with multiple items included. Sometimes the list won't apply to a specific site, so you remove them, but it should have everything from technical SEO to content analysis to even

Google questions about core updates to EAT. You then adjust that template depending on the type of audit the client needs."

What shouldn't SEOs be doing in 2023? What is seductive in terms of time, but ultimately counterproductive?

"Regarding SEO audits, less experienced SEOs usually rely on automated audits like Sitebulb. Practically any tool can generate a long, automated SEO audit with many pages and explanations. It is tempting to just hit 'Generate exports', however, you shouldn't do that.

Usually, the audit results will have nothing to do with how you want the site to look. Only you can decide whether a specific issue marked by the tool is really an issue because only you know the site's context, scope, and purpose.

Instead, create SEO audits and add your own commentary tailored to the site with relevant examples."

Olga Zarr is an SEO Consultant and CEO at SEOSLY and you can find her over at seosly.com.

Clean up your website—Bill Hartzer

Bill Hartzer believes that, as SEOs, we tend to get too involved in thinking about creating more content, more pages, and optimising said pages. He encourages you to start cleaning things up to make sure your current website is at its best.

Bill Says: "In 2023, we need to sit down and carve out time in our schedules to clean up our websites. Whether that's optimising current images on site to load faster, cleaning up widgets and website templates, or looking back at what content is getting indexed and what isn't. For example, there are lots of large websites that allow their internal search pages to get indexed and deindexed. However, do you really need all this extra thin content on your website?

Our main goals as SEOs are to get more optimised pages, more links, and create more content. However, have you considered the content you have currently? Always look through your existing content and update it accordingly - whether that's page titles, adding FAQs, or other general cleanup tasks. There's always lots to clean up, so why not address your current website in 2023 and ensure it's at its best in all aspects? It's not always about creating new content."

One of the things you mentioned is to look at what pages are indexed and not indexed. Is this a good place to start this cleanup exercise?

"Yes, that's a very good place to start. There are several ways to look at Search Console data, and various other data as well. Some tools enable you to see which pages are indexed and which pages are not. With Search Console, you can look at pages like coverage reports and go on to see which pages are crawled but not indexed.

There will be reasons why pages are not indexed, and sometimes pages get dropped out of the index for no apparent reason. If it's an important page to you, go back and refresh it. If it's an article or blog written years ago that's still relevant as evergreen content, you can go back and refresh and resubmit it to make it rank. Google might already know about it, so it will just be a matter of refreshing it so you can actually get it back in the index and so forth. This is all part of the cleanup process."

Why might Google deindex a page that has good content on it? Would it be because the internal links aren't directly from the homepage or significant pages to a site anymore and it's not getting that deemed authority from your site?

"That's one possibility but, in all honesty, we don't know why certain pages just get dropped. It could be internal links, it could be fewer clicks from search results. Sometimes random pages get dropped as a hiccup in Google's crawling and indexing processes. The main thing is: if it's a page where you can go in and change one thing and resubmit it, that page could be indexed again within 10-15 minutes. In this event, it might not have been the quality of the page that caused it to fall but some other reason that Google came up with.

It's important to do a bit more investigation into crawled pages that are not indexed. There are some cases where certain pages are just not indexed."

Could it be as simple as updating your titles if they're not deemed as relevant as other pages?

"Yes. By going back and tactically crawling sites you can figure out whether there's a reason why certain pages drop. Analytics comes into play too. If you have a list of URLs and there haven't been any traffic clicks to that page in a year or two, you need to determine why. Is it because it's not indexed anymore or is it because it's just not relevant content anymore?"

How much content is thin nowadays? Is it a certain number of words or is it just not answering a question sufficiently enough?

"When it comes to thin content, there could be a page that ranks very well and that's very appropriate, but has just 100 words on it. If this answers the question for the user then that's great. However, it's always best to look for duplicate content issues.

Many people make the mistake of writing a blog without using the alt tag that splits the first paragraph. In instances like these, 1,000 words of the blog post would appear on the blog post URL only. If you don't use that alt tag to split off the first paragraph - so that only the first paragraph will appear on the /blog page - you could have a situation where you have all of the content on the blog URL and all of the content on the main blog page. You'd have the same content in two places and could run into classic duplicate content issues that need cleaning up.

There's a correlation between thin content and duplicate content, and it is very close when assessing what pages to remove."

If you've got widgets on your blog, how can you tell if they're having a detrimental impact on user experience and even the search engines' perceptions of your site?

"Let's say you have a site you created ten years ago and it still gets traffic, however, there's a widget that pulled data or information from another site. If that site goes down, you'd have a widget that's just a black rectangle when the site loads. This happens with things that are supposed to load information somewhere or pull a logo from another site.

It could be another code, StatCounter code or any other code. This is all part of the cleanup. Another really important thing is who you're making it out to. Let's say you use a crawler that crawls all the internal pages on the site, but somewhere else you have an old page or other pages linking out to another URL. For example, most sites are now HTTPS, so if you can scroll through the external links you're linking out to you'll see an HTTP URL. All those main sites are now HTTPS and you'll be linking out to a URL that's a 301.

On the flip side, there's a link building tactic: to crawl your competitors' websites and find everybody that they're linking out to. In most 500-page or longer sites, you'll find they're linking out to a link to a domain name that's not registered anymore. In many cases, people would register that domain name and get the link back so that their competitor links to them. Your competitor could be doing the same to you, where you're linking out to a domain name that doesn't exist anymore and your competitor buys the domain name to get some of the traffic. It's always important to take a look at things and clean up."

What shouldn't SEOs be doing in 2023? What's seductive in terms of time, but ultimately counterproductive?

"Fairly recently we've been thinking about AI, machine learning, and AI-generated content. You can essentially put a list of keywords in and generate various articles and content. Some tools are better at generating AI content than others, but it appears to be a racing game between Google and the SEOs. As SEOs begin to generate AI content, how long will it be until Google fully understands what content is AI-generated and what isn't?

We had this situation years ago when people would create hundreds and thousands of doorway pages. People were curious as to how long it would be until Google figured out these were doorway pages and whether it would ignore them or penalise people accordingly.

There's a time and a place for using AI. If you're creating a site and your articles and content are all AI-generated, that's something you shouldn't do unless you're creating content for another site. However, on your main site, you should take a hard look at how much AI-generated content is being used.

AI can be very helpful if you have 100,000 products on your eCommerce site that need product descriptions, meta description tags, and a few accompanying sentences. AI could be very useful for crafting simple product descriptions, rewriting, and generating those.

What we shouldn't do as SEOs is rely too much on AI-generated content. Use it sparingly and only when appropriate."

Bill Hartzer is the CEO of Hartzer Consulting and you can find him over at hartzer.com.

Be selective about scripts, tags and other code items—Brenda Malone

Brenda Malone tells SEOs that third-party tag governance is going to be crucial in 2023 to maintain performance-compliant websites, and gives tips on how to select the right code.

Brenda says: "You need to be very judicious about every single third-party tag that's deployed on your website. Tags are the best and worst of things. There are little parasitic tags that reduce the performance of your website, slow it down, and can ultimately worsen your rankings. You should get control of those tags and only use them when necessary, as necessary."

Why are tags both positive and negative?

"Tags are extremely useful, especially to marketers, SEO folks, and business operations. Tags do many things: they tell us who's visiting a site, what's happening on the site when visitors are there, what they're doing, and whether they're successful in their mission. Tags let us know if they're able to purchase a product/service, they inform us about the pages which are very important to visitors, and they can also enhance performance. A lot of tags add animation dynamic actions to websites.

Some can be very useful but the problem lies in the fact that they're very heavy and come at a cost. They're very expensive to page loading and page performance. Going into 2023, you will need to manage that ratio of usefulness to detriment of website performance. Tags represent the best and worst of things."

Should each organisation have someone who can take charge of tag management and make the ultimate decision?

"Perhaps in a utopia. Currently, it is the wild wild west when it comes to tags. Seemingly, every department of an organisation, every developer, and every SEO has their own specific set of favourite functional or non-functional tags. Unfortunately, often they're all just tossed on a website with no thought as to what they do. Is it useful? Should we use it? How are we using it effectively? Most organisations don't have a designated party to govern these decisions.

In many cases, the developer will get a call requesting to put something on a site. They won't have the ability to question the business reason for the tag, and the SEO department may not understand the implications that a third-party tag will have on site performance. Many websites load a hundred tags on every single page and that's dreadful for page load and experience. With the new rankings in Google, you're liable to fail and have your developers running to the hills. They won't be able to improve performance as long as the marketing and SEO department are throwing dozens and dozens of tags on the website."

Elon Musk says that we should have to vote laws back in because they naturally expire over time. Should we employ a similar system with tags?

"That's a great idea and a brilliant way to phrase the whole problem. Maybe then the debate will be about the length of expiry. Before a tag goes on a site there should be a governing body that approves it - whether that's comprised of SEO members, marketers, IT members, or members from the business sector of an agency or company.

Police all of those tags, make sure the business case absolutely needs that, it's performant, and get your IT team and developers to ensure the tag isn't going to conflict with anything else that's happening on the website.

Maybe your developers have another idea, maybe they did not exactly know the reason why you needed that specific tag. Include developers in the conversation because they might not know the reason why a specific tag is necessary.

You should also include the SEO, marketing department, and tag manager. Only allow tags that have been improved, and that are in the library with an expiration date. Pull a tag off when it's not needed and only deploy it when necessary. For example, in A/B testing that tag will deploy across every page - and that's not necessary. A CAPTCHA form for security will also load on, every page and that's not needed. Use a tag manager, put your tags in order, and make sure that only approved tags which have gone through the vetting process are allowed. Also, have someone manage the expiration date so they can pull a tag off when necessary, put tags on a site, and manage, police, and use them properly."

If you've got a website with lots of tags on it, what's the best software to identify the biggest culprits?

"You should break it down with the waterfall chart. My favourite tool is webpagetest.org - an oldie that's been improved dramatically. It's at a level now where you can judiciously deploy and test what specific scripts do when they're turned on and off, and whether they're necessary. However, you have to manage them by looking at the page load and the waterfall chart to see the exact cost of that tag, how many seconds it's taking to load, and what else it's blocking.

Most tags are render-blocking, meaning when the tag calls back home nothing else can load on the website. Everything stops and waits for that tag to call home and come back with further instructions. Just stop it. Stop all those people from calling home. Don't allow them to slow your website down."

Is it possible for tags to fire after a partial load so that users can see everything above the fold and they can carry on scrolling?

"Absolutely. A tag manager could also do that. You can load it in layers and control when it loads, how it loads, and at what time it turns off. You can schedule your scripts to load asynchronously - which means you tell the website it's OK to load these tags together because they won't alter what's already being loaded. Or, you could load them deferred - which means that after all of the other critical website resources (your images, text, blocks of copy, headers and footers) load you can load those tags without them impacting performance as much as if they were loaded with higher priority.

For the tags that you absolutely must have, use webpagetest.org and look at the loading priority. This will help you determine the exact loading order priority so you can play around with different tests and see what will happen if you move the priority around."

You mentioned a tag manager a few times, are you just referring to Google Tag Manager or is there other tag management software that's just as good?

"Google is the elephant in the room. Most people are familiar with Google Tag Manager and it synchronises so well with all of the other Google tags, your analytics, search console, and ad tags. There are quite a few other tag managers too, though. Microsoft has a tag manager and Adobe Experience is useful too. Google Tag Manager can be exploited to do precisely what you need it to do. It's essential when you're governing your tag employment on websites."

What shouldn't SEOs be doing in 2023? What's seductive in terms of time, but ultimately counterproductive?

"SEOs should stop working in silos. Right now, we're a separate department with no coordination between the business units of the organisation. Sometimes the marketing department doesn't even know what the SEO department needs. The developers and IT department need to come to the table and there should be a seat at the table for SEO. Stop treating the SEO discipline as a separate cast-off division that just manages the website. SEOs should be present to save time when business decisions are being made and to increase productivity. Bring everyone together and stop operating silently in the background.

Emphasise business metrics and business ways of thinking about the time and productivity that can be saved. This is the type of language that an SEO should use to encourage top management to give them a seat at the table. Conversations with the business unit are a great way to prove your worth. Sometimes we navigate a difficult path when we should just divide the existence of SEO. If you're at the table in the beginning, you can develop parameters that will make it easy to gauge the effectiveness of SEO. This is better than working in hindsight after everything has been deployed or spent, because you'll just be playing catch up."

Brenda Malone is a Technical SEO Specialist at NP Digital and you can find her over at npdigital.com.

Review your content quality (or lack thereof) through content inventories—Charlie Williams

Charlie Williams believes that by using content inventories in 2023, SEOs can better understand the content quality that you are currently delivering across your entire website.

Charlie says: "Content inventories are a great way to get rich data and an actionable overview of all the pages on your site. You can then gain an understanding of all the content that search engines might use to rate you.

This won't just be for the pages you think you're putting forward or the ones on your main navigation, but for the entire site that's available. Though this is a tip that's existed for a while, it's more useful than ever in 2023. We're collectively embracing Google's new world of helpful content updates, product review updates, core updates, etc., and a content inventory gets us into the mindset of looking at the entire content experience of our site."

What does looking at the crawl index structure mean?

"The first step in gathering the content inventory is to understand all the pages you have available so you can pull in data for them. The first part of this is crawling the active website and the pages you have that are public facing. This involves looking at your main website and your XML sitemap, and crawling both to understand the active site structure. Once you've got that kind of information, you can expand out to other places where content might be available on the website, but is a bit more hidden away. For example, you can use the index coverage reports in Search Console to understand other pages that are indexed but aren't in that main active site structure.

You can use your performance reports in Search Console or your analytics package of choice. To see all the pages that have had organic traffic, you should use some of your favourite SEO tools to look at all the pages that have rankings in the search results. You can use a backlink tool like Majestic to understand all the pages that have backlinks, whether they're active or very old pages.

Speaking of old pages, the other place you can look is archive.org: the 'Wayback Machine'. You can use the site's API simply by entering a URL into the browser and it'll throw back all the pages it's become aware of over the course of time. This is a great source of potential pages.

You can put all these things together and, suddenly, you have a big list of all the pages that are active on your website right now. You can use this as the basis for understanding what your entry might contain."

What would you do if a page isn't indexed and you want it to be indexed? What are the typical reasons why a page isn't indexed?

"Let's say you have a website with 5,000 pages, and you notice there are a couple of hundred pages that have been crawled but not indexed. You can spot them and start looking for patterns suggesting why those pages might not be indexed. Is it a content duplication issue, a content quality issue, or something else around the pages? Is it a technical crawling issue? There are many reasons why that might've happened. The idea is to have a big inventory of all the pages so you can start spotting areas where things have gone awry."

Regarding typical areas, why would they not be linking to those pages? Could it be that you have inferior content there?

"Google is becoming more judicious about choosing what it wants to index or not. Before, it felt very much like Google would index everything and let the ranking part of the algorithm determine whether to show things in the search results or not. We're now finding that Google is choosing not to index as much. This means that when you look at these areas for a client, and spot these areas of content, it tends to be something to do with the content quality.

It could be a technical SEO issue that's causing near duplicates of pages, or it could be there are a lot of pages with very little content coming through. This could be because it's an eCommerce site where, if a category has zero products, it'll still show all the facets for it. It could be down to the fact that it's low-quality content that's not adding anything and so isn't being indexed by Google. The key is to be able to spot areas like this and put your SEO hat on to investigate further."

How do performance and load speed impact whether a piece of content is likely to get indexed or not?

"Load speed isn't necessarily an indexing factor, unless you're suffering from severe problems - for example, if Google decides to limit the crawl rate it's hitting your website with because it's finding it's very slow to load. This can stop them from crawling deeper into the website and will reduce your crawl budget accordingly. Though it's a rare occurrence, the crawl rate can drop due to the load performance being very poor. Sometimes Google doesn't crawl as deep into a site, so therefore pages aren't discovered and can't be indexed.

Otherwise, page load speed is more useful for Google as a tie-breaking ranking factor that's applied. It's great to have it in a content inventory in line with collating multiple data points, backlinks, organic visits, and internal links to see whether this content is indexed or not and whether you're putting your best foot forward.

If you have a site with multiple sections that have poor loading speed, not many internal links, and you're not getting many organic visits, rather than assuming it's poor-performing content you could say the content hasn't had a chance to succeed because you haven't linked to it much or it's not loading quickly. You can then focus on fixing those things, if you think it'll be valuable to do so, and see if that makes a difference. That's where page load speed can be useful as a performance indicator factor."

Are backlinks just external links?

"When talking about pulling the data, most of the time this refers to backlinks and external data. Does this content contribute to the backlink of the profile of the website? Is poor performance perhaps indicative of it being a competitive topic that this page is targeting? Would some backlinks potentially help?

Internal linking is crucially important from a site structure and architecture point of view. Is your content being referred to enough times internally regardless of the big number of visits? Are you positioning yourself to give those internal link signals to Google? Are you suggesting this is valuable content with internal links pointing to it, and the chance for users to discover it themselves through the journey of your website?"

Are you a fan of getting rid of content that isn't indexed?

"Yes, especially if it's not indexed because it's no good, indexed but never shown, or if we're seeing negative signals. You might also notice poor conversion rates, few people navigating to the page, and low content quality in general.

If the content isn't serving a purpose and it's not driving any benefits, how do you measure that? If it's not doing its job it's probably not worth keeping. Improve it or retire it in some fashion. You should make your website lean. Avoid having pages for the sake of it. Make the website as lean and efficient as possible. Start chopping things away and focus on the stuff that's important."

If you have some blog posts that didn't have any external backlinks and aren't getting any traffic, would you probably get rid of them?

"It's important to think about the goal of the content. If the content isn't getting traffic and it isn't driving backlinks or positive signals, when was the content created and who was it created for? What value could you get from keeping it? It'll still have value if it's blog content from years ago that can still be targeted to certain keywords, or if it's useful supplementary content for the blog post you're creating now. If you want to build expertise you'll need to show that depth of information, that you've been writing about this topic for a while at a high level.

If the content is still valuable and is still serving a purpose even without loads of backlinks, is it not getting traffic because you're not referencing it enough? Do you need to optimise it better? Is it not working because it's out of date? If it's not very good stuff and no one would want to read it anyway, it will become a clear candidate to go. However, don't throw the baby out with the bathwater."

Regarding content inventory, how often should this be done?

"You'll have to do an overview at the beginning. This is important in SEO and will be increasingly important for being aware of everything that's happening on a website regarding SEO performance. Doing the content inventory at the beginning will give you a month's worth of actionable ideas to work on. You can look at where you need to improve a section, remove a section, retire something, improve site governance, etc. By doing this at the beginning, you'll have a big list of words and can monitor your website more effectively.

There are website tools that monitor your website and tell you when pages have been added and deleted. These tools are becoming increasingly important, especially when combined with the content and venture at the beginning. You'll have a benchmark position to start from and understand everything you should be working on. Once you've done it well in the beginning (if you've got a strong monitoring system in place), you won't need to run it again for a while because you'll be aware of the new pages that have been added, deleted, or changed. You might not need to run it again for 18 months, but it's important to play to what your setup is."

What shouldn't SEOs be doing in 2023? What's seductive in terms of time, but ultimately counterproductive?

"The temptation is to follow a process-driven or assembly-line SEO strategy for every client. This is the counter of a content inventory. Some SEOs want to fit everything neatly into a box and follow exact processes and procedures.

Sometimes that can work, but it's difficult to apply a universal approach because everyone's tech stack is different, everyone's goals are different, and everyone's publication processes are different. The idea of assembly-line SEO is seductive. It's tempting because you will have a framework to go through. However, being bespoke to the actual needs of your customer is more important."

Charlie Williams is an SEO and Content Strategy Consultant at Chopped Digital and you can find him at chopped.io.

Prepare for the worst—Olesia Korobka

Olesia Korobka tells SEOs that you should prepare for the worst but hope for the better, so that you know your website can weather the inevitable storms that will arise in 2023 and beyond.

Olesia says: "To properly prepare yourself for the worst, you'll need to make a backup, write a workflow, and prepare to report on the circumstances that might arise."

From an SEO perspective, what might be the worst?

"Lately we've seen natural disasters, and some SEOs have even had their personal circumstances brought under fire. There have been lots of things happening and, as we shift into recession, we could expect the next year to be very bad for businesses in many ways. We have seen people getting laid off and this trend is likely to continue, if not get worse.

You might face circumstances and think that you are so experienced and can rely on your previous experience fully. The best analogy would be that you can always choke on your food or bite your tongue. Your lifelong experience chewing and digesting food won't necessarily protect you from this failure. The best way to prepare yourself for what might happen is back up your files, including a physical backup and cloud storage. These should be kept separately from the natural files you're working with each day. You can then create a written workflow of your typical daily tasks."

What specifically should you back up and why do you recommend taking a physical backup as well as a cloud backup?

"With cloud backups, some companies may decide to stop working with you. Some companies may get burned down, servers may get burnt, and you wouldn't have any access to your files. Alternatively, servers might be in a country that's experiencing difficulties. You can lose access to them. You may also find that people are storing backups along with their files on the same server. In these cases, whatever happens to the files happens to the backups.

A physical backup means that when anything bad happens, you can grab the disk or whatever files are stored on and recover them."

What data should you specifically include in the backup? Should you include your website and visitor data?

"All of your documents - your website, SQL tables, documents, passwords, and data entries. Most sales teams have lots of accounts and there could be multiple passwords to consider. It can be difficult to even remember the names of the tools you're using because they're all programmed into Chrome or elsewhere. You should have these stored independently to avoid forgetting about them.

Have backup data about all of your domains, and the links that you need to pay for after some time. Sometimes you won't get notifications that something is going to expire and you might lose access to your website, lose domains, backlinks, and lots of data in general. That should be a big part of your backup."

Is it an SEO's responsibility to think about all of this?

"Yes. You are someone who drives traffic and money to businesses. It's all about the money you can provide to businesses for them to maintain and grow. You should at least ask the questions because the success of the website will radically impact whether or not the SEO has been successful."

Could you elaborate on the importance of workflows?

"Some people think they're good to go just because they have backups of their documents and websites. They think they can use their brain because they have experience bringing up websites and assume they can remember everything. However, if anything unforeseen were to happen, they could become so concentrated on survival that their cognitive functions suffer.

Let's say you've always known how to perform a routine task and you're very successful with that. When the harder times come and you're under stress, you can't operate properly. You should also have these workflows written down for you. This might sound very basic and you might assume you know everything, but you won't. It's easy to forget everything. When you have your workflow written down you can open it in your backup and follow it."

If you have those documented workflows already, is it going to be much easier to get people working with you to replicate what you're doing?

"Sometimes very ordinary tasks will help you because you can forget how to do them under some circumstances. That might sound primitive, but that's the reality of what happens. Many people find this out for themselves. If you have that written down and you just open it from your backup, you'll be able to proceed with your work regardless. If there's a hurricane and you have your tasks written down, you could still execute them.

When something bad happens, pick one thing you're especially good at - something you're much better at doing than others. Write it down and make it something distinctive to you, something you can offer to other people in circumstances where've lost everything and need something fast to work with. Also, document everything."

You also talked about automated tasks, what are some examples of automated tasks that you should be backing up?

"Some tasks require you to do some very basic things, like tracking performance over time in terms of rankings. Set up alerts in the event of anything happening to a website, for example, losing a big portion of your organic traffic for some cluster. Something else that you can automate is adding content and optimising it. Look for entities and schema markup. These are mostly technical tasks, like monitoring alerts for your backlinks."

What are some specific automated alerts that every SEO needs to have set up?

"One of the most important is that your domain is up and running."

How do you go about setting up and receiving an alert if you've had a dip in organic reach? Should you target overall reach or specific key pages?

"Make your developer do that for you if you can. If you can do it yourself, that's great - you can automate it with Python or Console. Some people have very small websites, like local business websites, where there are very few landing pages that aren't specifically tracked. These are usually the pages that are bringing in customers. For bigger websites, you can automate that in clusters. If you see a significant drop in one of those clusters, you'll know that you need to go and see what's happening there, and why it's happening."

How do you bring everything together and turn it into a report that you can action?

"There isn't a one-size-fits-all solution for this. Most people turn to one of two options. Firstly, you could use Looker Studio and get all the APIs in there. Others use Power BI, which is very useful when you have lots of projects - for example, you're running lots of websites and they are more or less in the same niche. You want to see the performance for each of them at the same time because you're selling around the same across the board. You want to understand how they're performing altogether, not separately. Power BI is useful when you want to see all of your projects and track their performance in one place."

What reports are key to building inside Looker Studio?

"Organic traffic. You'll want to see how many people come from Google and other search engines, and what their flow is like across the website when they convert. You should also look at all of those associated conversions that brought them to buy. Some of them will be lifelong customers, so they will either subscribe to your newsletters or not. Analyse things like this by bringing them to the attention of the marketing department, or whoever else is responsible."

What are the key metrics you would recommend sharing with a general marketing department?

"If you have a service company, one of the key metrics would be sign-ups, the calls to your service, and how leads convert into customers. You should look at the leads coming into your system and how they convert afterwards. You should look at where they are diverting to and which clusters are the most popular. Do they all come to one specific page and are you dependent on that page or are you able to bring them to various pages? These are important considerations for eCommerce when you have lots of different pages but still want to see what customers are buying the most.

You can also work out if they buy anything else with that, and add that as a proposal to other customers to sell even more. It will be dependent on the type of business you're in, but you can look at things like sign-ups or things that people buy or add to their cart and how they convert after that. As an SEO, you'll see the correlations for pages and where they rank in terms of

Google and everywhere else. How much traffic is brought from that system to that specific page?"

What shouldn't SEOs be doing in 2023? What's seductive in terms of time, but ultimately counterproductive?

"SEO in 2022 was about AI. Now it's really happening, and lots of people are over-engaged in this. They try to invest lots of effort and resources into AI. This can consume significant energy and effort.

AI tools are only based on one or two of the same resources around the globe. It probably won't generate many benefits because, after testing, you'll end up spending more money than if you were to work with a human. Maybe in 2025 or 2024, AI will become less resourceful and more beneficial. In 2023, they'll still be testing a lot and the fact-checking for these types of content will be difficult, to say the least. You'll end up spending more on AI if you invest in that over real humans. Do not invest too much into AI in terms of content."

Olesia Korobka is the Founder and SEO Leader of Fajela and you can find her over at fajela.com.

3 CONTENT STRUCTURE

Core Web Vitals and content quality—Taylor Kurtz

Taylor Kurtz asserts that Google's algorithm changes mean SEOs should avoid churning out content for the sake of it in 2023, and also focus on your customer experience.

Taylor says: "My advice for 2023 is twofold. One, I want to emphasise your website's core vitals and performance. While it has recently become a primary ranking factor, it's often neglected if you analyse your competitors. It has also been stated as a primary ranking factor by Google - not necessarily a tiebreaker - so it can be an easy win against your competitors.

But more importantly, when it comes to these core vitals like the Largest Contentful Paint, First Input Delay and Cumulative Layout Shift, with certain tools you can easily get in compliance with Google. When they give you direction on what they need, you might as well do those things. Hence, one of the top tips is to focus on your core vitals and your website's performance - and share a good user experience.

Everyone talks about backlinks content, which is important. However, it all contributes to what Google really wants: websites that provide the most valuable information and the best user experience."

What are the important elements within Core Web Vitals, maybe starting with the Largest Contentful Paint? How would you summarise that?

"Essentially, Google's goal with this was to put metrics onto the user experience. The Largest Contentful Paint represents how long it takes for the biggest element or piece of content on your website to load, whether it be a video, a photo, an appointment, or an embed. Whatever it may be, Google wants that to load in two and a half seconds or less.

That can be easy to do, yet you'll often see people loading images that would look like they are designed for an 8K TV. On the phone, viewers don't need that kind of image. Hence, you can often use tools to identify what's taking a long time on your site and make sure it loads more efficiently. That will certainly help with the Largest Contentful Paint. Cumulative Layout Shift, however, is where most people have had to put their efforts.

Essentially Google was trying to avoid scenarios where you are travelling, you're looking for food and you find an interesting restaurant, you go to their website and see a 'View Menu' button, but as you click it, the rest of the website loads, and you end up clicking something else. That is the layout shift that Google wants to avoid, which most people spend their time addressing.

Either way, if you're really into SEO and you're on a micro level, your websites are probably already in compliance. For larger agencies or people without that level of detail, it's something that Google highlighted as important, which you might want to comply with. If you are working with a good developer, that shouldn't take so long."

How would you summarise the Largest Contentful Paint, Cumulative Layout Shift, and First Input delay?

"Cumulative Layout Shift is a metric that Google wants to keep under 0.1 seconds. That being said, the First Input Delay is essentially how long it takes to get a response when you interact with the website or click on something. There, a lot of times, people focus on hosting problems. For example, you'll have somebody that pays $3 a month, and they don't even know who's hosting their website. You'll notice that every time someone clicks on anything, there's a huge delay, because it takes a long time to get that response from the host.

Generally, those are the three vitals, and getting those in compliance will go a long way and set you up for long-term success."

From an SEO perspective, how do we measure the impact of improving webpage performance? Can we say that if we increase the Page Speed loading by X%, our rankings will increase by X%?

"If you increase or improve your performance at all, there's no chance you'll go down because of that. Say you have a web page that does well and competes with four other pages. If you pay attention to these vitals, you will not necessarily jump over them. Rather, you will, by default, climb the rankings if they do nothing. It is thus not a reward for your efforts, but you are not being penalised for ignoring those details either.

Will your page get higher rankings if you have the same number of backlinks and website age and type of content compared with a competitor - but you're doing a better job with website performance?

Most likely. So many factors go into it, so it is not a guarantee, but you can expect to see positive results for that."

Why should SEOs not neglect content and relevance?

"John Mueller (who is considered the Google Search liaison for Google) in August 2021, went on Reddit. When talking about these core vitals around the time of the algorithm update, he said, *'The algorithm of these core vitals are primary ranking factors. They are more than just the tiebreaker, but they do not replace relevance. At the end of the day, while we want a good user experience, if there's nothing of value on your site, it doesn't matter how fast it loads or how well it's performing. When I land there, I don't take anything away.'*

Although it is such a cliche thing to say - 'Content is king'. That's never been more relevant than now. In mid to late 2022, Google announced and then released the next week what was called the "helpful content update." Also, about ten years prior, the Panda update came out, which completely shifted the way people within SEO strategise content and set optimisation. It's been said that this new update is expected to have the largest impact of any algorithm update since that time.

The goal has always been content. However, Google now says it needs to be helpful and authoritative content intended to share and educate. What differentiates this update is that it's called a site-wide update. Typically, when Google releases any significant update, if you have a page that's not meeting whatever standards, it would fall in the rankings. With the helpful content update, Google said that if you have an unfavourable ratio of content considered unhelpful, your whole site will get penalised. That's what makes it dramatic - because so many people and companies are dedicated to churning out boilerplate content. Therefore, Google is trying to emphasise and reward those that provide valuable and helpful information instead.

Like John Mueller said, focusing on those core vitals is an easy win because you can get all those in compliance in less than a week. Then you don't even have to worry about it for years. However, that still doesn't replace the relevance or impact of content, specifically when Google is now prioritising quality. Google actually put out some guidelines and checklists along with that in August 2022. If you looked through it and they mostly applied to your website, you might be at risk. It covered issues like clickbait, summarising people's content, answering questions, etc.

Basically, it's trying to tackle people who write content to manipulate and please search engines. They want it to be written for people, not the algorithm."

Does that mean that Google expects your website to be a niche specialist and focus on specific content moving forward?

"There are several ways to go about it. You would often go through the site, either using a tool like Screaming Frog to crawl every page or going through the Google Search Console. Then, find the pages that have generated little or no clicks in the past 12 months and decide whether they are still relevant to your niche. From there, you will have three choices: rewrite the article, get rid of it, or redirect it to another page.

The other option is to add the noindex feature. That way, if you are concerned about a page that is not generating traffic but is still great to have on the site, you could add a noindex tag in the source code. When Google crawls it, they don't factor that into the index.

I have seen clients that have been producing content for over ten years, yet when you go back and look at blogs written in 2010/2011, the style of writing and the intent behind it has changed. A lot of times, the information is now outdated too. That becomes an excellent opportunity to refresh your content and boost yourself as an authority. Content remains king, so it is even more important to write with authority and be the expert in 2023."

Is there any particular style or structure of the content that Google prefers now?

"Google had that checklist of things to avoid/red flags, and one of them was writing for targets like the length. The general mindset has always been that longer is better, based on the fact that you are trying to be the expert here. You want to have more information than any of the other pages out there and leave no stone unturned.

At the same time, if you want to rank for a keyword, you don't want to see who's ranking in the top five and take an average word count. That would simply be writing for search engines, which Google does not want.

You should consider the question/topic you are writing about and whether you can address it in 100 words or 2,000. Overall, the goal is to be the foremost source of information. Google will consider whether, after checking out your content, the reader leaves to find out more information. Therefore, ensure all the content is valuable and doesn't leave people wanting more."

How do you select which keywords to target?

"A lot of it is client-dependent. You may get a client that produces Wagyu beef and, of course, they want to rank number one for 'Wagyu beef', which is the broadest competitive term in their market. You'll go through that and also find out what other search terms or industries represent the kind of audience you would like to attract, and then pull up more specific keywords related to Wagyu beef from there.

Are there very specific questions like, 'What is marbled beef?' Though that's a much more specific question, you can rank for that in a much shorter time. And that process has a snowball effect on where we want to go as we build up authority.

So when picking keywords, consider what the client wants, but also do more research to find less frequently searched terms where you can quickly capture the first spot or featured snippets, and continue to generate relevant traffic."

What shouldn't SEOs be doing in 2023? What is seductive in terms of time, but ultimately counterproductive?

"We are now going to have a huge focus on content, however, producing the content is one of the most time-consuming things, especially if you don't want to pay for a content writer. What many people do is find the best page on the topic they want to write, then copy the entire text into AI tools which can rewrite them in any format - and they don't have to worry about plagiarism checkers. This process can be quite tempting, especially with the amount of time you can save. In reality, it's all the same. You're not adding any new information, just rephrasing everything.

Google is not stupid; its algorithm is improving daily. It relies on AI, and as that gets more sophisticated, it will pick up on trends and patterns created by this artificial rewriting software. While it is tempting, the risk is too high. Before, the biggest risk was the page that didn't perform. Now, when you have a page deemed unhelpful, your whole site is falling in the rankings because of the new algorithm.

Essentially, the practice is one of those black hat tactics that give you short-term success but doesn't pay long-term dividends. At the end of the day, all the time you save will come back to bite when you are stressed because the website got penalised.

The tools are great and do a good job. If its whole purpose is personal, then no one will know, but if you're trying to manipulate search engines, that is the main issue that Google's new updates try to capture and avoid. It may work today and tomorrow but, eventually, it will catch up with those doing it and possibly have significant consequences."

Taylor Kurtz is the Owner of Crush The Rankings, and you can find him over at crushtherankings.com.

Focus on building your expertise, authoritativeness, and trustworthiness (EAT) as a brand—Jake Gauntley

Jake Gauntley feels that the best way for brands to prosper in 2023 is to focus on flexing expertise, authority, and trustworthiness online – and he gives you actionable tips on how to achieve this.

Jake says: "Building on your EAT is not only essential for organic success but as a way to instil online consumer confidence across all channels."

What should SEO content writers, websites, and publishers incorporate within their content to demonstrate expertise?

"Depth. Expertise doesn't solely stem from a single piece of content; it derives from the brand and the website itself. For example, if a brand wants to operate in the healthcare or finance sector, it will need to demonstrate why they're an expert within a respective field.

Therefore, from a content creator's point of view, it's essential to ensure you have links to the accreditations or social profiles of the people you're looking to write content for you. You should establish why that person is an expert in their field and why it would be relevant for them to address your proposed topic.

Being able to back up an author's profile with tangible qualifications and accreditations enables you to determine whether they're someone you can trust. It's important to think with expertise, authority, and trustworthiness, however, it's a two-way street - where authority and expertise build trust and vice versa."

What is the best way to demonstrate who the author of a piece is?

"Within the article schema, you can add all of the extra information about the author. It's advisable to link to social profiles, accreditations, and essentially anything that links that piece of content to the actual human. It's important to ensure your author is happy to link to their social profiles, however, if someone is an expert within their field they'll more than likely have an active social media presence.

Providing clear links to social profiles is a great way to confirm all of the other things they're talking about within that field. They should affirm that the person is not an imposter with a stock image, but an expert with links to verifiable locations where people can see they're active. By correctly verifying users, you can deem whether they're worthy of creating content and whether the user can trust this content."

From a social perspective, do Twitter and LinkedIn give the best bang for your buck when demonstrating who a person is and their expertise? Are there up-and-coming social platforms you would recommend as well?

"It's very much dependent on what the person does. Authenticating a doctor would naturally require vigorous checks for things like medical accreditations, for example. There's also no harm in linking to someone's TikTok profile if they're active within that space and their profile provides a fair indication of their status.

When there are different avenues to exploring who an expert is, they are well worth looking into. LinkedIn is the most professional option, Twitter is great if they participate in active discussions, and TikTok shouldn't be overlooked because it will offer additional, perhaps nuanced, insight."

Is it a good idea to link out to blogs and top newspaper sites where people might have published in the past? Will this risk driving traffic away from your website?

"If the link is within an author page or it's in the source of a main piece of content they've written about, there's less harm in traffic suddenly going away from your page. There's likely more benefit in having that link as a visible, credible way to back up your information. This is also a way to ensure information transparency - where your role as a content creator is to be transparent about who your writer is and where their information has come from.

Driving traffic away from your website is unlikely to be a big deal because you're probably not going to be competing against that page. Even if you are, the good things that come from having links to credible sources are likely to outweigh the negative impacts deriving from losing traffic to another page."

What are your thoughts on the styles that tend to be the most effective in terms of length and type of content?

"Authoritativeness can also stem from the offline factors a brand engages in. Many companies put on expert in-person workshops and offer information about these activities via their website. This is a great way to prove that your brand embodies a particular practice/culture rather than it being perceived that you're only doing something for SEO purposes.

Offline functions like these can help to back up your stories about why your brand is an authority within its space. In-person events can hold significant value outside of SEO and EAT for building your brand and business. If you want to be viewed as the best in the business, you've got to be doing all of these things anyway, they just so happen to be a ladder that leads to positive SEO benefits."

Can you gain trustworthiness by constantly making people aware of the content you publish?

"Absolutely. Trustworthiness derives from consistently providing accurate, trustworthy content you can back up with sources. You should also offer full transparency about where the information has come from and who created it. However, if you're an eCommerce business, it also comes down to whether people can trust you when they hand their money over.

Trustpilot and internal product reviews on your website are great ways to garner trust, respect, and authority. As a business, it's important to be seen as someone who does good business and gets good reviews from customers.

If you're not getting regular positive reviews from customers, there's ultimately something fundamentally wrong with how you're operating within the chain of your business.

However, if you are getting 5-star reviews, it's a great idea to integrate these ratings within your website. Many businesses show their Trustpilot ratings in a prominent place on their website - where people can get a great indication of positive customer dealings. This goes hand in hand with the content side of things, where you can show you know what you're talking about in terms of the information on your website, but also that you're a trustworthy business in terms of delivering on your promises when customers hand over money.

Both aspects contribute to trustworthiness, where you can firstly show you're a good business so people want to give you their money, and secondly prove your worth with real customer reviews displayed on-site."

Should every business have a process to ask for reviews or is this something that should be more organic?

"This is a sensitive one. Requesting reviews can be a normal business practice where companies follow up with customers, however, asking for reviews can seem needy if requests are ongoing. It has a lot to do with finding a sweet spot in terms of how frequently you ask people, but if nothing has gone wrong then there's no harm in asking.

You'll need to ask everyone for reviews if you want to purport an accurate representation of your business and act on negative experiences. These will allow you to focus on areas of improvement, where if things aren't great you can proceed to make them better. If you do have lots of questionable feedback, though, it's probably not worth promoting it on your profile."

Have you ever experienced someone asking for a review before you've received the product?

"It has gone a bit crazy, hasn't it? The frustrations are real - being asked for a review after a day, getting a second reminder a day later, then a week later and two weeks later. Often companies will request reviews after a couple of days when you've barely had time to experience the product at its full capacity. With this being said, reviews are less effective when they're merely a commentary on the early part of the customer experience."

What shouldn't SEOs be doing in 2023? What's seductive in terms of time, but ultimately counterproductive?

"In terms of counterproductivity, my biggest tip regarding things brands shouldn't be doing in 2023 is: don't stand still. Don't bank on previous success within SEO as a guarantee that your page will continue to rank and perform well. Companies often make the mistake of reaching a high position for a given search term and thinking the job is done.

Unfortunately, SEO doesn't work that way - especially in a constantly changing environment where many brands are fighting for the top positions. You can't afford to rest on your laurels, reach a high-ranking status, and put your feet up. If you do this, you'll start to slip over time and failing to update your SEO tactics can lead to you falling by the wayside.

A really good analogy for this involves looking at football teams or sports teams in general. The great ones will continually update their roster to give themselves the best chance to compete. If a season hasn't panned out exactly as expected, changes can be made in the offseason to retool for the future and promote a successful outcome.

Other teams may fail to have a successful season but still do nothing. Doing so would be a recipe for disaster that aligns with doing nothing to improve your SEO practices. Football teams will sign fresh players, promote player development, and ultimately operate with long-term success in mind. If they don't make sure they've got fresh talent and fresh ideas, they'll risk sacrificing the top spot or winning the next title. In this sense, it's essential to continuously strive for improvement even when you're at the top of your game"

If you've got a client that's ranking number one for a competitive keyword phrase, how do you justify spending a significant budget to keep that ranking when you don't necessarily know when those rankings will disappear? How do you calculate how much you should be spending on that?

"In this instance, a change of tactics can do you the world of good. You might've been doing loads of content and on-page technical work to get in great shape and reach position one. Once you get to position one, you can then revert to making sure you've got a steady stream of links going to that page. With this being said, it's not necessarily that you have to keep doing the same things over time. What's more important is to make sure your content remains fresh. With certain types of pages, the information will need to be changed over time.

You should ensure your content remains up-to-date and maintain a regular stream of links going to a given page. By doing so, you'll indicate that people still think it's a good page. You can't just drive a load of links to a page and be content with your number one position. If you get no links from that point onward, that's going to look even more suspicious than anything else.

If it's a money-driving page and, for example, you've dropped from position one to position five, you could calculate how that would impact the revenue that page drives over, perhaps, a set of keywords. If you are going to attach monetary values to potential decreases, you should consider investing a little bit of money in that page over the long term. This might not seem like that much of an investment compared to what your website could lose."

Jake Gauntley is SEO Account Director at Reprise Digital and you can find him at reprisedigital.co.uk.

E-A-T is a key factor to rank internationally— Gemma Fontané

Gemma Fontané recommends that you focus on creating content for human users that demonstrates EAT in 2023, particularly for small or

medium-sized businesses that are looking to make a start in new or international markets.

Gemma says: "My number one SEO tip is for small and medium-sized businesses. What I recommend for them is to really work on EAT, especially if you are starting an international strategy."

Why is EAT going to be particularly helpful for small and medium-sized businesses starting to move into an international space?

"EAT is about showing the expertise, authority, and trustworthiness of a page. It's not only YMYL content that needs to demonstrate EAT, but also websites that want to sell internationally or want to sell in a new market. It allows you to target your new audiences and gives you the opportunity to explain your products to them and the value of what you are offering. It is very important to demonstrate your expertise and knowledge online to show your authority.

SEOs working in these businesses should be asking themselves what their website is currently doing, what style of content they have, how they are sharing their expertise, authority and trustworthiness, and whether their content is primarily made for humans."

Why is it important for SEOs to ensure their content is primarily made for humans? How do you determine whether or not you're doing a good job at that?

"Whether you're working on EAT at a local or an international level, it's important to remember that you're writing for your user - for human beings - and not only for the sake of being first in the rankings.

You need to do topic research that covers all your users' needs and create the right content that is focussed to them. It's not enough to only do keyword research and just work on the keywords that you can find through your tools.

You should be working on content that is going to be useful for your users and is going to help them to resolve their needs, whether that's related to products, services, or comparing to other products, other websites, or other stores. Focus on intent."

What are your thoughts on using extensive automation to produce content? Would you ever use AI to generate content?

"No matter what market you are in, if you are using AI-generated content it is likely that it is not going to be focused on the human user, but only on ranking in search engines. I highly recommend creating unique content that is original and targeted at your users. Don't aim to just have a lot of content on your page and a lot of pages, without a focus on your products.

I don't recommend using AI to generate content if you want to build EAT on your website nowadays. Maybe it's a good source of content if you have other objectives, but if you want to show expertise then it's important that someone with a lot of knowledge on the topic is the one writing about it."

Why is trustworthiness important and how do you establish if an article is likely to be trustworthy?

"You should be asking yourself; would you trust the information presented in this article? What would your users think? First of all, is the content written by an expert? You need to validate that the author is someone that really understands the topic.

It's also important to work on the videos and images on your page, especially when you want to try to sell internationally. Users may not know who you are in a new market, they may not know that you're a store because you don't have a physical store in their country, for example.

That's one of the reasons why it's important that your content has a lot of trustworthiness, and you have a lot of content, images, links, and references that explain - in the best way possible - what you are offering."

Can you build trust from a third party, by having someone that is a frequent publisher of content in your industry publish content on your website, for example, to quickly build up authority based upon the fact that Google knows who they are?

"That is an option, although it depends a lot on the sector that you are in. There are a lot of factors to take into account.

My recommendation is that you create great content that's going to be spread around, and that people are going to share easily. You might not need to be the one looking for a third party and finding the experts. If you create really good content from the beginning, and content that's worthy of being spread around, then maybe they are going to come to you."

In terms of establishing EAT, what does it mean to create trustworthy original content?

"Originality is very important when you're trying to build trust and authority. You should be asking; does this article provide original content, original reporting, original research, and original analysis? It's not enough to be publishing original articles, you actually have to be conducting the original research yourself as well.

If you found your information through a book, through an article, or through another page, it's really important that you are linking your sources too. It's rare that you will be the only one that knows all about a single subject. You are not the first, so you need to reference the others.

You should share where you are getting the information from so that your users know that you're not just making it up. It shows that your opinion is strong because you have a lot of knowledge about this topic."

If you represent a small or medium-sized business and you don't have significant amounts of authority on your website already, but you've done some great research, where should you publish that?

"If it's possible to publish it on your own website, then that would be best. Other people may then reference it, but you need to be the one in control of your content and your research. I would strongly recommend that you publish your own research and your own data on your website, and then look for other people to share it and spread it around. You need to be the expert on that topic."

How do you make sure that your site is perceived as trustworthy for doing things like getting a customer to give their credit card information to you?

"When you're starting an international strategy it's important that people trust you, especially now that there is a lot of competition in marketplaces and big websites. They need to look at you as more than just a small website that might sell them a product - they need to believe that there is someone behind the page.

Do your research on the markets that you want to start expanding into. Check all their payment methods. Whether it's credit cards, PayPal, or whatever, it's important that people are used to the payment method that you are using and that they trust that there is someone behind the website.

Create a really good, specific About Us page with information about the store, the team, the products - everything. Also, create a Frequently Asked Questions page with answers that are not only about the products but also about things like international delivery, because that may be a way that you're going to sell your product.

Try to get reviews from users in different countries. Use certificates or references that validate your credibility. Include a chat so, in case of problems, users can contact you 24/7.

Make it easy for your users to trust you. Whether that's through your payment methods, reviews, or other tools that help you to build confidence, it's really important that you have that trust."

Should SEOs be encouraging customers to write reviews on your behalf, or should this be a fairly organic thing?

"Positive reviews should be an organic thing, however, there are small actions that you can take that will bring more in. For example, when you are selling a product, or when you are delivering it, you can include a small message explaining how the product works and telling them where they can come to ask questions. Or you can send them online notifications to rate their experience once they have received the product. It's not directly asking for a review, but it's encouraging them to comment on the product."

In relation to the content itself, how important are videos and images? Should every piece of research content also be available in video form and have images to accompany it or does it depend on the piece and the intent that you're trying to serve?

"I would 100% recommend using images and videos to complement all your content and all your information. It's particularly important when you are trying to sell a product.

Images show the quality of your product. Especially if you're selling internationally and people don't know what the product looks like, it's important that they can imagine it completely. It will help you to have higher rankings and higher visibility on search engines.

Videos are a good way of showing users how your product works and how they can use it, or it can be a way to compare your product with other examples."

How do you go about benchmarking how well you're performing for EAT?

"It depends a bit on the strategies that you're implementing. To measure whether you're achieving your goals you can focus, for example, on the number of referrals that you are getting. You can look at whether that's increasing or not, but especially at whether you are gaining referrals around the subjects that you're covering. If other websites or magazines in your sector, or other users, reference you, it means that your content is of quality and shows expertise, authority, and trust and is worth being shared.

To analyse whether you are becoming an expert or not, you can look at the new contacts that you are making - perhaps with journalists or other content creators online. You can look at the reviews and comments that you are getting from your target countries, and you can look for an increase in the number of people contacting you through the website, or an increase in sales in a specific country.

Last but not least, you can look at whether your rankings are improving or not, especially for the pages where you are focussing your efforts."

What shouldn't SEOs be doing in 2023? What's seductive in terms of time, but ultimately counterproductive?

"The worst thing you can do is create low-quality content. Content is not only a piece of text trying to rank on the first position of Google. It's a way to communicate your brand, to show who you are to your audience, to explain your products, and to persuade and convince your audience that you are providing something valuable.

Content is almost everything. I highly recommend that SEOs stop creating low-quality content in 2023 and start focusing their efforts on better content. It's going to help you to build your brand and improve your results."

Gemma Fontané is Founder of tiodenadal.online and Co-Founder of orvitdigital.com.h

Build a content plan to properly leverage the entity maps for your market space—Eric Enge

Eric Enge gives advice to SEOs in 2023 on how to keep up with Google's constant evolutions by focusing on mapping out your customer journeys so that you are constantly growing as well.

Eric says: "You should internalise what Google is trying to do with their updates, then map your SEO strategy to fit into that. That way, as Google evolves and releases new algorithms and updates, you grow along with them, and they favour you. Basically, get in line with the programme and stop fighting it."

You have previously stated that it's critical to understand the entity maps for your market space. What does 'the entity markets for your market space' actually mean?

"Ultimately, Google receives a user query - usually a few words, except if it's a long natural language phrase - yet it's still not a lot of information for Google to figure out what a user is trying to do. That phrase represents the start of a journey. Although there are sometimes the whole journey starts and ends with a single step, that is exceedingly rare in most of our interactions with users.

Google wants to map out that journey. They want to understand all the things that a specific phrase implies. For example, if we pick a good common term like 'digital cameras', there are millions of different potential paths that users could go down from this statement. Google simply needs to understand what all those different journeys are. This is where the concept of entity maps comes in.

Google wants to understand all the relationships between the potential things that users might be interested in throughout their whole journey. They start with entity maps, by understanding all the connections between things, people, time, and nature. They then build these complex maps to understand how things are interrelated because they know those user journeys tend to travel around the entity maps.

That means that if Google centres on understanding this and wrapping that into their algorithm, they will want to rank sites that are doing the same thing. They want to display people who understand their users and know how to build a map of all the potential user needs. Finding those sites is a home run for Google."

Does Google personalise entity maps based on the perceived user journey stage?

"They would probably love to get that far, but it gets tricky because of privacy concerns about how much Google can track. Now, they're mapping statistical distribution. That is the probability that a user is in the early, mid, or late stages. They are trying to show results at the appropriate ratio level.

That's why search results have a mix of informational, competitive, and comparison responses."

What key ways can an SEO try to ensure that their brand appears at the right stage and entity maps?

"You must go through the same exercise. You have a class of customers whose needs you're trying to meet. Map out those needs, find out what they are, talk to customers and prospective customers, speak to your customer service people, etc. Then look at site search to see what users are typing in, do keyword research, and thoroughly map out all the various need sets that apply to your organisation based on this.

From that point, you can evaluate your site and see how well you address a wide range of those needs. It is also great to look at analytics and things like bounce rate, time on site, pageviews per visit, and repeat visits. However, the real exercise is understanding your prospective customer's journey and how best you can help them. You can then figure out what pages, content, and services you need."

How do you decide on simple things like keyword phrases and the type of content to use to ensure that you're resonating effectively with your target market?

"It's great to start with keyword research because it's immediate and doesn't involve other people. You get to collect a lot of initial data, but you will need to filter some out because keyword research often comes back with similar phrases. Thus, you will need to break it down into the root phrases you need."

What are your thoughts on zero-volume keywords? Do you sometimes write for your clients, ignoring keyword volume?

"Having pages that address the long-tail needs of clients, even if they have zero search volume, is critical to ranking on other related pages. First of all, they don't really have ZERO search volume. Your KW research tool has suggested them because they have SEEN the keyword, but they're not attributing any volume to it because they don't see enough volume to be comfortable about how many searches per month it gets.

In addition: you need to stop thinking that SEO is only about the page you're currently on (what I call 'one page at a time SEO'). For example, suppose you have a camera page for 'digital cameras'. You have 150 other pages related to the digital camera journey that help that page about digital cameras rank for 'digital cameras'. It is the interaction of all these things together.

Therefore, you can't just look at something and assume it is a waste of time because it has zero search volume. Creating several pages that meet different user needs (even with zero search volume) will help that head term rank on the page designed to rank there."

Is there an effective way to measure the value of the interaction between customers and third-party sites where they find out about your brand and its impact on their decision to visit the site and purchase?

"There are ways to set up Analytics to track the data source. Knowing where users initially came from and ensuring you can track all the touchpoints involved in an eventual conversion is a critical activity. Of course, there are some businesses where things are highly transactional, while others usually involve multiple steps in the journey.

For example, social media is a tough investment for many companies to make effectively. Getting real value out of social media is tricky unless you are a visual-based business. Nonetheless, the main concern would be tracking and evaluating the activities that bring the best results."

What shouldn't SEOs be doing in 2023? What is seductive in terms of time, but ultimately counterproductive?

"Don't just spew content. You have to stay at the centre of this, which is catering to user needs. How are you using your site and your content to meet user needs? You must be SEO smart so that you can get the rankings you deserve from that content, however, don't just throw it out there."

Eric Enge is President of Pilot Holding, and you can find him over at pilotholding.com.

Craft fact-based content that maps to the search engine's understanding of entities— Jamie Indigo

Jamie Indigo acknowledges that the last couple of years has been a wild ride. The movement to digital has been dramatically accelerated by changing circumstances across the globe, and creating fact-based content will help SEOs to remain trustworthy in 2023.

Jamie says: "Our reality changed so much over the last few years that we were forced to order groceries online and use internet search to find out whether it was safe to go outside.

As consumers, we have collectively embraced a digital-first mentality. In 2023, we SEOs must keep step with Google as it's pressed to combat myths and disinformation in SERPs. We can do this by crafting fact-based content that maps to the search engine's understanding of entities."

Is Google getting better at combating myths and disinformation?

"Yes, it is - and it's had to be more vigilant in this area. Today, if a hot news trend emerges but there are no factual or authoritative sources speaking on it, you'll get a bit of a notice that indicates there aren't really any good answers. Google has had to acknowledge that, even as a search engine that wants to give answers for everything, there are times when those data voices can be weaponised and shouldn't give answers for everything."

How would you summarise the method that Google currently uses to understand what an entity is?

"The easiest way to understand it is using an analogy from The Hitchhiker's Guide to the Galaxy. It was a book that the main character, Arthur, carried around with him. It contains information on everything that exists in every person, place, colour, thing, concept, event, etc., all in one handy spot. Google has its own version of The Hitchhiker's Guide to the Galaxy which is known as *Wikidata*."

In the eyes of Google, is getting your entity into Wikidata the fastest way to get your brand established as something they understand?

"Absolutely; it's the cornerstone foundation. It's important to remember that, technically, entities are in two places. If you're just getting your business started, you're probably going to begin as an entity in Maps in Google Business Profile because you have goods to offer. This would be your first cornerstone. The larger scale suggests we look at the concepts that we try to rank for in our head-level keywords. These are our entities."

Are you thinking of schema? Are there different ways of marking up your business and different facets of your being as an entity?

"Absolutely. With structured data, if you were to go ahead and open up Wikidata on a specific subject, you would see things you recognized - perhaps from books, structured data markup, the year the book was published, the number of volumes it's had, etc. Those pieces are all copied over. When we talk about this great inbound Web 3.0, one of the cornerstones is an interlinked data structure. In the same way that we write up schema for Google to understand what the web page is about, they have their own schema to understand what our reality is about."

You mentioned misinformation and disinformation at the beginning. Are many websites marking up their data incorrectly and/or is Google having to fight this as well?

"Incorrect implementation of markup would not be the same as accidentally sharing misinformation. You read a headline, you write about it, and you don't fact-check it. Despite there being schemas in place to understand the world better, just like any other SEO elements, those are often abused."

You recommend the creation of fact-based content. What is fact-based content and how do you go about creating it?

"Let's say, for example, we were to have a well-informed conversation about Star Wars. We're probably going to casually mention Wookiees, Siths, Ewoks, and Jedis. This is all part of being well-informed on the topic. There's semantic interlinking, the same way that in Schema.org information you could mark up a book with characters for Wookiees, Siths, Ewoks, etc. - they'd have the entity mappings of the same things. They know how the pieces interconnect and create factual content it's going to relate to. Are you covering the facets and understanding of an entity expected to be considered an authority on it?"

If you're talking about Star Wars but you're not a film website, would Google not assume that you're going to be talking about the film Star Wars?

"It's not necessary to mark everything up, but if you're in your business starting out, it's definitely a great way to add a cheat sheet. If you're a site that is JavaScript-generated and you're all client-side, pass along the cheat sheet and initial HTML to let Google know there is a payoff that this page will answer in intent once they go through the trouble of rendering it all."

Is it a quicker way for a new brand to get Google more comfortable in what they're about and what their business is?

"Absolutely, when you contribute to Wikidata or Wikimedia Commons, you'll start adding in media elements like photos and videos to contribute to the understanding of an entity. Even, for example, with your home page - one of the boons is more traffic. When people want to understand the base construct of what a thing is, your site is the statement that says, 'You're not going to get this one, it's well covered'.

Wookiees are part of the Star Wars universe, so every relationship between two entities is made up of a factual statement."

Is it possible to automate this or does it need to be done on a manual basis?

"You can certainly try, but it's a community. It's similar to how Wikipedia was exploited with a pullback for people being able to edit it. It's the same kind of trust with Wikidata. You don't even necessarily have to start with your brand. Start with something that you are presenting, as a business, to be an expert on and contribute there."

Is traditional SEO still something that's very important for building entity trust?

"As we look at our use of heading tags, we're semantically structuring the content of the page. That's the same way that an entity is semantically structured and that product data markup is semantically structured. This is a repeating theme, both 1.30 and 3.0 are made of interlinking data structures."

Does Google have any preferences in terms of content length, content type, etc., when it comes to giving more trust to what an entity is about?

"There are no limits or requirements on length. If it's something super simplistic, they probably already know it and could tell you from search directly. If the factual data add that you provide can be summed up in a rich result, you'll need a better page that's more complete because no one will be flicking through yours.

If they had one question and it was answered just now, they won't go to your site. Zero-click SERPs aren't going away - they're powered by entities, so you need to be at the trusted source that provides that content. We're already seeing this change in how vaccine information was presented. MUM is powering those results and it's helping to give contextual news results. It's exciting and scary at the same time."

How does an SEO articulate the financial value of doing an activity like helping to define the entity better, inserting schema on every single page, etc., instead of more traditional SEO activities to senior business leaders and business decision-makers?

"Because these are the ultimate links, you'll have to submit any media to creative commons. Make an experiment and set KPIs. This is how you can define success, whether something will work out or not. You can share success on the first thing and then start building trust. However, SEO is a very esoteric field - a lot of the time it can just sound like word salad."

Does that mean it's better to just have a single domain to establish your reputation as an entity?

"When twelve clones are walking around, how do you know who the real one is unless there is a distinct value proposition, different audience, and a different tactic for engaging? Perhaps you've created top-level country code domains but also lost that domain property view that lets you see from one place.

Is everything working correctly? Are they all functioning the same? Are response codes returning the same thing? You need visibility to be effective and if your visibility is now spread out across all of these domains, how can you even spot when you're cannibalizing your own content if hreflang links aren't set up properly and all of these pieces are now fractured across the web?"

If you decide to change your brand and domain, is setting up permanent redirects from individual pages to the alternative individual page in the other domain enough to persuade Google that the entity has shifted? Are there other things that you need to do as well?

"There is some fun structured data markup you can put in there as well. If you have claimed your Knowledge Graph, you can update the information there. If you have a Google Business Profile location, that information should be updated there. One of the biggest markers will be part of the signals. They won't just be hearing from the one site that your name changed. They'll hear from five sites - from five trusted sources - that your business has changed its name."

What shouldn't SEOs be doing in 2023? What's seductive in terms of time, but ultimately counterproductive?

"Adding more third-party tools to the head of the page. You need to protect the head. Even if the sales guy says it's plug and play: 'Just put the script directly above the opening tag and then magic elves will run across your web page and people will convert everywhere!'

They may not know they're lying to you, so be kind, but also audit your page. Are you actually using everything that's on there? Are you accurately collecting data? If you fire your analytics via Tag Manager through this mousetrap-style machine of mechanism and machinations, are you sure this was done right?

You need good visibility to make good decisions and you need good data to make good decisions. If you have a bobblehead site full of single points of failure and render blocking scripts, plus far too many A/B testing loads, you won't need them on every page and you certainly won't need twelve of them. Protect the head. The bobblehead is out, the svelte head is in."

Jamie Indigo is a Senior Technical SEO at Lumar and you can find her at not-a-robot.com.

Treat translations like languages and your audience like humans—Isaline Muelhauser

Isaline Muelhauser believes your approach to translations will greatly affect your SEO results in 2023. She explains what it means to treat translations like languages and how this impacts SEOs.

Isaline says: "Treating translations like languages means that it isn't enough to copy the text you have written in your first language and directly translate it for another audience. I call this one-on-one translation and it doesn't work, because when you translate text for websites, you want to capture the intention. You also want to achieve similar SEO, visibility, and conversion results. Most of the time, just direct translations will not help. You will need a bit of copywriting work on top of the translation."

Is the optimum situation to get someone in the local country who understands the idioms, dialects, etc. to do that translation for you?

"Exactly. The ideal case scenario is that you have a localised copywriter or at least a native speaker of the target audience's language. For instance, if you hire someone from Germany to do a Swiss German website, it will not work 100%. That is because the vocabulary used in Swiss Germany might be slightly different from that used by Germans based in Germany. Of course, that depends on the subject too.

When I say treat your audience like people, it's the same. It means people across different countries are quite different. With language comes a universe of references and concepts that vary. That becomes quite obvious when you translate expressions like 'white as snow', which is an expression that you typically can't directly translate if you use it on your websites.

Therefore, you have to really think about the impression you want to give and what you are trying to achieve with your audience. Then you can deliver something with a similar impact in the country. Adapt and localise what you are trying to say for the people in the target country. Doing that means that texts also don't need to be exactly the same. Even when you have two articles, they don't have to be identical. Sometimes you might have a different definition or additional explanations - maybe because the people in that country don't understand a concept that is usually known among those that speak your first language.

This applies to expressions at the level of words and concepts at the level of ideas. That's why translation is often not enough on a website. For some articles, they can be, but sometimes you need to go further.

If you're speaking about an institution, for instance, do you have a similar institution in the target country that people can relate to? It's about the words, but it's also about the ideas you are conveying, what you're referring to, the links you use, etc."

Should you just focus on your higher converting and profitable pages for the type of translation that you're advocating? What about the other pages on your site?

"Realistically, a company will not have the same budget for every language. You might have your first language and realise you cannot invest the same amount of money for the second language - or at least not initially. A good plan is to start by listing all of the content. By all of the content, I also mean the architecture, the buttons, etc.

My recommendation here would be to focus not on a type of page but on a type of service you want to sell in the given country. For instance, in eCommerce, instead of translating all the products, pages, etc. - choose a category of products that is very relevant to Swiss German people. Then, there might be another category that is relevant for UK people.

The idea is to focus on a domain of expertise of service or category of projects and see how that works before you touch on other aspects of the site. Direct translation could be enough for elements that are not so important for the target group or where competition is still too high. You would not need to invest heavily everywhere."

Is there ever a place for automated translation?

"There can be. It depends on the amount of content you have to translate for your website. In that case, you can start with the less important parts - the types of projects on your websites that might not work as well in the target country - and start with an automatic translation there. However, you should have a plan to optimise it.

Very importantly, if you are only the SEO or project manager, you should clarify to the higher-level managers that this will not convert well. That will help manage the expectations of those who say 'no' or call for you to translate everything. You will need to explain to them the various levels of translation that can be achieved, and their corresponding levels of profitability.

Basically, you really can't do everything since it is expensive. Manage expectations and have a plan to do everything at the right time eventually. As you execute the plan, you should have your KPIs set. Then, examine the elements you already localised with translation and find out how well it works.

You will have the KPIs from traffic, from Search Console, and the rankings of keywords. However, also get some internal feedback from places like customer support. The customer support team are your friend in the company. Their feedback is important because they might be receiving lots of questions from a country. What are these questions? Find out. This is not something that can be seen as quantitative data. Nevertheless, you need to gather this internal feedback and know what type of questions they are always answering."

How do you ensure that you're covering the right keywords in another language if you don't speak the language? Is it necessary to employ a local SEO on top of a local writer in a country?

"I would start with translating the keyword research with automation. Get an export from a tool such as Ahrefs and Semrush, and then maybe choose the highest-ranked keywords. Afterwards, you can have the ones you plan to use checked by the copywriter. That would be the cheapest alternative, if you can't have a local SEO doing the keyword search.

In an ideal scenario, you have your local SEO who does the keyword research along with the copywriters - just like you do with the first language. That way, it is not just a copy and paste of the first language's content. However, this is expensive. You can do the first part yourself with the tools you have at your disposal, and then only check the essential keywords you plan to use when you do your URL mapping."

What shouldn't SEOs be doing in 2023? What is seductive in terms of time, but ultimately counterproductive?

"The first thing is to be careful with the type of work the client is asking you to do. For instance, if the client asks you to translate the keyword search. Translation work is very different from idea gathering and data management of keywords. You should be mindful of settling for translation or, rather, you should it with the client. Do they want you to translate the words and quality check them, or find better alternatives involving idea gathering, keyword multiplier, etc.?

Generally, do not just settle for work that sounds like translation because, often, clients expect cheap translations with big SEO results. The SEO process is different from direct translations so you must be careful with that. One of the risks I have encountered is that you translate the keyword search and check the words. Then, the client checks on their tool, discovers that there is an alternative and starts to doubt your work. I often have to explain that they asked me to translate the keyword search, which is different from the SEO process of idea gathering.

Basically, be careful with the client's wording and be sure of what they are asking for so that you deliver the results that they are expecting. Your keyword search should be two different documents, and then you can map the translations."

Isaline Muelhauser is an SEO Consultant at Pilea.ch and you can find her at pilea.ch.

Invest in the power of putting people first— Sarah McDowell

Sarah McDowell believes SEOs should invest in the power of putting people first in 2023 so that you are creating content and optimising your site for users rather than just search engines.

Sarah says: "Whenever you're creating or improving existing website pages and content, you need to be thinking about people first - the people who are actually reading content rather than search engines."

Why is this so important?

"Traditionally, SEOs create and write for search engines first and think about people second. We've been taught to think about search engines. People are often an afterthought, and that doesn't make much sense. Over the years, search engines like Google have become increasingly aware of this and want SEOs and website owners to prioritise people over them.

People are Google's customers. The experience people have on website pages is important, especially if Google want to maintain the high market share they have over competitors like Bing, Yahoo, etc.

If you look at the SERPs you'll notice a shift where Google is awarding sites that are people-first. There is a focus on the people who read the content rather than search engines. This is especially evident after Google's helpful content algorithm update, which rewards sites that create people-first content."

What does 'people-first' mean in practice? Does it mean that keywords don't matter anymore, should you just think about the user and write whatever comes to mind?

"Firstly, a special shout out to Lily Ray who works at Amsive digital as Senior Director of SEO and Head of Organic Research. She wrote a blog about the helpful content update after analysing the SERPs following the rollout. One of the topics she covers is how to avoid a search engine-first approach to writing content. According to Lily, Google says that if you answer 'yes' to any of the following questions, you probably have content that's written for search engines and not humans.

Question 1: 'Has the content been created to attract people from SERPs rather than made for humans?'

Question 2: 'Are you covering lots of topics in the hope that something sticks and works?'

Question 3: 'Do you have extensive automation in place to create content on many topics?'

Question 4: 'Are you summarising what others have said rather than adding your own value?'

Question 5: 'Are you writing about something because it's trending when you wouldn't normally bother?'

Question 6: 'Does your content leave readers with more questions and do they have to go elsewhere to get an answer?'

Question 7: 'Are you writing for a particular word count because you've heard Google has a preferred word count?'

Question 8: 'Did you decide to write on a niche topic just because you thought you'd get traffic?'

Question 9: 'Does your content promise to answer a question that actually has no answer?' For example, a release date for a product when one hasn't been confirmed."

Is it still beneficial to do some keyword research then optimise the title, incorporate the keyword in the title, have some H tags, and tweak the content to incorporate the keyword phrase you're targeting?

"Yes, as SEOs, we still need to optimise for keywords. We need to ensure we're mentioning the terms that people are searching for on Google. Going forward, it will be more about questioning content before you write it. You'll need to focus on writing to add more value to a topic rather than just rehashing something in the hope to rank and drive traffic to your website. Be strategic and go after topics where you have the expertise, can be helpful and informative, and also add value or maybe even a different viewpoint. For example, target topics you've got your own data on or where you have the expertise to cover what hasn't quite been covered yet.

What I would recommend doing is using tools like People Also Ask, Also Asked or even Google's 'People Also Ask' to see what questions and queries are relevant to a certain topic. Go a step further and use questions you get from your clients and customers too. Ask people what they like and dislike about the content you publish on your website, e.g., a form at the bottom of blogs with the title 'How did we do?' and a space for them to give their feedback. This will provide valuable insights because you can understand what people like, what topics you didn't get right, and what questions you didn't answer. You can see where you haven't quite answered a question and work out how you can improve it."

How do search engines determine that a piece of content was written for humans and should be ranked higher than other pieces of content that weren't written for humans?

"Google has a couple of things they can use to their advantage. They will consider dwell time, for example - how long someone is sticking on a page and reading content. If dwell time is low and people aren't sticking around to read content, Google will know that piece of content isn't helpful because the user experience hasn't been great.

They can also use expertise, authoritativeness, and trust (EAT). Google is getting better at knowing what is authentic and expert content, not information that's been regurgitated and doesn't offer anything new. They're getting better at analysing content, who wrote it, and who's behind it. They'll continue to get better at this.

Not only should we be asking those questions that we highlighted earlier and avoiding writing content for search engines, but we also need to think about how we can show Google that content has the expertise and authority to be trusted. You can include things like author bios, links to research you've done, and links to mentions. These are the types of things that will become more and more important to Google."

If someone's writing an article for you, is it essential to have an author bio or an author page, or at least be linking that article to the individual author you're trying to build credibility for?

"100%. That's really important, especially for content that is deemed 'YMYL' which stands for Your Money and Your Life, so content that talks about topics that could impact someone's life, e.g., health or money and financial stability. In these cases, it's definitely important to reference the author because the claims you're stating must be backed up. Who are you to say that? You need to show that the author behind what you're writing knows what they're talking about and they have the expertise and qualifications."

Let's say someone started to talk about Star Wars having never covered this before. Could Google start to think that the company is about Star Wars and associate some of that author's previous knowledge with what they're likely to be writing about in the future?

"Relevancy is always going to be important. There are many factors that Google takes into consideration when ranking pages, but relevancy is always going to be one. When it comes to ranking for Star Wars-related queries, is it realistic for you or your business? What have you got to offer to Star Wars fans? Can you compete? If you think you can genuinely create content that will be informative, educational, fun, engaging, etc. then go for it!

When you're thinking about the content you're writing, you need to be thinking about E.A.T, but relevancy is also crucial. This goes back to the earlier point of not writing about a topic or putting a piece of content together, just because you want to go after a trend, see it as a traffic generating opportunity etc. Relevancy is definitely important, so the content you're writing has to be relevant to you as a professional or what your business offers."

Does Google get confused about understanding who the entity is and what its expertise is in?

"Yes, Google isn't perfect and will get confused about understanding who the entity is and what its expertise is in. That's why we need to make it as clear as possible on our websites. Make use of author bios, talk about industry-recognised qualifications, link out to media and industry mentions, etc."

What shouldn't SEOs be doing in 2023? What's seductive in terms of time, but ultimately counterproductive?

"SEOs shouldn't be getting too hung up on Google algorithm updates. Whenever there is an announcement that Google is tweaking their algorithm or a core update is out or on its way, it causes panic in the industry, and SEOs may want to drop what they're working on at the moment to focus on that update. It can be a scary time. Yes, look into these things if you are seeing a dip in traffic and visibility, or if it aligns with current projects or business goals, but don't get hung up otherwise.

However, know that Google is always going to be updating and improving its algorithm. They do something like 2,000 per day, they did around 4,500 back in 2020. Yes, be aware of them, and act accordingly but don't get too hung up. Make a plan and make sure to prioritise the right things for your website and its performance."

Sarah McDowell is SEO Manager at Captivate and you can find her at captivate.fm. She also co-hosts The SEO Mindset podcast.

Go headless and leverage structured content for scale—Lidia Infante

Lidia Infante suggests that SEOs in 2023 should go headless without losing your head and understand that the world of SEO has become about much more than just the search bar.

Lidia says: "Move to a headless CMS. SEO is going omnichannel and it has moved way beyond the search bar.

There's a blog post every SEO has read where Google came up with the name 'multi-search' to talk about their proposition with Google Lens. This involves searching on the search bar, but also with your camera. If you have an android phone and you're using your Google widget, you've probably seen a little pop-up that says 'Tired of typing? Search with your camera'.

Google has widely acknowledged that search has moved beyond the search bar and, as SEOs, our roles have evolved significantly. We're not only tied to the 10 blue links anymore. We have a plethora of different widgets, rich results, and other stuff going on in the organic search results. We now have to start caring about how businesses are being searched on social media, such as Instagram and TikTok. We have to care about how we're getting found on Pinterest and visual searches in general. It's about much more than just a search box."

Why should SEOs be concerned about what brands do and how people search for us on social media? Does that impact things like click-through rate and brand click-through rate on the conventional Google SERP?

"We should be concerned about this because we're not Google optimisers - we are Search Engine Optimisers. The moment users are searching on Instagram, TikTok, Pinterest, or with their phones and cameras in general, we should be concerned.

SEO sits in the marketing department and SEOs have a commercial function. SEO supports revenue quite heavily, especially for businesses in eCommerce or SaaS. With any searches, we have to get the right information in front of our users where they are looking for it. It's not that we are concerned about posting daily Instagram stories, that is the job of social media managers; we're more interested in what happens when someone searches our location on Instagram or TikTok. We should respond to user queries where they are happening.

There are some verticals that are simply more inclined to be searched using visual media - for example, food and travel. Industries like these are more conducive to video results and you're going to satisfy your user intent better with video. We already assumed and understood this when we started to look
at YouTube SEO. My point is that search is happening omnichannel - it's not only happening on Google
anymore. A few years back, you would start a product search on Google,

now many of us are starting it on Amazon.

The world of search engines is evolving and has been evolving for a few years. Circa 2015, even Facebook was convinced that they were going to be the next big search engine and they were encouraging their users to search on Facebook. It didn't work for them, but it definitely worked for Amazon.

Lots of SEO roles are moving to optimise a brand's exposure online as opposed to traditional SEO. Does the name SEO need to change?

"Maybe. We've always been marketers, despite some people pretending that we're programmers or data scientists. We're marketers that use some resources like Python and some technical lingo. We're quite close to the technical side of things - and we have to understand it for our jobs otherwise we'd never rank for anything - however, we're marketers and we've always been marketers. There's no point thinking that we're better than a social media or PPC marketer. We're in the marketing department most of the time."

How do you leverage structured content and scale?

"It's really difficult to explain and grasp for yourself. Structured content involves treating content as data. Instead of thinking of documents, you're thinking of fields. Instead of thinking of a product page for eCommerce, you're thinking of a template and what goes in it.

It's like the page template is the recipe and the content is the ingredients. The page template calls for a title, a picture, some feature information, a description, a price, related products, and maybe some tags. Imagine being able to do this as a publisher.

If you're thinking of fields instead of thinking of documents, you could program an API to push out all of the titles as Instagram stories and maybe include a link. You should essentially just tag the content you have and organise it into types, with attributes and relationships between them. It's difficult to grasp but it's like a massive mental map of everything."

This could be very useful from a publisher's perspective, but what about other types of businesses? Is it just as easy to take advantage of?

"For eCommerce, definitely. This also brings us back to the business side of things. We've got direct-to-consumer brands - for example, Adidas sell in major retailers and in their own stores. However, why would you go to the Adidas store over any other shoe shop in the UK or US? You'd go there for the brand experience. You're walking down the street, see a brand that you like, identify with the store's values and enter. You go into the Adidas store and it's got a special type of music, a specific look, and a specific smell. The people that work in the store are representing the brand. You'll see sales assistants there to help and exclusive products on offer. You'll have personalisation options that are not available anywhere else.

On the other hand, for eCommerce, you'll have the same experience in the online Adidas store as you do on Amazon. There is no experience and no differentiation. This is a big loss for D2C brands, because their distributors will be the ones getting the consumer insights and data. D2C brands will also be losing margin because their distributors are going to be selling at a similar price or lower. Price-sensitive users are more likely to go with the distributor, and the distributor's margin will make a dent in the brand's final revenue.

It is expensive for B2C brands to not offer a brand experience aligned with the brand's values online. Brands can tackle this issue by using structured content to bring their brand experience online. Think about this: most product pages look the same. You'll see a title, a breadcrumb, a picture, the product title again, a description, the price, reviews and then maybe a full accordion menu where you can go to dimensions or product descriptions and learn more about a product. There'll normally be a line of related products underneath as well.

That template is being used both for super high-end lifestyle products and for the simplest purchases. Imagine you have an electric bike business. The electric bike itself is a lifestyle product and people can use it to commute. Maybe customers are interested in health and fitness, maybe they want to take their kids to school on the back of a bike and are interested in safety, or maybe they're super into mountain biking and want an electric bike to power their hobby. In this sense, your target customers are making a lifestyle purchase. Then you'll have parts, like someone wanting a bell for their bike. Prospective customers could be browsing those parts via the same templates you've used for selling bikes - and that doesn't make sense.

These two categories of products should be presented differently because the buyer's journey and the emotions are different for those sales. D2C brands can make this happen by structuring their content on their backend, and creating different templates for each product type. For parts, you could use a classic Amazon template, and then for bikes, you could have a video and maybe an image of a mother or father looking happy and safe taking their kid to school. It can be very detailed, but also beautifully highlight the features of a product. Is this fast charging? Is the battery detachable? How long does it take to charge? Are there specific security features? Are the wheels sturdy? If you can explain the features clearly you can make the user feel like they're making a very important purchase in a very informed, inspirational way.

This is something that Apple absolutely nails. When you go on their new iPhone page, you're shown people that look like you and are doing the things that you want to be doing. There are going to be aspirational images – a beautiful way of displaying product features, characteristics, and limitless possibilities. Their accessories are just that. They have a clear set of features and a prominent "add to cart" button. That's what you can achieve with structured content."

Will everyone be moving to this type of structured content? If so, where's the differentiator in future and what opportunities do you have to demonstrate that you're better than the competition?

"In 2023, the differentiator is going to be using structured content to highlight your products better. This will be very helpful for publishers who can make their content go omnichannel in a better, faster, more efficient, in an API-driven way.

In eCommerce, using structured content is a competitive advantage, since very few people are creating product pages that don't look exactly like Amazon's. This matters most to D2C brands because where there are endless wins to increasing your margins and owning your own user's data.

Things will probably look a lot different in 2025. It's exciting to see the headless and structured content approach, because it is an enabler for creativity. What will creators do next? They're no longer constrained by the limitations of their CMS and page template. They can literally plug anything with an API into their content. It's impossible to know what people will do but it'll be curious to see. When you give your editors
and creators a single source of truth to take care of, you'll be freeing up their time to do other essential things. You could even run a guest authorship program, which as a publisher is super interesting. This could enable and encourage authors to create amazing articles and make them SEO-optimised from the outset. You could create brilliant editorial experiences for your writers and editors that will improve the productivity of a publishing business."

What shouldn't SEOs be doing in 2023? What's seductive in terms of time, but ultimately counterproductive?

"Stop obsessing over Google updates. Google is going to Google and it's always going to be in August when you're on holiday. Don't waste your time looking at what Google is doing specifically with each update. You've already been told the route to go down, just look at the Google Quality Rater Guidelines. Create trustworthy, authoritative, expert-led content and publish
it in a way that's user-friendly and doesn't absolutely drain your customers or
user data plans. Don't obsess over minor updates."

Lidia Infante is Senior SEO Manager at Sanity and you can find her over at lidia-infante.com.

4 TARGETING

Think like a machine—Sante J Achille

Sante J Achille informs SEOs that thinking like a machine, and challenging yourself to truly understand the inner workings of today's algorithms, can reap massive dividends in 2023.

Sante says: "This is a challenge that stems from a paradigmatic shift. If you want to manage SEO at a certain level in terms of quality and an understanding of what's really happening, you need to delve into the nuts and bolts of SEO. What is really driving the fundamentals upon which the algorithms have been built?

You can start at the very beginning, with Natural Language Processing (NLP), and try to understand what is behind it. Not everyone can tackle it at the level of sophistication that may be required. There is a lot of Mathematics involved and computer science too. However, everyone can do their best to push the envelope and push their limits to the point where they feel like they can't take it anymore.

If you go down this path you can get a feel for what's going on and truly understand things. It might be a difficult road ahead, especially if you don't have a technical background, but it'll definitely be the best approach to better understand exactly what's going on. If you want to at least try to understand the goal and general direction you're moving in, NLP is definitely what you need to do."

How have machines changed the way we think we can use a word like that?

"Let's say you go back and study the basics of NLP. If anybody starts venturing off on this path they'll read of things like 'a bag of words.' There was a time when articles and so-called stop words like 'a', 'the', and 'them' were excluded because search engines couldn't understand them. Now they can actually understand a sentence as it is.

There's been quite a jump in terms of the evolution of algorithms. They're smarter in this regard - for example with the BERT algorithm. There's an interesting video from Google when you search for the BERT algorithm. It helps you understand the technical jargon and embrace the general philosophy and approach."

Now bots are better at understanding natural human writing, does that mean it's less necessary to incorporate keyword phrases within natural writing?

"No, it is still necessary to incorporate keywords. You should appreciate how far a search engine has developed an understanding of a certain niche. Things change significantly. There isn't a one-size-fits-all approach to algorithms and verticals. Different businesses have different ways of behaving and processing things.

The best thing to do is to research the SERPs and put lots of work in. You'll have a certain list of terms that work and your client can come back with a set of money terms. They know what terms are converting from the analytics. You'll want to go into the SERP and look to see how many other competitors are using those keywords. If you move away from that keyword - keeping the same meaning but changing it slightly - you can see if the same pages show up on the different SERPs. They may change and that will give you a clue; a signal that says, if they are shifting then there is a difference. Fortunately, the algorithm has the ambition to fully understand even the smallest of differences.

It's an algorithm and it can fail, so you need to look at those phrases and the system/pages that are ranking. Try to understand the intent behind those pages. You might have a main phrase you're looking for, but there are going to be other concepts around that phrase. You can push these so that Google understands that people searching for that phrase are interested in the concepts surrounding the main focus of that particular SERP."

What are the trends that you're seeing in the SERPs? What's Google preferring to rank at the moment?

"A bit of everything actually, especially if they are not sure about your intention. If the query you're throwing at them doesn't disclose a clear intent, it'll be populated with things that are related to the search but completely different. It's no longer a case of looking at the SERP and searching for some kind of a signal, clue, chain, or connecting thread because they can be totally unrelated. This will depend on what Google see as the best options around which they can develop an understanding of your query and answer it in the best possible way. They'll give you a menu of sorts."

Does Google infer intent from search history?

"Yes, you can see this by clicking. For example, you can have up to 10 browsers clicking on the SERPs. With different browsers, you can use a proxy that will allow you to search from different countries to try and understand the general picture. What you observe will be different from the general picture, which will in turn be different from what visitors see. The uncertainty principle that was spoken about in 2022 still rings true. You need to take the order of magnitude of things to survive and make a sustainable, stable proposition - based on this uncertainty principle as a driver."

What is your preferred way of defining intent for a keyword phrase? What do you do as a result of defining intent for a keyword phrase?

"The best guide is the Search Console. Somebody will write a piece and you can optimise it, let it brew, and then go back to the Search Console after maybe a month. Here you can see the search terms Google has proposed for the page. You can also check the metrics like impressions and click-through rate, to see how they fit into the bigger picture of what the page looks or reads like. Is it actually matching the intentions we had when we wrote the piece? Do they fit the queries and the searches that Google has associated with your page? If it's not showing up then you'll need a bit more of a boost.

You'll need to do some link building and promoting on that page to give it a bit more of a push. It might also be going off in the wrong direction, which would mean that the algorithm is failing you and isn't understanding what you wanted to say on that page. That's where going back to the drawing board and tweaking it pays off. Your SEO skills must be sharp and you must have the intuition to align your content to the search terms you want the page to line up with.

Alongside Majestic, another tool that's great to use is the Grammarly tool. This is great for everything, where even if a piece is written properly it can come back with suggestions. These are useful more often than not because they come from a machine, which will tell you when it's not clear what you've written about. Within limits, you should reshape the phrase, rewrite it, cut it into pieces, and re-modulate it so that Grammarly (or an equivalent) understands it and will tell you it's good. If the AI understands it you can be more confident that Google will understand it."

What shouldn't SEOs be doing in 2023? What's seductive in terms of time, but ultimately counterproductive?

"The trend for people is to use a lot of tools. The landscape has become so complicated and the marketing has been very aggressive in terms of promoting tools. There are lots of tools out there and they all have an incredible amount of information to share. That's not necessarily wrong, but it's best to avoid going down different rabbit holes chasing details that aren't that relevant.

When you live on a website, the extreme details become important. You should have all of your bases covered. However, when you have a website where the structure is all over the place, your client won't listen to you. They'll write things in a different way, the web server will be slow, and your core vitals won't work. In this case, it doesn't really make sense to start looking at the tens of signals sent from tools. One of the seven hooks we've been hardwired with is the alarm one. We're encouraged to create alarm - to create this sense of agitation to act on all of these things.

Many of us fail by being hooked on the fact that there is so much that needs to be done, including all of those other little things. If you put all of your energy into this, days will go by one after another. You'll be looking at the trees but you'll miss the forest."

Sante J Achille is a Search Marketing Consultant and you can find him over at achille.name.

Include zero-volume keywords in your SEO strategy—Mark Williams-Cook

Mark Williams-Cook tells SEOs in 2023 that it's important to build most of your content research around zero-volume keywords and intent proximity, rather than monthly search volume and related keywords.

Mark says: "When we talk about zero-volume keywords, we're not referring to keywords that have no searches a month. What we're really talking about are the gaps in information that exist in the tools and data we have access to.

When a tool doesn't know how much traffic a particular search term gets, it will show it as zero. Professional SEOs have been known to discount these, however, that'll be an ill-advised approach going forward. From an SEO perspective, the bigger, more progressive trend is thinking outside of the individual keyword phrases you're optimising for.

There are lots of ways to write queries that mean the same thing in Google. You may know that searching for 'my blue men's running shoes' only has a few searches per month, but you could rewrite the same query multiple ways. If each iteration has 5-10 searches per month, you could quickly get to thousands of searches per month for something you may have otherwise completely overlooked."

What percentage of keywords out there have search volume but no listed keyword volume that can deliver traffic?

"The top line mostly. It depends on what data you're looking at. Many modern SEO platforms have reported that within around 90% of the keywords they track, there are less than 20 searches a month for many of the search terms. This is partly due to the changes in user behaviour we've seen over the last decade. Interestingly, when search engines are a bit more basic, people do a lot more searches around one or two words because the algorithms are a lot more basic at finding that information.

Now people know that if they're specific in their searches, the technology exists to get better results. When you're doing keyword research, you still need to look at monthly search volume, especially when you look at site structure and how categories should be structured. When it comes to producing this sort of content, you need to realise that people are doing specific searches, so if you write specifically to answer all of the branching questions that a single intent has, you're going to satisfy users and rank better."

Is it easier to rank for longer tail keywords without noticeable search volume? Is it easier to rank for these keywords than trying to rank for keywords with higher volume?

"That's definitely true at the moment, and partially true over the last very recent timescale. We've seen some updates that Google have made like BERT and passive indexing. These have increased the opportunities for these specific key phrases to rank. Since the Google helpful content update, lots of people have been looking at spam sites created around mining Google's People Also Ask questions and scraping or generating results from them. Some of those websites have gone from zero traffic to over a million visitors within 8-12 weeks.

That would certainly suggest there's potential to rank very quickly, which is also what makes it an important thread of SEO strategy for most websites. The majority of websites can't easily rank for big head terms, especially if they're new. This strategy gives an opportunity to get meaningful search traffic to smaller websites very quickly, providing you can research and produce content effectively."

If SEOs dive into tools like People Also Ask, they can quickly find themselves drowning in thousands of potential opportunities to rank. How do you suggest that an SEO or content marketer goes about selecting which phrase to write for if they're all zero-volumes?

"Once you know the topic you're writing about, you can try to find a root question that might not be zero-volume but just low-volume. There are loads of ways to go about this. If you have things like live chat on your website or a site search, these are great ways to see the specific questions that people who are already engaged with you are asking. You can then make sure you have the content to answer them. There are other tools like AnswerThePublic that use Google suggest, which is different to People Also Ask because it gives a bird's eye view of a topic where all of the questions aren't necessarily related to an intent, they're just thematically created. This is a great place to start and get that root question.

People Also Ask data is great because of intent proximity. Let's say you put in an initial question that's specific - for example, 'does pet insurance cover dog poisoning?'. If you enter this into a traditional keyword tool around pet insurance, it will essentially just give you a list of questions that contain the word pet insurance. They'll all be thematically related but not close in terms of intext proximity.

Intent proximity means someone has asked a question and to fulfil their search journey needed to ask multiple follow-up questions. If you put this type of question into People Also Ask, you'll see that one of the closest related questions is something like 'what does a vet do with a poisoned dog?'. That'll show that this is what the person wants to know but might also panic the user that their dog has been poisoned. If so they'll Google whether their insurance will cover it and then look at what the vet might actually need to do.

Once you've established a root question, using People Also Ask specifically will give you a mirror from Google about what they are expecting users to ask. Apart from just the raw questions, the most powerful part of that data is the relationships between those questions. Interestingly, the results you get from People Also Ask differs depending on your starting point.

For instance, if you do that search around pet insurance, get four or five questions and click on one of them, you'll get some more questions. If you started the query from that second level, you would actually get a different set of questions because Google has learned there could be a slightly different intent path and different intent proximity to other questions. This is a great way to determine a starting point with other data points. What should you include? What questions should you answer? What topics should you cover in a particular niche?"

Should you have one question for one page or should you have separate pages for every single question that you try to answer?

"No. You shouldn't be creating separate pages for every single question. Most of the time, the proximity of the intent means that if you answer three or four of the closely related questions on the same page, that's better for the user - because they're going to want to know that next thing.

Don't place an extra burden on the user. Don't add extra friction and make them click and wait for the latency of another page load. There comes a sensible point where you'll stop answering questions, but that's why it's good to group pages together based on how related they are.

If you're using things like header tags, it should be easy for someone to scan through your content. Then, even if they're interested in the second or third answer, they can easily see that within a few seconds on the page, and that'll be faster for them than clicking on individual links to each of those pages."

How can you help Google to perceive your answer as authoritative for that particular question, or to feature your answer as a featured snippet within the SERP?
"There are lots of tactics you can use for the actual optimisation of the content, especially where you've got advice that goes against the grain. However, do you want to have a succinct answer that's good for the user or should you write a really detailed answer to show expertise? You can achieve both of these things by taking heed of how newspapers write stories. If you have a particular question, you can give a one-paragraph summary of the answer and go into details below that. By doing so, you'll be giving search engines an easy job to understand this is the answer to the question. It'll also be small enough to show in a featured snippet, and you'll have the longer answer there to cover other search terms and to inform users that want that answer.

You can use structured data too. FAQ page schema gives you a better chance of getting rich results. Also, you should think about the format that is being used to answer those questions. Google is really helpful when you put in a question.

For example, let's consider a tourist website where people are searching for things like the height of The Shard. When you delve into the question, some people will be searching for how high it is in feet, others in metres, and a whole host of people searching for how tall The Shard is compared to the Eiffel Tower. '300 metres' as a statistic doesn't mean a lot to some people, but maybe they're a tourist from France and they know exactly how tall the Eiffel Tower is. Showing this in an image format can be really helpful for them. Using multiple different types of format - and the right format for the answer - can increase your chances of ranking high for those kinds of terms."

As an SEO, how can you justify spending time on zero-volume keywords? Also, what sort of ROI do you look for from people landing on your pages from top-of-funnel questions?

"Firstly, examine the traditional strategy - of looking at certain keywords because they've got X search volume, and if you rank position one, two, or three you'll get this much traffic which contributes to our target. Visually demonstrating to people how they are targeting a minority of search terms is helpful. Show them that they are leaving the majority of searches on the table, and that those search terms are in a way zero-sum games.

If you've got a 20,000-a-month search term and manage to knock off whoever is ranking position one, they're not going to say 'oh never mind, that was nice when we ranked one' - they'll fight you for it. Realistically you need to budget for the fact that competitors will up their game and input to win that ranking back. This can become an expensive way to compete.

You should then think about how you're going to do things like build links to these pages. In nearly almost all the cases I've encountered, it's difficult to do things like build links to pages that are commercially driven because you're asking people to sell for you or link to very commercially focused pages. The strategy you can adopt at the top of the funnel is using those pages to internally link to our commercial pages and increase those rankings.

The final part of all this is in terms of strategy and the bigger marketing picture. Where does SEO fit in there? The gold standard of marketing is around brand building. The idea is that, rather than people googling your product or service, they'll be googling your brand, then your product. Why? Because they know you're number one and therefore they want it from you.

Most people wouldn't just google 'running shoes', they'd Google 'Nike running shoes' because they know they're the best. One of the ways you can do that is through helpful top-of-funnel content. You'll be getting that brand exposure, winning that affinity with customers, and helping them with that. When they panicked about their poisoned dog, you relieved them and thus they'll be motivated to share that answer in the future. Start to build that affinity with them. In terms of measurement, you'll see results from zero-volume pages much faster than you'd expect. You can sometimes see results within weeks of publishing content, and it'll stack up nicely as you start seeing links coming in.

Then you can start measuring if you're going to link to a specific set of your commercial pages and look at how that's impacting the longer term there. There are lots of very good commercial reasons to go after this which aren't as obvious when you're putting everything into a spreadsheet - though there is value in doing that."

What shouldn't SEOs be doing in 2023? What's seductive in terms of time, but ultimately counterproductive?

"Regular disavowing links that some third-party tools label as toxic or bad links. This is still happening - some practitioners assess and disavow links on a monthly basis. They have intentionally bad links, and Google tends to deal with this by ignoring those links rather than applying a negative weighting to them. That's understandable because if Google applied some kind of negative weighting to a 'bad link', they would create a very easily manipulatable system. It'd be very easy to damage your competitor's websites by sending spam links to them rather than adding value yourself. By simply ignoring them, Google doesn't create that kind of bad economy that's going to make all of our jobs harder. They negate any easy ways to buy or spam links and know if they're not working.

Even if you buy links (though this can still work in some cases), the difficulty is those links may get ignored and you won't know because you won't get a notice saying 'you've got a penalty for these links'. SEO is all about building equity over the long term. Everything we've discussed today is user-centric. If everything you're doing is user-centric, you'd still be adding value to your website/brand even if search engines didn't exist.

There are other cases where there is a kind of one-off bigger disavow. This is less worrying, but some people have shown some anecdotal results where they've seen an uplift that's reversible. You can put things into disavow, take them out again, and notice varying results. Google says you can just take stuff out of the disavow file and it'll go back to being counted. Some people run experiments where they disavow all links and then remove the disavow file and notice things not returning to how they were. Disavowing is something that isn't worth touching unless there's a known problem, like if you've had a message from Google saying you've got bad links that need to be addressed."

Mark Williams-Cook is a Director at Candour and you can find him at withcandour.co.uk.

Focus on the searcher's intent to connect demand with supply—Nitin Manchanda

Nitin Manchanda believes that SEO is a demand-based growth channel, and that through this way of thinking you can open yourself up to new opportunities and better target potential users in 2023.

Nitin says: "It's easy to miss out on important opportunities, but if you look at supply and demand parameters, you'll position yourself to uncover new prospects."

How do you establish what the demand is?

"Perform detailed keyword and competitive research to understand what people are searching for. You can then create clusters referred to as 'demand parameters'."

What are the most effective ways to establish which keywords you should be aiming for? How do you determine relevance and optimum keyword phrases to target?

"There are lots of parameters to consider in keyword research. Keyword difficulty is also important because it tells the story of how easy or difficult it is to crack a particular keyword. Keyword search volume is important because it tells you how many times a keyword is searched in a given month, geography, etc. It's also worth looking at CPC, which will tell you if it's a keyword that's being targeted by brands. If so, that'll mean there's demand and you'll have a great chance of converting.

There are some parameters you can look at to understand how important a keyword could be for a brand. Regarding relevance, you can look at the keywords and work out whether you have a good supply for them or not. For example, if you're in an eCommerce company and you see a huge demand for 'black dresses' you don't have the supply for, you'll know not to go for that keyword. In this situation, if you were to create a landing page and generate traffic, you wouldn't be able to fulfil commercial intent queries. Any rankings you'd get wouldn't be sustainable and users wouldn't convert."

Which platform do you use to establish keyword difficulty?

"Semrush is a great tool because it's reliable and easy to use."

How do you work out if you're likely to rank for difficult keywords?

"It depends on what kind of domain you're working on. If it's a fresh domain that doesn't have strong authority, you should implement a strategy where you're focusing on long-tails with less keyword difficulty. When you start gaining Google's trust and begin ranking for these, you can gradually move on to more difficult keywords. Alternatively, if you're working with a well-established eCommerce brand, they'll be looking to create a ranking page and rank for it immediately. For example, established companies target super high-term keywords with massive search volume and high keyword difficulty. They'll have a better chance to thrive because they already have amazing authority in their particular niche.

For a domain name or website that's new, it's important to consider whether you should publish content as a blog post, where it should go on your website, and whether or not it should be published at all. What also matters is the type of content you're publishing. For example, if you're expecting traffic where people are searching for 'black dresses', you should create a category page as opposed to a blog post. You can then put useful content there so you're answering all the questions users might have. That's how you should think about the quality of content for a specific page."

How do you go about establishing a user's intent?

"Semrush is a great tool for this because it will have data which is at least 70% reliable. You should also perform a manual check so you can understand whether the main keywords are important keywords. Avoid blindly trusting how a tool is putting a keyword into a category. The first step will resolve roughly 70% of your problem. Then you can do a quick scan to determine how keywords are mapped in terms of intent."

How do you define and determine what to supply? What content should you create in order to satisfy the intent?

"Once you know your demand parameters, it's very important to understand whether you have the right supply. You won't want to generate traffic that doesn't convert; traffic that leads to a high bounce rate but then the user never returns.

From the supply perspective, you'll want to see if a user's intent is informational. You'll also want to determine if a user wants to buy or do something on the website. If you don't provide that something for the user, then you won't have that supply. It's important to understand that when someone searches for 'black dresses' online, they won't necessarily be looking for pages that just talk about 'black dresses'. Even if your page was optimised for that particular URL and you started ranking, you wouldn't be able to retain those rankings forever. You'd need black dresses in your inventory so that users could buy black dresses on your website."

Are there any other buckets you can put people in regarding intent?

"The four intents are informational, commercial, navigational, and transactional. It's easy to go through Semrush and assume you've covered everything, but there'll always be more to consider than you realise."

How would you define navigational intent?

"Navigational is mostly branded, where someone is looking for a particular brand and it's clear they want to land on that brand's website. For example, if you're searching 'Amazon' on your iPhone X, that's more navigational than commercial because it's clear you want to go to Amazon."

How do you define transactional?

"There is a good overlap. There's a lot of confusion between transactional and commercial because transactional also looks at when the user wants to transact. There is a very thin line between commercial and transactional, so you can use either of the two. Transactional intent comes at the bottom of the funnel."

What are the parameters that don't matter?

"Many big companies over-optimise because they get behind something Google has said. However, this can be ill-advised. For example, let's say you're working for a company with a Core Web Vitals performance score of 90. They want to touch 100, so they rush to it because Google said it's an important ranking factor. They get behind Google's recommendations but then realise it's a master task from an effort estimation perspective. It would be important to not purely focus on getting behind Google's fancy numbers and instead focus on the user experience. If you think going from 90 to 100 would take a lot of time, you'd be better off spending that time on something built for users."

What trends are you seeing in content types that are really effective at the moment?

"It depends on the kind of niche you're in. For example, in eCommerce, video is trending a lot. Amazon Live is only available in the US but there are early-stage startups building similar products globally. Video is a hot trending concept in general. In the travel industry, people are more likely to gain inspiration from videos. They'll want to see things like mountain ranges and get a visual overview that words can not describe.

It really depends on the type of content you're producing and for which niche. Words can't always do things justice. However, sometimes users will want to see images and read content too. Therefore, it's important to embrace an integrated approach dependent on the situation at hand. For example, if someone wants to buy insurance they'll probably just want to read an article about details or look directly at product pages and compare policies. Your content should be crafted around the niche you're in."

Are you seeing any particular trends with live video and the types of brands that are achieving success?

"It seems this concept is still in the development phase. There is another American brand called Whatnot.com that does something similar to Amazon Live. They're successful as established players in the market with lots of categories. Users can search for things like category names followed by the term 'video sale' or something similar.

Their concept is rather new and is still developing. The brand is spending lots of money educating users that video sales are possible and that you don't have to go to Amazon by default. Whatnot.com has product pages and category pages where you can look at products. They also provide opportunities to receive advice from experts on why you should buy something. They're essentially using Amazon Live to drive customers off Amazon."

Is demonstrating that SEOs need to be thinking outside the Google box an important metric or message?

"Yes. Even though you are an SEO, you should have a growth mindset. Think outside of the Google box because there'll be lots of opportunities there. For example, if you're working with a publisher, most of your traffic will come from Google news. This has a different set of parameters which aren't really standard SEO.

Alternatively, you might work for another brand where 70% of traffic is coming from Discover. If so, you'd have to play a different SEO ballgame altogether. From a growth perspective, you should jump at every opportunity that can get traffic to you. SEO is not just SEO anymore, it's evolved into much more than that."

Nitin Manchanda is the Founder of Botpresso and you can find him at botpresso.com.

Intent-driven search will become much more important—Jess Maloney

Jess Maloney believes that all-around search intent will be more important than ever in 2023 and that understanding what your users actually want is the key to creating successful websites.

Jess says: "The Google helpful content update wasn't really anything new, most SEOs were already doing everything that falls under the update. Not many have been hit terribly. Google is putting out these updates and sharing that it's really important to focus on the user more than the search engine. This will play into making sure you're getting the right search intent for the right users and how you're going to rank because of that."

How do you define search intent? Is it thinking about the intention behind someone typing a keyword into Google?

"Yes, absolutely. There are typically four kinds of search intents that everyone typically focuses on: navigational, commercial, transactional, and informational. There's going to be a lot more nuance around that though. While everyone has been focused on these four previously, next year we're going to have to take a deep dive into these to determine what people are searching for.

For example, if someone is looking for a website with navigational intent or commercial intent looking for a certain brand, are they actually looking for that website or are they looking for a review of that brand? They might be looking at where they can find something in the store. There will be a lot more nuance to these intents that we've perhaps never considered before."

Is it reasonable to ask a tool to automatically categorise intent or should intent be categorised on a manual basis?

"Tools can be helpful but there's not really an exact way that they can know. There are lots of tools that do this - like Semrush, Moz, etc. They provide this intent for users, but when you drill down and look at them it'll be different from when you look at things manually. Always look at intent manually and not only at what the search engine is presenting. Use a bit of common sense and logic to determine what people are searching for when they enter a search query."

With informational intent, do people have a brand in mind or just a general query in mind?

"Informational is typically for people who are searching for 'who', 'what', 'where', 'why', and 'how' question-based inquiries."

What about commercial intent? What does that mean?

"Commercial has a lot to do with the different brands and searching for something within that brand. So, looking for something branded and where you can find those certain brands. Whether that's Nike within a different kind of store or something like that."

What is transactional intent?

"Transactional is about the kind of people who are wanting to buy something. They are at the buying stage of that funnel - whether they're looking for the best price or where to buy certain things. They're at that stage when they're ready to make a purchase."

Is the next step to map content to fulfil exactly what people are looking for? How do you decide on what content to write for a particular search query?

"When looking on a query-by-query basis, people commonly look at what Google is presenting as the result. Google typically thinks that people who are searching for something are targeted with a certain intent, and most people will begin to write content for that intent. This is a great way to see what Google thinks that intent is so it's a great way to go.

One thing that people haven't considered is the format of the content that's being created. For example, if you wanted to make content about how to make a chicken soup, you could go to Google and see the top result is a YouTube video. Traditionally you'd see that and think you need to make a video to target this, but that wouldn't be considering all users. Maybe 50% of people want to watch a video to learn how to make soup, but that wouldn't be considering the other 50% of people who like to learn by reading. Consider making multiple pieces of content in different formats, whether that's videos or blogs to target different users within that same intent."

If you were to do that, would you want to incorporate different forms of content on the same page or publish it on different pages?

"It takes a lot of learning, but sometimes one page might not suffice. It could be that you create a video and add a transcription of that video and that covers all bases. Alternatively, you might create multiple pieces of content and have a hub around that topic."

How does Google go about determining that you have satisfied the intent of the user?

"There's not really a true answer to this because Google is just using an algorithm. They don't fully know if you are satisfying the intent. What they're looking at is how people interact with the website, and website owners need to consider how the search intent is being hit as well. You can look at things like engagement stats, whether they are spending time on the site, whether they're finding what they need straight away, or whether they're bouncing. More onus should be on the website owners than on Google because it's just an algorithm."

Can certain queries just require a quick answer and the user could be satisfied within five seconds of visiting a site?

"Absolutely. A lot of this plays into the stuff about no-click searches, where websites now have to make sure they are getting clicks through and satisfying that search intent. Encouraging the click is key because a lot of what people can get from the Google SERP is all they need. It's about giving them a little bit and enticing them to explore for more."

Can it be an SEO win if the answer from your site appears directly on the SERP and the user is satisfied with that?

"It depends on what kind of website it is. If you're looking for brand awareness and you want your name out there, that'll be great because people will remember your site and hopefully come back. If you're at the stage where you want people to click through and do something on the site, it can be an issue if you're not getting the clicks because you're not targeting the keywords with the right intent."

If you are targeting those kinds of phrases and intents, how do you measure the success of that if you've got a fairly long sales funnel? Should you accept that visitors are worth X amount or is there a better way of defining the value of early-stage intent?

"You can track the brand search interest. If it's not a big brand that everyone has heard of, you can drive content to get that top-of-funnel stuff. You can start to track search interest in their branded terms. You can see how their impressions are growing and use Google Trends to see how that is changing over time. You can also start to look at repeat users and what they're doing, when people are coming back (whether that's through organic or direct), and what's the next stage. It's all about tracking the user journey in these situations and seeing if users are landing on the content straight away. Then, further down the line, you can track them and come back to what they're doing."

Is it best to focus on commercial and transactional keywords initially - bottom-of-funnel phrases - or should you work on all stages of intent at the same time?

"It's worth considering everything and considering all kinds of stages. With the bottom-of-funnel stuff, it'll be a much longer turnaround to start driving leads. If you're working with a client, they're not going to be happy with just clicks from the get-go. You'll want to show them some form of valuable results.

Take a holistic approach across the board from an early stage. You should split out content in the early stages across the four areas. If you start testing early on, you can start to see what kind of content is working well for your brand and what isn't. You can also look at the user journey from the different types of content and use that to inform the rest of your content strategy."

Are you seeing any trends in terms of what type of content Google is more likely to serve up for different stages of intent?

"It depends massively on the different areas. A lot of it is definitely focused on the user. When you're looking at long-tail terms, it's more specific and you're getting more in-depth content appearing. When you're looking at the top-level stuff (the short-tail keywords that are typically harder to rank for), you'll find more general stuff. It depends on how long the keyword is and how detailed the user search is. This will dictate how detailed the answers are or how general and top-level the answers are."

What shouldn't SEOs be doing in 2023? What's seductive in terms of time, but ultimately counterproductive?

"Stop focusing heavily on algorithm updates. When an algorithm update hits and you notice a negative impact on your website, it's easy to focus on this without another care in the world. It's important not to solely focus on what's happened and instead try to fix things.

With all the different algorithm updates, once you've been hit you can't really resolve that drop quickly. You need to make sure you're doing best practices all around. You could spend time trying to figure out why something has happened, but you'll never know because Google will never give you the full results. You could spend a lot of time focusing on this when it could be better spent making sure you're hitting best practice across the board."

Jess Maloney is an SEO Partner at Open Partners and you can find her over at open.partners.

Matching your content to what searchers want—Andrew Cock-Starkey

Andrew Cock-Starkey persuades SEOs in 2023 to think more deeply about the concept of intent, and all of the different areas of SEO in which intent is so important.

Andrew says: "The number one thing for people to consider in 2023 is intent."

What does intent mean to you?

"When I was thinking about what I should talk about, I chose intent, and I decided to deliberately leave it quite broad so that we can kick around ideas about all the different things that come up when we talk about intent.

Intent is really important in SEO, and it should play a key part in all the planning and processing you are doing. The most obvious question is: what is the intent when somebody is searching for something? When somebody Google's a query, what is it they're actually looking for and what is the answer that they want? The aim for us, as SEOs, is to try and match our content to that, and show that we know what the user is looking for and that we've got that answer.

It goes a lot broader than that, though, and there are many different types of intent. It comes in even before that point, when people are doing their keyword research and looking into the queries and things that they want to rank for. You need to consider, what is the business's intent? That is something I bring up with clients. They want to produce more content, but why are they writing it? What is the intent for this piece of content? Often, the answer is very simple: it's that they want to sell more stuff. However, you need to consider what that stuff is, who you are selling it to, and how often - all those kinds of things.

To bring it back and bang that 'intent' drum again: what do you intend to do? What do your customers intend when they're searching for that thing that you're trying to match this to? I am keeping the idea of intent deliberately broad, but it's really important across all kinds of stages of SEO."

When establishing intent, what comes first? Is it the customer, the business, the product, or something else?

"It has to be the customer. You might have the intent as a business owner to rank for 'Facebook'. Great. Are you Facebook? No. Then you're not going to rank for that, and you shouldn't. Businesses generally already have answers to these kinds of tricky questions - about who their customers are and what they mean when they're looking for these kinds of things. They often say that they don't know, but they really do. They'll have customer types, they'll have user journeys, etc., and there are some great ways that you can show them how SEO feeds into these things.

Businesses have these lovely funnels that we're aware of, like awareness, consideration, conversion, and then retention. However, as much as I love funnels, I also hate them because almost no customers do that. If you map a user journey, from when they first started thinking about something that you sell to when they buy it, they very rarely flow perfectly through the funnel in that way: where they're unaware of your brand, then they're aware, then they consider you, then they convert, and then they're happily retained forever and ever and they pour all their money into your bank account. It never really works like that.

People mess your funnels up all the time. They'll constantly zigzag around, they'll jump up and down through your funnel, they'll think about one thing, get halfway down, change their mind, come back and consider another product, then consider their budget, the colour, their availability, etc. It's never a beautiful, linear journey.

You have to think about that from a customer point of view, and then show how that maps with SEO. Put the pieces of content that a website has onto this funnel. You might be able to show that you've got 50 pieces of content that are all top-of-funnel, you've got 10 pieces of content that are all bottom-of-funnel, and you've got nothing in the middle. That shows a really big gap.

All these people are looking for stuff in the middle to help push them to that last stage, and you haven't got anything. You've got content for users that have never heard of you, explaining who you are and what you should be considered for, but there's nothing then pushing them through those next stages of the funnel. Mapping that kind of thing - from the intent of customers to the content that they've got - to those funnels and user journeys that a lot of companies already have, can be really eye-opening."

What are some questions that you tend to ask top players in a business when it comes to the intent behind the business or the product? How do you establish that for the first time?

"For a lot of companies, you will first ask, 'Who's your target audience?' The stock response is, 'Everyone. Everyone wants our stuff.' If you pick into that a little bit more, they don't. It will be a new modern piece of kit, like the latest flip phone, and they'll say, 'Everybody should have a flip phone, it's amazing!', but does my mum need one? She's in her 70s and she struggles with her basic Nokia. She doesn't need it and she doesn't want it, so she's not your target. You have to ask those kinds of questions - really picking into who their target audience is.

You also need to make them think about what kind of things they want, and what they need more of. That's often a question I start with because clients will have all these really broad things that their business does. There are very few businesses that just sell one product. If it's a service industry, they'll have different scales of products that they'll offer. If they sell cars, they might also do servicing, they might sell spare parts, they'll have training courses, and other things as well.

It is often a case of getting them to focus on the right things. You'll ask them, 'If I could get you 100 more customers tomorrow, who do you want? Do you want more people buying your cars? Do you want more people booking your services?' That will make them think. Buying the cars might be nice because that's where they make the most money, but what actually sustains them through the long winters could be people getting their cars serviced. They might decide that what they really need for the business at the moment is 100 more of those because it's retained business. People buy a car, and they never come back again for 10 years, whereas a person who has a really good service will come back once a year, every year.

I'm often asking those kinds of questions: about who their most profitable customers are and which customers they want more of. The standard response is always, 'More of everything, please?' but you need to be more focussed. Try to push clients to make that kind of decision. 'If you had to choose one type of customer that you want more of, which would it be and why?' That can be really interesting."

How do you go about mapping intent to the different stages of the user journey, and targeting the right consumer at the right time?

"Most people will understand a lot of the types of intent that we talk about. They will either have done this themselves, or they'll be marketers and they'll have come across these terms before. There are informational queries when the user is in the early stages of exploring a topic - where they want to know who did something, they are looking for ideas about something, they want a definition for something, etc.

There are also navigational queries, where the user already knows what they want. They might want Majestic, so they Google 'Majestic', or they might even Google 'majestic.com'. For those queries, they already know what they want or they're looking for a particular place. Sometimes, they'll want to go to the coffee shop they went to last week, and they'll search for the name, for example.

Then, there are transactional and commercial queries - like consideration and purchase-oriented decision-making - and Google talks about those too. In Google's documentation and their guidelines around these kinds of things, they use the terms: 'do', 'go', and 'know'. A user wants to 'do' something, 'go' somewhere (like a particular website), or 'know' something. Analysing the intent of these queries matches up with what Google is saying. They're trying to do this too, and they're trying to steer people towards these ideas with their content as well.

You have to look at what the types of queries are. Looking at qualifying words is particularly helpful, like transactional terms. First, people will go through the stage of looking at all the options available, like 'Mercedes', 'Porsche', 'Lexus', or whatever products they're considering. They will narrow it down to a shortlist and then, they might search for a voucher. If they're searching for 'your brand name + discount code', then they're telling you (and Google) that they already decided what they want to buy and who they want to buy it from, they are just looking for some money off.

Adding those qualifiers - like 'voucher', 'coupon', 'buy', 'price', 'deal', etc. – to keywords and queries shows you the intent behind that. If they're asking 'who', 'what', 'where', 'why', and 'how' questions, then they're probably slightly higher up the funnel. They're in the informational area, kicking around ideas.

There is sometimes a conflict between what the business wants and their intent, and then what Google wants and Google's intent. Google is always a key entity to consider in this. When you look at Google, and you look at their search results, they'll often have indications of what people want. I was reading a piece by Tomasz Niezgoda from Surfer about this. When people search for hairstyle ideas, they don't want 6,000 words - they want pictures. When people search for, 'How do I fix my dishwasher?' or 'How do I fix this issue on my car?', they want videos - they want somebody to talk them through it and explain.

Google will show that. Google will have video boxes, they'll have image boxes, and they'll start to bring in the most prominent bits of search. If it's a quick answer, like 'How old is Barack Obama', it will just be right there on the search results. That can show you what Google thinks people are looking for.

You can try and hijack the search results and force what you think is the right answer in there, but sometimes it's a longer process of persuading Google that it's the better answer. You have to try and find the match between what the business wants, what customers are looking for, and what Google is showing people. That's the sweet spot."

How do you determine whether the content that you produce is most likely to be a close match to someone's intent?

"An important way to think about this is to consider the intent of the page. What do you want them to do next, once you've got them on that page? If you know that they're looking for information, or they're looking for something transactional, are you helping them to reach that goal? Goal completion is something that Google has also talked about, although nobody's quite clear on how they measure it. That goal completion could be finding an address or the phone number of the company, or it could be buying the socks that they wanted to buy. You need to think about whether your content matches up to the goal of the user.

Businesses are very good with this kind of commercial thing. They will say that they want their users to buy something, so they're going to write some content saying it's lovely and that they should buy it. It's not often that easy. Sometimes, for informational queries and things that come higher up in the funnel, what you want them to do next is read another piece of content, sign up for your newsletter, or just go away and think warm, fuzzy things about your brand. That kind of purchase journey is a lot longer.

A lot of the companies I deal with are not B2C, with users directly and immediately buying a pair of socks. Nobody buys huge pieces of industrial medical equipment on a whim, for example. You don't just drop 3 million pounds on a huge microscope that you're going to put into your lab. That's not an impulse buy like a pair of socks; it's much more of a considered journey. There might be things that they need along the way, to help persuade their CEO or their financial director. It might be that what you actually want from this piece of content is for them to download the 'Persuade Your CFO' pack - that could be the conversion.

What do you think the customer wants? What do you think Google wants? What do you want them to do, and does your page help them with that goal completion?"

What shouldn't SEOs be doing in 2023? What's seductive in terms of time, but ultimately counterproductive?

"One issue I often see is what I call a 'word soup'. There are some great tools out there that use things like the People Also Asked questions and 'related searches', and they'll grab all these possible questions and combinations around the target query that you're going for. The temptation can then be to write one absolutely biblical piece of content that covers every possible additional question, follow-up question, and question that questions those questions.

When you're not quite sure where you're going to aim a piece of content, it can be really tempting to just aim at everything, throw it at the wall, and hope that some of it sticks. There are times when that idea sort of works. AlsoAsked.com is a great tool for that kind of initial research around a question, particularly with financial stuff. With a query like, 'What's the best mortgage for a first-time buyer?', there will be related questions like, 'How do I get a mortgage?', 'Which is the best bank?', or 'How much deposit do I need?', and those are all related things. That's good - it makes sense, and you should put those in with your content too - but then you can find yourself going really deep down the rabbit hole.

What you end up with are these 'word soup' articles. People often point AI writing machines at these kinds of things. They pull out all the headings and the AI-generator goes wild. It's really tempting, it can be fun - and it can occasionally be effective - but it can be dangerous too. It's often much better to just think of Google as one of your customers, and bear your end customer in mind as well.

We've all arrived at an article that's 6,000 words long and you just think, 'I haven't got time for this. I'll go somewhere else.' Think about your customers. Yes, it might be a good idea to get all those additional questions and related searches in, but that could be over two, three, or even ten articles. You don't have to word-soup it into one ginormous piece of content."

Andrew Cock-Starkey is the founder of Optimisey and you can find him over at optimisey.com.

Consider intent when you create content—Julia-Carolin Zeng

Julia-Carolin Zeng encourages SEOs in 2023 to ask themselves: What is the intent behind the keywords that you are creating content for? What is the user actually trying to do when they are typing it into search?

Julia says: "My number one SEO tip for the coming year is to look more at intent when you create content. Don't just say, 'This is my keyword, so this is what I write.' Really ask the question: What is the intent behind this keyword? What is somebody trying to find out when they type this into a search engine?"

How do you go about defining what intent is?

"By looking at the search results.

Initially, I identify keywords using the standard tools. Semrush and Ahrefs are my go-tos, and I sometimes use Keyword Planner as well - depending on the client and the industry. Once I have identified the keywords, I will put them into Google to see what actually gets brought up for that keyword, and what the intent really is. What is the question behind that keyword? When somebody is typing a keyword into Google, they are usually not looking for that particular word – there is a question that they want to be answered.

The search results can give you a lot of information on what your content should be about. You can look at the title tags that are displayed there, the meta descriptions, the Featured Snippets, the People Also Ask boxes, etc. All these are hints that Google is giving you as to what it understands about what is behind the keyword, and what it thinks the best answer is for somebody searching for this particular word. Then you can get good ideas for what your content should be about to fulfil that intent, and to answer the question."

Do you believe that manually determining intent will give you higher-quality results than relying on software tools to guess what that intent might be?

"Yes. A tool can help you to start classifying whether a keyword has informational intent, transactional intent, etc. You can classify your keywords and decide that, for example, certain content should sit in a glossary because it is informational intent and other content will be for product pages because it's all transactional.

When it comes to the stage where you are actually writing the content (or in my case, creating a content brief for a writer), it is important to look at the actual search results. You want to see, what is the question here? What is the information that needs to be provided on this page (for longer-form text content)?

It's not about using the keyword hundreds of times anymore, it's really about: What is the searcher trying to find out and is that content actually answering that question? If it does, you can rank the content without even mentioning the actual keyword - if you meet the intent and provide the answer."

Can you target a keyword without incorporating it within the text?

"Yes, you can. What I always say when I brief somebody is that we want to make it easy for Google to understand what your content is about. In my opinion, that's what it's about these days. Make it easier for Google by using things like structured data, even if they're not displayed.

You can have the greatest FAQ schema on your page, and I will still hear from clients, 'It's not displayed on Google!' Yes, but it still helps Google to understand that this is a question/answer type of content. It might appear in certain contexts, and it helps you rank better because it makes it easier for Google to assign an overall topic, determine what the content is about, how it's structured, etc. The same is true for things like bullet point lists.

I still recommend using the main keyword - in the title tag, the H1, and so on - but just to make it a bit more obvious what it is about. It does depend on competitiveness and which industry it is, but you can still rank that content if you don't mention a keyword at all, as long as you are meeting the intent."

Are there other buckets of intent that you use, besides informational and navigational?

"Commercial intent. That's a keyword where somebody is ready to buy a product. The page that should rank for that keyword needs to make it easy for the user to actually buy, otherwise it won't work. I've seen pages where there's not even a 'buy' option.

You know what the user is trying to do, and you are still sending them through three to five more clicks before they get to the point where they can buy the product. It should be easy and straightforward for the user."

What do you incorporate in a content brief to try to ensure that the content writer targets the correct intent?

"Usually, I give a little summary in a bullet point list. It will say: 'These are the paragraphs that should be on the page. These are the things you should mention.' Then, I include something like, 'We should have FAQs on this page' and if it's not necessary I don't mention it. I can determine this by looking at what comes up in the search results. What are the top-ranking pages doing? What are the subtopics?

I also give the writer keywords, but not just one keyword; I give them all the synonyms or other words that should be targeted as well. That could be a long-tail keyword, where the answer is just answered in one sentence or one short paragraph. Those are useful because Google now does something called 'passage indexing', where it will pull out one paragraph from your content and display it on the SERP and, when you click on it, it brings you directly to that paragraph. You don't need to create a separate page for something that is answered in one sentence, you can include that on a page where it fits in topically.

I will include all of these things in the brief that I give to a writer: 'These are the paragraphs that should be there. Here are the keywords - use them as inspiration, you don't have to use all these words on the page.' I also give some competitor examples or pages that are ranking for those keywords that I think are good examples of what I want the content to be. That will mean that the content the writer is creating is a bit of a mix of what the top competitors are doing.

I will also include anything else that I think could be useful. These could be examples of images or graphs that somebody else has. If I expect the piece of content to become quite long, then I tell a writer that I want a table of contents early on so that we can add page jump links. With passage indexing, it's not really necessary for SEO anymore, but it makes it easier for Google to understand the structure and which passages to take out for passage indexing."

Do you give an indication as to the kind of length that you expect or is that up to the writer to decide?

"I usually don't give word counts unless somebody really needs a word count. Sometimes the client might need one for payment reasons - so that they can pay the writer or so they know how much to put on the PO. Then, I just take an average of what the competing pages are doing and say, 'Let me know if you need more'.

If I can avoid it, I don't give a word count. I don't want a writer to feel that they need to fill it with more words if they've said what they need to say in the content. I also don't want a writer to have to cut it short. Sometimes they just want to add two more sentences to really explain something, but they need to cut words. That's not what we're trying to achieve.

I've never experienced content becoming super long or super short if there is a detailed brief of what I want. I'm also getting great feedback from the writers, saying that they know exactly what is expected and what they should write."

Do you ever map multiple intents to a single keyword and try and deliver on multiple intents on a single page?

"No. I try to deliver on multiple keywords if the keywords have the same intent, but not on multiple intents. If the intent becomes different, then it should be a different page."

Is it possible for a singular keyword to have multiple intents? If so, do you try to rank for those keywords on separate pages?

"That does happen. I think we need to redefine how we look at keyword cannibalization in SEO. I sometimes have clients that say, 'I use this tool to track my rankings and I constantly see the pages swapping, is this keyword cannibalization?' and it kind of is, but you have to think about the person searching for that keyword.

It could be that they are trying to find different things under different circumstances, which means it is actually a good thing that Google swaps out pages to better match the intent for that specific case. People are concerned about data, but Google knows so much about the individual. It knows: where is this person? What is this person doing? What are their personal circumstances? What have they been searching for before? So, if they now type in a particular question, Google will decide what it is that they probably want to see, and it might decide to display a different page.

In your data, it might seem as though keyword cannibalization is happening but it's not, really, because the intent is different - even though the word might be the same. It's language; one word can have different meanings and people can be after different things.

This is also true with click-through rates. I had a client a few weeks ago who asked me, 'Can you look through our click-through rates in Google Search Console and see what we can improve?' I looked at the data and I said, 'Those keywords where your click-through rate looks bad, on paper, are actually keywords where Google provides the answer in the search results.' You see this with these featured snippets, answer boxes, etc. Somebody just needs a definition or wants to find the age of an actor, and that is displayed in the Knowledge Graph. You don't even need to click on anything to get this information anymore. The click-through rate for these keywords will always be a bit lower than for other keywords.

What I say to my clients is that it's still brand visibility. If you get that featured snippet, the user in front of that search engine will still notice who is giving them that answer. It's a good thing, so it doesn't mean you should not go after these keywords."

Are click-through rates the best KPI for measuring how well you're serving intent?

"No, because of these instances where some keywords don't even require a click anymore. One good indication is to look at bounce rates and, of course, conversions - all these numbers together. When you're analysing the data, you need to think about the reason why somebody came to the page.

When I have a product page where I tried to sell something, it's very obvious what the measurement should be: did I make the sale? Did somebody sign up for my newsletter? The conversion numbers are a good indicator.

Content groupings will help. If you have a bucket of informational keywords, and you are looking at a glossary, all of that traffic is not intending to purchase anything. They're so early in the funnel, that you just want to get them to your website. You want brand visibility, and maybe you have a newsletter signup but maybe not.

A lot of marketing psychology is involved to really understand what the person wants. Why did they come here? Does the data suggest that they found what they were looking for or does the data suggest that we're doing something wrong?"

What shouldn't SEOs be doing in 2023? What's seductive in terms of time, but ultimately counterproductive?

"We already mentioned it and, for lack of a better word for it, I still call it keyword cannibalization. I often see websites that have already created the same type of content in the past, that meets the same intent - they were just thinking about a different person.

For one client of mine (a software product), they were trying to map one page to somebody in HR who might need the product, and then somebody at C-level, and then the line manager, etc. In the end, they all have the same question. It's a problem of internal communication. You don't need to create a separate SEO page for all these different personas if the intent behind the question is the same.

That's something I would really advise everybody who has a website to stop doing. Stop publishing the same piece of content five times, delivering the same answer. That is the kind of keyword cannibalization we're trying to avoid."

Julia-Carolin Zeng is a Freelance SEO Consultant and she writes at charlieonthemove.com.

Create or update your content to satisfy user intent— Irina Serdyukovskaya

Irina Serdyukovskaya explains to SEOs in 2023 that content is still king, but you need to be more specific about the type of content you create and understand what your users are actually looking for.

Irina says: "My number one tip for SEOs in 2023 is to create or update content to satisfy user intent. As an SEO, you shouldn't be doing something just for SEO if it doesn't benefit the user and customer UX.

You need to create a website that is not for Google. Don't think about how to rank, first you need to think about what customers or potential users are going to see on your website. Content is still king in 2023, but now you need to understand how to create the type of content that users are looking for and be more specific about what you actually put out there.

There are already thousands of websites even in just one market or industry. To be competitive, you need to think about the customer first and not about the keyword research first, because of the level of competition in the space. In the end, that just might not be your audience."

How do you create content that is different, distinctive, and better than your competitors?

"I would recommend (and this is what we are doing for our clients) that you speak with customers and potential customers - and use the feedback from customers to create content.

Don't just use a keyword research tool, but actually go to the customers and ask them what questions they would like to find answers to on your website. What benefits are they looking for when they would like to buy your product or pay for your SaaS tool?

That's the main difference. Instead of creating content based on keyword research, go to customers and ask what they are looking for. Then, you can match this with the data that you have."

Is it sufficient for a customer service team to simply ask an additional question or two when they are communicating with customers or do you have to set up a separate, more intensive conversation?

"I think it's both. You might have a group of customers who are open to giving you more detailed feedback, and if they are a fan of your business then they will appreciate the opportunity to take part and make improvements.

To have broader data, however, you might ask questions after you talk with the customer, or you can listen to the questions that your customers ask. You don't always need to directly ask them what they would like to have on the website.

The customer team can give you a list of questions. They will be having hundreds of calls during the week, so they will know what questions are coming up. People might say, 'I don't know how to cancel' or "How can this tool work with another tool?' You can get these queries from the customer team directly without asking any questions of the customers themselves.

Conversations with customer service teams often revolve around negative feedback, so you do need to be proactive in reaching out to your more neutral customers as well. That will reflect a broader section of your audience. You could have a focus group so that you can reach the customers who are maybe not that satisfied with your tool or the customer service in general. All of this information is really useful for making improvements to your business and the content on your website."

How often would you recommend getting a focus group together?

"Once per year should be enough, unless you are launching a lot of new products, new tools, or new features for your tool. It takes a lot of investment to actually organize a focus group - perhaps not from a financial perspective, but from a time perspective - that the team needs to put in to get it done properly."

You mentioned that SEO should be a broader part of the whole business, including conversations with marketing teams, product teams, development teams, etc. How does SEO better marry itself to different parts of the business?

"SEO is part of marketing because, when you create content, you need to understand how you can share it on social media, how you can promote it through your email marketing campaigns, and how it could help you with your PR activities or your brand awareness.

If you can achieve all of those goals with one piece of content, it's a win-win for the business. If you only create content for SEO (e.g., to rank on Google) that's a fair goal but, if you can match it with other marketing channels, you will get much more out of that one piece."

What are some key aspects of content that should be included?

"First, it should be written by an expert - either from your company or externally. There should be some expertise in your content, not just rewriting the content that is already out there.

The second thing to think about is: will this content be shareable? That's very important. Do you have any data, for example, that could be interesting for your audience and that they would like to share, download, or save? Is it newsworthy? If you have these three things - newsworthiness, shareability, and expertise – then you will probably have created some really good content."

What makes good newsworthy content?

"It could be related to something that is happening in the news at the moment, or it could be something that should be popular or important every year. We have New Year, Black Friday, and the summer holidays every year, for example. During April and May, the media is writing about where you can go for your summer holidays, and in October there will be content pieces about what you should buy during Black Friday.

You need to get this kind of content planned in advance. When it's something reactive, you need to be very fast and this isn't always possible for marketing teams. You might not have the capacity to react, but there are other ways that you can plan ahead."

If you want to have your brand featured in news media for Black Friday, for example, is it best to publish an article in mid-November? Should you be reaching out to journalists directly and should you be publishing content yourself?

"There are different strategies that you can apply. If you have the data, then it makes sense to publish it as a press release or put the research up on your website. It is also best to prepare these things in advance and publish them early on, particularly if that data is about how to prepare for an event like Black Friday – which is something that needs to be published before the event itself. Then, you can pitch to the journalist, and they can mention your content and link to your website, because you have data there.

If you write your content and publish it earlier, you have more time to promote it and pitch it to a journalist. You will get more publications and more mentions, compared to content that you create reactively during the event - although you can still get a lot from reactive content as well."

If you should never be creating content just for SEO's sake, should SEOs not be building links unless they are sure it will drive traffic?

"It does still make sense to build relevant links, even if you would not necessarily gain direct traffic from them. However, they need to be the right contextual links – where a website has mentioned your brand.

People generally don't click a link mentioning that a company prepared some research or data, for example. They are not necessarily interested in who provided that data, they are interested in the data itself, which was probably already published by the journalist. However, you still need links like these, because they are relevant and they build authority.

On the other hand, if you add links that lead to promotional pages and places like that, people will not click on those, and they do not provide authority. That's not a strategy I would recommend."

What shouldn't SEOs be doing in 2023? What's seductive in terms of time, but ultimately counterproductive?

"First, stop buying links from low-quality websites or buying links from comments. People still do this, and I would not recommend it. Second, don't create content if you can see that there is a lot of high-quality content for that keyword already. It's very tricky to create better content if you can already see some of the best content possible.

Before you start writing any content, you should look at the SERP. If you see that the optimum answer already exists, then you should be aiming for another keyword phrase instead.

You should only create that kind of content if you don't have any other ideas and you have already written thousands of pieces of content. For most businesses, you will still have less competitive keywords that you can create content for, where you have more expertise and can provide more value."

Irina Serdyukovskaya is an International SEO Consultant, and you can find her over at irinakudres.com.

5 CONTENT PLANNING

Have a clear content strategy and invest in content the right way—Kevin Gibbons

Kevin Gibbons gives SEOs in 2023 a series of steps on how to have a clear content strategy, making sure that your content is actually engaging your customers in the right way.

Kevin says: "My number one tip is to have a clear content strategy. Since we arranged this interview, Google announced the helpful content update, which further solidifies the importance of this. I've always been a strong advocate of having a very clear content strategy, investing properly in how you produce your content, and making sure that you're doing everything in a way that can attract potential customers across the journey.

Having the right content strategy, for me, means you carry out a full content audit. Don't create content until you know what you have already, and how well it's performing. Also, carry out a gap analysis against competitors, and understand where the opportunities are for you to grow. Then, you really invest in content to make sure that it's working for you.

It's not a tick-box exercise – where you are just creating pages about a topic. It's thinking about how your content is actually engaging with your customers. Invest in content so that it works for your site in the right way."

5 Content Planning

In order to carry out a gap analysis, how do you establish who your competitors are?

"We use some in-house tools that look at a set of keywords and, depending on the brand in the niche, that could be a hundred keywords up to tens or hundreds of thousands. Based on that analysis, you will start to see trends for which competitors rank highly and have the strongest visibility for those keywords.

There are also external tools on the market that you can use, to show visibility and how that ranks versus competitors, who is most relevant, and where the overlap is against your competitors. We normally do that based on the keyword set that we want to rank for, and then we build outwards from there.

If you don't look at the keywords, you might rule out competitors. A lot of people say that Amazon isn't a competitor, for example, because they do everything. Actually, Amazon often is a competitor. If you sell trainers, so does Amazon. You don't want to compare your own performance against Amazon for everything that they do, obviously, but if you have a niche product and Amazon is ranking number one, why would you discredit them? If your research is done on a keyword basis, you're looking at the visibility of those keywords and the brands that are most relevant and performing highly for those keywords.

That's the first step and then you can build outwards. Start with keywords - and at scale so that you can notice the trends. Equally, you might find that you have multiple product lines, and you have different competitor sets across those product lines. If you're a fashion retailer, you might sell jeans for men, and you might sell dresses for women, for example. There would be some competitors that do both of those as well, but you'll also have competing brands that are more niche and specific. You have to factor that in, from the top level down to the product level."

What's the best content to start with? Is it content that there are gaps for, or are you better off writing about the key content that is directly related to what you do as a business?

"I wouldn't start with the gaps; I would start with your customers. What are the most important topics for them? Google Ads is still something that I would go to in the early stages because you can see how much revenue you're making on a keyword level. There's much more data available around that versus organic search. You can also understand, from your own analytics and from an organic perspective, which pages are making you the most money. There are ways to link that up to Search Console and get keyword data as well.

Start with your own audience. What is it that you're finding converts the best? If you think of it in terms of the awareness, consideration, and conversion stages of the funnel, I would start backwards. That means starting from conversion. What is it that's going to drive sales? Quite often that would be branded keywords or product keywords, which people overlook. You might assume that you will be number one for your own product or brand, but that's not always the case. Start by making sure you are number one, and also secure number two and some featured snippets around that, if you can, to maximise and own those pages as much as possible.

Then, start to look at what your top converting keywords are - the ones that are going to drive sales and revenue. That way, your content strategy becomes prioritised by value in terms of the revenue that will be brought into the site. Then, you can start building out into awareness topics.

There will be some gaps. You probably haven't 100% nailed what your customers want to be finding you for, or what you may be relevant for, but I would start with understanding what you have already and how well it works. Look for any gaps between your own PPC and your SEO because, if those keywords are performing well, you might have content for some of the best opportunities already, it's just not doing enough. If it's on page two and you can take it over to the edge onto page one, that's a great initial starting point. You might already know it will convert – if you've got data that shows that traffic to those pages (or for those keywords) always converts highly - and you just want to get more traffic from what you already have. Invest in that content. Build it out and make it as strong as possible versus your competitors.

The metrics can be a bit flawed as well. It's not just about traffic and it's not just about rankings, either. It could be about improving the click-through rate from your existing pages, improving your conversion rate, lengthening your average time on site, reducing the bounce rate, etc. Investing in content from a user perspective, and a customer perspective, is really important. Conversion rate optimisation would overlap here, as well. It could be that you can turn a page into more revenue without actually increasing traffic.

There's a lot to look at in what you have already. You can go on to the gaps afterwards, but don't create any new content until you audit and understand what you have already. It's quite possible that you will already have pages around the topics that you need to be writing about, it just might not be working to its full effect."

What software do you use to have a look at seasonality trends and what are you looking for?

"Google Trends is pretty good, and having Google's own data is useful. Certainly, if it's a client, we would look at their analytics and what trends we can see from a traffic perspective. We do some market research insights for the eCommerce sector where we understand what the trends are, and we've actually done an interview with the head of retail at KPMG so that we can understand seasonal and economic trends that could be coming for different sub-sectors.

You want to know, from a search volume perspective, what's popular in different areas. Some are more obvious, particularly for recurring seasonal events. Christmas is pretty predictable, in terms of when people are going to start shopping. There could be others, however, that are more of an economic trend. With COVID, for example, DIY, home and garden furniture, and online groceries had a big spike, whereas luxury fashion may have gone the other way.

You need to be aware of not just the seasonality of what happens year-on-year, but also potential changes in the economic climate. Then, you can factor that into your prioritisation. This is key for seasonal products, of course. If you're a fashion brand in the northern hemisphere and you're advertising winterwear in May, you're probably not going to be doing particularly well. Equally, you don't want to leave it too late when it does come around.

It's important to prioritise when you focus on these so that you can secure the rankings in the right way in order to get traffic. Invest in that content at the right time. Think about the people. If your blog is full of content about winter fashion in summer (because you're trying to secure rankings ready for winter) then who's going to read that? You've got to think about the timing from a customer perspective, instead of just lining everything up for Google."

What does a content strategy roadmap look like and how often should it be revisited?

"Through a combination of the audits and gap analysis, you can create a forecast. That's where you see the potential upside of actually doing this. Quite often, brands won't know how much to budget, or they might have a fixed budget, but it might not be right. You could take a fixed budget, and build your roadmap around the best way to get value from that budget, or you could present it as an opportunity to grow and what you achieve will depend on the budget that you're given. That would factor in the roadmap as well.

If you've got a low budget, and you want to create tens of thousands of pages, that's obviously not going to work. You might have to look at the 80/20 rule and focus on getting the most bang for your buck. Then, you would build that roadmap prioritising by value first, and looking at the revenue opportunity of different pages and topics. Once you know what that revenue opportunity is, you can overlay seasonality. You don't want to be waiting 12 months for that to turn into revenue - you want it to have a shorter-term impact.

You need to understand the capability that you have, and the budget that you have on the production side. If you create a full content strategy that looks at absolutely everything you could do, but you don't have the internal resource of copywriters (or budget externally) to create that content, then you're wasting your time. Build a forecast and build a case for what you would do if you had an uncapped budget versus what your budget actually is, and how you can use that in the best way possible. Then, you can prioritise.

Also, think about how you are going to invest in the right way to make sure you've got content that is good enough to rank against your competitors. It's not just about how far the budget spreads to create as many pages as possible. Then, you're playing a game of 'how much content you can get for the budget' and, in that game, the cheapest copywriter wins. On Google, however, the highest quality content usually wins. Make sure that you're aligned in what you're doing and why you're doing it."

How do you forecast how long it's likely to take to achieve the rankings that you want to get?

"It will be based upon the difficulty of achieving that ranking against competitors. Take Amazon. If you're a startup with a lot of other competitors, and you're trying to outrank them for book titles, then it's not going to happen overnight. However, if it's a more niche product and the competitors are fairly light (maybe outside the top two or three), then you would factor that in and potentially aim to be on page one for those terms within six months, and in the top three within twelve months.

Take your competition into account. Fashion is a great example. In our eCommerce report, I think we have about 50 brands just for fashion retailers alone, and trying to become part of that top 50 is really difficult. Ranking for the most competitive terms, like 'black dress', 'blue jeans', etc., is not going to be easy.

The sweet spot to aim towards is finding the highest volume where you have a realistic chance of winning over the next six to twelve months. Think long-term, but you need to be able to show progress toward that. You will have to start to show an ROI against your efforts and your work, so that you can prove that it is working, it's on the right track, and it's sustainable from a budget perspective - because you're self-funding and reinvesting the profits from your work into getting you into higher positions longer term."

What shouldn't SEOs be doing in 2023? What's seductive in terms of time but ultimately counterproductive?

"I think SEOs can often get too tactical. You have to start with a strategy. I wouldn't look at any tactics until you know the strategy of where you're going. SEOs can focus too short term. You need to be aware of algorithm updates but, equally, know what has value to the business, and understand what it is that you're trying to achieve.

If you're looking to maximise revenue, then look at how you can focus on top-converting keywords. It's not necessarily always the tactical items. Focus on a longer-term vision, and a plan that works towards that in the short, medium, and long term. Don't get too distracted by everything that's happening in terms of the tactics around it. Understand what you're trying to achieve and work backwards.

Going back to the content strategy perspective, there are two ways of doing things. One is to maximise traffic, and the other is to can maximise revenue. For me, maximising revenue is easier because you're focusing your effort on what's going to work for that brand, not just what's competitive and popular in Google.

Don't get too distracted by what everyone else is talking about and focus on the business metrics. This will certainly help to delight your clients because you're making them money, and that's the most important thing. Keep focus and, on the flip side, don't lose that focus."

Kevin Gibbons is the Founder and CEO at Re:signal and you can find him at resignal.com.

Quality over quantity—Ian Helms

Ian Helms believes that quality over quantity will matter more than ever in 2023, so you need to be hyper-focused on delivering the kind of quality that Google is actually looking for.

Ian says: "Lots of junior content-focused SEOs and agencies make the mistake of focusing too much on output and reaching a certain quota. With the news of the helpful content update starting to roll out from Google, we should be hyper-focused on crafting high-quality content. Avoid just churning out content to get quick keyword rankings."

Are you referring to everything or specifically zeroing in on content?

"It's a little bit of everything. There is a technical side to any content that you create, but there's definitely more on the on-site content-focused side of SEO. It's important to dive a little further and not just churn out content that includes keywords for a random topic.

You should think holistically about how organic search can fit into your broader, integrated campaign. It's about aligning your keywords with user intent and targeting what your customers need. Tie your unique perspective and business values into offering something more helpful, relevant, and genuine. For example, if you're writing that water is wet just because it's a highly searched keyword, that's an ill-advised approach. Focus on establishing proper breadth and depth on a particular category so you can demonstrate your expertise and authority around the topic."

Regarding high-quality content, is there any particular length or content type that Google prefers?

"It's a cliche of me to say, but it depends. Whenever you're creating a new piece of content or looking to launch a campaign with an SEO component, you should always look into the terms you want to target so you can get an overview of the landscape. You can then see exactly what Google says users are looking for.

Google will always try to prioritise ranking the best content on page one. By looking at what's ranking - whether that's a How-To, listicle, specific opinion piece or other - you can model the content you create on what you find there."

Let's say you visit Google and discover a listicle in the Google SERP. Would it be a mistake to build a different form of content that targets the same keyword phrases?

"It's probably best to avoid doing anything different. What works best for the user when they get to your site will vary depending on the line of business you're in and what you're talking about. Think about the primary piece of content and align the quality of your content to what Google is showing. Then you can think about different iterations and other formats that your content can take.

For example, there might be a downloadable aspect that you can link to from that page. There might even be a different form of content that you can link to from that listicle. Use Google as a guide - as a ramp to divert traffic based on what you think the user will be looking for. Your audience might resonate with types or formats of content that are outside of what Google suggests."

If Google is already listing a certain type of result for a certain keyword phrase, will going against Google make it harder to rank?

"Yes, but it's not always as simple as that with some SERPs. Some results pages have many different types of content. When the search landscape changes as it has over the years, some forms (like category or shopping-focused content) may no longer perform. Google can show more results on the editorial side, like how to style a particular type of clothing or the best materials for the type of clothing a user wants to buy.

When you align on a topic and content format, remember it won't be a set-it-and-forget-it type of situation. There are many ways that content can fit into other pieces or related keywords you're targeting. Continually check back and see whether something is doing as well as you'd hoped. You should also look at whether Google has changed the way it assumes or determines that people are enjoying the content. You can then evolve your strategy from there."

How often should you check back? Also, how often should you use some kind of formal analysis on the type of SERP that exists for your target keyword phrases?

"This can be done based on either the amount of content you're creating or bandwidth. Time is always a luxury that we have at a minimum. You should focus on performing a yearly overview of retroactive content performance. If you churn out content for the sake of churning out content, you'll get lost in the shuffle of project managing 1,000 pieces of content every month.

If you don't take the time to do a yearly reflection and look back at how well your content is performing, you'll keep going down the wrong path. Google will not reward you for what an SEO doesn't benefit from, regardless of the situation you're in. Quarterly content is great too, but when it comes to diving into the content you're touching, creating, and involved in, a yearly minimum review should come into play."

Regarding the intent you mentioned earlier, is the type of SERP result also an indication of the likely intent of a keyword phrase?

"It's certainly not perfect in most cases. Tools like Semrush have launched new intent-based keyword markers for when you're doing keyword research. However, they're rarely perfect. If you're targeting a broader keyword, you could shape the intent with some of the secondary and tertiary keywords you're writing about. These might have a different intent than the broader keyword topic you're writing about, which can shift the narrative and guide people down the journey you want them to take on your site. Also, once they're stuck on your site and you keep them there, you'll be pivoting them to an area where you're getting them to do what you want them to."

How can SEO more effectively work in line with other forms of digital marketing?

"Just start a conversation. A lot of SEOs get siloed or they feel scared about going over to the paid side. Why? Because of the way paid media teams are treated differently - their budgets vary, and their preference is more short-term than long-term. By having those conversations, you can reach out, extend some olive branches, and secure testing opportunities.

Some of the most successful campaigns are fully integrated across teams. You should assess situations by, for example, recognising that 10,000 people are looking for something on a monthly basis and working out the structure your content should take. You can incorporate internal links to get visitors to stay on-site. You can then request that paid search teams use these landing pages as a starting point to create a remarketing tool. Also, paid social can get your content in front of people who aren't searching but could be interested because there are so many people proactively searching.

On the email side, it's kind of twofold, depending on if you're emailing prospects or existing clients. It also depends on whether it's a loyalty or acquisition style of play. Think about what email nurtures are already in place, like the welcome series on the email side, and identify ways your SEO content can fit into that.

This is a really great way to build bridges between teams for greater success, excitement, collaboration, and integration. Then you won't be looking at things purely from an SEO perspective. You'll be able to zoom out and say that this category content ended up influencing our organic search rankings, and drove this much social media, this much email traffic, and this many conversions. You won't just be siloing yourself. You'll be breaking down the walls and preferably getting extra buy-in and more priority. From an SEO perspective, prioritisation is the next big thing to achieve."

Does email send signals to different platforms that say your new piece of content is getting views and is worth being considered for organic rankings?

"Absolutely. Email has always been one of the more difficult channels to work with, especially on the agency side. Why? Well, often email runs sales content, or is really trying to get people to convert on the bottom of the funnel. However, the content you create from an SEO perspective is usually on the top-of-funnel side. Therefore, your content won't always naturally fit into the strategy. There will often be times when you don't get the positioning for proper visibility. Your content could look unsuccessful just because it's hidden at the bottom of a really long email or something.

The other challenge is when you're trying to do a regular newsletter and you don't have the content output. This goes back to the notion of quality over quantity. If you're not going to churn out five or six blog posts a month, you're not going to have to fill out a newsletter either. That's when you can get to thinking about whether there is evergreen content you can mix in with new content. Repurposing existing content is a great tactic. It's not always about new content but thinking in a retroactive way. What content can you redo, that is already performing well but could be distributed on other channels?"

What shouldn't SEOs be doing in 2023? What's seductive in terms of time, but ultimately counterproductive?

"People are starting to chop up old content from their sites or get rid of content they don't feel is relevant anymore. However, it's not as simple as that. When it comes to your organic search, visibility, and rankings - if you declutter your site by deleting entire sections, this could easily have a negative impact on your rankings.

You should look at things objectively and focus on repurposing, refreshing, and updating content. Old content often has good bones and was written with good intentions. Reassess the original intention behind a piece and think about where the content falls short. You can then work on fixing it (perhaps in line with SEO best practices) instead of just getting rid of it in a way that potentially damages your site or keyword rankings."

Ian Helms is the Director of Growth Marketing at Q.Digital and you can find him over at ianhelms.com.

Create quality content and topical authority— Sara Taher

Sara Taher informs SEOs of the ways that the industry has changed in recent years. She breaks down the three key areas that you need to focus on in 2023: content, context, and control.

Sara says: "SEO in 2023 is very different from a few years ago because there have been several major changes. Now, three things take centre stage: content, context, and controlling how results are displayed in search."

What is so critical about content in 2023?

"We need to shift our mindsets from keywords to topics and topic clusters. Search volume and keyword difficulty mean less now. Hence, we need to change the conversation to user intent, buyers' journey, and how our content should satisfy both. We must approach creating content in topics and topic clusters and how these are related and support each other.

Also, it now matters who is writing your content. Producing great content means working with writers who have subject matter expertise. It also means you'll need to vet your copywriters, which makes producing good content quite expensive. That is where understanding buyers' journeys and prioritising your content accordingly will come in handy."

What does this mean for the outsourcing of content? Do you have to get a named writer or can you use a pen name to get someone else to write the content on your behalf?

"If you want the content to be more authoritative and show expertise, you want someone with some experience in the field. For example, if you're writing about travel, you want a travel blogger or a traveller to share their expertise. It improves the quality of the content and makes it more personal.

When you hire someone, ideally, you want to have the author's bio and link back to their profiles to show their expertise. They don't need to be the biggest name in the industry, but they must hold some relevance and authority. This gets more important if it's in medical or finance."

If you link back to their profile, aren't there some concerns that you're taking authority away from the core website?

"Linking back to authoritative websites is a good practice; it shows the credibility of the information you're sharing."

What are the key elements that you should include in your content nowadays?

"Firstly, we often use exact match keywords, but synonyms would also work. You need to diversify the way you use your keywords. It's no longer about using the exact keywords several times in the body of the content and the titles and calling that great content.

Secondly, structure your content in segments, bullet points, or sections with clear subtitles. While the content is for the user, there's also a bot that will be reading this. Thus, titles need to be very clear about what the section is about.

All these add up to how you want your content to be. It's no longer just writing 1,000 words and stuffing it with keywords and ranking."

Does that mean that you need to identify different sections of content that are, by themselves, distinct ranking opportunities?

"You need sections for two main reasons. First, it's better for a mobile experience, which covers most of your users. If you have long paragraphs of text, they'll look like one solid block of text on mobile and that creates a usability issue for the users.

Secondly, you need to structure the content for both the user and the buyer. You can have multiple sections talking about different things, all under the same topic. For example, if you're talking about summer destinations, maybe talk about how to choose the best destination for your family and budgeting, all as subsections. It's vital from a usability and SEO standpoint."

What do you mean by context?

"First, writing one piece of content on a topic or a handful of issues does not make you an authority. You need a lot of information and more resources to show that you're an authoritative figure in that area. Plus, even with the target topics, ensure that you are covering them thoroughly.

Secondly: the URL structure. It is big in SEO but not very impactful, according to Google. Many SEOs confuse URL structure with the information architecture of the website. Google has also mentioned several times that it does not specifically need a clean URL to understand the structure of the content on the website. We need to stop asking our clients to change the CMS or hard-coded URLs because the impact doesn't match the effort. Instead, focus on internal linking, breadcrumbs, and other things that show how your content is structured."

Suppose that you are putting together a key pillar article and then some supporting articles with related content. Is there an ideal way to link the different pieces to ensure that everything gets indexed and potentially ranked?

"The main guide should link to all those subtopics naturally, when possible. Then those subtopics should also link back to the main topic. Some practitioners say that if you're targeting different topics - for example, 'summer vacations' and 'winter vacation' – then you should not interlink them. Instead, you should keep them separated. Although it is a good point, there isn't much evidence that it is necessary to do."

What do you think about a circular approach, where each sub-article is linked to the next article in a chain, then back to the pillar article?

"The purpose of internal linking is to show hierarchy. You want to show the pillar piece of content - which is the most important and subtopics. The most important link in that situation is the one from the pillar to the subtopics, and then the one from the clusters right back to the main post. Although it is not as essential, ideally you should use this structure.

We've been doing this in the SEO industry for a long time, focusing mainly on blog posts. However, this can be done differently - like with product pages. The pillar page does not necessarily need to be informational; it can be a commercial page. The reason it has been maintained as an informative page is because of the technicalities around the CMS. You are limited in WordPress or Shopify, where you cannot have a blog post URL in a subfolder from a product."

For SEOs on commercial websites, should they be thinking about building subpages of content on the same domain that link back to key category pages, which would then act as the central hub page for that section?

"They should use that option. Then, at the bottom of that commercial page, they can have resources related to this main page and linking to the top related resources."

What do you mean by 'controlling the way results are displayed'?

"How Google displays results has changed a lot and has become so diversified compared to the past. Many things are involved, like images, videos, the People Also Ask section, etc., and therefore we need to play big, and right now our major focus and efforts are directed to on-page content.

However, we have somewhat side-lined the click-through rate (CTR). There is more focus on creating and updating content but less on CTR. We need to experiment with schema - getting schema markups and testing titles for CTR. That's a big chunk of traffic we're not getting because we are not planning for it. Generally, since SEO is becoming more and more challenging, you need to utilise and leverage every single opportunity."

What shouldn't SEOs be doing in 2023? What is seductive in terms of time, but ultimately counterproductive?

"SEO shouldn't be focusing on and obsessing over search volume and keyword difficulty. What matters is whether the topic will bring value to the business. There are also a lot of other valuable considerations. Zero search volume keywords are essential as well, and should not be ignored.

Secondly, there should be a mindset change around SEO being separated from other marketing functions. SEOs are marketers and need to remember that when dealing with content and working within a marketing team. For example, there's plenty of opportunity to work with PPC."

Sara Taher is the SEO Manager at Assembly Global, and you can find her over at sara-taher.com.

Focus on content quality and FAQs—Marco Bonomo

Marco Bonomo believes that 2023 presents a fantastic opportunity for SEOs to focus on content and content strategy, specifically designed to please and delight your users.

Marco says: "You should ensure that all of the content within your website is unique. Rather than focusing on providing an ultimate guide for a specific topic, you should really reach in and think about introducing some extra elements.

For example, if you're having a conversation with a specialist, you could incorporate some visual data, charts, etc. to consolidate the unique thoughts shared throughout the conversation. Ensure that your content is specifically made for users and not for bots."

So the focus is shifting from pleasing Google's algorithms to pleasing users?

"Definitely, but the bar is getting higher and higher. Google is getting smarter at understanding how granular a topic can be, which means we must learn to adapt. Content is one of the main pillars of SEO, so we need to make sure that what we write is comprehensive, simple to understand, and easy for most users to read."

How do you bring stakeholders into the discussion, incorporate them into your content strategy to inform them of your SEO desires, and develop a content marketing strategy that appeals to all?

"Most businesses have a department strictly for PR. You need to work on trends. For example, in the vaping industry, you might look into the future of disposable vaping devices. You should work on specific data to discover the current trends. Each market is different so you'll have different shades of the same topic. The content you present must be unique. Different marketers will have different approaches, but the content must be really direct to the specific user that is going to use the specific content.

PR efforts are important but, at the same time, if you're working as a manufacturer to produce specific items, you can go to customer service to help limit the number of people that call with queries. This can be achieved with informative content via your FAQs, which should be updated regularly for all the products you sell. Proper content will offload the time your teams will have to spend contending with calls from customer service. Optimise with the resources you have and provide better service for the end user."

How do you determine trends that aren't popular yet but are likely to be in a few months' time?

"If you work in a large organisation where you're selling to multiple markets, you can try to split your approach in waves. Every year you could have six to eight waves of content. Though it's difficult to predict what's around the corner, the core point is that you'll be able to identify what the primary trend is.

For example, you'd know that disposable vaping is a growing market. You'd know where users are moving, how they interact with devices, and how the legal framework is changing over time. You must have a strategy that tries to comprehend all the little shades needed. Not everything is going to be up to date right now, but you should try to follow the trends and anticipate the needs of the user and what's going to be up to date in a year to two years' time."

How do you publish FAQs on-site? Is it important to publish all of your content on one page or do multiple pages appeal to search engines?

"You can have single pages talking about a specific FAQ or you can have FAQ category pages. For example, you could have one for a dedicated pillar of your content. The risk of adding a singular page for each FAQ is that Google will not consider that particular FAQ as worth enough. If you have a page with a couple of lines of content, will it really be worth crawling these pages for more indexing?

Always put yourself in Google's shoes. If you try to create a proper category page and interlink, you'll develop the content and be able to explain things in a more simple way. You could then link all the categories together and improve internal linking to signal whether you're a manufacturer, sell physical products, sell software, or do something else. Being really focused on FAQs will make your end users' lives easier. If you never work on FAQs, now is the time to plan, improve existing sections, or make new ones."

Let's say your business has a relatively short list of FAQs on one page. Is it easier to get each answer ranked if you have everything on-page as opposed to on individual pages?

"It's probably easier to create a single page, like a category page for FAQs. You can publish an additional layer of content for maintaining structured data. Creating categories is probably more beneficial than single pages.

Also, publishing FAQs and having structured data with rich snippets could cause you to lose traffic if the user gets their question answered on the SERP and doesn't click through. It'll be a trade-off between providing better content for the user and securing more clicks."

Would you classify appearing directly in the SERP as an SEO win?

"Yes. Your ultimate goal will be to have happy customers that keep buying from you. Even if you get fewer clicks, what matters is how you serve your end user. Did you do a good job of informing users? If you did, you'll align with Google's end goal."

How do FAQs fit into the helpful content update?

"The update should stop us from simply copying and pasting content from manufacturer descriptions. Google is honing in on looking at how much additional value you can provide the end user. Why should they consider your content when the same content is already listed in the original corporate funnel manufacturer? FAQs are very particular and niche, but at the same time useful for the user. They must be highly allocated and provide specific answers."

If you're focusing on the user, will it matter where you provide that value for them, e.g. on social media, review sites, etc.? How does Google treat your brand being found on third-party websites?

"Going forward, Google will have an enhanced understanding of whether it's a good brand, whether it provides good customer service, etc. When you launch something, you'll always focus on the 'wow factor' because things have to be big. However, how good will your particular brand be at keeping promises, listening to social media, providing support, and helping the end user?

Further in the future, Google will provide a bird's eye view where you can figure out whether something is worth buying or not. It'll be about more than having perfect SEO and complementary content. You'll have to look at how users determine whether something is worth buying, whether a company is good, etc. The value of SEO is becoming more intangible."

Is it becoming harder and harder to measure the ROI of SEO? How do you prove the value of what you're doing internally?

"For the next few years, the value of SEO will focus on driving traffic to the web for certified ROI. Google is just an advertising company, so SEO is definitely going to shrink, though it has somewhat already. You'll also have Google providing FAQs that didn't exist a few years ago. SEO will still be a part of the bigger picture. Justifying SEO as a pillar in your overall strategy won't be more difficult, but it will need to be more integrated with other channels."

Do you think SEO will die?

"No. Google is relying on users looking at specific query results. These users can be described as 'freemium' - with Google, pay-per-click, and YouTube representing the same philosophy.

There has been an Amazonification of Google, which is an irreversible trend. Amazon is getting much more aggressive at taking over the eCommerce world, so Google must expand to maintain its position. Google needs to adapt, so we need to adapt to what it's providing as a service."

What shouldn't SEOs be doing in 2023? What's seductive in terms of time, but ultimately counterproductive?

"It would be great to see content that isn't as flashy and useless as we've seen. When you do product reviews, for example, you should avoid clickbait and focus on what the product will include, when it will be released, etc. Also, avoid content made for the sake of producing content. If a copywriter is forced to create a specific article within a specific timeframe on the same topic, it'll provide practically the same low value.

Hopefully, the Google content update is going to provide clarity, and maybe exemplify how intrusive the ads on publishers are. If you discover content in five parts - encountering a video and an audio stream before getting to the main piece of content – it's probably not going to be worth reading."

Marco Bonomo is Global SEO Operations Lead at Phillip Morris International and you can find him over at marcobonomo.co.uk.

Perform a content consolidation audit—Andrea Paternostro

Andrea Paternostro has a four-step process that will help SEOs in 2023 to consolidate their content and strike a balance between freshness and intelligently reclaiming existing content.

Andrea says: "My tip is to perform a content consolidation audit. If you think of the word 'CoCoA', it's easy to remember. We should strike a balance between the freshness of our content and the need for consolidation - the intelligent reuse of existing content."

I know that you've got a four-step process. What is step number one?

"My first step is to avoid low page quality. We should mention Google's Quality Raters Guidelines, which is a document that is very important for us. Dan Tayler wrote about this last July on Search Engine Land. He went deep into this process and the need to look at the Google Search Console and see what prevents some pages from being indexed.

It's good that not everything is going to be indexed – as not everything we publish has value - but we should try to have some pages that have a high value proposition and concentrate our efforts on taking care of these pages. Another negative consequence of low page quality is cannibalization. We might be aiming at the same keyword rankings on Google with different pages, but only one is good for our revenues."

What is step number two?

"Number two is to make intelligent use of existing content. In a survey, Orbit Media found that bloggers who update all their posts are three times more likely to get a result. Updating posts and reusing content is so important for driving better organic results on Google. Sometimes we don't need to create new content. Why not concentrate on what we already have?

There are a lot of ways to do that: third-party tools, Search Console, etc. I live in two different realities. Irion, which is a B2B software company, and Milano Weekend, which is a B2C daily newspaper about events and leisure. Different customer journeys, different complexities, and different SEO goals.

At Irion, what's important is lead generation - as a marketing team and for branding. We need to communicate the expertise, authoritativeness, and trustworthiness of the company (the famous acronym 'EAT') supporting a very complex customer journey. Sometimes, we merge all three pieces of content into only one. In regulatory reporting, for example - which is a complex topic about regulations, laws, and what banks should do for compliance.

Our business goal is lead generation and not traffic. We don't have to look at the traffic. We may sacrifice some page views in order to drive better leads. Instead, we look at the long-tail model and see what opportunities there are for ranking in the long-tail.

At Milano Weekend, on the other hand, we aim for traffic. We need more traffic, and we need more domain authority to appear in SEO tools and to drive our sales. For a lot of companies all around Europe and the world, their SEO agencies are writing to us and ordering a guest post, for example. You can only be good at selling guest posts if you have good domain authority, and your rankings are good. That's a very different context and objective."

How do you know it's the right time to start updating your content?

"You can set up various tools for lifting data about your SEO rankings, but I think you need an expert eye in your team that can strike a balance with the possibility of writing new content. It depends on your company. Do you need to hire another writer or can you write something by yourself or with your collaborators? It depends on the organisation.

Usually, the more often you can update your posts, the better. In the publishing business, for example, an exhibition, an event, or a concert might come to the same city year after year, and you might use the same URL. You don't need to change the URL, just write the new content straight into the page.

For a B2B business, on the other hand, evergreen content is so important. When you're looking at regulatory reporting or another complex topic - like data management, data quality, or data governance - things don't change as often. You don't need to make many contributions, so you don't need to look at reports every week. You need to fulfil the business's needs. For some topics, you may give a monthly look at ranking reports, for other topics that may be every three months. It depends on the business.

Align with the business and talk to your top management, then you will know when it's time to prioritise a content operation because your company needs to sell a product at that specific moment."

How do you know which articles to merge together?

"It's good practice to make some templates. For blockbuster and product pages, we have two templates at Irion. All the content produced five or six years ago might have a different template. While you are porting the old content into the new template, you will discover more things to do.

You'll discover that you can reword the title, you can add a description, and you can add a fresh image to rank in Google Images - and this happens a lot for complex topics and business topics. Google Images is so powerful for being discovered.

You can do a lot of content operations by just getting started. Open your CMS and start doing things. You will discover many things that can be made better in your content."

What is step number three?

"Number three is to ensure the alignment between business metrics and content strategy. This is something that we need to learn as marketing teams: we need to speak the language of the business. Sometimes we talk about content KPI, pageviews, service validation, etc., and top management doesn't care at all. Top management just wants to know about revenue and sales: 'How has updating my content contributed to better sales?'.

I can show that some of the leads that have been made in my company in the last 18 months have visited our website. In their complex customer journey (their 'messy middle' as Google calls it) they had a touchpoint with our website once, twice, three times. What has our website communicated to them? Expertise, authoritativeness, and trustworthiness. The three things that today's Google wants in order to rank you in competitive markets."

What is step number four?

"Go deep into Search Console analysis, because there are some things in the coverage report that can explain why some pages are not correctly indexing.

You can look at the duplicate pages, for example, or the soft 404 - which often comes out in the Google Search Console notifications. For some soft 404s, if they are useful, you may choose to manage them with a 301 redirect or you may choose to go canonical, because there may be a problem with categorization. If it's not useful, I usually go with a 404, but I know some people prefer the 410 HTTP code. It depends. When Google comes into a website and crawls, it is often able to understand that 404 pages should not be taken into consideration anymore.

It depends on the user experience. Some websites find a good result with the use of 404 and some find better results with the other codes. The only way to find out which is the best situation for your website is to test a lot and understand that a resource can only be useful or not useful for the user."

Would you ensure that each page that you want to rank can be found and crawled by search engines?

"Yes. Not only found and crawled but, if we really want that page to be indexed, we need to focus on the reasons why it may not have been indexed yet. We should push for manual indexing through Search Console if we need that page to be indexed.

Sometimes the guest post pages asked for by our clients absolutely need to be indexed, because some clients want to appear in Google News as soon as possible. They value our website, and our publications, because they are included in Google News. Sometimes you need to give the Googlebot a shake. Often, you get a good result from a manual push."

What shouldn't SEOs be doing in 2023? What's seductive in terms of time, but ultimately counterproductive?

"Being too frenetic about the changes and fluctuations in your Google rankings can be very bad for your mental health, and for the overall outcome of the project. Have weekly notifications via email for your rankings, if not monthly.

Google is changing too fast, the search engine results pages are changing too fast, and there are too many fluctuations. We should not worry because it's not a good thing to concentrate too much on the quantity of fluctuations.

When we communicate with our clients or stakeholders, whether we are an agency or we are in a company, we don't need to take these fluctuations to our top manager every week or every month, because they don't need this information. They just need to know if the content operations have led to more sales or not."

Should SEOs set up an alert, so that if their rankings fall below certain parameters, then they can go and check them?

"Yes, we should set up the correct alerts for our business needs. Today, SEO reports are too thick, too long, and done too often. We should communicate better with our clients and our top management, and we need to have the courage to communicate concisely - to say just a few things. Focus on business metrics and leave out the technical part that they don't want to listen to."

Andrea Paternostro is a Technical SEO and Content Strategy Trainer, and you can find him over at andreapaternostro.com.

Map out what you're creating and why you're creating it—Paige Hobart

Paige Hobart shares her frustrations with creating content for content's sake and implores SEOs in 2023 to have a more focused idea of exactly what you are producing, why you're producing it, and what it is supposed to be doing for you.

Paige says: "My tip for 2023 is born out of a little bit of frustration from the past few years. It's to better understand your SEO content - and make sure you actually understand what you're producing and why."

Why do you think the word 'content' is massively overused?

"I hate the word 'content'. Some of you might know me from the SEO SERP Features Glossary - I'm all about trying to help beginners and experienced people in SEO all use the same language. If we're all speaking from the same hymn book, we all understand what we're trying to achieve and what we're producing.

The word 'content' is too broad; it describes too many things. I have been asked to 'do content' by many clients over many years, and every single one will have a slightly different understanding of what it means and what they actually want from that. I want us all to really dig down into what 'content' is, why you're producing it, and what it's supposed to be doing for you."

What's a better word for content?

"Get more specific. When you're talking about website pages: Is it a product page? Is it a category page? Is it timely content? Is it a guide? Yes, it's all content, but dig down into what it is, why you're producing it, and what it's supposed to be doing.

A lot of the time it's rankings. We're SEOs. We want that content to rank for a certain keyword or group of keywords, or we want that content to convert (we want that user to buy that product, to be inspired by something, etc.) - or we don't want it to do any of those things. We might just want to be able to put something out there that shows that we're experts in our industry, that we have an opinion, and that we should be a thought leader. That's valuable too. It might not rank for anything, but it's still inherently valuable to us as SEOs."

How do you map out what you're creating and prioritise what you're doing?

"I actually created a map. It's slightly based on something that you've created, David, because I took a lot of inspiration from your Pump and Funnel model. I produced a white paper when I was still working for ROAST about what content is (that you'll find on the ROAST website).

In there, I made a map where you put into boxes how the content that you're producing fits each of the descriptions. You can really dig down into what that content is and, more importantly, what its KPI is. What's it supposed to be doing for you?"

Is it possible to measure the KPI of every piece of content?

"I think so. Some KPIs are softer than others. Rankings, conversions, coverage, views, links, etc., are all KPIs. They don't have to all do the same thing - and they shouldn't all do the same thing - but there should be at least one goal that a piece of content is trying to achieve."

How does SEO get itself involved with content across the entire business, and does it have the right to do so?

"I think we have to. Shifting from agency to in-house has been a huge eye-opener for how inherent we are in every single element of the business.

I am currently writing a webpage - just one page for the entire website - and I'm speaking to the sales team, the implementation team, the client success team, and the product team. Everybody has a right for that website to work for them. The SEO's goal is to tie it all together in a way that makes sense to users and search engines, and make sure that content performs and hits those KPIs."

What kind of conversations have you had with sales teams? How do you initiate them and what information are you seeking?

"For this example, I'm looking at one page and just one feature of what we sell - which is the employee app feature. I'm asking the sales teams: 'What are the common questions that you're getting asked? What are the prospects asking you about this particular feature?'

Then, I'm asking the client success teams: 'How are your clients doing? What problems have they fixed by using this feature?' Ideally, I can take a nice little quote to boost those CRO scores on the page and show that we have really cool clients that have really succeeded using this.

For the product team, I'm asking: 'What are the key features? What are people looking for? Is it something that integrates with iOS and Android? Then let's make sure that that's front and centre', etc. As an SEO, I don't know all of this information, but I can bring it all together in a really optimised way."

What happens if your sales or client success teams use phraseology that doesn't get significant search volume? Do you use what the sales teams suggest, or different phraseology with the potential to drive more traffic from your keyword research tools?

"Phraseology is such a common issue for SEO - where the phrase that's being used internally is not the language customers are using. We have to be educating the teams and helping us all to sing from the same hymn sheet.

Make sure that we're all using the same language, and guide people by saying, 'We might call it that, but the customers are still calling it this'. You should be able to get that buy-in from people like the sales teams by asking 'What are your customers asking you, as opposed to what you're saying to them?"

Should you be creating more generic sales pages first, or higher search volume content (like the questions that your typical customers ask)?

"I think it's all the same thing. I want my sales page to contain those common questions, and cover those common FAQs. If you're thinking about that specific feature or that specific product, you've landed on that page. It's not efficient for them to then go through to the sales team and ask the same questions all the time.

If I can put those questions front and centre on that page, and make everybody's life a little bit easier, we're going to have more qualified leads and save the sales teams time."

Should you integrate content the business produces in other areas, that's not necessarily crawled by search engines (hardcopy content,

copy for trade shows, etc.), and ensure that the phraseology and style are matched across the organisation?

"I think you should, particularly when you're talking about technical features. However, it all goes back to those KPIs. What is that piece of content trying to achieve?

If it's thought leadership, and you're using a few lofty terms, then that's fine. It doesn't always have to match - you can have a bit of freedom, depending on what the goal of that is.

If you want it to rank and you want it to convert and be really clear, then make it really clear. If you want it to be thought of as something loftier, then you can be a bit more creative."

If an SEO in an organisation receives pushback from sales teams and creative teams, what is the best way to get buy-in from those conversations?

"I was recommended a few books to read before I went in-house. There's a really good book by Eli Schwartz about product-led SEO that you should all read (*Product-Led SEO: The Why Behind Building Your Organic Growth Strategy*). It really helps you understand internal thinking.

I'm lucky where I am, in that collaboration is something they are really pushing as a culture. I am always inviting people to give me their opinions.

Everyone's got an opinion. Although they might not see it come to fruition in the way that they're thinking, by at least giving everyone the opportunity to voice that opinion you'll always get something. Even if it's not hugely helpful, at least you've engaged with those people in your team and your company."

Has the SEO job role completely changed nowadays, becoming more like internal consultants liaising between different departments and less technically focused?

"I have worked in an agency for over seven years, so consulting is kind of what I've always done, but now I'm really in it. I'm under the skin, as opposed to this external insect buzzing around going, 'Please do this! Please do this!' and not seeing anything once it goes inside.

It's really interesting coming to the 'dark side' of in-house (as some of my SEO colleagues would have said). I get to actually put a webpage together, go into the CMS, build it, mock things up, bring people into conversations, and go and find people to talk to.

An in-house SEO is a very different role from an agency SEO, but we don't have to be less technical. Tech should always be the foundation of what you're doing and why, because you're going to need to use that to back yourself up. If people say, 'That doesn't look very nice, though.' you have to say, 'Well, you're gonna need it anyway.'

As an agency SEO, you're saying: 'You're paying me for my opinion, here it is.' Clients won't always implement that - or they'll implement some things but not other things. Most agency SEOs will find that very common and incredibly frustrating. It's a big change going in-house."

What shouldn't SEOs be doing in 2023? What's seductive in terms of time, but ultimately counterproductive?

"Content for content's sake. It's such a frustration when people just publish. There's still a lot of the 'I have to do a blog post every day for SEO' mentality. No. Stop doing that. If you're publishing every day, but your industry does not need you to do that, then you're not saying anything of genuine interest or anything genuinely helpful.

It's just the same churned-out rubbish that everyone else is talking about, like the same old top 10 lists that everybody does. I just want everyone to think: 'What am I doing? What is it trying to achieve? Is it genuinely helpful to my users or my community?'

It's not that the days of an opinion-based corporate blog are numbered, you just have to actually have an opinion. Stop being bland. I like to use Martin Lewis from MoneySavingExpert as a perfect example. What a spokesperson! What an author, for your EAT signals, to be out there having an opinion and talking in the press. That's an SEO's dream, to have an author on your website that is that prominent. Let's all be more like Martin Lewis."

Can you train someone to write like that?

"I think you have to find those people in your organisation that are willing and confident enough to do that, but also create a safe space. I was that person at ROAST for many years. I would go out to events, I would represent the company, and I would stand on stage and give people my opinion.

Even today, I'm giving my opinion, because I've been brought up in the industry to feel that it's okay to do that. Especially in SEO, everyone tries stuff. Not everything works out for everybody, but it's a safe community for us to have those conversations and build on each other's work."

Paige Hobart is SEO Manager at Unily and you can find her over at unily.com.

Get more buy-in from stakeholders—Gus Pelogia

Gus Pelogia recommends that SEOs invest more time in 2023 getting the buy-in that they need by communicating with stakeholders. That will give your projects a chance to actually work out in the way that you hope.

Gus says: "My number one tip for SEOs in 2023 is to actually spend more time getting buy-in from stakeholders when you're executing your projects."

Why is this so important?

"I think this is really important because there are so many directions you can take in SEO - and they're not as clear as they would be with some other channels.

If you're doing a commercial for TV, everyone understands what it is. They've seen a commercial, they get the idea, and they can picture what's going to happen. If you're working on PPC it's also easier to say, 'We're going to spend this and we expect to make this amount of money or bring in this number of bookings'. People don't really need to do to know the nitty-gritty to understand what's going to happen in a project.

With SEO, however, you're talking about what the algorithm thinks, or what people are doing. The outcome you're going to get is not as clear and it's much harder to make predictions and estimations.

If you don't get buy-in from people before you start working on this project, it gets a lot harder to actually bring them along, going from start to end, in the way that you hope."

What are some of the important job titles that SEOs need to start reaching out to and building relationships with?

"In my case, I'm essentially looking for engineers, department heads, directors, and product managers. I tend to get as close as I can to the work they're doing and the language they use so that I can see how we can actually work together."

What kind of conversations do you have with people working in content?

"I try to understand the process that they use right now. When I started talking with them, I discovered that we had content writers on the team, and we also have career coaches that are writing. They're quite specialised in what they're doing, so the quality of content they produce is going to be at a much higher level.

As you start talking to people, you discover who's involved and who's doing what. In one of these conversations, I realised that someone I was talking to about written content we wanted to create was also managing our YouTube channel, so she does a lot of video content too. This person is not looking at keywords and rankings - she is thinking, 'Am I helping job seekers?' As you start talking with them, you will discover a lot more about the people that are involved."

How does she measure that? Does she look at the audiences and analytics on YouTube to see who's watching the videos?

"Certainly. She's going to look into analytics and she's looking at who is coming to the website. I can come up with a list of keywords, or a cluster, and say, 'We need to cover those areas.' That person is not going to say, 'Well, we have the H1 and H2 and we'll put those keywords in here.' She's trying to answer that question holistically, so there will be a lot of moments where there will be no keywords in mind.

That person is writing fully with the intent of helping someone who's looking for a job or someone who wants to get better at their job. We can come back and do some SEO behind it and see if some other areas weren't covered as part of this content, but a lot of this is not written with SEO in mind. Honestly, it's a very good direction to go in these days. Google is a lot smarter at understanding content, context, what is being answered, etc.

It's very interesting to have these conversations with different people, and you stumble upon different solutions that may already be happening - you just didn't know about it."

Should you be understanding their objectives, understanding what they're trying to achieve, and then having an open conversation about how you can help them to achieve that, rather than speaking too much about technical SEO?

"Absolutely. You shouldn't be making them feel bad about the fact that they haven't incorporated keywords into their content. They're doing a great job creating content that resonates with people. It's about tweaking that, rather than completely changing what they're trying to do.

It's also about learning their thought process. I try to get to know people before I have a specific project with them in mind. I'll give an example. The UX team was working on creating some more classifications for content. They wanted to release new types of pages to help users by classifying content that is only about a specific profession.

SEO had a similar project, before I joined, where we wanted to do something along those same lines. Some of the thoughts we had were a bit manual, and a different team came up with a way to automate a lot of this process.

They were not looking at which professions had a higher search volume on Google, or which professions would bring more people, but, holistically, do we have enough content related to all of these professions? Are job seekers at Indeed looking for these types of professions and do we have these jobs on the platform?

I would have loved to lead the project, but once I got to see what was on the table, it was clear that SEO wasn't really the right owner for it. The thought process that was already put behind it by a different team was way more advanced than I would have thought. So, I just joined forces.

This is a very important part of getting buy-in on a lot of projects. Sometimes you can be the lead on something, but sometimes you can join something that is already in motion because someone else might own it or know it a lot better. Maybe you want to release an 'estimated time to read', a table of contents, or something else that has some SEO reason behind it, but SEO might not be the best place to actually start.

We can benefit from it, and we can give our input, but there are other people and other teams that will know the project a lot better. It's about not having the ego - not thinking you should own something or that SEOs know best - but actually partnering with people that are already owning that project. They could be the ones that you would have to get buy-in from, but they have already done that hard work for you, perhaps for different reasons, and you're just joining forces on something that is already in motion."

When it comes to conversations with heads of product, are you trying to understand what's coming down the line in terms of new products, then maybe consulting and assisting them with things like phraseology and targeting?

"That is absolutely right. You have to be smart in order to join forces on all of these projects. Some of them will be relevant to you, and some might not be as relevant. You need to measure what the impact is going to be, for your team and your product.

I join forces at every opportunity that I have. Another example is when we were doing some work on PageSpeed. There's an engineer that is not part of my team, so I don't talk with him very often, but I saw that there was a ticket with his name, and he was leading a project. So, I dropped him a message and he was available for chat, maybe half an hour later. In that half hour that we were on the call, we built a very strong relationship, because I had a lot of thoughts about things that were already in motion.

I could just support the project. There were some hints that maybe certain pages weren't performing well - for reasons A, B, and C - and I could come back to him and say, 'I believe that you're right. I can get the arguments for you to prove that this is the right way to go.' Equally, I might do the analysis and realise that it's not.

The project was already there - it was already discussed in a different meeting with different people. I was just giving a little SEO touch, and I can claim all the benefits. The engineer will get credit for the project, but I can also say, 'Look at all the results we're getting on SEO because of this project.'"

In a COVID (or post-COVID) world, more people are working remotely. Is it more difficult to build relationships with people virtually?

"I thought it would be very hard, but it's completely the opposite. Pre-COVID, you would start at an office, meet 20 people in a day, and you won't remember their names or know exactly what they do.

It once happened to me that I got a job at an agency and the person that interviewed me and offered me the job was my boss, so I thought I knew who my boss was. After a couple of days, someone else came and talked to me as if he was my boss. He was very friendly, but he was planning for me and telling me what I should be doing. He never actually introduced himself to say that he was also managing the team alongside the person who interviewed me. Over time, I realised (doing some digging on documents) that both of those people led the team, and they had the same power over the team.

In a digital post-COVID world, or a remote world, you don't have that. People introduce themselves to you one-on-one. Having those one-on-one conversations with everybody is really helpful. You get some time to meet the person and work on that connection. For me, it was much easier to build that over time.

Also, because a lot of people are remote, you don't have too much friction. You don't have to deal with being outside of a bubble, because everybody is kind of outside. For me, it is much easier to build connections, book calls with different people, introduce myself, and understand what they're working on. Often I don't really have a project to work on together, but I can picture that I might in the future. If this person already knows who I am, and I start suggesting things that I could do for them, it makes the initial connection much easier."

How do you persuade someone to partner with you when they're not that keen, to begin with?

"I actually had a situation like this not too long ago. I was talking with an engineer, and I wanted to do something that I thought was very simple, but he felt it was very complicated and we would need to rebuild a lot of things. It was almost a plain 'no'.

I had already discussed this with different stakeholders and they were on board so, instead of just having the conversation again, the next time I came in with a spreadsheet. I wanted to show: 'This is what's happening. If we don't do this, these are the consequences.' A conversation that I thought would be very difficult turned out to be, 'Okay, I get it now. I think I have a direction for it.' As it turns out, there was an easy solution and we managed to put that into production in around two weeks.

I needed to come ready for that next conversation. Instead of just saying, 'I talked with A, B, and C, and they're all on board, so you have to find a solution.' I came in with a spreadsheet and showed what wasn't working if we kept it the way that it was. I could show exactly what was happening and the amount of money we were losing. Then the conversation was very different.

Sometimes it's about changing the argument or preparing a little bit better for that conversation. In that case, we have recurrent meetings. Instead of coming in with a list of things, I can decide on just one to discuss. One thing might be very important, and I would rather get it done instead of talking about 10 things and maybe not getting to the really important ones."

What shouldn't SEOs be doing in 2023? What's seductive in terms of time, but ultimately counterproductive?

"I think we shouldn't go crazy on fully generated AI content. This is not just because of the helpful content update - which really scared everybody - and the conversations they had with SEOs that made it sound like it was going to be huge.

You might use it for some bits and pieces of your content, but I wouldn't trust AI to run all the content on a website. I don't think you're going to get good results. Regardless of Google being able to identify all of that, I think there is a much higher chance of things going wrong than things going right."

Gus Pelogia is SEO Product Manager at Indeed, and you can find him over at @pelogia on Twitter.

Demonstrate excellence at what you do—Eilish Hughes

Eilish Hughes believes that you should put your best foot forward and demonstrate both excellence and honesty with your content in 2023, and you should avoid taking actions just because everyone else is doing so.

Eilish says: "If you've decided that, in the wake of the climate crisis, 2023 is the year your brand should talk about ESG, sustainability, or other topics that can align your brand with 'doing good' you need to demonstrate that with action and facts. You can no longer nod to movements without being able to substantiate your claims."

You also shared that there's a need to demonstrate excellence and honesty. How do you do that as an SEO?

"As an SEO, it comes down to writing truthfully and usefully. Everyone has seen the latest algorithm update that Google has dropped aimed at rewarding helpful, valuable content. Now more than ever brands need to ensure that if they are taking part in conversations around climate change, for example, they're participating in them in a meaningful way.

If you're an energy provider, your onsite content should discuss climate change in relation to your organisation's roadmap to net zero, transitioning away from fossil fuels, and moving towards a circular economy. These topics would be far more valuable coming from you for Google's index than repackaged advice on recycling for families. Whilst climate and energy-related, consumer recycling isn't in your area of expertise, so your site would not be the most 'helpful' source of information on the subject."

Does that allow you to publish unique content and rank because you have your own angle or you have interviewed someone unique?

"That comes back to one of my favourite topics - expert content and leveraging your in-house experts. It is something we should be trying to bake into all our SEO strategies: making sure that real, recognised people are on your site.

Make sure they've got a LinkedIn, a profile page on a website, marked up with schema, etc. It will give them an actual digital footprint, which can be scary to some people who don't want to have one. Yet, it's essential if you're writing about any topics that could potentially impact big groups of people."

How do you demonstrate that you are the best option in your field or industry?

"It helps to be measurably the best, though it can be hard to leverage onsite! You need case studies, original data, statistics, reviews, and quotes. It's no longer enough to write an article or just have an opinion or thought piece.

You must have more substantial signals of expertise, authority, and trust that Google's crawlers, the Search Quality Guideline Raters, and users can all see to back up your claims. Everything within the Google ecosystem needs to be supported with links, ratings, certifications and schema – it's now much more than simply writing great content."

Is it possible to fake excellence in any way? Can you feed five-star reviews to the various platforms people look at in your industry?

"If it is possible to trick Google at the moment, it won't be for much longer.

An example of why you shouldn't even bother trying to fake it is looking at Glassdoor. If there's a company on there that has a pretty toxic profile that is then suddenly flooded with positive reviews, it's clear that the company has been on a big push to get existing employees to write reviews to bring the average rating up. If it's that transparent to people, it will be evident to Google. You can't game these things; you need to tell the truth. That's where the excellence comes from."

Something else you talk about is aligning your SEO with your brand. How do you do that in practice?

"SEOs and web teams, you need to talk to your branding people! Without connecting, there can be a real missed opportunity if the two departments go ahead and progress two different content streams across multiple channels. We see this with many brands when they repeat subjects in content in separate and disjointed areas of their websites. When this happens it's usually the result of resource constraints leading to poor communication, which is such a shame because when you team up you access more experts and data.

Imagine that you've got an SEO content stream based on keywords and excellent content briefs, and you push out an article. Then, your PR news team pushes out another article on the same topic, but it's got a quote from your CEO and a case study that you didn't even know existed! Combining these two projects could create one stellar deliverable that would really stand out in the SERPs as well as being enhanced for PR distribution by being informed with SEO competitor insights."

Are our brand departments generally more aligned with SEO than they used to be? Or is it still a struggle to get both people to do the same things simultaneously?

"It depends. With some brands, it works well, and with others, it doesn't. Company size, senior stakeholders' understanding, and creative and tech resources are all factors. To get everyone working together, there needs to be an educational piece at the front that explains what SEO is and how it can support the brand. It's not taking away from the brand but rather elevating and collaborating with it.

All departments will have their own micro KPIs and timelines but, as marketing teams, we're all working towards increased sales, revenue, and awareness. Branding and SEO teams' micro KPIs and deliverables should align to avoid duplication of work and achieve the most from each team's outputs."

If an SEO takes the time to understand other departments' goals, objectives, and targets and tries to assist them with achieving that, will they be more receptive to what you're trying to encourage them to do?

"Once you get that initial buy-in, you can have the test pieces and show that it's working. That's when people start to have that 'Aha!' moment and realise rather than creating work, you're enhancing what they've already done. If SEO teams don't take the time to understand other departments' goals, it can be left to brand teams to figure out what's right and try to align things.

Instead, if SEO teams can get sight of the other departments' plans you can show them how your keyword & seasonal data, audience and tech insights can easily slot into what they're doing and, in some cases, take research tasks off their plates."

What are you referring to when you talk about a world with changing priorities?

"Everyone knows now that Gen Z is here to save us. They don't just care more about the planet – they're committed to action in a way that I certainly wasn't in my teens. Personally, now I'm terrified about where the world is going – and, as a consumer, my habits have changed to reflect that. I'm lucky to be able to switch up what brands I buy and how often I buy them, where I go, and how I travel, and more people are doing that. When people and consumers can't make those purchasing decisions, they are making choices on who they will interact with and what they share online.

Now, brands that are seen to not be taking climate change seriously - who are a couple of steps behind in terms of equality, understanding, and togetherness, or are indulging in greenwashing – will see engagement and loyalty fall away."

There's a great quote: you have to "skate towards where the puck is going". Where should an SEO be looking to future-proof their keyword targeting efforts?

"When it comes to predicting search volumes where you don't necessarily have any historical data, there are several things you can do. You can look at similar keywords or topics and their exponential growth. You can start to look at how they've changed in the past in similar periods and think about using those trends to forecast.

You can also look at different data sources and get data on how much things have been trending on social media, for example. It's just about thinking outside the box, playing around with things, and knowing that SEO is tricky to forecast at the best of times, let alone in unchartered territory. Take as many data sources as you can and start there."

Should SEO have greater involvement with business decisions? If so, how do they go about having that kind of impact with senior business decision-makers?

"Backing up with all the data as much as possible. A straightforward way of explaining this is with buying and merchandising teams - determining what you should be buying at a time, what you should be leveraging, what competitors are doing, etc. That's an excellent B2C way of looking at it. When we are thinking more about B2B or branding in general, SEO teams should lead on uncovering sentiment, audience conversations, and likely future trends.

If you're pushing for visibility in the merger and acquisitions section of a fintech site, you need to have your finger on the pulse of that world. How has the industry been impacted by recent government budgets? Who are the key option leaders? What is the trending pain point for your potential customers?

This can help you identify if there are areas of the business you can productise, or any historic white papers that should be refreshed and pushed out as online resources. These tactics can help you to identify new pages to be linked in the primary navigation to get an instant uplift in visibility. Think about what you can dig up from the existing content to package up to drive leads."

What is an ideal SEO Department's position in a progressive organisation?

"It is more of a circular relationship with no department positioned above or below another. SEO teams act as great turntables, feeding in data, optimisation and identifying points of synergy across teams.

SEO teams, I believe, are uniquely positioned to predict and identify trends as we have access to, and understanding of, multiple data sources that marketing can then amplify across other channels. Then, of course, SEO should also feed into the IT department, similarly to marketing. It's all about being cogs in a machine that are all working together, with no break, all spinning simultaneously."

What shouldn't SEOs be doing in 2023? What is seductive in terms of time, but ultimately counterproductive?

"Jumping on things just 'because', without thinking about the impact on your site. We have seen many people doing audits and talking about EAT, yet these factors are not make or break for every site. The EAT process for Krispy Kreme wouldn't be the same as a fertility site.

Also, if your website is in pretty good technical shape, look at your broader roadmap to consider reprioritisations. Do you need to do as many dev and tech audits when there are huge content gaps that should be filled? You'll find an SEO checklist in your head that grows every time you go on Twitter because there is something else you need to think about or look at!

Half the battle with SEO is understanding what will impact your site the most and tuning out all the LinkedIn and Twitter noise."

Eilish Hughes is an SEO and Content Director at Mindshare, and you can find her at @dorkyeilish on Twitter.

6 CONTENT PRODUCTION

Focus on information responsiveness rather than just information retrieval—Koray Tuğberk GÜBÜR

Koray Tuğberk GÜBÜR advises SEOs to change their way of thinking so that you can stand out in 2023 and navigate the labyrinth of semantics by providing responsive information and developing knowledge domain expertise.

Koray says: "Focus on information responsiveness rather than just information retrieval."

What does information responsiveness mean?

"It is a concept from Google's research papers, particularly the work of Dr Metzler and Dr Najork. These two names are really important for the future of Google as they are like Amit Singhal's successors. Google is actually publishing many fantastic research papers about corroborating web answers, finding new knowledge domain experts, understanding who has the real expertise on the web, and what kinds of filtering methodologies can be used.

Information responsiveness is highly connected to the latest Google update, which is the helpful content update. It focuses not on relevance, but on the quality of the information: whether it is accurate, whether it is rich enough, and whether it is responsive to the need behind the query. To be able to do that, SEOs need to focus on information extraction."

How would you define 'knowledge domain expertise'?

"I can give my definition first, then I can give the definition from the Googlers. The knowledge domain is slightly different from the contextual domain because a knowledge domain actually consists of multiple other entities around a specific type of topic.

When it comes to the contextual domain, you always have a context qualifier. These are usually created with functional verbs, like 'for', 'on', 'in', etc., which are used to unite multiple other entities around a certain knowledge domain. Google is actually dividing the entire web into different knowledge domains and different contextual domains. This makes indexing much easier and cheaper.

In one of their latest pieces of research, they even tried to change their indexing structure. Rather than using phrase lists - or even entity lists - they actually started to focus on triples, and especially the predicates. To demonstrate the prominence of these declarations, I can tell you that if a search engine changes its indexing structure, it means that all the rules of SEO will change. That's how important it is."

What are the key rules that have changed?

"Since 1999, most search engines have tried to create phrase lists, then they start to create word vectors, or context vectors, and different combinations of phrases to understand the topicality of a specific document. For the last 10 years, however, Google has focused on balancing the PageRank based on the quality of the information.

Every time they improve their language understanding capabilities - thanks to different language algorithms like BERT, MUM, or T5 - they can understand more of the tiny details and minute context differences. It helps them to focus on the information in the content, rather than just the PageRank or the PageRank holding. With links, everyone is manipulating them, in a way.

Rather than focusing on just what kinds of phrases appeared, and the PageRank, they focus on what kinds of questions are answered, and what functions these web page offer. That's why they are thinking about the predicates in the triples. Take the phrase 'Tom Hanks acted in Philadelphia.'

In this case, after the named entity (Tom Hanks) there are probably around 600 other predicates that you could use, but according to the predicate that you have chosen, all of the nouns (or objects) that you might use will have certain constraints. These constraints help Google to divide entire indexing shards - or create an index hierarchy. According to the predicate, noun, or subject in the triple, they are able to separate entire pieces of documentation.

Google usually wants SEOs or website owners to choose a certain context, a certain main entity, and a certain topic for an entire document. They want us to focus on a single area. There is a research paper on context-based person search that will help people to understand this. It will help you to see, especially in the news industry, why these things are really important."

If you publish a wonderful piece of contextual content that Google understands, is it easier to get that ranked than it used to be?

"Yes, it's much easier without the links. Lately, however, there is another problem related to AI content generators. I have a website which generated 6,000-8,000 clicks a day. The entirety of the content was generated using AI, and the content was high-quality – but just six days ago we received a manual penalty. Now the site is at zero clicks. In this case - even if your documents are really high-quality, responsive, and contextual, and you configure them in the best way - search engines will still want to block you if you are generating content using AI.

Exploring Natural Language Generation was actually my suggestion for SEOin2022, but that doesn't mean that I am the expert there. That's why I'm saying that finding a knowledge domain expert, and understanding that this person is really the expert on that topic, is much more important than just producing responsive content. If you're able to provide expertise, and you're able to prove that expertise, then search engines will try to prioritise you further.

One more thing on AI-generated content. If you are generating 50,000 websites every day, with 10,000 pages each, it means that you are trying to erase the real experts from the web. Then, the real experts will have to do whatever you do, because they can't compete against the AI. This would create an SEO culture in which everyone uses automation, and no one does any research.

That's why AI-generated content websites are a little dangerous from Google's point of view. Between 2000 and 2010, we gave more weight to

PageRank and information retrieval. From around 2010 to today, we have gradually given more weight to semantics, linguistics, and real information in order to find topical authorities and experts. Today, AI is able to generate millions of pieces of content every day. This means that Google might need to give more weight to PageRank - because we can generate 50,000 pieces of content a day, but we can't get the links that quickly.

To prevent this situation, Google will need to fight against fake experts. It might be easier to rank with your responsive information, but you also need to provide a really strong brand identity, and expertise identity, for that topic."

Is it now a bad idea to ever use AI-generated content?

"If you are using AI to outsource your content production, then Google will probably find you eventually, and you will have a manual penalty (as I have experienced myself). However, if you are providing expertise and you only use AI for speed reasons, rather than for complete production, then you can use it.

With AI, I can write a perfect article about the treatment of a type of cancer, but it doesn't make me an expert. I can even harm people if they reach out to me. Thanks to AI, everyone can imitate expertise - but they can't have it. That distinction is something that Google needs to focus on further and further every year."

Is it still okay to use AI to generate content for product pages?

"Yes, you can use AI in these areas and it shouldn't put you in danger. If you have 40,000 products, you can't use humans to generate that content. You can use different automation to give certain types of structured information about the products.

However, when it comes to proving your expertise for these products, you will need to define many concepts, many parts, many types, and many use purposes - and you will need to create guides or guidelines. Even if you use AI, you will need to provide an identity to show that you are accountable for the information and the product that you are actually providing."

What does 'corroborating web answers' mean and why is it important?

"It's the name of a research paper from 2007, and it's important because every Googler today still cites the document. Minji Wu and Amélie Marian carried out this research with queries from Yahoo. Around 2007, Yahoo was a really strong search engine, alongside Bing and Google. Google started dominating after 2010 and 2011, mainly thanks to Chrome.

Google launched three or four different blog announcements lately. One of them was about information quality, one was about information literacy, and the other was about content advisories. If there is no proper or helpful content on the search, Google puts out a kind of warning. They say that the content of these pages is always changing, and they are all saying different things.

Corroborating web answers is collecting all of the answers from multiple sources. Then, you use all these answers from different sources to find a fact - or a factual grounding. Sometimes, you don't have an exact fact and you need to create a truth range, or factual range, especially for numeric values.

In the research paper, they used the mileage of a 2007 Honda Civic. They found that even Honda.com gave contradicting information. One page says that it is 51 and another page says it is 38. In these situations, to have a consensus and 'groundedness', the search engine needs to collect all the answers from all the different sources, and they need to collect all the evidence. To construct a more accurate Knowledge Graph, they need to understand certain methodologies and corroborate these things in order to present the facts. Callouts in the featured snippets, according to Google, are a consensus – they are grounded facts.

If you check the LaMDA research paper, you will find six different metrics. One of them is interestingness: they want LaMDA to give interesting answers rather than boring answers. Another is safety: they don't want LaMDA to tell you to hurt yourself and they always try to find answers with positive sentiments. Another metric is groundedness: they want their AI to find foundational, grounded answers or information.

If they can't find a consensus, sometimes search engines will provide multiple features in pairs, or multifaceted featured snippets by giving answers from multiple sources. Then, they try to understand which one is better and which one should be the main representative snippet. The others will probably only appear in around five or six percent of the SERPs. That is what corroborating web answers means."

How can SEOs implement or utilise the knowledge that you've shared, perhaps in a piece of content or by evolving an entity?

"To be able to create responsive information, or to have query responsiveness, you will need to give the answer in a direct way – and a more direct way than your competitors. You will also need to variate every declaration that you make. You can say that a product is best for a specific temperature, but for lower higher temperatures you might need to change some of the attributes of the products. In other words, giving a certain declaration or answer is not good enough - you will need to variate it for multiple other things.

Let's say I asked, 'How long does language education take in Germany?' According to Googlers, or search engine engineers, there is no explicit question. Every question has some implicitly. In the question that I asked, I didn't mention what kinds of language education, what parts of Germany, in what century, and for whom - for professionals, children, or others. You need to use uncertain inference here. All probabilistic search engines try to understand probabilities in the questions and the queries.

If you're able to list all of the different variations, then you can actually use some smart defaults. You can give a main representative answer, by saying 'In total: three months. Per day: three hours. Per week: twelve hours.' When you include 'How long?' in the question, the search engine will focus on units of time. In this case, if your main answer (the earliest point of the answer) doesn't have any units of time, then you will most probably be filtered out. If you don't multiply your answer (if you just say 'six weeks') you might also be filtered out, because you didn't say how many hours per day. Also, using different methodologies. With personal, practical learning, it might take longer. For children, it might take longer as well.

To be able to have appropriate information responsiveness, you will need to think about every query and every question, and then you will need to order all these variations. You will need to answer all of them one by one, without breaking the context. That's why semantics is like a labyrinth. You're playing a kind of mind game with the search engine."

What shouldn't SEOs be doing in 2023? What's seductive in terms of time, but ultimately counterproductive?

"First of all, you shouldn't write articles for the sake of writing. You don't have to publish more content all the time. Instead, go back and increase the quality of your older articles, and you will find yourself in the safe zone. For every website, 20% or 50% of their URLs don't actually generate any clicks within the last 28 days. You can check that.

If these web pages don't generate any clicks, it means that there is a quality issue there. If you don't fix these web pages, your new URLs will also be affected. Instead of focusing on always writing more content, go back and increase the quality of the pages you already have. Also, you can create more internal links, or check for any wrong information that you are providing. If you are giving out any wrong information, the search engine won't forgive you.

I have one more concept that might help. In an article, you can find three types of errors: structural errors, conceptual errors, or information errors. Structural errors mean that you are using long paragraphs or grammatically incorrect sentence structures. Conceptual errors mean that you are giving useful information for the wrong concept. Let's say you write a sentence like 'Search engine crawlers rank.' Technically, they don't - search engines rank, search engine crawlers just crawl - so that is a conceptual error.

When it comes to information errors, the search engine doesn't forgive you. It is the biggest sin; you can't give false information. If you do that, then you will start to lose authority in a really big way. Go back and check your current webpages, rather than just trying to focus on new content all the time."

Koray Tuğberk GÜBÜR is the founder of Holistic SEO & Digital and you can find him over at holisticSEO.digital.

References mentioned by Koray

Metzler, D., Tay, Y., Bahri, D., & Najork, M. (2021). Rethinking Search: Making Domain Experts Out Of Dilettantes. *ACM SIGIR Forum, 55,* 1 - 27.

https://arxiv.org/abs/2105.02274

Wu, M., & Marian, A. (2007). Corroborating Answers from Multiple Web Sources. *WebDB.*

https://www.semanticscholar.org/paper/Corroborating-Answers-from-Multiple-Web-Sources-WuMarian/d746cd387522d826b2ab402cb37c96059fa04261

A. A. Shah et al. (2020). Web Pages Credibility Scores for Improving Accuracy of Answers in Web-Based Question Answering Systems. *IEEE Access.*

https://ieeexplore.ieee.org/stamp/stamp.jsp?tp=&arnumber=9153749

Fan, A., Jernite, Y., Perez, E., Grangier, D., Weston, J., & Auli, M. (2019). ELI5: Long Form Question Answering. *arXiv preprint arXiv:1907.09190.*

https://arxiv.org/pdf/1907.09190.pdf

Haveliwala, T. H. (2002, May). Topic-Sensitive PageRank. *In Proceedings of the 11th international conference on World Wide Web* (pp. 517-526).

http://www-cs-students.stanford.edu/~taherh/papers/topic-sensitive-pagerank.pdf

Roy, A. (2021, March) Progress and Challenges in Long-Form Open-Domain Question Answering. *Google AI Blog.*

https://ai.googleblog.com/2021/03/progress-and-challenges-in-long-form.html

Gupta, N., Venkatachary, S., Chu, L., & Baker, S. D. (2022). Context Scoring Adjustments for Answer Passages. *U.S. Patent No. 11,409,748. Washington, DC*: U.S. Patent and Trademark Office.

https://patft.uspto.gov/netacgi/nph-Parser?Sect1=PTO1&Sect2=HITOFF&d=PALL&p=1&u=%2Fnetahtml%2FPTO%2Fsrchnum.htm&r=1&f=G&l=50&s1=9,959,315.PN.&OS=PN/9,959,315&RS=PN/9,959,315

Sandell, T., Malik, W., & Ahmed, J. Supervised Fact Extraction from Web Pages. *Stanford, CA.*

https://web.stanford.edu/class/archive/cs/cs224n/cs224n.1194/reports/custom/15791700.pdf

Whang, S. E., Gupta, R., Halevy, A. Y., & Yahya, M. (2017). Extracting Facts from Documents. *U.S. Patent No. 9,672,251. Washington, DC*: U.S. Patent and Trademark Office.

https://patft.uspto.gov/netacgi/nph-Parser?Sect1=PTO1&Sect2=HITOFF&d=PALL&p=1&u=%2Fnetahtml%2FPTO%2Fsrchnum.htm&r=1&f=G&l=50&s1=9,672,251.PN.&OS=PN/9,672,251&RS=PN/9,672,251

Galland, A., Abiteboul, S., Marian, A., & Senellart, P. (2010). Corroborating Information From Disagreeing Views. *WSDM '10*.

https://www.semanticscholar.org/paper/Corroborating-information-from-disagreeing-views-Galland-Abiteboul/edcd2884e7e4050e15f9c2e351f3f07dcf5ed974

Dong, X., Gabrilovich, E., Murphy, K.P., Dang, V., Horn, W., Lugaresi, C., Sun, S., & Zhang, W. (2015). Knowledge-Based Trust: Estimating the Trustworthiness of Web Sources. *Proc. VLDB Endow., 8,* 938-949.

https://www.semanticscholar.org/paper/Knowledge-Based-Trust%3A-Estimating-the-of-Web-Dong-Gabrilovich/117da44f01ef45ef8223bec8f9c2346b131321f4

Dou, H., Li, Q., & Zhang, Y. (2010). Find Answers from Web Search Results. *2010 Seventh Web Information Systems and Applications Conference*, 95-98.

https://www.semanticscholar.org/paper/Find-Answers-from-Web-Search-Results-Dou-Li/d7a2a11b167cfc26cd14c3ddf1b60b5a6e7f7f60

Shakeri, S. (2021, May) KELM: Integrating Knowledge Graphs with Language Model Pre-training Corpora. *Google AI Blog.*

https://ai.googleblog.com/2021/05/kelm-integrating-knowledge-graphs-with.html

In-depth answers will be favoured over one-sentence answers—Nikki Halliwell

Nikki Halliwell tells SEOs in 2023 to look for keywords with a high number of impressions and reveals other opportunities for making sure you are providing in-depth answers to the right questions.

Nikki says: "There's a really significant opportunity to capitalise on keywords that have a high number of impressions in Google Search

Console, but a low number of clicks in comparison. A lot of people are talking about this on SEO Twitter, WordPress, and those communities.

Someone's created a tool called Query Hunter, which helps to do exactly that. As a result, you can improve your rankings, and it works really well. It is geared more toward WordPress sites, but there are ways around it that you can use on non-WordPress sites as well.

For WordPress, it's a plugin that you can download, and it allows you to see your Search Console data within each post while you're editing. You can see the keywords that get a lot of impressions, but very few clicks. Therefore, you can easily see the posts that have the potential to bring in a lot of traffic. You already know that they're being seen in search because of the number of impressions that they have.

What we can deduce from that information is that they might not be completely fulfilling the intent of the query, because they do have so few clicks by comparison. You can then look at opportunities within that content and see whether you need to write a new post around that keyword - or those select keywords - or if you need to cover them more thoroughly in a separate post.

Something else that you should do, either within this same tool or manually within Search Console, is look at the keywords for posts that are ranking around positions 3 to 11. That is really useful, and I think it's going to continue to be useful throughout 2023 and beyond. They're already doing well, they're on the first page of the SERPs, but you can then look at what pages are actually above you - in positions 1, 2 and, 3.

In some cases, it can be as simple as ensuring that you've mentioned the keyword enough times in the content, or you can go a little bit deeper and find keywords that have actually not been mentioned in the content at all. That's a really powerful opportunity. It essentially means that you're already ranking for those keywords and getting impressions for those keywords, without actually mentioning them in your content. Then, look for natural ways that you can integrate the keywords into the content to facilitate that boost in rankings.

I've been looking at this for my own clients, both with and without this tool. You can do it manually by looking in Search Console at a page level. It is more time-consuming, and it involves a fair amount of searching and sorting through the data, but it's certainly useful. I would love to set up a dashboard that pulls the data in, which would make it easier to roll out to other websites. I've been able to do it on Magento websites that have blog content using this more manual method, so it's certainly not just WordPress specific."

What similarities are you noticing between articles that are performing well and pages on your site that aren't performing as well for Google?

"The frequency of keywords always helps, but I've actually seen that internal links have made the most difference. Also, making sure that the keywords are going from your content to the main money pages, with the appropriate anchor text. That's something that's often missed, and it's something that I've been working on with my clients.

Make sure there's no generic anchor text, like 'click here'. Update it with those target keywords that we know can be improved a little bit, and use those as the anchor text to drive traffic to the money pages - as long as it's in a natural way, and it makes sense. Obviously, we also want to avoid anything that's even slightly spammy.

If it doesn't make sense to do it, then I'm not going to add internal links or make any changes. I'll always look objectively, and make sure that it is actually going to be helpful for the users."

You're a fan of creating long-form content, so how long is long-form?

"I try to stay away from a word count. That's not something that I think about when I'm either writing the content myself or working with copywriters. How I try and approach it is by thinking, 'What's going to answer the query in the best way?' If it's a simple question, like, 'How many legs does a horse have?' (which is a common one that I see going around at the minute) then I don't need 1,000 words to say that the answer is four legs.

I will look at other pieces of content that are ranking and see how well or not they're answering the content. If they're not doing well, I will look at how we can do that better and provide added value. I don't think in terms of, 'To rank number one on this, we need 2,000 words.' because that's not what's actually going to be helpful to the user and our target audience.

If writing just 500 words on a piece of content succinctly answers the question, actually provides value, and gives our target audience what they're looking for, then that's completely fine."

When you're providing in-depth answers, are you just thinking about the users or do you ever have search engines in mind?

"I do and I don't. I try not to fall into the trap of creating SEO content just for the sake of SEO content because Google is not my target audience. Google, or any other search engine, is the tool that we're using to be able to get out there and reach people.

I've had more success thinking about the users and writing for them. I think that's the way much more people, and particularly copywriters, are also approaching it."

Does more success mean higher rankings and more traffic?

"Exactly. Going back to what we were saying about internal links: having these detailed answers that get straight to the point (if that's what the query deserves) means we can then use the internal links to drive traffic and attention towards our money pages, our calls to action, or whatever it is that the business is focused on."

How do you go about selecting which questions to answer?

"I do it in a few different ways. We'll do initial keyword research, especially if it's for a new client, that will give us all of the broad terms that people are looking for. However, what I've started doing more recently (and it's something that I'm definitely going to be rolling out more throughout 2023 and beyond) is looking at Reddit and sites like Quora as well.

I use the internal search features of these websites, as well as the reviews that people are leaving for the businesses that I'm working on - whether that's on Trustpilot or Google Business Profile, or wherever. I actually look at the language that is being used in reviews and internal searches, because that can inform the questions that we then answer, and the language that we're using ourselves. Internal jargon, like the terms that the business uses to refer to its products, might not be quite the same language that the audience is using.

I had a client that makes plastic containers, packaging, etc. - and they sell their lids separately. What they call them internally is 'closures', and that's what the manufacturer calls them as well, but the customer calls them 'lids'. They want plastic bottle lids, so that's what they search for. We were able to restructure the site and change the way that the language is used throughout the site, in order to reflect that. Very quickly after the content was reindexed, we were able to see the change that made to traffic, and the increase in conversions that they had as a result.

Use the data that's already available. That's something that not everyone looks at; they don't think to look at internal search results that way. In that example, people were searching 'lids' in the website's Magento search features, and that's how we found it. We were able to position the content in the right way as a result."

Do you also check People Also Ask on Google?

"Definitely. I use it for informing header choices on content as well. We can look for ideas on Reddit and Quora, and in reviews, but you can also just look for that topic on Google. When I look at People Also Ask, I tend to pick those questions out as the headings, answer that question in various headings, and then mark it up with the relevant schema as well - if it makes sense to do so."

Is it a better use of your time to answer new questions and create new content, or update answers to questions that already exist on your site?

"I would look at the detail that's been answered in those existing questions. Is it a quick 'yes or no', that's been answered, but your competitors have actually gone into more depth? If that's the case, then that is something to look at. You don't want to increase the likelihood that users are getting the answers that they're looking for on your competitor's sites.

Look at that first, but if the questions have been well answered on the site already, then look for new questions and look at ways that you can solve problems for the clients that other people aren't solving. I do both, in essence, but look at what has been done first, and look at what poses the biggest opportunity."

What shouldn't SEOs be doing in 2023? What's seductive in terms of time, but ultimately counterproductive?

"I think it's an over-reliance on AI-generated content. Don't get me wrong, I use tools like this myself –I certainly have in the past for short-form, quick answers. I might also use it to get me started on a question for my own niche websites, and then write the content manually myself.

However, I think there are websites that have an over-reliance on AI-generated content. They are almost guilty of creating content for content's sake, rather than thinking strategically about how it ties into the overall strategy.

It comes back to the question of providing value to customers and users. I think it's always been the case that AI hasn't answered questions fully, but that became more true when Google rolled out the helpful content update. It's interesting to see how that impacted content.

Ultimately, my tip is not to rely on AI. Don't create content for content's sake; focus on providing value that's genuinely useful and solves problems. That will be the best way to continue to have success. AI content does have its place, but use it sparingly and in moderation."

Nikki Halliwell is a Technical SEO Consultant, and you can find her over at nikkihalliwell.com.

Create powerful content for even the smallest searches—Adelina Bordea

Adelina Bordea tells SEOs in 2023 that, to keep up with the competition, you need to be generating truly powerful content - no matter what size of search you are targeting.

Adelina says: "My number one tip is that we have to start creating very powerful content even for the smallest searches. The competition is very high and we need to provide an answer for our audience Many people think longer content is better but it actually doesn't matter. As long as you provide a brilliant answer or brilliant content, it is going to rank."

How do you define smaller searches and what is powerful content?

"Powerful content is content that answers the user's search, and a smaller search is something that is more niche. It means doing a lot of work with long-tail keywords, which is how you're going to find that required content."

What's your favourite way of finding long-tail keywords?

"I use a lot of tools. I go over my website and I try to find relevant searches for my audience, then I do keyword research with Ahrefs - and I also use AnswerThe Public. I will then mix everything together, look for that search intention on Google, and find the perfect content for my audience.

AnswerThePublic is very useful but it doesn't come with any associated keyword volume, which is why I use Ahrefs as well. I also try to select keywords that have relevance to my business. You have to create content for people, but you also need to make sure you have an actual audience who you can sell your product to."

How do you decide on which keyword phrases need longer form content and which keyword phrases can be answered just with one answer?

"I study my competitors. I look at what their answers are and how we can do it better. It's basic content SEO; you see what is going on in the world and then you try to improve it.

Sometimes it's just about the text but sometimes is about adding something new, like a photograph, a video, or any kind of multimedia item. That way you can offer a better solution compared to your competitors."

How do you decide who your competitors are?

"It depends. If you are working on a project, then you have clear competitors. If you are writing something new, however, you should be looking for some context first. The first three search results are obviously the ones that I look at the most because it means they have something that really appeals to my audience and to Google.

Sometimes, checking those first three results will give you a hint as to whether that is the right content for your audience or not, because that search intent might not be exactly what you need for your product.

You start with the idea of what the keyword phrase and target audience might be, that you think you want to write content for. Then, you can look at the SERP for that particular phrase. If those first three results are actually talking about something completely different that doesn't suit your target audience, you might rethink the value of making that content."

When you're improving on what your competitors are offering, how do you decide whether to include an image or a video and what's likely to appeal to your target consumer?

"This is something you learn after working for some time on a project. It really depends on what you are selling. If you're selling information, then a video or an infographic is likely to be more specific and useful, depending on the content. If you are selling a product, however, a comparison table can often be more useful to the consumer than a picture or a video.

It really does depend on the product – I know SEOs love that word, but it's just true. What I've also learned is that, when you are spending a long time working on the same project, the content you are releasing will tell you what works and what does not. You can make decisions based on that as well."

If you were to incorporate a video as part of your content, would it be an embedded video from YouTube and would you be attempting to rank on YouTube as well?

"Why not? We can do SEO on YouTube as well, and try and pick up some new users that way.

There are also some websites where, if you upload the video and it's not embedded, it's going to be really heavy. That means it will impact your WPO, which is bad for the website as well. There are a lot of things you can do to improve that, but an embedded option is easier - and faster as well."

What sort of process do you go through to try and get more people to view your content, and get your content ranking reasonably quickly? Do you reach out to journalists to get them to mention your piece?

"It depends. If you're writing for your website's blog, then you are just going to try and create the best content possible. Then, you make sure Google is indexing and ranking it, and you are carrying out fundamental optimisation and looking for anything that you can still add to that article. This way, people are going to link it in a very natural way and there will come a time when you don't have to worry anymore about a paid link building strategy.

If you're launching something, then you might want to reach out to journalists and newspapers. I've also worked with ads: Google ads, Facebook ads, and social media ads in general. Pinterest can be a good option if you have visual content. When I worked for a DJ, YouTube ads were great for pushing my SEO strategy.

Study your product to see what channels are better. Look at the money and the hands that you have as well, that's very important. Then, create a plan that will push your SEO-based strategy. For me, SEO is fundamental. Everything else is just going to push that base strategy."

Is there a certain type of content that you find resonates more with different countries?

"Yes. Infographics are very relevant for USA audiences, for example, which actually surprised me when I first started working in the American market. They aren't as relevant for Spanish people; we are not as accustomed to them.

You need to really think about your target audience. Think about the kind of content that they actually want, rather than assuming that everyone around the world is going to resonate with the same thing.

Something that does work worldwide is short videos. They are a big thing right now, and we need to implement those into our strategy as soon as we can."

What shouldn't SEOs be doing in 2023? What's seductive in terms of time, but ultimately counterproductive?

"We have this 'great' thing called AI, and automatic content, which is something I highly recommend SEOs stop doing. Google has recently released a new update specifically targeting these kinds of websites.

I know it's hard to rank a website. I know it's time-consuming and costly in terms of resources, but I can assure you that it is worth it. If you do a good job and produce high-quality content, it's going to bring you a lot of money and traffic in the long term.

You might use AI to generate content if you don't really care about a particular website, or if it's a project or experiment that you want to try out. However, don't use it on your main website. It's unlikely that it will work out well."

Is it dangerous to use AI content even on pages that don't bring in a lot of traffic? Does it potentially send a signal to Google that you're publishing inferior-quality content on your site?

"It depends on the size of your website, but sending these kinds of signals is never good.

If you have some URLs that don't bring in as much traffic, then ask yourself: 'What is this useful for?' Maybe it's not an SEO page. It might just be something that you have for your return users, or something that mentions a tool or feature of your company that shouldn't be erased. If that page isn't useful anymore, then try and blend it with another piece of content on your website.

I would suggest that you never use those kinds of automated and AI tools without supervision and detailed monitoring. I don't know if Google is going to change the rules of the game and we will be surprised by a sudden positive shift towards using AI, but I think it's unlikely."

Adelina Bordea is an SEO Content Specialist at Freepik and you can find her over at her work-in-progress adelinabordea.com

Never underestimate the power of reactive PR—Eva Cheng

Eva Cheng stresses the importance of never underestimating the power of reactive PR, and explains how this type of work can make a big difference for your SEO in 2023.

Eva says: "Reactive PR can be expert comments or general requests, creating proactive campaigns related to awareness days, relaunching past campaigns, etc. It's all about keeping an eye on what's happening now and less about planning for evergreen campaigns which can last more than a year because of production and outreach."

Should you have a particular channel in mind when using reactive PR?

"Purely through publications. It's all about building links and really tailoring campaigns to target niche publications which are harder to gain links in. If you were to create a small proactive campaign for an automotive client, let's say - if it's relevant and timely it'll be more likely to get covered within those kinds of publications."

Is reactive PR about seeing what relevant stories are out there and then adding to that by providing a slightly different angle or interviewing someone?

"That's one tactic of doing reactive PR, but it's very much about knowing what's coming ahead. It's like with seasons; you always know what's coming so you can prepare in advance. Going back to the automotive example, if you know the winter is coming and the roads will become more dangerous, you could write some campaigns covering aspects like safety tips for driving in the winter."

When you talk about never underestimating the power of reactive PR, are you talking about the power to build links?

"Yes. When launching reactive PR and corrective campaigns, you'll gain more relevant links within publications. For a mattress client, for example, it would be easier to gain a link within an ideal home when they are looking for someone within that area of expertise to offer advice."

How do you track of which stories are current and which stories to write about?

"Keep an eye on the news and create a digital PR plan. Know what awareness days are coming up, what people are interested in, and also look at Google Trends. On AnswerThePublic you can enter a topic like 'electric vehicles', and it will give you the most asked questions that people type on Google. You'll then know that people are searching for the topic and it'll give you a good idea of what's to come."

Is the aim to rank in Google News?

"Not necessarily. It's to build the backlink profile so you've got more relevant links to your client. For an automotive client, you'd never try and target a beauty publication because it wouldn't be relevant. If they were getting spammy links it would impact their backlink profile. Google would see that as a negative and the rankings would be impacted. Google has said it looks at the backlink profile of websites to value the trustworthiness and authoritativeness of the site."

Do you reach out to people with a view to them linking to your content? Do you ideally want to build organic links to it?

"Most links that are built are purely organic and not so repetitive, and therefore more unique. This builds that trustworthiness with Google. It's like sending a trust signal towards them that you're not just posting all over forums as part of a spammy practice. Niche publications are harder to get into and it's harder to get links within big publications. Creating campaigns that are effective and relevant gives the journalists more reason to cover them because they'll be what people are looking for."

What type of content do journalists like?

"It's a big mixture at the moment. There are big hero development campaigns which are landing links within relevant publications. There's also reactive stuff like, for example, a sleep campaign around 'How to stop storing' when it's National Snoring Day. It's very hit and miss when deciding on the main gain of getting links."

Is there an online resource people can use to find national days?

"You can just type in national days of the year and you'll find some great resources. Don't just look at national days, but look at charity awareness days too. If it's a mental health charity awareness day it could be a great opportunity for brand collaboration and sharing advice.

You can even do the same with evergreen campaigns. The reason it's great to focus more on reactive PR at the moment is because of the substantive effort that goes into making things look brilliant on-site. Reactive PR can be a great way to get a quick win. If you have blog content on your website already and it becomes relevant again, you can relaunch the campaign and potentially send journalists to your content. It's like creating a hook for journalists. You have to be very aware of what's going on around you and never be afraid to refresh old content and bring it up to speed with the latest societal developments."

How do you find and build relationships with journalists?

"You can just do a news sample. Go on Google News and search for electric vehicles. If you've got a campaign around electric vehicles, you can find journalists that have already covered the topic, get their names, and start doing a deep dive into their internet profiles. Check their information online and try and get their email address, etc. You can also check media database websites online."

What initial message resonates with journalists and is most likely to get a reply?

"It's tough because journalists don't really have much time to build a strong connection with PRs, especially in digital. It's a lot easier within product and physical PR because they want to converse about things, do product reviews, arrange giveaways, etc. In digital PR you might not have the physical resources to achieve the same. You should put your headline as the main hook of your campaign in the subject line of emails."

What's an example of a headline that works?

"It really depends on what time you're sending it and who you're sending the email to. Adding 'revealed', 'data reveals', or 'experts say' to the start of an email headline would traditionally increase the open rates. However, these terms have become overused and less effective. If you change your headlines and mix up the wording you'll stand out much more."

How do you measure the value of reactive PR?

"You should partially look at the links that you build for brand new clients - whether that requires building the link profile or a diverse set of links. They might already have syndicated links across regional publications which are great for their backlink profile. Then, you need to analyse what the competitors are up to.

If a client got a link within Motor One but your client hasn't got the link in Motor One, you should target those backlink gaps in order to compete with your competitors. Once you achieve that, it should essentially raise you in the SERPs and you'll climb higher."

Will journalists automatically link to you if they know you're the resource or do you have to make sure you ask them for the link as well?

"When you launch a campaign you should add 'if you want to use this data please credit...' and then link to the relevant post. Alternatively, if it's an expert comment and you're jumping on it, you could ask the client if they can link to a relevant category page within your site.

For example, for an automotive client's site, it could be a landing page on EVs or hybrid cars because that article would be relevant. This will also be considered a trust signal from Google because all of the content around it is talking about electric vehicles. If you get linked with this content on electric vehicles or cars, Google will see this as a trust signal because everything is interconnected and relevant."

What's the future of reactive PR? Is it going to be more about using social media platforms or will blog posts and traditional journalism still be relevant?

"Both. You can use the traditional blog posts that you have on there, but if you want a quick win you can look at social media and analyse TikTok and such. It's good for internal PR teams to work with social teams because they might spot something you can monopolise to complement your existing plans. If you have content writers who are writing blog posts for a client, it'll be great to see the content plan so you can get the media list, email templates, journalists, etc. ready for outreach. Once that's ready and it's live, you can just hit that link in there and send it out to journalists in the hope it gets covered."

What shouldn't SEOs be doing in 2023? What's seductive in terms of time, but ultimately counterproductive?

"Building links for the sake of building links. We used to think a high volume of links was a trust signal to Google, but when you do a deep dive on a business's backlink profile you might see they've got spammy links, loads of forums, directory sites, and things that aren't directly related to their business.

Relevancy is the key to 2023 because it does impact your search. If you're an automotive client and you've got links within a beauty publication, how is that going to drive sales and traffic to the site? If someone is interested in beauty they're less likely to be interested in cars."

Eva Cheng is a Digital PR Consultant at Evolved and you can find her at evolvedsearch.com.

Prepare to compete with AI-generated content—Chima Mmeje

Chima Mmeje warns SEOs in 2023 that you need to be ready to beat out those who rely on AI-generated content by using AI to your advantage and looking at the bigger picture, so that you can create great holistic content that is both useful and relatable.

Chima says: "My advice is almost more of a warning: we are going to drown in content in 2023, because of AI.

Those of us who look at SERPs to get results, we're going to drown in content, because there's going to be too much of it. There is already a lot of content out there right now, but there is going to be even more as AI content adoption increases.

In 2022, Google released the helpful content update. Many SEOs assumed, and rightly so, that those who are depending on AI to create content are going to be the worst hit because they are relying on AI-generation tools to write the content, come up with the brief, and do everything short of hitting the publish button. In the short term, some of these websites will suffer but, in the long term, the tools are going to get better at creating briefs, writing content, and optimising that content with semantic entities. They are going to get better at creating content that ends up on SERP.

Is it usable? Is it useful? Who knows, but we are going to see it on the SERP. As they get better at giving Google what it wants, we're going to see AI-generated content that is scalable. It's scalable because you can type in a keyword and it generates the brief, writes the content, and you hit publish. You can do that 20 times a day just covering one keyword and building clusters. It makes it easy to scale content marketing and build authority faster. This is what we're going to keep seeing on SERPs, because they are producing content faster and at scale in a way that no one else can even dream of competing against.

Now, what does that mean for SEOs and content writers? Instead of trying to fight AI, we can use parts of AI to figure out how to create better content. We can use AI to improve content optimisation and find the most common questions or subheadings that pop up for a specific keyword. Then, we can optimise our content for those questions and subheadings. That way, we're giving Google what it wants. We can also use AI to determine search intent, understand the ideal word count for an article, and even plan the structure because all these things matter.

However, when it comes to beating those who rely solely on AI-generated content, we need to create content that is useful and relatable. At the end of the day, if the content that we're writing satisfies search intent to the extent that the user doesn't need to go back to the SERP and click on other search results - if they find the answer they're looking for in your content - then you always have a better chance. Not just at ranking for one keyword, but ranking for multiple keywords and gaining legitimate authority that lasts, and drives results.

Machines don't have empathy. They can't see the bigger picture, and they don't have the human element that gives us the bird's-eye-view. This is the biggest advantage we have when creating content to beat those who rely on AI in 2023."

Should SEOs be using AI just to generate content ideas and concepts, rather than to create content in its entirety?

"Yes. We can use AI to find content ideas and automate the manual process of trying to understand search intent, content length and the most important questions we should be answering for a specific keyword. AI can help us get those answers very quickly.

However, we should not be using AI to write content. We can use it to create a brief and to understand what should go into the brief, but not for writing the content."

Will AI miss keyword opportunities to optimise for? Can you trust AI to generate that for you?

"While AI tools can help you to find the most important questions that you should be asking, it doesn't give the full picture that you get by manually opening SERP results. You need to look at what each person is covering, and especially what they are not covering - because that's where the gap and, by extension, the opportunity lies.

What are they missing that you can exploit and do better? I don't think you can get that from AI because it tells you what already exists and analyses that information to do more of the same. AI doesn't help you find your 'X factor'. You can only do that by manually analysing the SERP. That's a strategy that humans will always do better than AI.

Let AI support you by automating word count, understanding search intent, and finding the most important questions, but, when you want to create holistic content, you still have to look at those content pieces that are ranking - to understand what is missing and what could be better."

Will AI also be replacing podcasts, videos, and content like that anytime soon?

"There is already AI for videos. If you go on AppSumo you will find lots of deals for tools that will create videos for you. You just need to put in a keyword and maybe some ideas about your brand, and it will make the videos using vectors. They already exist, but is it good? Is it engaging? Does it make you want to act? No. I haven't seen any of those videos that made me feel anything. That is why the human element is better.

For podcasts, AI can potentially help you plan the structure of what you should be talking about - that's something that AI could be doing soon - but for speaking one-to-one, I don't see that happening."

Can you beat Google and make it think that AI-generated content has been created by a human?

"People already do that. I used to work in a content mill and that was practically half of our job. You just need to make sure that the article is up to snuff lens-wise. You make sure to throw in a few infographics (that can be auto-generated with some tools), add a few stock pictures, optimize the images, and make sure that it's using as many entities as possible.

We use entities because, when the search bots are crawling the page, those are the words that help them understand what that page is about. Apart from optimizing for entities, we built backlinks to those pages, linked internally to other pieces to get the content to rank.

Most times, it worked because Google is a machine and machines can be tricked. I don't care what Google says, I don't care how many algorithm updates they release: machines can be tricked. I build content briefs as part of my job, and I analyse at least 20 pieces a day. I see a lot of thin content on SERP and content pieces that were clearly written by AI. Across all of them, I see the same thing: they are doing this by building backlinks, populating their websites with a lot of content, and optimising for semantic entities."

Is Jarvis, now called Jasper, one of the better tools? Are there other tools that you'd recommend?

"Jarvis has to be at the top of the food chain when it comes to AI tools for content, but I really like what NeuralText is doing.

When you create content and you want to promote it on social media, NeuralText can help you jumpstart creativity. It will also produce 5, 6, 8, 10, social media posts. It can help you write meta descriptions, intros, ad copy, and a ton of other stuff that I have not seen any tool out there doing with AI. I started using it recently and it just has so many options for how to automate copy, it's insane.

The part for writing meta descriptions can be very useful as well. I don't write ad copy, but I believe that it could be helpful to give you a rough idea that you need for inspiration so you can write better copy. It can give you the first couple of lines, maybe. It's the same for writing a blog introduction or writing the first couple of lines of a subheading."

Most people seem to be thinking it's okay to use AI-generated content on descriptions of products or less trafficked pages, but they wouldn't use AI-generated content on high-traffic pages, blog content, or home pages. Do you agree with that perspective?

"Partly. You can use an AI generator to write meta descriptions because they're not a ranking factor. You can use it to write social media copy because that's not going on your website. However, for any content that is going on your website - I don't care if it's a lower traffic page - I don't want to see AI-generated content there because you don't know what the next algorithm update is going to be.

I always want to be on Google's good side, so that I'm not panicking when there's an algorithm update. The best way to do that is to make sure that every single piece of content on your website is written by a human and is written for humans first and search engines second.

The machines focus 100% on writing for SEO. What we keep seeing with every update, is that Google tries to force SEOs to write for humans first and search engines second. That is the opposite of what AI tools do."

What's something that SEOs shouldn't be doing in 2023? What's seductive in terms of time, but ultimately counterproductive?

"As I've already said: don't use AI to write all your content. I know there's a lot of pressure to create as many content clusters as possible and get those clusters to rank quickly and generate results fast. Nobody wants to wait three months or six months, and the fastest way to get results is always going to be to create more content.

I understand that pressure but do not give in to the temptation to use AI to write content on your website. At some point, it might bite you in the a**, and you can quote me on that."

Chima Mmeje is Content Strategist at Zenith Copy and you can find her over at zenithcopy.com.

Expand your content strategy into other formats—Lily Ray

Lily Ray encourages SEOs in 2023 to expand your remit into new formats and take advantage of what Google and other search engines have to offer in order to stay ahead of the curve.

Lily says: "This year, it's going to be especially important to think beyond the 10 blue links. Google continues to innovate with different rich results, new types of accordions, thumbnails, carousels, and all kinds of SERP features that are changing the landscape of organic search.

If you're not expanding into new formats to take advantage of what Google (and other search engines like TikTok) are doing with images and video, then you might be left behind."

What does that mean in terms of tracking your SEO success? Are software tools getting better at incorporating other search engines, and things like images and video?

"I can't think of a tool that comes to mind in terms of capturing a brand's entire organic presence in the search results across a bunch of different search engines, social media platforms, and everything else. That's a big opportunity for the analytics tools to think about.

There are different ways that you can piece things together in terms of how your site is ranking across different sites that you own, or different social media properties. You can then cross reference that with the analytics tools that you use. Within Google Search Console, you have a lot of different reporting features that you can look at as well."

How do you measure the benefits of appearing high in the rankings on other search engines, where converting traffic is perhaps less directly measurable?

"It's getting more and more challenging over time. A lot of us have relied on tools like Google Analytics, which is going through a big change in 2023. It's changing to GA4, and it's going to take a lot of the SEO industry, and the analytics industry, a long time to adjust to that.

Attribution is getting harder across the board, not just for SEO, but for paid channels as well. It's challenging. A lot of the time, we just have to try to get a good understanding of how valuable it is for a brand to appear in these different places, and do the best we can in terms of tracking attribution across different platforms."

Is there a particular attribution model that you favour?

"It's case by case. We like to take credit in the SEO space because people often encounter our content first - months before they make a transaction. In that sense, first touch is great. It's really hard, however, to keep track of the role that organic plays in a customer's search journey. There could be so many different touchpoints where they encounter us organically, or they may just search for the brand at the very end - even though they've read a lot of our content before that point. It's getting trickier and trickier."

What should brands be doing on these different platforms to be more successful?

"Platforms like TikTok and Instagram serve as places for your brand to rank in Google's organic results for your brand name. To that extent, everybody should be there. I waited a really long time to join TikTok, for the same reasons many people don't want to join, but I realised that brands and individuals are starting to have their TikTok pages rank on the top page of Google when you search for their name. There was a big algorithm update early in 2022, and a lot of the TikTok pages for brands like Starbucks started to rank on page one of Google for their names.

Controlling all of those different assets is a reputation management strategy. You don't necessarily need to try to become famous on TikTok, because it's hard to do, but you should maintain a brand presence there. If you can start to figure out your niche - there may be some cute videos that you can make about your company, for example - then you should definitely take advantage of that."

If you're on these platforms, do you need to stay active, and keep checking them and publishing content on a regular basis?

"It's hard to say. With TikTok, it's hard for a lot of brands to fit the vibe. TikTok has quite a particular audience, and there is a certain type of content that resonates with its audience. For some brands, it can be really hard to create that type of content and make short videos that explain what the brand is all about while finding a way to entertain customers. If you're a B2B company, for example, it might be hard to do that.

Just having a presence there is enough to get started, but you should definitely be keeping a pulse on how people are interacting with you and whether they're sending you messages, etc. Of course, that should be part of a brand's social strategy anyway."

As long as you're publishing content regularly and you're not targeting highly short-tail keyword phrases, is it easier to gain visibility for your brand's activities on other platforms, and other search engines, than on Google?

"Definitely. Starting to think beyond Google, and starting to think about all these different places where your brand can convey expertise and provide expert content, is definitely something that companies should be focusing on in 2023.

Google is getting better at understanding audio content and video content. One thing that I always recommend is to use the experts at your brand. First of all, whatever content they are creating (if they're doing podcast interviews, for example) you should be leveraging that content as much as possible for your own site. Maybe you can embed a Spotify podcast or YouTube video on your site and add a transcription.

There are also a lot of great ways to use the search engines of stores like Spotify or Apple Music as a place to show up for different types of queries as well. Taking inventory of all the different search engines that are available is a really great approach."

Is it important to have other platforms in mind when you're creating content?

"Absolutely. If you're recording a podcast or a video show, you could think about sound bites or questions that are likely to be appealing on social media. Then, you've got something that you can share on multiple platforms.

Also, consider the transcription capabilities that a lot of these tools have, including Google and YouTube. Google is now serving up both audio and video content as an actual search result for queries, if they found the answer to a question within something like a podcast or an interview.

You might ask how to pronounce something, and Google can actually jump to the middle of a YouTube video where it says, 'This is how you pronounce this word.' They're getting better at understanding the text that's within a video and audio file. The more that you can do to think about the actual content quality within something like an interview is going to be really helpful.

You might do some keyword research on People Also Ask content and incorporate those questions as part of your content, which can then be transcribed or published as well. Structuring questions and answers in a way that people search is always best practice, both in text and audio."

Where does something like a TikTok video, a podcast episode, or a social media post sit into the overall content marketing strategy?

"I tend to recommend this type of approach for any business that's focusing on leveraging in-house experts as part of their content strategy. If your expert knows something about a given topic and they're able to go and share that knowledge with the world (through podcast interviews, video interviews, etc.) then that's a great way to show Google that you have in-house experts that can use their voice across different platforms. A lot of the time, Google will show a YouTube video result for a given search query, so having your experts in all those places is really important.

As far as TikTok goes, then it's almost a different team, or a different area of expertise, than traditional search marketing. At my agency, we have TikTok social media people that are making TikTok videos, and we also have a video production team that's making TikTok videos. That's not SEO to me. Of course, it is a search engine and there are ways to tag it properly for SEO, but it's more about creative capabilities and finding a hook and a type of video format that really resonates with people."

Do you think SEOs in the future will have to be completely aware of other search engines, rather than completely focussed on more traditional, highly technical SEO?

"SEO is becoming more fractured, in a way - particularly in terms of the skill set that's required to do SEO. My team contains more than 30 people, and we have people doing local, people doing technical, people doing content, etc.

You should probably know a lot about all of those things as an SEO specialist, but there is a depth of expertise that people have in different areas. It's really important to hone in on what you're good at. There's so much knowledge out there, and it's hard to be an expert at everything."

How would you decide on what you're good at?

"What you're good at and what you enjoy doing becomes clear the longer you do SEO. We have certain people on my team that love Local SEO, and they're obsessed with Google Business Profile, so they should spend their time getting to know local as much as possible. That way, when we have local clients, they can specialise on that. We also have technical people who have an IT and coding background, and that's their thing. They don't love content optimisation as much.

That's not to say that every SEO has to find their area of expertise, but if you do have something that you really love, then go down that track. You'll probably see better results that way."

What shouldn't SEOs be doing in 2023? What's seductive in terms of time, but ultimately counterproductive?

"2022 showed that Google is becoming a lot stricter in terms of fighting spam, but also some content strategies that SEOs might not consider to be spam – like a lot of the grey hat automated SEO strategies that used to work really well. Google's cracking down on these, with the core updates and the helpful content update.

Google's very focused on EAT now; they're very focused on reducing thin, duplicate, low-quality content. A lot of sites over the years have tried to take shortcuts with their content strategies, and have perhaps relied too much on

AI to the point where the content doesn't make sense. Those types of strategies are going to work less well over time, for sure."

Lily Ray is Senior Director of SEO and Head of Organic Research at Amsive Digital and you can find her over at lilyray.nyc.

7 GUIDE THE BOTS

Google is a child that is thirsty for knowledge, and you need to educate it—Jason Barnard

Jason Barnard explains that to prosper with SEO in 2023, you should treat Google like a child and make sure that you are educating that child about who you are and what you do.

Jason says: "We should tap into Google's childlike desire to learn and educate it accordingly."

What kind of child is Google?

"Google has a Knowledge Graph: a massive machine-readable encyclopaedia of knowledge. This is its understanding of the world. It makes sense to see Google as a child because Google has a little knowledge, and is trying to learn absolutely everything about everything in the world. As SEOs, our job is to teach this child about the small corner of the internet we're interested in.

It is our job to teach Google who we are, what we do, and which audience we serve."

What kind of education and nourishment does Google need to effectively learn about brands?

"In terms of brands, the thing that Google needs to focus on is entity understanding and entity identity. Google's understanding, and its confidence in that understanding, are the cornerstones of absolutely everything we do in SEO. EAT (expertise, authoritativeness, and trustworthiness) is fashionable at the moment, and there are signals for that. If Google understands who you are, that'll send a positive signal their way. If Google has to guess who you are, then it can only apply these signals in a dampened manner.

Being in Google's Knowledge Graph means that Google fully and explicitly understands who you are. In this case, any EAT signals you're working on will be fully applied. Going forward, entity understanding and your entity identity will be the most important things for SEO."

If you're launching a new brand next week, what would be some of the initial things you would do to increase Google's confidence and understanding of who you are as a brand/entity?

"At Kalicube we have the Kalicube Pro platform - which was built in-house. It was designed to provide a way to analyse how Google learns and where it gets its knowledge from. What we've learned from the platform is that Google gets its knowledge for each entity from different sources. You can't always assume that a specific source you're looking at is going to be a source that works. You should instead look at each entity. From this perspective, you need Google to understand who you are, what you do, and who your audience is.

The best place to start is on your website or entity home: a page on the website that represents your entity. Google refers to this as the 'point of reconciliation', where they need your version of the facts on a page of a site that you own. Then, when Google goes around the web and discovers fragmented information about the entity, it can use its explanation to understand how all the information fits together.

The first thing to do is to identify the entity home, and the second thing to do is to write a clear description that Google can understand. At Kalicube, we use Google's NLP to analyse the text and understand whether it explicitly understands the entities in your text. This description can be placed on the entity home so Google can easily and clearly understand who you are, what you do, and which audience you serve. You can then spread that description across the web as confirmation corroboration and indicate this corroboration from the entity home using either links or schema markup.

It's interesting to note that schema markup supports all of this. It's a way to communicate those three things to Google in its native language. It can then fully and explicitly understand where the entity home is, who you are, what you're doing, which audience you serve, and where to find the corroboration."

Regarding the entity home, are you talking about specific pages on your website or your domain name/site in general?

"It's a specific page: one single page that represents the entity. Ideally, it would be an About Us page for a company but, as you would expect, Google tends to default to the home page. However, if you make an early start working on Google's understanding of your entity, you can get it to use the About Us page as the entity home. This is preferable because the homepage already plays an important role as the representation of the website. It's also an incredibly important landing page for your audience when they visit your website.

If you can get the entity home to be an About Us page then that's much better, but if Google has already chosen the home page you'll have to go with Google."

If you've focused on the About Us page as your entity home, does that mean there's a chance it will be the number one result in the organic SERP as well as for your brand?

"No, they're not linked at all in that sense. Google will always understand that the homepage is the correct one to put at the top of the SERP for a search on your brand name. However, the About Us page will appear in the rich site links just underneath. That means you won't run into any danger of the About Us page dominating the homepage in terms of Google search results.

You will want it to dominate, however, in terms of where Google looks for information 'from the horse's mouth'. They'll look at who you are, what you do, and who your audience is. Most brands tend to sit back and assume 'Google gets it, Google understands, I'll just leave it to Google.' That's a foolish assumption because, though Google understands a great deal, it will at best understand reasonably well and at worst get everything wrong.

Confidence is vastly underrated too. Google's understanding is very important, but the confidence in that understanding is the single biggest insurance that future Google updates won't impact you negatively."

What sort of phraseology should you use? What's an example of a way that many brands write that just doesn't work well for Google?

"Brands tend to talk about where they started and this usually makes it difficult for Google. For example, stating that your company was formed in 2015. However, the first thing in the description is perceived to be the most important and currently relevant information, and what you'll want Google to focus on. Generally, that will be what's happening today, and why your current audience is looking for you, etc.

In terms of writing tips, semantic triples are incredibly powerful. In more simple terms, these can be viewed as 'subject, verb, object'. By keeping those semantic triples as close as you can, Google can more easily get to grips with what you're saying. Make sure that what you're writing is clear because this will be a big signal for Google.

It's important to remember that this machine doesn't have a sense of humour, a sense of irony, or a sense of poetry. It doesn't have a real understanding of culture. That means the mission statements that many brands add to their About Us page aren't helpful to Google. One could argue they aren't very helpful to the audience either.

It can be argued that when you focus on being clear for Google that will translate to what's helpful for users."

How do you measure if you've been successful with that, and ensure that Google understands what you do?

"There are a couple of ways of looking at this. Firstly, you can look at the Brand SERP: the search engine results page for your exact brand. You will see that the better Google understands you the more that Brand SERP will represent the brand message you've been projecting to your users.

Secondly, the Knowledge Panel that triggers when somebody searches for your brand name. This indicates that Google has not only understood who you are and what you do but that it's incredibly confident in that information. Otherwise, it wouldn't show the Knowledge Panel. It's great to track both the Brand SERP and the Knowledge Panel, preferably with a knowledge system to see how stable, rich, and representative they are. You can also try to measure how Google's confidence in its understanding is progressing.

That's exactly what Kalicube Pro SaaS does. It's exciting to be able to look at just how confident Google is - whether it's 50% confident, 60% confident, or 70% confident. The confidence in this understanding is your insurance. It's your safety harness for every single Google update you'll encounter over the next few years."

Are there many different scenarios where the Knowledge Panel wouldn't appear?

"It's a great question because there are lots of different aspects to this. Ambiguity can be a huge problem and is often the reason a Knowledge Panel that exists in Google's 'brain' doesn't appear on a Brand SERP.

Another one is geography - for example, names being spelt differently from location to location. Whether an entity is relevant in the user's geolocation can 'make or break' a Knowledge Panel. Additionally, Google's confidence in its understanding about the entity. It won't show a Knowledge Panel when it isn't confident in its understanding of the facts. There are lots of brands and people who have Knowledge Panels who don't even realise because they've never seen them. The reason they haven't seen them is simply that Google isn't confident enough to show it, or it hasn't got enough information.

The last point that's worth thinking about is search history. What's interesting about Knowledge Panels is that, if you're researching an entity by doing multiple searches around the name, or clicking on items in the Knowledge Panels, the search history within the search session is going to have a massive effect on what you see in the Knowledge Panel: it will tend to become richer with more information. Try that, then close the browser and start again. With a new session, you're going to revert to whatever it was to start with, meaning it's very much session-based.

For example, if you close your laptop, but don't close the Google Search result, when you open it the next day you'll remain in the same search session and you should see a continuation of that rich Knowledge Panel rather than seeing it revert to its initial status. We're getting this incredible, personalised experience but it's still session-based."

What shouldn't SEOs be doing in 2023? What's seductive in terms of time, but ultimately counterproductive?

"I strongly recommend getting into the Google Knowledge Graph. In order to maintain SEO performance in the years to come you need Google to have a solid, explicit understanding of who you are, what you offer, and which audience you serve. I would avoid going the wiki route, whether that's with Wikipedia, Wikidata, or one of the pseudo-wikis out there. Doing so will hand control of your brand message over to anonymous wiki admins. An additional huge problem is that, if your Wiki page or article is deleted, you are likely to lose the Knowledge Panel, and recreating a Knowledge Panel in this scenario is ten times more difficult than creating one without a wiki in the first place.

Avoid wikis as much as you possibly can, and build your Knowledge Panel through your capacity to educate the child that is Google. Keep control of Google's understanding of you and, by extension, your brand message on Google."

Jason Barnard is the founder of Kalicube, and you can find him at kalicube.com.

Use structured data to market to machines— Jono Alderson

Jono Alderson stresses the importance of using structured data to market to machines so that you always have the permission you need to actually access an audience in 2023.

Jono says: "The simplest and biggest machine to market to is Google. You also have to convince a raft of essentially omniscient AIs that your products, services, etc. are a good fit for their audiences. Otherwise, they won't have an incentive to rank or surface you algorithmically.

Processes like algorithmic sorting have been around forever, but they have become less about where they rank you and more about whether they'll include you - and the criteria for excluding people entirely.

Let's imagine Google says your price isn't right and your reputation isn't good enough. They're not going to feature you in emerging rich result formats or when people search for things on, say, Google Discover. In this case, you wouldn't have a way to access an audience. You wouldn't be able to market, spend, or advertise to these people because you wouldn't have permission to reach them. This appears to be the future of SEO and a huge transformation in the way marketing works."

Do AIs really know everything?

"The fact that they don't is a scary thought, especially when they're attempting to understand concepts like quality and reputation. However, they're really quite limited in the tools they have to do that. They'll look at the words on your webpage, and the ways you describe yourself, or are described by others.

An emerging way to tactically influence this is through structured data and Schema.org. If machines are looking for clues as to whether a product is good, a brand has the right reputation, or whether the content is suitable for a user, you can use structured data to explicitly describe specific things so that the AI can determine what you have to offer.

There is an increasingly large selection of tools for chasing rich results and holistically describing who you are and what you represent. You can do this in a way where the omniscient AIs can use your information to decide whether your brand meets its criteria and should be shown. These are the clues they're looking for."

What would you say to an SEO that says 'if you just focus on people the machines will follow'?

"That's a lovely sentiment when it comes to content, product-market fit, branding, and messaging. However, it does overlook the fact that the way we access audiences has changed. You need to start thinking about Google, Facebook, Pinterest, Twitter, etc. as bouncers and gatekeepers of their own audiences. They are choosing what people get to see. The secret to accessing and solving user problems is to do the things they want you to do - things that are valuable and good. You can do this in a way that considers some systems will decide whether or not you get to play.

It's important to have as much of the right structured data as you can reasonably implement in a meaningful way. Lots of people are just scraping the surface and assuming things, like Google is supporting star ratings. Sure, you can get tactical rewards from copying and pasting a snippet from a blog post and inserting it into your page, but this approach fails to take long-term considerations into account. If we want systems to be able to understand our content, we need to think about the relationships between the entities that we need to be describing."

Is there a best way to install and manage structured data?

"If you're using Yoast SEO on WordPress, most of this is done for you automatically. You can use an open standard and an API to customise and extend data in a way that's logical, sensible, extensible, and stable. If you're not a WordPress person, you can go look at the Yoast SEO documentation at developer.yoast.com. There you'll find a standardised approach that describes the exact process. That means that, even if you're doing unrelated stuff (for example, JavaScript activities), you can take the approach Yoast has defined and use that to build something equivalent in your own ecosystem. Copying and pasting what's in Google's documentation will only get you to step one."

What are some key SERP features that display your content because of structured data?

"People are underestimating the impact of Google Discover. It might be very Android-centric at the moment, but it is rolling out to other parts of Google. Discover preemptively give you articles it thinks you'll be interested in based on a combination of search history, implied interest, etc. Its decisions are hugely influenced by structured data and Schema.org. It's very sensitive to headlines and image sizes and ratios - where the standard social image size is slightly too small for Discover. You need to be looking at your schema markup and consider using different images, different treatments, etc.

It's worth diving into some of Google's documentation on how article schema works. You can do so much more than list a headline and an author. You can define the copyright holder, the primary image of the page, where the author went to University, etc. There are lots of things you can do to enrich that and increase your chances. You can then go through their documentation and look at things like recipes, articles, breadcrumbs, logos, and organisations - and do as much as you can."

What should people be doing to explore the possibilities of Google Discover? What's the future of Google Discover, are we looking at some sort of social network?

"Maybe! Google is always talking about journeys, where they're trying to understand the overarching journey users are going on. If you plan to buy a car, for example, and conduct multiple searches on multiple devices, Google will try to understand the discrete behaviours and processes and marry those up to help guide people on what's the next step and what are the best results.

A combination of something like Discover and structured data could help Google preemptively suggest your next step and describe what your page is about.

There has been significant exploration around what replaces cookie-based marketing. One potential route is a system whereby websites and users exchange information about the content they're interested in and what content websites publish. Schema is going to be a huge part of accurately defining what your content is about in terms of website features, topics, etc.

Joining all of this up and thinking about the technical aspects of how you tell stories is going to be really important going forward. It will be beyond writing good content for users and more about marketing to machines, using their language, and qualifying it to users."

What does this say for the future of search, could people get lost in a pyramid of different possibilities?

"Google is keen for search to be an assistive handheld process, where you just get shepherded through to a set of results. The worrying thing about this is that it could really impact - and potentially break - the commercial model of content publishers. In this event, what would be the point of creating great content, answering questions, and solving problems? Google will just take that, put it in front of a user and not allow them to access my website.

We're stuck accepting that Google is changing the ecosystem. The industry is currently split, with half of the professionals chasing rich results and clicks and the other half not using schema or structured data because they think it will devalue the content on their site and reduce the incentive for Google to send them visitors.

It feels like fighting Google on this is not a good strategy. We need to give Google content so it can reach its objective of solving user problems. We can then configure what that means for our commercial models. Opting out of the entire discovery funnel, and the entire top of your marketing funnel, doesn't feel like a good play in the short term."

Is structured data in a good place to service this more discover-orientated web? How is structured data likely to evolve in the future?

"As a standard, Schema.org is reasonably mature, because the tools exist to describe our content in ways that social media platforms can, and already do, read and extract. Google Merchant Centre and Facebook marketplace can scrape your page, read the schema, and use that to update product information in real time. Therefore, if your price changes or your stock levels change, they'll read the schema and update your catalogue information. Your website can then be more like a real-time database of the truth of your business. This is an interesting model because it's not just content and marketing for humans, but also the information that you use to service other platforms and systems.

This enables individuals to build something that consumes that schema because everything is explicitly labelled. Conversations surrounding this are all happening on the Schema.org GitHub repository, where people in Google are requesting specific schema based on a given spec. Google can then introduce this schema and incorporate them into the merchant centre, broader schema, Discover etc.

If you want to see where this is going or shape and influence those conversations, you can get ahead of the competition by going behind the scenes and seeing how things are unfolding. Look at what's going to launch in the next month or two and get that ready to implement."

What shouldn't SEOs be doing in 2023? What's seductive in terms of time, but ultimately counterproductive?

"People should stop staying in their lane. SEO is now so broadly interwoven with, affected by, and integrated with everything that just doing 'SEO' isn't going to be enough to succeed. We need to prevent people from thinking that they're not allowed to challenge quality, a product, or a business. Your biggest SEO opportunity might even be to change where the CEO eats lunch, invest in training your customer service team, or (if you're a restaurant) source better ingredients.

Historically, we've been able to paper over poor product-market fit by doing more SEO, to the detriment of consumers. You can get a bad product or page to rank if you throw enough money, links, and SEO at it. It's going to get harder and harder to accomplish things this way, so you need to invest in making the thing itself better. SEOs need to look further than marketing the thing and focus on improving the product, service, brand, and reputation.

We need to stop optimising and start improving. If all the evidence points to your product/service not being a great fit, it's going to get harder to convince machines. Historically we've gotten away with that - where previously we could attract an audience and then pitch and sell. Now, we can't access that audience we need to stop optimising and start improving. If you're not addressing the fundamental reasons why a system might choose to not rank you, you're not going to achieve anything."

Jono Alderson is Head of SEO at Yoast and you can find him over at yoast.com.

Manage your structured data like a financial portfolio—Martha van Berkel

Martha van Berkel advises SEOs in 2023 to handle your structured data like a financial portfolio in five key ways: manage and maintain your structured data, prepare for volatility, test new investments, treat SEO as a team sport, and view machine learning as your 'blockchain of schema'.

Martha says: "It's all about managing your structured data like a financial portfolio. We'll dig into how those things are related, but as the world's financial systems are going up and down, your structured data is also changing."

Why is it necessary to manage your structured data?

"Back in the early days of structured data (2015, 2016, 2017), you did your schema markup and then left it. It wasn't very volatile and not a lot was changing. Those times have changed. As we enter 2023 it's important to manage your structured data and maintain it.

Just like you would with a financial portfolio, you need to be looking at what
elements you have, and which types of rich results make up your structured data portfolio.

You also want to measure what's performing. Do you have diversity? If FAQs change with an algorithm update, do you have something else in place that you're either experimenting with or testing? You need that diversity to ensure performance"

What does effective diversification of your structured data portfolio look like?

"When we talk about diversity, we want to see different types of rich results.
Such as FAQ, How To, product, articles, and video. If you go to your search appearance in Google Search Console, and you look at all the different rich results that you have, you want to make sure you have more than one or two.

We're seeing that SERP change. One key thing that happened in 2022 that was different from 2021 are the very visible changes Google made in the SERP, and updates and changes to structured data What's changed? In June, we saw clicks from FAQs come down, but they came back at the end of the month. We saw the SERP change with regard to video rich results - where they pretty much only gave YouTube video rich results on desktop and everything else went under the Video tab. Again, Google serving themselves by changing the SERP and how they're using structured data.

We also saw really big changes in recipes. This time, recipe markup actually started performing really well, out of the blue, with 1000% increases across the board. Most of these changes started in June, similar to the other big changes in the algorithm, core content updates, etc.

Google is investing and changing things around structured data. That's why it is so important in 2023 to be managing it. You need to have a plan and be proactive about having that diversity."

You've come up with five key ways that you manage your structured data in a similar way to how you manage a financial portfolio. How do you manage structured data like a portfolio?

Tip #1: Measure what you have today and put a plan together for diversity.

"That means having a look at what you're getting today. What is your plan? What do you actually have in play? Also, do you have a process for maintaining this?

Structured Data is in the mainstream now, it is no longer just for early adopters and innovators This is just like everything else that you have to do on a regular basis - whether it's checking your financial portfolio or putting money aside every month. Just like you're doing keywords, looking at your page performance, and checking your vitals on a monthly basis, you should also be checking how your schema markup is performing. So that's one thing, alongside ensuring that you have that diversity."

Tip #2: Expect changes in Rich Results.

You also mentioned volatility as part of your second tip, what do you mean by that?

"Considering the changes that Google made in 2022 (with regards to FAQ changing, recipes, video, and the SERP changing) it meant a lot of volatility. You might be getting a lot of clicks from FAQs or How Tos on your blog, but you want to have a plan for when those things change. You need to already be working on what that next piece is and planning for what type of rich result you want to achieve with that new content.

If you're in a large enterprise, you're perhaps not as agile as a small organisation, so it does take planning. You need to be thinking about what those experiments are, in order to be ready for that volatility and the changes that Google is going to make. They are going to happen. Things are going to go up and down (Welcome to the world of SEO; that's why we all have so much fun here!) and being ready is important."

Are there any less obvious causes of volatility?

"Changes your organisation controls include content changes. Where the IT team suddenly changes something and messes up something up on the site or content gets moved something without people knowing.

Changes you don't control include things like the helpful content update. This algorithm change is all about what is of service to your customers. You need to really think about what that content is, and what purpose it serves. Last year, we talked about specificity. It really comes back down to whether or not you have FAQs or content that's really specific and of service.

Did something change in the performance of your website and Core Web Vitals that's impacting things? Or was it a broader change - like a competitor coming up or Google changing how they're proposing things?"

Is it possible to prevent these fluctuations from happening or do you have to have something else ready and a plan in place?

"That's where my first point - maintenance and monitoring - comes in; make sure you're managing your schema markup. That's for everything. It's not just the performance and outcomes, but is it still accurate? Are you getting more errors and warnings? Is it still covering the pages that you expect it to? At Schema App, that's what we're great at and what we do for our customers, but everyone needs to be in that mindset: that this is an ongoing, repeatable process.

Tip #3: Try new Rich Results types

Also, you should always be producing new content, which ties into my third point about investing in new things. Just like how the schema markup portfolio has to be managed, you also need to be reaching out to those other teams and saying, 'What is coming up next in our blog? Are they adopting the best practices? Are we thinking about rich results as we're producing new content, instead of it being an afterthought?

This is where I really see schema markup as a team sport – which plays into my fourth point here.

Tip #4: SEO is a Team Sport

If the SEO team is doing their job well, they're educating and pulling in content to help them and they're making sure IT understands what happens when they change things for fun. It's about understanding what that dynamic is and working cross-functionally.

The fun part is diversifying and testing different things, and testing and measuring those new investments."

What are some typical schemas that people can implement on blog posts?

"Blog posts things are typically articles, news, or blog postings. The reason I'm saying that you should try different things within a blog is that there's a lot of flexibility around the content. Where getting copy updated for your product might take lots of teams, and lots of cross-functional buy-in, restructuring the type of content in a blog can be done relatively easily.

Another example would be if you're seeing changes and you really want to try out 'How To' content to see if that's appropriate fo your audience, for example, you can write up a brief for the content team. They're producing content weekly, ideally, if not monthly. Within 30 days, you can actually start testing and measuring results.

If you're writing up a blog on a specific topic for a specific audience, you could make it an FAQ instead, and put it as questions and answers. It could be an article that is the subject of an FAQ, or you can just do it as an FAQ page, but it allows you to test more, and within a more free-flow area.

The other thing about blogs is that they have authors. Authors are important because a lot of the changes that we're seeing in the latter half of 2022 have a huge tie-in with EAT: expertise, authority, and trust. Expertise, authority, and trust all come into play when you talk about the author. Who's writing this? Do you have an opportunity to call out an expert? You can do that in your articles, your blogs, and your news pieces - and then use structured data to elaborate on who that author is.

Why are they an expert? What authority do they have to talk about this specific topic? It could be talking about their education, how they're tied to an organisation, or what they're a member of and what affiliations they have. That's a great way to tie in that EAT, which is another theme I'm seeing a lot of in the Google updates. It's not called out specifically, but the helpful content update has EAT written all over it.

That's why I see the blog as a fun place to experiment and test things."

Tip #5: The Blockchain of Schema is Machine Learning

Using your financial portfolio analogy, you said that the blockchain of schema is machine learning, what do you mean by that?

"For my most 'out there' recommendation, I started thinking about two things: semantics and machine learning.

Machine learning is one of the other themes that I'm seeing across the announcements and updates from Google. For example, in a podcast that came out in April of 2022, Ryan Levering was talking about structured data and what it's all about. He talked about how structured data was really built in order to be a baseline to help machine learning with regard to understanding. He talked about how it is still evolving, and how they're still using it to check in on things.

I was also reading and listening to Alan Kent (also from Google) about the product update. He was talking about how machine learning is looking for trends and patterns, specifically around product reviews and content. If you put those things together: the structured data is helping Google to understand trends and patterns in order to determine whether or not content is helpful.

We're seeing this across the board, in different areas. Structured data is helping Google to learn, using their machine learning, which is why you should invest in it and manage it as part of the 'financial portfolio' for your organisation."

What shouldn't SEOs be doing in 2023? What's seductive in terms of time, but ultimately counterproductive?

"Don't keep your head in the sand and try to get everything done on your own. More and more, especially in large enterprise, SEO needs to be a team sport.

You're starting to build that relationship and making sure that they understand that they can have an impact on performance, by thinking ahead and working cross-functionally. That's why points three and four are so important. Test and measure, and involve your team. This is: 'How, within the organisation, do we work together to get those outcomes that we're trying to get?'

There's so much that we know, as SEOs, that can help other teams to have a bigger impact on the financial outcomes of the company - which ties it all back to the overall theme.

We have to be educating, sharing those best practices, and getting them to share in both the 'doing' and in the wins. Don't keep your head down. Don't just think of the SEO team; think of that broader team that you can impact."

Martha van Berkel is CEO at Schema App, and you can find her over at schemaapp.com.

Take unstructured data from the webpages into structured format using the JSON-LD Schema markup—Suresh Kumar

Suresh Kumar reveals the power and importance of metadata to SEOs in 2023, and recommends that you start getting to grips with the JSON-LD code and apply schema to your pages.

Suresh says: "It's all about the metadata: the metadata of the website, web pages, and so on. That is where we need to be implementing schema.

Back in 2011, metadata was almost entirely the meta description, but there is a lot more to it these days. People are pumping a lot of data into their web pages. Even in videos and images, we have metadata. An image will have EXIF data and for a video, a lot of data will be there also.

When it comes to the data on the webpage itself, that is where we can use schema (Schema.org) and the JSON-LD code to help search engines to understand exactly what the page is about. That includes the topic we are talking about, the entities that are present, and a lot of other things as well.

What are the key elements of metadata in 2023 that SEOs don't know enough about?

"When SEOs do focus on the metadata, they often rely on automatic generators to make use of something like JSON-LD. These generators can be wrong, and that means that SEOs are not getting the maximum that they can from their metadata. Once you start learning the JSON-LD code and how it works - and you can expand on what is already there in the code - then you can make the most of it.

I have carried out single variable testing on it, and it works. I am finding a 90% success rate. That's exactly what I do full-time: I consult on schema, and I go through all of this, along with technical SEO consulting. That means that I see exactly what happens when we deploy custom schema on a client's website. Within days, or sometimes weeks, we see a lot of big movements in the rankings."

What makes JSON-LD so important?

"Google uses JSON-LD, and they recommend JSON-LD. It is the easiest way to get the data from a web page. We should keep JSON-LD in our heads, as it's the simplest code.

Some people will try and hide their JSON-LD code somewhere (like on the footer) because they think it will slow down the speed of the site. It doesn't work like that. JSON-LD does not affect PageSpeed at all.

By using JSON-LD, we are just saying exactly what different pieces are, like the header, the title, or exactly what topic we are talking about. We can also use entities from places like Wikipedia and Wikidata as a kind of vocabulary.

For example, if you are from London, you can find the entities for London. You can take them from URLs like Wikipedia and Wikidata and put those into that code block. That way, Google can easily understand (for something like a Knowledge Graph) that you live in London. It works in the same way for entities about your job. Search Engine Optimisation is a topic on Wikipedia, so you can use that as well."

What is the easiest way to implement JSON-LD?

"As of now, if you have no idea about what it is, then the easiest way to implement it is to pick up some generators. Start filling out the details, get the code, and implement it in the site headers.

While implementing, make sure that you implement one code for each page. That's how it should be. People just put it in the headers, and it will be the same code all over the place. I've seen a lot of cases where homepage schema will be present on inner pages. That's bad because you are then confusing Google about which the homepage is."

Can this easily be incorporated into most CMSs? Is there a plugin to do this for something like WordPress?

"Yes, you can do that as well. If you have no idea how to implement it, you can always reach out to a freelance platform, like Fiverr, and find someone who can help. You can also find help through support channels.

Something that I wouldn't recommend is GTM. Google Tag Manager has to load, it has to deploy the JSON-LD code, and it has a very long rendering time. You don't want that to be happening for Googlebot."

What are some of the key schema markup opportunities that SEOs are still missing out on?

"One of the most important ones that I have seen recently is the Clip operator for video. Actually, Google has recently created their own documentation on video Clip data. With video, you want to try and find any juicy parts that are particularly helpful. When you have the answer to a question in a YouTube video that you are embedding, you can identify the key clip with a timestamp, and it will link to the exact part of the video that is relevant. We can add this to the schema as well.

The schema type will be the VideoObject, and the Clip will be the structured data that tells Google what key moment to look for within that VideoObject. By adding this Clip information to the schema on your website, you will get more featured snippets.

That same Clip schema can be used for audio clips as well, which is something else that SEOs are not doing. You can implement this for audio-only content, like an mp3 on the page. Most SEOs are not even upgrading their schema codes - they just leave it as it is. We have to keep upgrading and implementing the new things that Google is offering."

How does schema help users as well as search engines?

"Every time there is an update, users often have a hard time finding relevant results. People have to browse to the second or third page of Google to find the relevant information that they need.

The more information we can give in the metadata, the better Google can figure out and process that information. Then, Google can get the relevant results to the top of the SERP, visitors can click those URLs and come to the website, and we can obtain those high-intent visitors. That's exactly what we wanted. It's a win-win scenario. Now, Google gets the high-intent visitors, we get the potential customers or readers, and the user finds what they are looking for."

Is it easy to measure the amount of increased traffic or brand exposure and ROI that you get as a result of implementing this kind of metadata?

"There was an update to Google Search Console recently, and now this kind of improvement data can be seen there directly.

Once we implement the code for video schema, for example, the thumbnails will appear in the search results, and you can use a third party to find the attribution for that. I like to use HockeyStack to track where visitors have come from so that I can get that attribution when they sign up for something or make a purchase.

You can use Google Analytics, which is also fine, but the data is skewed, which is why I prefer third-party software.

Measuring things like CTR is simple. If you implement schema for something, you can split test between a couple of pages to see if it has an impact or not. After it has been implemented, just make sure that you have reindexed the same page. People will often forget to do that. The schema has to be indexed so that the information can be processed, and you can get the results."

When it comes to split testing, what are you testing and what are you looking for?

"The first thing we are looking for in split testing is getting more CTR on the search results. The second thing is the Time on Page, which is always a goal. If we have a video that appears on the SERP, people have to visit the page that the video was on so that they get what they want.

It's a good signal because the more time they spend on the page, the more likely it is that they are a high-intent visitor. It's also a good signal for the Google algorithm, to say that these visitors have spent this kind of time on these pages."

Is this something that SEOs have to do after the fact, or can content creators define where to utilise schema within their content?

"We have to do it after the content has been created; It's our job to work on this. Content creators handle the content part, but they can't actually work on the code and all of that. The SEO or web developer has to be there to make the most of it, which is something that you can also automate.

In WordPress, there is a plugin called ACF, which is a Custom Fields plugin. We can also use that software for text tags on other kinds of websites. Based on your requirements and whatever you already have, you can still make use of schema.

SEOs should know what they want so that it's as easy as possible to convey to a developer. You should make a template for pages that will have the same kind of schema so that a developer can easily deploy them using those variables.

SEOs have to be present in every stage of deployment, including the creation of strategy and advising content creators on what to include."

What shouldn't SEOs be doing in 2023? What's seductive in terms of time, but ultimately counterproductive?

"There are too many tools out there and SEOs are often missing out on the Google Search Console data. They will see things like keyword gaps and content gaps, but they don't see something called "intent gaps". Each keyword has its own intent gap. You have to see the data from Google Search Console, and you have to implement it, but everyone sticks with their Ahrefs or Semrush data.

I have tested this using different intent keywords on my test sites. It is a game changer for me: the KGR, or Keyword Golden Ratio. Look at the intent and find similar keywords where no one is competing, so that you can make the most of it. This has to be done manually using Search Console and regular expressions.

When you have skin in the game, you will be able to identify that intent. Once you understand the business, you understand the intent far better. You can also serve more than one intent on the same page using subtopics.

SEOs should not be relying so much on their tools and should focus more on Google Search Console data. You have to make the most out of it because you don't get it anywhere else.

You can take that data and put it into somewhere like Bigquery so that you can understand things like queries, number of clicks, impressions, etc. - or you can just use the simplest, which is Google Search Console."

Suresh Kumar is Technical SEO Consultant at Gondi Media and you can find him over at sureshkumar.digital.

Index specific faceted search pages you don't have categories for, and style them as categories—Kevin Indig

Kevin Indig explains to SEOs in 2023 that, in the right situations, indexing facets can actually be a game-changer for an eCommerce or large aggregator site, and gives advice on how to make sure those pages are still relevant and valuable.

Kevin says: "Faceted indexing has been a controversial topic in SEO, especially over the last few years in eCommerce. If large eCommerce sites index targeted facets, under the right circumstances, they can significantly increase their organic traffic and revenue from it."

Is there not a danger that these pages could be perceived as thin content that doesn't offer much additional value?

"That's the crunch point. When we talk about facets, there's a high overlap between the facet and the root or canonical URL. However, there are instances where long-tail versions of the short head keyword have lots of search volume. It's often the case that there's not a lot of competition for the long-tail versions. There'll be an opportunity to go after them with facets of a category or subcategory.

There are two ways to make content on the facets relevant. One is by product selection, where you ensure the narrower categories filter to create that facet. You'll want to ensure the product section really reflects the filters that are relevant for the facet.

The second way you can do this is through content on the facets. Some of the best eCommerce companies use this strategy and add a little bit of unique content to the faceted category page in the form of text. The aim is to make sure that Google understands that a page is relevant for a slightly different keyword, or variation of the keyword, for the canonical category."

How do you identify the faceted pages that you want to index?

"Firstly, you'll want to drag all of the keywords that are important to you. Secondly, you should group them by category. Thirdly, look at the long-tail and short head keywords for that specific category.

Look at the signals so that you can decide whether you want to create a faceted category and let Google index that to see who is ranking for what. If you see the same competitors ranking for short head keywords in the same category, and for long-tail keywords with the same page, that'll be a signal to not create a faceted category version. However, if you notice that the same sites that rank for the short head keywords of a category are not ranking for the long-tail version of that keyword, that would be the signal to create a facet and index it to Google.

The meta point, or the key to being successful, is to have the technical ability to create facets and decide when Google indexes them or not. In many cases, this is a manual effort but there are ways to automate that. Companies that automate have a huge competitive advantage over others."

Is this not something that can be completely automated or are you always going to be able to do it to a higher standard manually?

"It's possible to automate this with the right set of tools. You'll probably have to build a custom logic, but you can monitor short and long-tail keywords for your most important categories and who ranks for them regularly. If you can monitor this on a weekly cadence, if not daily, this type of infrastructure will tie that to the creation indexation of facets.

This is a powerful way to automate things, but it will probably take some sort of data leak or intelligence that unites these strings of data and is attached to the CMS. It should create a facet or let Google index that facet. There are companies that can help you accomplish this."

What are the key style elements commonly associated with category pages that you should use with these faceted pages?

"You should have a selection of products related to the category/subcategory and filter. For example, if your facet is for 'blue t-shirts' you'll want to make sure that the t-shirts are really blue. This is an important criterion to provide more filter and search functionality for the users.

What often happens is that users come through facets on a category page and still browse around or filter until they have the right product. Don't just make this a landing page with no filter options; you should make sure it's a category page where users can keep exploring to find the right product for them."

How do you ensure that Google finds them?

"Internal linking. Ideally, you'll have some form of internal linking for several facets. It could be something like 'other users also bought', or complementary products around what users are already looking at. You can also use HTML sitemaps. Ideally you'll create a unique HTML sitemap specifically for facets. This is an old-school internal linking trick that still works very well. If you can get indexed or open facets into an HTML site quickly, that can help Google find the pages that might not have been accessible before."

What's the best practice for content on these pages? Is it all about having a good UX or do you need a reasonable amount of relatively unique content on these pages as well?

"Reality shows that unique text on category pages still helps Google better understand the relevance of a category. It's still deemed necessary, but the question is: what type of content is important and how much content is important?

With facets, you won't need as much content, but a couple of sentences could be helpful. In the case of eCommerce, you should make it very buyer guide-focused and really hone in on what additional information you can provide to help users make a better choice. For example, you could talk about the material of the product and how there are differences, providing specific context around it.

There are lots of ways to provide helpful information, and that doesn't always have to end in a wall of text. It can sometimes just be an elegant paragraph that gets users the right amount of information to make the right choice."

Is it completely satisfactory to have the text underneath the items you're selling on the page or is it more effective for search engines to have the text above them?

"The verdict is out on this one. Sometimes it's fine to have the text at the bottom of the page, but more and more users are getting used to scrolling and exploring a page. If the text is really helpful and provides extra information, it should live at the top of or on the side of the page.

The challenge is that we're yet to see enough A/B tests of different placements of text to determine the perfect way to do it. In reality, different placements work and there are also versions where you can have a bit of text at the top and then a bit of text at the bottom. This will allow users to click a button that leads them to the bottom of the page. Be creative and mindful that we're still waiting on the body of research to inform us on the best way to do it."

What are your thoughts on the creation of content using AI?

"You have to have really good inputs. It's possible, but the quality has to be high. AI content is generally considered to be of lower quality. The reality is that there are lots of companies or people who use AI to generate content, it's just that they need to spend the necessary time to vet and edit it to make sure it's a high standard, usable, and easy to read.

If you have these resources then there's not necessarily a problem with automating content generation, especially when you have several inputs for every category and want to create lots of content for lots of different categories. This is totally possible, but the inputs have to be right and the outputs have to be of high quality. It all depends on where you start, and what kind of information you have available to create that content."

As Google gets better at determining which section of a website a user should be driven to, will you still need to create very small niche faceted search pages? Could you just create big pages with different sections on them?

"Yes. There are trade-offs in terms of performance, though. This has much higher importance in eCommerce than in SaaS and other types of SEO. There are trade-offs in terms of internal linking, performance, Core Web Vitals, and user experience. It's interesting to see how some of the big players do that. For example, Amazon indexes lots of search pages that sometimes seem to be overlapping in user intent or product.

Google can understand that there are fine differences that lead to a much better experience for users. There could be a world where very large categories rank for all sorts of long-tail queries. However, it seems like this is getting harder and harder because there are lots of players that successfully create very targeted, narrow filter pages to hit precisely what the users are looking for. It's a bit of a trade-off, but the best in the game test one against the other and make a data-driven decision."

Is it important to create friendly URLs for search engines, even when there are so many sub-sections that pages can be built out of?

"In the context of the content, the user experience, and things like Core Web Vitals, price, delivery, etc. URLs are less important than they were five or ten years ago. However, you still want to aim for creating a taxonomy that makes sense and is short and to the point. Working with subdirectories or scanning with subdirectories is a great approach because they translate into breadcrumbs which can be shown in rich snippets and give users a feeling of whether they're at the right address or not.

It depends on how large the site is, what the scale mechanisms are, and how many facets you want to index. It's all about taking an iterative approach - not indexing thousands of pages overnight, but undertaking small experiments and seeing how they go. If these are successful, you can proceed.

You can take a similar approach with site structure and friendly URLs. Avoid building a huge construct of millions of pages and start with categories then build subcategories and facets. Take a slow, iterative approach to rein in problems like URLs being too long."

What shouldn't SEOs be doing in 2023? What's seductive in terms of time, but ultimately counterproductive?

"SEOs shouldn't be going after overly competitive keywords that they have no chance of ranking for. It's juicy to see some of these short head keywords that have lots of search volume and potential traffic but are highly competitive. The problem is that going after these types of terms and not ranking well for them can mean that you lose a lot of trust and credibility, especially in-house but also with a consultancy or agency. You could create all these expectations and high hopes with customers or stakeholders but then not deliver on the promise. You typically need lots of firepower to compete with these keywords. In my mind, what SEOs shouldn't do is jump the gun and go after super competitive keywords.

What you should do is develop a very good understanding of the keywords you're eligible for and where they can rank. Maximise that potential, and then build on top of that like a pyramid and iterate toward those competitive keywords, rather than going after them right away. This would be a rookie mistake that's worth avoiding because it could cost a lot of credibility and trustworthiness, both internally and externally. It could even go as far as causing you to lose funding or lose a client."

Kevin Indig is a Growth Advisor and former Director of SEO at Shopify and you can find him at kevin-indig.com.

8 SERP SEO

Adapt your strategy to capitalise on the changing SERP—Louise Heap

Louise Heap believes that SERP optimisation is a key part of SEO in 2023, particularly considering the features and formats that have reduced the SERP click-through rates to standard organic listings.

Louise says: "To give your site the best chance of driving traffic and visibility, you need to be optimising for the SERP and not just for your keywords."

How has the SERP changed recently?

"We're not that far removed from the days of having paid listings at the top and organic listings underneath. The organic listings were pretty standard and the URL and metadata were all that you saw.

More recently, we've seen the introduction of lots of different types of formats and features. We've seen Knowledge Graphs, featured snippets, FAQ rich results, reviews, maps, news, and more. We've also seen images and videos being directly removed from the standard SERPs. Things are much more varied than they used to be. Google has been introducing and testing in the SERPs for a while now, and it's likely to continue into 2023 and beyond.

This could be perceived as a move to a more holistic and comprehensive way to address user queries. The MUM update is further evidence of using in-depth world knowledge to gather additional information through formats like text, images, video, and audio."

How do you optimise for a constantly changing SERP? How can you give a brand a decent chance of featuring in those new features by marking up code on-site?

"Firstly you can identify what features and formats are appearing in your key SERPs. This varies a lot from industry to industry. Certain tools can scrape the SERPs and show the features which are appearing, including common ones like featured snippets or PAAs. Some tools will even show you who owns those features, which is something you can do within the tools by plugging in a keyword and seeing what features are generated.

Another thing you can do is manually look for your head or primary terms - not the entire keyword set but the terms that matter to your brand. Manually look at what's appearing in the SERP because it'll be subject to regular change. Also, the tools won't necessarily pick up on all the latest features and formats that are appearing. Have a look and note those features and formats down.

You can then look at who owns them and consider, why? Generally, it'll be because Google feels that particular feature or format best answers the user intent. For example, if it's something like a featured snippet that's appearing for one of your head terms, look at who owns that, where the format is, and what format the featured snippet is written in. Is it a paragraph or a list? You can then look at what type of content is there when you click through from the featured snippet to see if that reinforces why they own that particular feature.

If the content on your site is in a paragraph format and the featured snippet for the query you want to target is in a list format, consider restructuring your content to match the format that Google is showing for that particular query. This is true for features and formats too. If there's lots of video content appearing in one of your key SERPs, reach out to your video team and see if they can produce some video content. If there are things like FAQ rich results being pulled through into the SERP, make sure that you're marking up the content on your site with schema to increase the chances of FAQs being pulled through your site as well."

What's the best initial featured snippet strategy? Is it to look at competitors and try to do better or look at keyword phrases that don't have a featured snippet and create content to serve that?

"You should look at whether your featured snippets are appearing. We know that Google will see those as key SERPs that you need featured snippets, because they're the best at answering that particular intent. Once you've achieved this, it's good to future-proof your strategy and aim to put features where they're not appearing at a given time.

Certain SERPs which have ranked highly might have a really high search volume too. However, there might not be many featured snippets or other types of results appearing in those, which would suggest it's more than a traditional listing. You should look at which types of SERPs are generating those features first.

Ultimately, you should think about intent and understand what the audience wants to see. From here, you can try and get ahead of Google a little bit to future-proof your strategy. For example, you might assess your in-house audience data for a certain type of query and discover that people prefer to have their questions answered in video format. Therefore, you should make sure you're ready with that format, in case Google decides to pull that particular feature in."

How do you financially justify the importance of trying to appear in more featured snippets? What's the ROI of getting more featured snippets and are there more click-through rates from the SERP that you can measure as a result?

"Even if you rank well for one of your top queries, because more features are appearing in the SERPs, the click-through rate to those traditional organic listings will reduce. This is a common occurrence across various industries, so it's about maximizing that visibility in the SERP. You should aim to get in those PAA and featured snippet boxes."

If you've got the brand appearing in a featured snippet, does that provide value as well, or are you always looking for the click-through?

"Ideally, you would like people to click through to the site so you get traffic. However, the reality is that as search changes change so does the overarching ecosystem. For example, there are no-click searches where people can receive quick answers to questions via featured snippets.

Google has started to recognise this and is serving those, but it's important to raise the awareness of your brand to show that you have authority and can answer a particular question. Then, if somebody has a follow-up question that requires a more detailed response, they're still likely to click through."

How do you optimise for personalized search?

"It's about understanding the audience's intent as much as you can. If you've got a research and insights team that truly knows who your audience is, you can better understand the SERPs they're seeing so you can try to capture them. It's difficult because what we see when we look and try to optimise our strategies is different to what a potential customer would see. Therefore, it's really important to understand who they are, what they might see, and what features they might be shown."

How are you seeing user behaviours change in terms of how they search? Are people searching for longer-tail keyword phrases, perhaps even using voice search or something else?

"Voice searches are interesting. Going forward, the way we search will be much more varied than simple keywords. Lots of broader searches will still be really valuable, as will performing specific searches.

You need to be able to answer queries with really comprehensive content. Though it's important to make SERP optimisation a key part of your strategy, that doesn't mean you should completely disregard keywords. It's important to look at those, but consider what might be appearing on the SERP so you can target those keywords in the right way."

Do the user's search preferences depend on where they're from, their age, the device they use, etc.?

"Yeah, that's fair to say. Today's generation consumes media very differently from their predecessors. We've seen the rise of video in today's younger demographics. Perhaps Google recognises this and is consolidating more video searches onto the main SERPs. That's something that's becoming more prevalent. With the younger generations, if they are using voice search more, that's something we should factor into our strategies as well."

What shouldn't SEOs be doing in 2023? What's seductive in terms of time, but ultimately counterproductive?

"Stop relying purely on keywords. Really think about intent, how you can best answer that, and capturing the best format to answer that intent."

What are your best sources for discovering audience intent? Do you use software tools for that or do you need to manually go through different keywords to work out the intent behind each phrase?

"It's a mixture. There is a certain insight you can get from tools, but what's even more useful is qualitative data or audience-led research from your research or insights team, brand, or customer care teams.

If it's a brand that people bring up and ask questions about over the phone, that will give you really good primary data that you might not see reflected in search results. Use as many resources from as many different channels as possible to build up a comprehensive understanding of who your audience is. By doing so, you'll be positioned to better understand their intent."

Are you a fan of optimising for zero-volume keywords?

"It's important to take a holistic approach because something might not be reflected in tools at the time but lots of customers are inquiring about it. If it's not reflected just yet, it's still worth having that content appear.

Get insight from your customer care team about something that's been asked. Then you can produce a piece of content to get a decent amount of traffic. It can take a while for the number of people searching around that intent to be reflected in Google data. Always try to address audience intent with your strategies.

If you know something is an intent or an area of interest for your audience, you should always address it."

Louise Heap is SEO Content Strategy Manager at Stickyeyes and you can find her over at stickyeyes.com.

Get ready for more dynamic SERPs - paid and organic content blending together—Navah Hopkins

Navah Hopkins recommends that SEOs in 2023 need to get ready for the dynamic Search Engine Results Page and be prepared to incorporate the two worlds of paid and organic even more in the future.

Navah says: "This may come as a shock as a PPC in an SEO conversation, but my number one tip is to get ready for a more dynamic SERP. Get ready for PPC and SEO to be collaborating far more than they already are.

When we think about how much PPC and SEO work together - that has escalated tremendously - but the biggest catalyst for that is how much the content for paid media is blending with organic. You can see this in shopping, you can see this in images, even in traditional search - you're starting to see tests where organic takes the former right-hand side of the page, where it used to just be a stack.

Get ready for those complexities. I'm especially excited about this when it comes to local, because there are far more exciting local placements to be had, but even in shopping. Particularly video and images, as PPC now has the Performance Max campaign and you're going to see a lot more folks producing video and image content. Get ready for those search result pages to really be a blend.

From a branding consistency standpoint, we want to make sure that we're on point, we're carrying the same message through, and we're being mindful that we're not stepping on branding toes as we communicate with our audience - either through paid or through organic."

How often should SEO teams and PPC teams sit down and analyse the SERP together to devise a strategy for the optimum way forward?

"There is no hard and fast time that needs to be set. When I ran the paid arm of a tech SEO agency, we had a weekly meeting that was just our wild and crazy innovation time - where we chatted and collaborated. All client communication ran through everyone, and we were all on the same page, but that might not be tenable for some brands. It might be a quarterly conversation.

What matters is that you are building in automated workflows to get that data from the paid team into organic, and from the organic team into paid, so there's a constant flow. Also, that you're not growing complacent in analysing our search result pages. You really want to have a sense of, not just what is happening in your world, but what's happening across the aisle.

One really powerful tool for this (especially if you haven't run a paid campaign but you need to get a sense of things): Google Ads has a free Ad Preview and Diagnosis tool that will give you a sense of what those SERPs look like. If you don't want to create SERPs in the wild, that actually count against your metrics, this is a really powerful way to get an idea of what's happening on the pages. It can also give you a sense of what's happening in the account and what might be causing the paid campaigns to not serve.

I definitely recommend, at minimum, a quarterly connect. You can connect every day, you can connect every week, the point is that you're collaborating and automating as much data sharing as possible."

What's something that an SEO team can do to make their results suitable for a dynamic SERP, i.e., the results will be just as effective in multiple environments?

"There are two really big things. Number one is to remember that, from a paid standpoint, a lot of the good is going to borrow from organic. When we think about paid versus organic, one of the common misconceptions is that paid is for transactional and organic is for research. That's just blatantly untrue. Organic is just as powerful, sometimes even more so, at driving that value. Make sure that when you're looking at your creative (your landing pages, your title tags, etc.) you're building in that transactional intent - and building for humans, not the machine.

One of my favourite stories about 'average creative' is that when the human mind comes up with average ads, and Google does their automated ads, then the automated ads perform better because Google gives more attention to the ads that it created. So, if you build average creative - if you build average experiences - you're going to perform poorly. Whereas, if you take the time to really think about how you can drive more value, direct the user to the right spot, and engage them in a meaningful way - so they consent to be tracked in this first-party data world - you will do so much better.

The other really important thing is to be very mindful about what kind of domain structure you want and how you are setting yourself up. In a lot of cases, people will try to share domains, and then you fight and you're stepping on each other's toes. If you know that there is always going to be conflict, you might want to think about splitting things so that you have a subdomain versus a main domain; you have your main domain as your organic and subdomain for paid. That way, you can really control how users are engaging with you, and you can have that really beautiful tracking.

A lot of people, especially in eCommerce, will try to force all of the traffic to go to the main domain, and there are some instances where you do want to have that separate domain. If you have to share, make sure that you're being mindful about tagging for out-of-stock, you're being very upfront, and you're building in enough leeway time for redirects - because redirects cause disapprovals. Be mindful of that. There's nothing worse than paying money to drive traffic to a bad page, being in that top five organically, but your page is just bad. Be careful there."

Does Google advocate AI-driven content for paid but hate it for organic?

"I had a really fantastic conversation about this with Cindy Krum. She is one of my absolute favourites in the mobile spaces, particularly mobile SEO. She was caught really unawares by how much close variants are a thing in paid. In looking at the most recent update in August of 2022 (being upfront with your creative on the SEO side - don't try to cheat the user), AI content is not necessarily the answer. The answer is content that is good.

Google is inclined to believe that its tools are good. If you lean into Google's automations - whether that's the ads that it automatically creates, leveraging Smart Bidding, leveraging Smart Campaigns, PMax, etc. - they tend to get more screen time than a campaign or an ad, if both exist alongside each other.

If you just have things that the human fully owns, it's a little bit easier for that to get screen time. You have to be mindful that when you use automation it can do a lot of good, save a tonne of time, and do amazing things, but the things that you specifically create might struggle to get screen time - even if your thing might be a smidge better."

How do you measure the value of a dynamic SERP, where a result is going up and down, appearing in Local Packs, etc.? How do you keep track of things like click-through rates and traffic from the SERP?

"One of the things that I focus on is brand lift - whether I'm getting more brand lift off of Local Map Pack versus traditional listings, for example. That's something I monitor quite a bit. The other thing that I look at very carefully is how much I am getting paid queries for traffic that I'm also getting from organic, and if the bounce rate is better, worse, or the same.

If I see that paid is weaving its way into organic SERPs, but the performance is poor, I will start to exclude some of those queries. I want to let organic shine - I don't want to pay for that traffic. Conversely, if I see that paid is doing great, I might double down on paid so I can really own that SERP and still have that organic placement there for when I need it. Then, I will start to build out content so I can get those supplemental SERPs.

This includes video. I cannot overstate how important it is to build video into your strategy because there are more and more SERPs that require video. Particularly in eCommerce, but also on the local side. This goes for local service ads, Google Business Profile posts, etc. Video definitely improves engagement, so video is pretty powerful."

Is it best for brands to have a YouTube channel and embed YouTube on their website, or have their own self-hosted video or video service?

"I am always Team YouTube - but also place on LinkedIn, and place on Facebook, and host yourself. The more domains where you have that content, the better. If your goal, though, is to improve Google placement - YouTube is one of Google's toys. You will improve your standing by playing with Google's toys. That's just feeding the content into the system.

That said (and this is a shameless plug for Microsoft) a lot of Microsoft content can actually be pulled from Facebook. Especially if you love what you get from Google, but wish you had a little bit more control and it was a little more transparent on the data, Microsoft ads and Bing can be super powerful. The content that you get from those other hosted spots definitely feeds into Bing, so you don't have to do as much work.

Get your video everywhere. If you care about Google, prioritise YouTube first, and make sure that you write out really documented descriptions, so they're highly searchable. But equally, don't be afraid to post that content on Facebook, LinkedIn, etc., so it will serve not just on Google but on Bing, and drive that much more traffic for you."

How do you optimise for the user experience?

"Microsoft has a free tool called Clarity. It is one of my absolute favourite gems - every single digital marketer needs to get this installed on their site. It does not impact site speed in any meaningful way, and it will give you full transparency into user behaviour. From recordings to heat maps to comparisons to running A/B tests. It's fantastic. I strongly recommend Microsoft Clarity. It has a lot of the same functionality as things like Hotjar, but it's free.

Once you have that installed, you can see what the user journeys are. Do you find that people are clicking on things that they think are buttons, but they're not? Do you find that people are getting stuck in a weird render and that explains why people are bouncing: because something is rendered poorly?

Obviously, things like site speed tests are great too. Also, be mindful of colours and the subconscious feelings that people have around different colours on the internet - and fonts. However, the most actionable advice I can give is to get Microsoft Clarity installed on your site and look at what your users are doing."

What shouldn't SEOs be doing in 2023? What's seductive in terms of time, but ultimately counterproductive?

"One of the things I find very troubling when it comes to seasoned professionals is that we get very confident and comfortable in what we know. We start to lose the lustre of the industry because we get so comfortable. We have our game plans when it comes to algorithmic shifts, and we have the same cycles.

We need to test more, and we need to be willing to fail. We need to get out of our comfort zone and test one new thing a quarter so that we can make sure that we're staying current and providing value to the brands that we serve.

One of the worst things that you can do is to assume that you know everything because then you will know nothing. There is definitely a pattern where we get to a certain level of excellence and then we plateau. The biggest challenge we all face, as incredibly talented digital marketers, is how we can make sure that we're keeping our teeth, and that we're remaining current.

Test one new thing every quarter. Come up with a wild and crazy idea and test it. If it fails, then you have data that shows it doesn't work, and you can test something new. If it works, you just found something really amazing and incredible. These tests don't have to just be in content or tech SEO. They can be in CRO, you can test something with your paid friends, you can test something with social, you can test something with in-store marketing, etc. Don't lose your fearlessness. Don't get complacent and risk-averse."

Is there one resource, or one software platform, that you would recommend to assist with testing?

"I've said Microsoft Clarity a lot, and it is really fantastic, but this is going to be more of a holistic answer.

Find a testing accountability buddy. Find someone that you love and respect, that may be in a completely different company or industry, that you come at things the same way, you can share your tests and your ideas, and have that sounding board and check-in with. This isn't your boss; this is your friend that you don't want to let down.

Yes, there are tools out there like Clarity and Hotjar, you can look at Ad Preview and Diagnosis to review the SERPs, and you can look at Google Trends. There's a plethora of tools, but a friend that will hold you accountable for running tests, that you love and respect - that's priceless. That is the best tool I can suggest."

Navah Hopkins is CEO of Navah Hopkins Consulting LLC and you can find her at navahhopkins.com

Check the SERP and build your personal brand entity online—Sara Moccand-Sayegh

Sara Moccand-Sayegh advises SEOs in 2023 to look directly at the SERP for more information about what is actually being shown, and also ensure that you are presenting a clear and consistent personal brand identity across the web.

Sara says: "Check the SERP. It's so important. We have tools that support us, but sometimes they don't give us all the information that we need. Some tools, for example, will not give you position zero, but you want to know what is there – at the top of the search results. Tools often start from position one, but you have position zero before that and you have so many other features in between. It is always better to check.

I was doing some tests on myself, as it's sometimes easier to test on yourself rather than on clients. I realised something weird was happening with my images and Google was having some difficulty understanding them. I was only able to see that because I was checking the SERPs.

For one presentation that I did for BrightonSEO, they literally changed the picture for my presentation. That was one example. Another was with some other images of mine; it was showing the source and where it came from, which was strange to see."

When you analyse the SERP, do you also go behind the SERP to see where Google is getting its information from?

"Yes, exactly. That is what helps you to progress, analyse, and understand the system. That is also part of the job: to try to figure out how the system is working and why it's doing what it's doing. In my case, for example, I was questioning why it was treating my images that way."

What trends are you seeing in terms of where Google is more likely to get their information from, compared with a couple of years ago?

"Now there is the machine learning system, obviously. We have all the entities, and they are creating all of the connections. That is the main driver, but you still have to create the entity itself, and you still have to understand the system. Part of all of the tests that they do is trying to better understand what they can see. It's all about understanding."

How do you give Google greater confidence about who your entity is, what it represents, and why it should be authoritative in a particular field?

"That is a tricky one, and it's a big part of the job. A lot of it is about giving consistent information. Don't give completely different information on one site than on another. Be consistent in the information about you online. There are also other things that can help with Google's understanding, like schema.

In terms of where you want to have that consistent information, being on a wiki is the dream. Everybody wants to be on Wikidata, Wikipedia, etc. but, from experience, it's not that easy. The community is very strong, and they check very often. You need to collaborate with those communities. Sometimes, SEOs want to be smart by adding their own information on a wiki without being consistent elsewhere first – that's counterproductive.

Don't start with the end in mind. A lot of people go directly to Wikidata, for example, because they want to achieve that listing - but that should be your final goal. Before arriving there, you need to do all of the other work. You need to be consistent in your social network, in your company profile, on your entity home, and all over the web.

This can be difficult. If you are a single person, then you can create your own brand first. If you have your own brand and it becomes strong enough, then you can start thinking about going to Wikidata, Wikipedia, or wherever you want."

How should someone go about creating a personal brand?

"When creating your personal brand, the entity home plays a big role and Jason Barnard (CEO and Founder at Kalicube) explains it like this: 'The entity home is a web page recognised by Google as the authoritative source for factual information about a given entity.'

The entity home, in most cases, is your homepage and has the biggest influence on your knowledge panel. However, I have seen some exceptions, especially for people who do not really have a website but are very well-known on a social network. These individuals can still receive an accurate knowledge panel without having a website as their entity home. This brings me to the conclusion that having an entity home is fundamental for creating a personal brand, and this can easily be achieved by having your own website. To sum up, your website acts as the central source of true information about you online, and will confirm the information that can be found everywhere else."

Should a business or corporate website build personal profiles for the authors that create blogs for the site, so that those profiles can function as the entity home for the brand of those individuals?

"I work for a company that does exactly that, even for people who don't write that many blog posts. You can see the effect directly by typing my name into Google. What comes up is the page that contains all of the information about me, and a list of my blog posts connected to that. Clearly, that is important.

In my case, my entity home is my website, which you will also see in the SERP. That is the site that I am using (through the About page) to confirm the information about me and create consistency on the web. That is because of the tests that I am doing and how I have structured my information online.

If you have a corporate website, it will also help to have one page there with your name, some clear information about who you are, and the blog posts that you have written."

Can your LinkedIn profile act as your entity home, or is it always going to be more beneficial to have your own domain name?

"I actually found some interesting research about this recently. I was looking at the SERP for Aleyda Solis, and she has a Knowledge Panel. What I realised was that the information in that Knowledge Panel has been taken from LinkedIn. That shows how important your LinkedIn profile is. So, you should make sure you are putting together your profile really well, and being consistent within that profile.

However, I still think that Google needs to confirm all of the information that they have, no matter where they take it from. Having your own website - with your domain and your information inside - will be a place for Google to double-check what other people say on the web. They can ask, 'Is that correct? Okay, we can see it in your domain, and we can see it outside your domain as well.' They will be able to get confirmation of what you're saying."

What are the best first steps to start building your own personal brand online?

"What really helped me was to start speaking. Speak at some conferences, for example.

Twitter is also very helpful. My Twitter profile is the first result that you find when you search for my name, and I don't have a lot of followers. You don't need to have a huge profile on Twitter, particularly if it is very targeted. Like a lot of people in SEO, I tweet regularly and I interact a lot with people in the industry. Start with a consistent profile, then you can interact and use more of your social network in the right way, like using your LinkedIn profile as well.

Even better is if you can start speaking at webinars, conferences, and things like that. That will really help to build your own brand. It's about creating an understanding of who you are, across all the information about you on the web."

What shouldn't SEOs be doing in 2023? What's seductive in terms of time, but ultimately counterproductive?

"I often feel that SEOs are a bit too obsessive about Core Web Vitals. They are important, of course, but you shouldn't be spending hours and hours of your own time, and hours and hours of your developers' time, trying to arrive at a perfect score. Having less than 2.5 seconds for your Largest Contentful Paint is great, but it doesn't matter when you don't have any content or links.

Even if your Core Web Vitals are average, that's okay - especially if your competitors are not doing great."

Sara Moccand-Sayegh is an SEO Specialist over at Liip, and you can find her at liip.ch

Create video that ranks on Google—Dre de Vera

Dre De Vera highlights the importance of video for SEOs in 2023 who want to dominate page one in Google. He explains that it's now about more than just being at the top: it's about pixels on the page as well.

Dre says: "It's not that difficult. Being on page one is awesome, but owning more pixels on page one is even better. You can have your page one ranking with your blog, but when you have a video pop up you'll be taking up many more pixels on that page. You'll be taking up so much valuable real estate that's incredible to have. Also, if you optimise your videos correctly you can get the time stamps in there and get even more space. Dominating the pixels on page one will get you that click-through rate, authority, and expertise."

Regarding timestamps, does that mean taking a section of a video?

"You can actually do this with schema and stuff like that. You could also have YouTube do some auto-chapters that auto-segment content and pull those chapters. These will translate into the Google SERPS."

Is it essential to do this if you're serious about ranking videos on the SERPs?

"Yes, or at least have it turned on so Google can do auto-chapters. If you decide to turn this option off, make sure you add them in with some very keyword-rich headlines and timestamps."

Is there a certain type of video that Google prefers? Is there a favourable video length, answering question type, or certain style?

"There's definitely more of the answering question type. One thing you can do is look at the Google SERPs again and see if there is a video carousel on there. If there is, you'll have a much better chance to get your video ranking. If you see a little straggling video on the second or third page, do a video yourself and you'll pop up a carousel and have a great chance of ranking."

Does 'pop up a carousel' mean including your video alongside other videos as the answer to that question?

"If you do your research and see it's on there, then yes. When videos are long they have a better chance to rank. Fifteen minutes plus is a good target. You can also take your SEO-optimised blogs and convert them into scripts. Take the exact same content, put it on camera, and add everything to do with your video optimisations. Once you've done your high-quality video production and know how many words are on screen, you'll have a much better chance of getting a video and blog ranking on page one. You should also publish both pieces of content at the same time.

Sometimes it's a chicken and egg situation. Is the blog helping the video or is the video helping the blog? This is definitely worth checking out."

Should videos solely be produced to rank them on the SERP? Will you get just as much value from these videos also generating traffic directly on YouTube itself?

"It's definitely both. If you look at the video and it's not only ranking on Google, but within the top 5 of YouTube itself, that will indicate it's really helpful information people want to hear and see. This is something you can implement on your page as well, like the schema to actually make them pop up. It's more important than ever, especially as Google recently put the video index reports in Google Search Console. They are paying attention to which videos are being indexed in Search."

What format of video titles and descriptions would you recommend? Is keyword research also important?

"Keyword research is still important. You can do research for an SEO-optimised blog and see if Google can see that within your video. You should use your tool of choice for content optimisation, get your blog ranking, and then do that exact same thing within the video. This is working like gangbusters right now. The value of owning more real estate on YouTube or Google is extremely high."

What type of keywords works best for that? Are you talking about really long-tail keywords, informational queries, or others?

"You'll be ranking for regular keywords. For example, 'What is cloud infrastructure security?' When someone types 'cloud infrastructure security' you could be the blog and even the video ranking there. Sometimes, when the competition is higher (like with 'VPN alternative'), you could get both a video and blog ranking, only for them to eventually fade off. The SERPs fluctuate. The blog may always be there but the video will probably pop back in and out."

Where do you lie on zero-volume keywords and should you test trying to rank for zero-volume keywords to see if they bring any traffic to you?

"With zero trust long-tail terms, you can test these by scheduling live video on YouTube. Google loves showing these lives instantly on SERPs. If it's long-tail enough, it will pop up there. If you just want to test something out to see if it will show up, do that first. Schedule a live video on YouTube and see if it shows in the results. This is a great way to see whether you can use video to take up more real estate. For the most part, you should go all in. When you see a keyword you're going after, your strategy should be to make sure you have a video to complement it."

YouTube wants you to build up a certain amount of history on a channel for it to recommend your videos to other people. Is this same sort of history and authority important for ranking videos on the SERP?

"Yes. Your account has to be strong enough to display on SERPs. One of the things you can do is tie your videos in with another piece of content. When you do that, you can include videos within your press releases for massive distributions. This is a valuable approach because ranking on Google and getting backlinks to your YouTube videos counts too."

Is there a particular niche that this works best for? Is it B2B or is it just any type of business that can take advantage of this?

"B2B, but you can even apply this advice to personal branding and testing. It may be something that any company or industry can work with. It's more for very educational queries - for people looking for an answer and it comes up. Google can see the content within each video and just pulls it out, ready to serve you up. Timestamps are very important because you'll be helping Google even more.

Does Google want people to view an embedded video on the SERP or click through and actually land on YouTube? What's the ultimate goal here?

"The ultimate goal is to take up more real estate so Google can define you as a brand builder. If your blog doesn't stick out on page one, they're going to see your video. One component of SEO that runs even deeper into 2023 is short-form vertical videos. Google is already indexing TikTok videos on SERPs. It's being tested and it's likely to become bigger and bigger. Even now, the Shorts algorithm within YouTube has been promoted by Google. You can easily garner millions of views posting Shorts, and this will eventually start trickling into the Google SERPs."

Are you saying that it's actually possible to incorporate videos from sites other than YouTube?

"We're seeing this already. You can search for some of your favourite TikTok influencers on Google and their videos show up as a TikTok carousel there.

Every company is becoming a media company. People are trying to put up more videos. The way to optimise content to make sure you have more visibility is by getting it on Google. Upload your video wherever you can, whether it's on TikTok, Twitter, LinkedIn, or Facebook. You can then at least see your videos from other channels on the video tab and have your actual pages show up there. YouTube will give more benefits to ranking your video on page one of Google, but you can still use better videos to have your own page rank with it."

Should every brand be on TikTok?

"Yes, but it depends on your business. If your crowd is there, then it's worth experimenting with it. Lots of companies use Instagram as a place for company culture and stuff like that. If you want to get noticed, use video."

What kind of ROI can you measure from video content?

"Be sure to use your UTM tagging. Tag your URLs. When some influencers post YouTube videos, you could even get leads just from people clicking links in the descriptions. You could see them coming in because of the UTM parameters there.

Companies should start building. Content creation is huge; we have a huge content economy and more B2B businesses are going to hire content creators going forward. When it comes to content creation, there's a certain style that can generate connections between potential customers. Your content should build relationships with people."

Should you include lots of relevant call-to-action links within the description of your videos and have UTM parameters on there so you can track whether people will click on those links?

"Yes. When you hire influencers and they ask their audience to click the link below, they'll generally click the link below. You'll see leads come in from their particular channel just from a UTM-tagged URL."

What shouldn't SEOs be doing in 2023? What's seductive in terms of time, but ultimately counterproductive?

"SEOs shouldn't be leaving out no-search-volume keywords. You'll be missing out on opportunities if you do. Use industry research from companies like Gartner or Forrester, see the terms they're using, and go after them. By the time the industry has caught on, you'll already be on page one. That's one way to go after zero-term query words.

Alternatively, you can go for other zero-term keywords where you see impressions on the Google Search Console. If you're getting a bunch of impressions there and you're on page two, you could miss out on an opportunity just because third-party tools said they're zero. Use your first-party data effectively. Talk to people internally, talk to customer service teams, and talk to customers."

Dre De Vera is Head of Growth at Twingate and host/producer of the SEO Video Show. You can find him over at dre.me.

Use technical SEO to control your website performance on Google—Kristina Azarenko

Kristina Azarenko believes that SEOs in 2023 should definitely make sure that their pages are indexed and visible to Google but, equally, you should avoid creating content just for SEO rather than users.

Kristina says: "You should ensure that Google can see and index the content you're putting out there on your website."

How big a problem is this? Are there people publishing content like blog posts and not even realizing that Google isn't indexing them?

"Today, there is much more JavaScript used on websites than we used to have. Now, people know that Google can understand JavaScript - which is true, but only if you make it understandable to Google.

For example, let's talk about the content. Sometimes people invest a lot of energy and money in creating content without making sure that Google can actually index it. If Google can't index it, then it can't rank it. And if it's not ranking, you're wasting money and time instead of working on being found and generating more leads."

What are some typical reasons why Google may not be indexing content? Is it not having internal links to a page or is it JavaScript-powered sections of a page?

"One of the reasons might be the quantities involved. You might have just a couple of paragraphs or sentences on the page, which is not enough for it to stand out in the search results. However, if you have good and thought-out content created by good writers, the problem can revolve around Javascript issues. That is especially the case if you're using single-page applications or if there are recent changes on your pages that don't allow them to be indexed appropriately.

Another thing would be website structure and internal linking. A website is an organism, and every part of it should be connected. Every time you add a new page to the website, you should have a process for how to integrate it. You must ensure that your entire website is accessible and that all the content you want Google to see is in the rendered HTML."

Is there software you recommend for identifying pages that are no longer indexed or pages that aren't as crawlable as they should be?

"Google Search Console is one of the best tools you can use because it gives you first-hand information. You can see how many resources are spent on HTML requests versus JavaScript, and you can also see any changes in your pages, rankings, and impressions on Google. It shows you what pages are discovered but not indexed, or crawled but not indexed.

Another tool would be Screaming Frog because it can show you how much of the content is text-based vs JavaScript-based."

Is there any particular alert you recommend setting up within Google Search Console to know when something goes wrong?

"Google Search Console sends many alerts, but not all of them need your attention - especially mobile-friendly ones. So, it could also be safer to use Content King for that. You can also do the same in Google Analytics every time a page undergoes significant changes.

How can you use technical SEO to control your website performance on Google?

"There are three pillars of technical SEO. First, there are pages that you want Google to index. Secondly, there are pages you don't want to be indexed or crawled by Google. And the third is basically about page experience. As a technical SEO, you have to have control over each stage.

If you identify the most important pages and want them to be indexed and crawled, you must ensure that they are not disallowed in robots.txt. Internal linking should also be properly set up and, generally, these pages have priority on the website. Google also considers whether there is an XML sitemap with the correct tags, like 'last modified'. These things will help you ensure that your website is up properly, you actually benefit, and you see those benefits much quicker from the content you're creating."

How do you decide which content to revise to make sure you are delivering a unique, distinctive, and high-quality user experience?

"It depends on the percentage of the entire site that needs to be revisited. For example, if a website has, say, 80% of the website outdated, then it could be a big issue. If they're just a couple of pages, then maybe it's not a priority.

The next thing would be to decide if there are pages you need to remove, but this can come with several options. Some can be improved, and others merged. You just need to make sure that the old pages have external links pointing to them.

Generally, it is a whole large project, and you want to ensure you understand the process before making serious decisions about removing pages."

If you see a negative impact after a migration, how do you identify which technical changes might have had the most significant effect on rankings?

"Usually, the best way is to queue the changes and not make them all at once. For example: don't change the domain at the same time as the website structure or any redesigns. That way, it will be much easier to see what worked and what didn't, and then fix it. It is common for seemingly minor issues to cause a great decrease in traffic and rankings.

Then, if everything is right but there is still a decrease, Google needs more time to review and re-evaluate the website. It is quite easy for Google to pick up all those clues and changes on your website, so it definitely needs more time.

Finally, you need to understand that any migration involves some risk. The more changes you make, the more risks there are. It's unrealistic to expect results in the early stages. Even if everything is in order, it does not guarantee that there will not be temporary decreases in traffic, because you can't control it fully."

What shouldn't SEOs be doing in 2023? What is seductive in terms of time, but ultimately counterproductive?

"Stop doing things purely for SEO. In most cases, this would be creating the so-called 'SEO content' - which is the type of content that is written only for rankings rather than for helping users by providing valuable information. We all know about the helpful content update, and how it is easy to get caught up doing multiple optimisations while missing the full picture of what your users actually need.

Overall, it should still be all about the users and finding ways to serve them better. SEOs need to zoom out and focus on the bigger picture. Remember that SEO is only one avenue of bringing the right people who can convert to the website. Therefore, it needs to align with all other strategies, as well as the actual experience of your users."

Kristina Azarenko is a Founder at MarketingSyrup SEO Academy, and you can find her over at techseo.pro.

9 USER-CENTRICITY

Focus on users—Filipa Serra Gaspar

Filipa Serra Gaspar stresses the importance of focusing on the user experience as an SEO in 2023, and keeping your audience as the central point of everything that you are doing on your site.

Filipa says: "Creating content with the user experience in mind will increase engagement significantly. You should write content for users, focus on the UX, and have them at the centre of everything you do."

Why is it an SEO's job to focus on UX?

"SEO and UX go hand in hand. They are obviously two different things, but to have a great SEO-performing website you must create a good UX. The user experience will be negated if your website isn't designed with them in mind."

Is it possible to directly measure the impact that UX has on SEO?

"Yes and no. You can see how the website performs and use heat maps which are correlated to show what users do on your page. Let's say you're just focusing on keywords, and that's getting people to land on your page. If your visitors are not doing much when they reach your website that will tell a story. If they go back to the SERP straight away and don't do much on your site, that can send signals back to Google."

What does having content written by people, for people, mean to you?

"Sometimes content is written with consideration to search engines - particularly how they'll find it, read it, and so on. In the wake of the helpful content update, it's really important for the user to be the focus. If the user isn't happy, then the search engine won't be either. Search engines are developing significantly in their ability to look at websites in the same way that users do."

How do we judge the happiness of our users?

"We should start by answering their questions. If a user enters a website looking for something, they should find the answer - and preferably promptly. In terms of measuring satisfaction, the bounce rate is good and bad. It's a metric of how long a user stays on a page, but this isn't as helpful to know in today's times.

Bounce rate is vulnerable, but it can be good for comparing like-for-like pages. It's a useful initial indicator and can work if you have two blog posts targeting different keywords. Let's say one gets a bounce rate of 30% and the other 50%. You could use this information to work out whether there's something different you're doing on those pages, or about the users you're attracting to those pages."

How do you decide on the question and the phraseology within that question?

"You can look back at old keyword research to find out what users are looking for and the intent behind their searches. When someone searches for something specific, you should assess the intent behind the keywords they're using."

Should you establish the intent yourself or rely on a software tool to tell you what the likely intent is?

"You should search yourself and see what comes up. Why? Sometimes different users will search for the exact same keyword when they're looking for something different. Try to find out what the majority are looking for while appreciating there are always variations. You can answer different questions at the same time.

Regarding how your content is shown, it helps to open a page to see how it looks from an SEO perspective. Focus on visual appeal and the user experience in general. Make sure the information you present is clear and easy to find. This will ensure users are satisfied when they visit and find exactly what they're looking for. If a user is interested, they'll keep looking and stay longer - but your content should always be objective."

What happens if you do a good job of answering the user question within the first paragraph, the user is satisfied, but they only spend ten seconds on your site and then leave? Would that be a negative signal?

"This is very tricky. Let's say you've done so well at answering a question that Google shows your answer on the SERP. In this case, the user would never actually get into your website. However, we're advised to encourage the user to keep looking, and to keep reading. You should answer the question they've asked but promote and incentivize them to learn about another topic you're sharing within the same piece of content.

Make your website feel like a trustworthy source, so that when a user has a question in future they'll come back to you for more answers. If they trust your information they'll be back."

Can a client benefit from Google taking your answer and using it directly on their SERP or is this just bad for SEO?

"Well, it would definitely mean you're doing SEO right and that the website is optimised and well-functioning. It can be good if someone finds the basic information on the SERP and has a desire to learn more. If so, they'll explore further and develop trust in the source. However, if someone has a basic question answered on the SERP and doesn't need to know anything else, being featured would be less beneficial. In the end, if your website is not showing up there, someone else's website will.

If the reader has more information to uncover then having the SERP listing would provide greater exposure."

What are your thoughts on where SEO intersects with CRM or capturing someone's data? When is the right time to do this?

"If it's eCommerce, visitors are often immediately asked to sign up for a newsletter for a special discount. When information pops up straight away and says 'Subscribe!', that's probably not a good indicator. The user should be on the page for some time before they're asked.

Sometimes, CRM interests clash with SEO interests - where it's hard to satisfy differing interests within the same website. It's best to avoid showing information straight away because that can be a bit too aggressive and even bad for SEO metrics. It can be a fight between people wanting leads and people wanting to stay on your website as long as possible. This could represent an SEO metric where the conversion is the newsletter subscription. It varies a lot in the end, because it all depends on the website you're working on."

What shouldn't SEOs be doing in 2023? What's seductive in terms of time, but ultimately counterproductive?

"Perhaps avoid AI content, themed content, and anything that's not specifically thinking about the user. The main action for 2023 is to always ensure the user is happy. I am not gonna deny that AI works in some specific cases and it really depends on the goal of your website and so many other things, but I still wouldn't recommend it for an E-Commerce, for example."

Is it acceptable to experiment with AI content on pages that are low traffic and perhaps not converting?

"Yes. There are even cases where people populate entire websites with AI-generated content and it manages to get good SEO traffic. I would say that AI is best avoided, but in SEO it always varies because there are no rules.

The most famous SEO phrase of all is 'it depends.' AI can get results but it could work less and less well over the years, or it could start working better and better. Who knows? AI is getting smarter, so maybe content could be written by AI but seem like it's been written by a specialist. We have an uncertain future ahead of us."

Filipa Serra Gaspar is an SEO Consultant and you can find her at seolipa.com

Create a user-centric strategy—Maria White

Maria White promotes the value of user-centricity to SEOs in 2023 and helps you to understand how to target your strategy to please the right users in the right way.

Maria says: "You should continue to focus your SEO strategy on users. This is said from the perspective of working in-house for one of the largest fashion brands in the world.

If you work in a similar niche, no matter the size of the brand, you should focus your SEO strategy so it's user-centric and not overspecialise or hone in on just one element within the SEO strategy."

If you're looking to identify the right users, how do you go about identifying where they are within their shopping journey?

"You could discover this via a virtual machine and lots of research; you could use several sources of rich research to determine who your customers are so that you can better attract them. You can also use analysis from brands - performing big analyses on where your customers lie based on engagement and several sources of data.

In terms of SEO, you should look at Google Analytics, data from physical stores, the conversion ratio of people who walk into a store, and the characteristics of those people. You can look at several sources to be able to determine the type of customer that likes to buy a product.

Look at the data you get from Google Analytics and paid teams. You can also include the data you get from physical stores. This is a great way to find out who your customer is and work out how they consume content and from which platforms."

What software can you use to identify where they consume content at the start of their journey?

"When you've found out who your consumer is, it's not easy to use Google Analytics to find out where they come from. If you're a large enterprise brand you can use an agency like Kantar that focuses on research and tells you the types of audiences that tend to consume a type of content from a given platform.

For example, you might find that it's TikTok or Instagram, WeChat in China, or perhaps Mercado Libre in Mexico. If you're able to find out where your content is consumed for entertainment then you can get an idea of where prospective customers are likely to start a shopping journey. If you discover they consume most of their content on Instagram, there's a good chance they'll start their shopping journey on Instagram."

Regarding Instagram, what are you trying to influence that impacts your SEO? Are you hoping to increase brand awareness via Instagram in the hope they then search for a product on Google?

"This is very interesting. Paid teams can focus their efforts on attracting relevant consumers from their current location. They would start the campaigns in various places, including Instagram, TikTok, Google Ads, etc. You could then see the engagement with the ads and perhaps how some people don't convert when they engage with the ads.

Sometimes there's a correlation with direct searches when you launch a campaign - it could be a strong digital PR campaign that involves national press or a very aggressive paid media campaign. There might also be evidence to suggest a correlation between consumers engaging with ads but not converting and going back to Google. They might then search for the brand separately and convert. In this case, it would be like the ad has worked as a source of influence for the consumer to then return to the transaction in Google."

So you're using SEO as a retargeting channel?

"In a way, but more in terms of how brand SEO works closely with paid media, PR, and engineering. My team sits right in the middle of all of those monsters. For paid media, we do use SEO as a retargeting strategy.

Another thing that worked very interestingly was creating campaigns for a Mexican audience in Mexican Spanish, which isn't the same as local Spanish. Localisation is important. Consider Portuguese and Brazilian. When checking the translations for the Mexican audience, you'd think about tweaking and optimising here and there. When we ran these experiments in Mexico with Mexican Spanish and optimised different aspects, we noticed a hugely significant impact on direct. It's interesting. As a campaign succeeds on paid media there can also be a spike in direct searches."

Is it about identifying the keywords that are a little bit different in Mexican Spanish or is it about the whole phraseology being more targeted on the whole web page?

"It's not just about localisation and translation. You can run an experiment where you use popular search terms on the ads, being super careful not to use keyword stuff. When you use popular search terms and phrases in the context of paid media, there can be a significant spike in direct searches as well. That's where SEO works with paid media for a large brand.

You should focus on significantly improving the user experience. Last year, in June/July 2021 there were some significant changes in Google. There were changes in consumer behaviour too, where people started to go back to work in the aftermath of the pandemic. This had a big impact on consumerism as people were spending less time on-screen and buying. Traffic and rankings were healthy, but revenue was down a bit. Also, we had a platform migration that affected rankings and organic. This year, one of the biggest things you could focus on is Core Web Vitals. Work with the engineering team to monitor changes that you can test on the SERP for a group. You can then monitor the Core Web Vitals when you deploy changes in that group of pages. You can then deploy them across the entire website and the whole brand.

As you might notice, we went from SEO working with paid media to SEO working with engineering and PR. Don't overspecialise and keep focusing your SEO strategy on the ways your consumers like to read, consume, and engage with content. Provide a good experience rather than going for keywords."

Regarding conventional areas of SEO, like ranking generic keyword phrases in Google search, is that not important for you anymore?

"It is. Let's say someone is looking for a specific type of boots and walks into a store but thinks, 'I'm not going to spend $100 right now.' They go back home and start looking around for that pair of boots and enter 'women's boots Nike'. They'd either get results from a third-party retailer or the Nike website itself. If there was an issue, or the product was out of stock on the Nike website, one of Nike's concessions could rank and the seller could go to them instead. When you work for a big brand you'll be close to number one for every single keyword among branded and non-branded terms."

Is it not just about getting the sale, then, but getting the sale in the right place?

"Yes. You could fluctuate from position one to three and that could mean that another one of your websites is ranking first for some reason. Maybe your competitors show first at a given moment. What are you doing about this?

Strategy is looking at this. Looking at how the numbers are different for specific products, or perhaps removing one brand and a specific model and making it available on just one website. Maybe that's what we're moving toward rather than just having the same product available everywhere."

Does an SEO need to be aware of the overall business, profit margins, and different products and where they'd prefer to make the sale from?

"That is reflected in budgets. Obviously, if you make more money on one brand you're going to have more and more budget than you would be spending on other brands.

Something very interesting that we learnt this year was that when a product is out of stock and someone searches for it, your concessions can easily go up to number one. Then the client could go there and buy it, which is still revenue because it's a concession. We sell products via concessions like Harrods, John Lewis, etc. Rankings are important when a concession brand is similar to the brand you're working for. Rankings are important, but you need to make sure you're not losing ranking against concessions or your own brands."

What shouldn't SEOs be doing in 2023? What's seductive in terms of time, but ultimately counterproductive?

"Overspecialisation, and just focusing on one topic. We've all been guilty of that in the past. If we've nailed one topic when we want to write about it, talk about it, carry on, and suddenly it's been a year and we've only focused on one thing because that's the one we want to dominate in.

Overspecialistion is not good. If there is a young new SEO reading this - in the early years you should focus on one channel first and build it up from there. As you gain experience you can become more of an all-rounder. Focus on being a digital PR and not a content strategist or technical SEO because that won't be sustainable. If you start as a digital PR, you'll progress to content strategy and then technical SEO and so on.

As you advance in your career and you're in a job where you move from department to department, you'll need to be able to explain the effects of everyone's work in SEO. You'll finally be able to specialise when the time is right. If you tried to do this from the outset, it wouldn't be sustainable, nor good for your mental health. Be cognizant of the classic saying: Jack of all trades, master of none."

Maria White is the Head of SEO at Kurt Geiger and you can find her @Maria_Amelie on Twitter.

Quality and user experience will rule in 2023— Pedro Dias.

Pedro Dias believes that your focus as an SEO in 2023 should be on enhancing the user experience and the quality of your content because these are Google's main priorities.

Pedro says: "Given the recent Google updates, it would help to be selective regarding the quality of what you put out. SEOs will scrutinise the kind of pages they put out and place less emphasis on the technical side than the qualitative side of things. And this pairs up nicely with past conversations around UX.

For instance, looking at Peter Marvel's UX Honeycomb, you'll see value at the centre, surrounded by all the other disciplines - like usability, fungibility, and desirability. To be able to create value, you need to hit all of those areas; otherwise, you will leave stuff on the table. That's where SEOs should focus and start to explore areas within the UX realm."

What does it mean to be selective with pages? Does that mean you shouldn't publish a page unless it's absolutely necessary?

"You should be more mindful before you create pages. Ensure that what you want to put on those pages is valuable and helpful to some extent, because Google is hinting that that's what they want, and they're being selective on what they index.

In the early days of SEO, we were more engulfed in discoverability because the web was very new, and websites were less accessible. We were using technologies that wouldn't obey conventions. Now we have more widespread use of good technologies because we know that some things should abide by certain criteria for development. It's hard to launch a website today that is not minimally optimised in some way, which wasn't the case in the old days. Then, you would just launch a website and worry about if you will be findable afterwards.

Nowadays, you launch a website, and it's already half-baked into what you need to do. Because of this, search engines can become pickier regarding what they select to be indexed and ranked. Before, search engines would crawl everything and have varying indexes for different things.

We are turning to a stage where search engines can just choose not to index something because they know it won't be helpful for anyone. You need to be much more mindful about investing money and effort in purchasing or producing something worthy of being crawled and indexed. That way, it can guarantee some value for the business. Basically, that's going to be where SEOs should focus and switch their minds to the more qualitative side of things, such as overall value."

Is the difference between you and a competitor now about your content rather than something like a plugin that provides slightly enhanced SEO?

"You can already see that if you look at WordPress. Even if you install WordPress without any plugins, you can easily have friendly URLs, which was hard to do in the old days. You'd have to do rewrites on your server and configure several things to get those friendly URLs. As technologies progress, WordPress has Sitemaps built-in already, and you almost don't need a plugin to generate them anymore. They are tearing down the technical hurdles. Google has said that they always prefer something that's qualitatively better over something that's technically correct. Otherwise, there would be a lot of spam.

It's still possible to exploit some holes in Google's algorithms, but not as much as in the old days. This change should drive SEO minds to think more critically about their sites and check whether they need to add more value to them. Plus, it's not necessarily about more text but about helping the user - because every page on the website should fulfil a purpose. Otherwise, it would still fall short, no matter how technically sound it is."

How do we measure if the page helps the user?

"Another thing that SEOs will be discovering is that you should not look as much at chasing algorithms. Instead, you should speak to your user base more about it. We see this with a lot of big companies that have UX teams. The teams usually have people who do UX studies, look at the user journey, and then think about other user experiences.

Then there are those who do UX research and interview other people. They try to find out what the website lacks, the ease of navigation, which one is preferable, etc. You should try to team up with UX research folks to try and understand your users more and define what they want.

Sometimes, you might want to launch a website and assume many things about consumers. You assume they have similar cultures and that they will automatically understand and relate to what you are putting out. You need to be more conscious of your audience in order to actually know whether they are happy or not."

Think of yourself as a business and narrow down the specific goals you want your users to accomplish with your business. For example, if you are a bank or a credit card business, you want your users to be able to distinguish the benefits of the credit lines or cards you're offering. Therefore, you need to understand how literate that audience is regarding credit. The main goal here is to assess the knowledge of your users and put out the content accordingly.

SEOs often make a mistake by trying to create large chunks of 'complete content'. You create over 7,000 words on a topic, yet sometimes the user just wants a small piece of information. Now you have a whole page with a lot of fluff the user doesn't need, and they have to dig around the whole thing to find what they are looking for. It should be all about delivering to the user what they want."

Are usability and UX interchangeable? What's the difference between the two?

"Usability is within UX, while UX oversees everything. UX is how users experience something and the perception that they have overall. On the other hand, usability is how easy it is to use your website: how pretty or how valuable and desirable it is. UX is a much broader area that exists even outside the digital world.

Usability is more about defining how usable your website is. For instance, if someone comes to your page, would they automatically identify the drop box, the menu, the drop-down, etc.? Would they complete and submit the form without overthinking? Usability is a more a much more tangible thing. One could say that usability is a tactic, and UX is a strategy."

What shouldn't SEOs be doing in 2023? What is seductive in terms of time, but ultimately counterproductive?

"Stop worrying too much about how long your website content is and assuming that a high word count is the most useful element. All these misconceptions stem from chasing Google algorithms, which can be counterproductive and time-wasting.

Every time you go on Twitter, you'll see a tweet about how Google's algorithms are working now, and analyses on how things should be done. It keeps you from doing the obvious. You already know where Google is heading: it's the happiness of your users. If you speak to your users instead of chasing Google, you'll be in a much better position because you will be on par with what Google is after.

Not to say that you should switch your SEO mindset off. By all means, keep yourself informed. Just don't go overboard and spend most of your time over-analysing Google algorithms instead of speaking to your users and tapping into all these UX areas that will be much more helpful."

Pedro Dias is the owner of Visively Ltd, and currently Technical SEO Consultant at eBay. You can find him over at visively.com.

Prioritise the user experience—Grace Wei Hou

Grace Wei Hou recommends that SEOs in 2023 put the experience of your users first when putting together your SEO strategy, to please Google, encourage effective conversions, and ensure that you are achieving profitable growth.

Grace says: "This is a very exciting question. My number one SEO tip for 2023 is to prioritise the user experience in your SEO strategy, and there are two main reasons for this. The first reason is that Google has been focusing on the searcher experience, which is reflected in its core algorithm updates, new features, and new products - including PageSpeed, Core Web Vitals, product reviews, and the most recent helpful content update. These are all about delivering the best page experience, or user experience, to searchers - and this trend will continue in 2023.

The second reason is that, given the current economic climate, businesses have shifted towards profitable growth rather than growth at any cost. Turning traffic into conversions and achieving a higher customer lifetime value has become more important than ever. It's not just in SEO, it's in every other marketing channel as well, and user experience is a key component in achieving profitable growth."

What does prioritising user experience look like when you're putting your SEO strategy together?

"Conventionally, when we plan an SEO strategy, we tend to look at the three aspects of SEO: technical, on-page and off-page.

However, I want to recommend some tactics that I think all SEOs should consider testing out. The first one is very simple but very powerful: communicate with your users and ask for feedback. Let the users tell you what they like and what they dislike on your site. Then you would understand, in a straightforward way, what you should continue doing and what you should stop doing or improve."

What is the best way to communicate with users? Can it be done virtually, or should it happen in person?

"This kind of communication can be done through direct user research, such as interviews and surveys. I've used both methods and they are very helpful.

In addition, there are a lot of insights that can be discovered by talking to the customer-facing team, i.e., the sales and customer service team. All of these methods of communication are very effective, based on my experience."

When you are carrying out direct user research, how do you decide what questions to ask your customers? What kind of format do those conversations have?

"Probably I could share a user interview experience that I have had. Recently, we've started to optimise and localise an English eCommerce site for a different country – in a different language. Luckily, we've received some immediate traffic and conversions from the target market. This made us interested in communicating directly with the real customers on that site.

Before having those conversations, my user experience designer and I discussed the goal of this interview, and what we mostly wanted to get from this direct communication. We also wanted to make sure that we asked the right questions and that we could implement the feedback we got from the customers with our bandwidth.

Once we had determined the interview goals and scope, we introduced those questions in the flow of a natural conversation with the users."

What kind of goals did you have for those interviews?

"One of our goals was to understand the impact of content localisation primarily powered by AI translation on the eCommerce site. I asked customers what they thought about the product descriptions on the localised version of the website. They gave us some of the most important feedback to help us shape our strategy and prioritise tasks.

One user said that it looked like the content on the product description page had been translated by a machine from the original English content. They could understand every word, but the content didn't help them in the conversion process. The customer actually had to rely on the product description on a third-party local eCommerce platform that was selling the same product to learn more. It was mainly the price that attracted them to convert on the brand's eCommerce site. Such feedback is so valuable to us."

How do you respond to marketing directors that believe the role of the SEO team is to focus on links and the technical health of the website, and not on conversion rate?

"If a director said this a few years ago it might have been valid, but the world of SEO and the whole digital marketing industry is evolving. Now, conversion has become an objective for every marketing channel.

Why would Google want to send traffic to a website that doesn't have a good user experience, where the users are disappointed and there are no conversions?

There is a strong trend out there: Google wants all websites to provide a first-class user experience. A user-centric SEO strategy will delight both users and Google, and conversions will follow.

In a nutshell, the goal of SEO team should be in line with the goal of the business. And we all understand conversion is one of the most important success factors for a sustainable business.

Is conversion rate the best way to measure a positive impact on user experience or are there other metrics that you also look at?

"In terms of the success of user experience, from an SEO perspective, there are two ways that you can measure: quantitative and qualitative. For your quantitative measurement, you can look at the metrics in your analytics tools, such as organic conversion rate, bounce rate, session time, returning users, etc.

Your qualitative measurement can be done through user surveys, customer reviews & feedback, and direct conversations that you have – where, after three to six months, you revisit the users you have interviewed before and ask the same questions again to see the difference. I believe these measurements are super important now. SEO is no longer just about getting a lot of traffic, but knowing whether you are getting effective conversions."

How is user experience going to evolve? Are there any other aspects of user experience that Google will focus more closely on in the future?

"Of course, Google has rolled out the helpful content update recently and this is an ongoing effort from them: to reduce low-quality content and to make it easier and easier for users to find content that is authentic and useful to them through search. Google wants us to focus on people rather than search engines.

Another aspect of user experience I would emphasize is you've got to make sure that your site is loading fast. Ideally, you want it to load within three seconds - or two seconds if it's an eCommerce site. Reports show that 40% of consumers will wait no more than three seconds before they abandon a site. It's very, very expensive to have a slow site, and it costs retailers around $2.6 billion a year in lost sales.

Monitor and test your page speed regularly. This will help you to discover and fix loading issues, such as unnecessary scripts, images that are too large to load, and redirects that slow down the loading speed."

What does Google mean by authentic content?

"One thing that many SEOs do is copy the content of their competitors and try to optimise it and outrank on keywords against those competitors. This kind of content is not authentic, because the drive behind it is primarily about gaining impressions and keyword rankings.

Authentic content should primarily address the user's needs and pain points. It should solve a problem they have, instead of working for rankings and traffic.

Google's AI technology is only getting smarter. They are using AI to decide what to rank, while some content creators use AI to generate content. It will be very interesting to see how these compete with each other over the next 12 months."

What shouldn't SEOs be doing in 2023? What's seductive in terms of time, but ultimately counterproductive?

"Linked to what I've just said, I think SEOs should stop creating content that is primarily driven by impressions and keyword rankings, instead of addressing people's needs and pain points.

A great tip for creating helpful content is to ask questions from the user's perspective, and put yourself in their shoes to understand what problem they want to solve exactly from the content you create."

Grace Wei Hou is a Growth Product Manager at Samarkand Global, and you can find her by searching 'Grace Wei Hou' on LinkedIn.

User experience should always be the top consideration in all aspects of your strategy—Sophie Brannon

Sophie Brannon believes that SEO in 2023 should be all about making the user experience as smooth and streamlined as possible, particularly in regard to visual elements and the arrival of multimodal search - which is just around the corner.

Sophie says: "You should streamline the user experience for video content and images across multiple forms of searching - at every touchpoint of the user journey.

It's all about the users and satisfying their intent in the quickest and easiest way. With the goal of achieving this, UX and SEO will be more combined than ever going forward. Visuals will be hugely important for eCommerce sites. With the multimodal search on the horizon, images and image quality will be even more significant. They need to be a high resolution without impacting site speed. They must also be properly optimised, have proper alt text, attributes, title text and be visible on multiple devices and screen sizes. A lot of websites are struggling with this at the moment, but it's going to play a really big part in picking up traffic across different types of searches.

There's lots of speculation about the next generation of searchers and their preferred methods for accessing content. They'll probably want to access information quickly and easily without reading through reams and reams of content. TikTok has even suggested expanding its services into a search engine capacity.

With the help of Google Lens, multimodal search is going to be a big player going forward. Since Google Lens was introduced, we've seen some interesting developments. The helpful content update that recently rolled out could have an impact on sites that have lots of content which isn't particularly helpful. Perhaps, going forward, an image or video could be more helpful in explaining a particular subject. Everything will need to work in close collaboration and the user experience is going to be a big part of that."

Regarding multimodal search, can you clarify what that means for SEO?

"Multimodal search is more around the way searchers are searching for things using multiple platforms and new technologies. The whole purpose of Google Lens is to take a picture of something and derive search results for your query. You can then assess information about that particular thing, go shopping for it, see videos around it, and learn lots of other things pertaining to that image."

Let's say you have an eCommerce store and you want to optimise for more progressive forms of search. How could you optimise your existing content and future-proof the way your results appear in search engines?

"Going back to the basics is really important. There's not that much information about whether there's a particular way to optimise for multimodal search. You should focus on doing certain things in order to be visible, but ensure your images are of the highest quality. If you've taken a picture of something, your image should be shown and be one of the most visible. You should make sure that it loads quickly and on multiple devices. Images are often displayed inaccurately, which is something that's influenced by what devices the images are viewed on. In these cases, the consumer won't be able to see what they're trying to purchase.

Rein your approach back and focus more on the user-friendly side of things. Be on top of the latest developments, and be experimental with what you're doing. Make sure your alt text and title texts are really well optimised for the types of things people might be searching for. Try not to go overboard with it. You'll need to do lots of experimentation over the coming months and years before you'll get a true appreciation of what you need to be doing. The basics will always apply."

Is it best to use a CMS that will automatically create images in multiple sizes, optimised for different platforms, and send different versions to different devices?

"That's certainly one way to do it. It's really important to do more of a manual test as well. You can't always just rely on automation and lots of CDN platforms. Cloudflare will work well to import, export, and show images in certain formats and sizes depending on the device it's viewed on. Make sure the original image is of really high quality without impacting site speed. That doesn't mean simply getting loads of high-resolution images across all sites. This could cause everything to slow down to the point where people can't access your site. It's all about striking the right balance."

How would you define a high-resolution image based on pixel size?

"It's difficult to state exact numbers, but numbers aren't always everything. It'll be about how the image displays. It's about testing and experimenting. Test and test again until you find the right outcome. See what people like and see what you can do to make sure things don't slow down."

How do you optimise video for better UX and how does that improve your SEO?

"That's a really interesting question that's developing with the multimodal search and everything around that. A lot of the time, the way SEOs approach SEO is by writing reams and reams of content. Hopefully, the helpful content update will have an impact on that and prevent people from pushing out lots of content for the sake of it.

There's lots of research to show that people interact well with video. In many cases, a video can show more to the user and be more aligned with the search intent. The way you'd look to optimise a video is around the descriptions, whether you're uploading it to YouTube or embedding it into your website. Make sure that it's tagged correctly with all the information Google needs for the new Search Console report that's started to roll out and pick up whether videos are being indexed or not.

Video will be important and Google will be paying a lot more attention to them. In fact, you can observe this in the search results already. Whenever you enter a search query you don't really get 10 URLs anymore. You get images, carousels, social media posts, featured snippets, Knowledge Panels, etc. Being aware of all these things – of what's ranking and how it's ranking - means you can direct your strategy around that. Users are generally interacting very well with video. This shouldn't be disregarded just because you feel like Google can't read video. If it's good for the users, Google will start to prioritise it."

Is it worth having self-hosted video nowadays or is YouTube the all-encompassing beast you need to embrace going forward? Will using YouTube videos help you get organic traffic from YouTube itself?

"YouTube is always going to be a big player in the market. The way search results are at the moment, you can see Google does prioritise YouTube. But there's also that site speed factor to consider. If you're embedding videos, that will have less of an impact on your site speed than hosting the actual video on that page.

It's all about that testing side of things, to make sure you're learning from your experimentation. You can see what works better, what engages the audience in a faster way, etc. Make sure your user is able to get the information they need as quickly as possible.

As experienced SEOs, we can give all the tips in the world. We can establish what we know works or have seen work with clients. However, every website is different and every audience is different. Take what you feel will work based on the knowledge of your audience and just try things out. This is a recommended approach to SEO in 2023.

Optimising performance is a matter of trial and error. Some things will work, and others won't. We can see the direction that Google's going in with multimodal, which is why you should have lots of different types of multimedia on your site. We are moving towards a strong user experience more than stuffing some keywords in a piece of content. Try out all the different ways you feel you can satisfy your user's intent and what your users are going to best engage with. This is the best way to approach any kind of strategy."

What is Google looking for in written content and how do you deliver great UX through written content?

"The way people write content and Google's understanding of good quality content has evolved over time. The landscape has changed, but many people haven't evolved with the times. People are still producing keyword-spammy content - especially small businesses with location pages. It's not as easy as inserting terms regularly within your content and assuming Google will like it because your site is well-optimised. That's not really how things work anymore. You should always go back to user intent. It's all about knowing a topic and being an expert on that topic. The EAT guidelines are not a ranking factor, but they are a great indication of what Google sees as good quality content within the search quality rater guidelines.

It's important to have really comprehensive content around a subject that's both relevant to what you're offering and engages users. Make sure you've got strong authorship and people who are writing/checking that content off. Ensure that whoever your content will be associated with, it's going to be a strong signal. If you're in a content-focused industry heavily impacted by big algorithm updates, you'll need to showcase your expertise even further.

Ensure you're not just writing a certain number of words simply because an SEO told you to. Avoid having a big chunk of content at the top of your eCommerce page category, so people can't find the product they're looking for.

It's all about balance, but content will never die out. We need to understand our audiences. With things like TikTok, it's evident that new generations want information quickly. Big volumes of content won't necessarily help your strategy. The way you should develop your content strategy is around understanding your audience, knowing who you're trying to target, the stages of the user journey you're trying to target, and being available at every single touchpoint of that customer journey. Position content so it's focused around their issues. Ultimately, people will search for something when they've got an issue or they're trying to find something. You should understand every single point of the journey through to the point of conversion.

People are reading content, looking at reviews, watching videos, and doing comparisons more than they ever have before. Why? Because they've got access to vast swathes of information. It's about being available at different stages to balance how the content needs to be, based on that journey. Do you really want to list lots of content like a PDF at the point where people will convert? No, you'll want them to see why you're better than competitors. That's the kind of content you'll want at that stage. If the searcher is not quite sure what the problem is or they're trying to understand what they need, this will be a great opportunity to offer informational content.

Content should be focused on users. User experience and SEO should be side by side."

Is it possible to improve what you're doing from a links and UX perspective at the same time?

"From a UX perspective, it's difficult to align that with links. You can look at your creative content and focus on strong creative content that's user-friendly and acts as an asset. That's the kind of thing people will want to link back to anyway. Things like really strong video content are going to be great for the user experience. If it's a really valuable asset for users and it provides a lot of information, you might also find it's going to be a really valuable asset to drive links back to the website. It's all about finding that balance and testing the processes. Links aren't going to be something that will die out soon. How we build and gain those links will continue to change with things like digital PR."

What shouldn't SEOs be doing in 2023? What's seductive in terms of time, but ultimately counterproductive?

"Don't push content out for the sake of it and don't keyword-stuff content. This sounds like really basic advice, but we're still seeing content like this emerging day-to-day. Maybe this will eradicate over time. In the wake of the helpful content update, lots of SEOs are hoping for content improvements. In 2023, make sure all of your content is hyper-focused on your audience and what they're searching for. Don't just push out content for the sake of it."

Sophie Brannon is an SEO Consultant and you can find her at sophiebrannon.com.

Don't do anything at the expense of the user's experience—Olga Tsimaraki

Olga Tsimaraki encourages SEOs in 2023 to worry less about the technical side of your websites and focus more on providing helpful content that is accessible and useful for your users.

Olga says: "Stop forgetting about your users; you need to remember that they come first. Google has been pushing us towards the users a lot lately, but they've been saying this at least since the Panda update in 2011. We're very focused on technical SEO fixes, following best practices, and the technical odds and ends on the site. We keep forgetting that Google's mission is to organise the world's information and make it accessible and useful. Accessible and useful have been the two key words forever.

Google's users are our users. Whenever you have someone coming to your site, you need to be helping them solve their problem. You need to be answering their questions and giving them something useful and accessible that's well-designed, legible, and enjoyable. That's what you should be doing. If you do that for your users, they will appreciate it, and they will buy, subscribe, or do whatever you want them to do.

Conversely, your users are also Google's users. If you give them useful and accessible content, Google will appreciate it and rank you higher. A big part of everything you're doing should be focused on that. It shouldn't be about fixing the speed or getting a perfect score on Core Web Vitals. That is important, but if the content on the page is not really useful - and you're leaving your users hanging by not giving them the entire answer that they're looking for - then having the perfect score and speed won't solve your ranking problems."

Is speed something that SEOs are focusing on too much?

"It has been, mostly since last year. We've been talking about this with our clients for years, but Google has recently been pushing toward user experience a lot more. Since last year, with the user experience update and the new Core Web Vitals, everyone suddenly got into a craze about fixing their speed.

It is extremely important, I'm not saying it's not. All the technical fixes that we're doing, the XML sitemap, the robots.txt files, the small optimisations that we do for the titles and meta descriptions, schema, etc., are all important. However, if we don't think about solving the user's problem first, whatever you do technically won't solve your issues. It won't make Google like what you do."

Can you positively improve SEO and improve things for users at the same time?

"You can, but it does depend a little bit on your capacity, and who you are. If we're talking about a small business, then you probably can't do everything on your own. If we're talking about a big business with a marketing department, or a full agency working for them, then you can probably do both at the same time.

What I've been stressing to most of my clients for the last three or four years is that they're focused on doing the technical things, but they're not as focused on the other part. They think that the technical things will save them, and that's how they will rank higher.

It's about not forgetting your users. We keep forgetting about the easier aspect: thinking about your users, making sure to have FAQs, having simple to-the-point content, etc. We start doing keyword research and stuffing keywords on a page, just because it's going to bring more people to the site.

Even if the keywords are there, if the content itself is not actually helpful then it doesn't make sense."

Why do SEOs tend to forget about the user so often?

"I may be biased because I'm mostly on the agency side. We depend on a lot of things from the client themselves. We're not in their company and we don't know everything about their company, but we see what they need to be doing. We point them in the right direction, but they need to actually be doing the work on their own. It's not that SEOs don't know what's important, but it always depends on the business owner and whoever else they're working with."

Should SEOs be pushing more to be involved in content strategy meetings at the beginning of the year and being a part of setting that?

"That would be very useful. I think all SEOs are slowly going towards that, especially since the helpful content update. It's easier to explain this to your clients now because it's right there in the title: Google is telling you that you need to have helpful content and not just content that has the keywords, or that's generated in bulk by AI.

What everyone knew was the idea that content is king. Write content, write articles, put the keywords in there. That's something that a business owner understands, but SEO is complicated to explain sometimes. When you're trying to push them towards a different direction, but they're not 100% sure about what that direction is or they think that the technical side is more important, then you get into conflict."

Does helpful content have a measurable positive impact on SEO?

"Helpful content is not actually a tangible ranking signal. However, user signals like bounce rate, new engagement rates that you see in Google Analytics 4, time on page, click-through rate from search, etc., are all signals that you can see improving with more helpful content.

Essentially, these are signals that Google is looking at. Nothing is verifiable, obviously, but if you look at old tweets and old communications from Google, you will see that they keep insisting that SEOs should focus on that. It might not be a ranking signal 100%, but if it's improved, then your rankings will improve. It helps your SEO overall."

How do you go about creating great content for users today?

"Try to give it a more personal twist. Do the keyword research, of course, because you need to see how people are searching for things, and you have to think about search intent. It's not just about the exact keyword. If someone searches for 'SEO services', they probably want to buy SEO services. If someone just searches 'SEO keyword research', however, then that doesn't necessarily mean that they need to buy it - they might just want to learn how to do it.

Search intent is very important. You need to know: 'Are they looking to buy so can I use it on a service page? Or are they looking for information so I can use it in my content?' Structure is also important - having a legible article with lots of spaces, small paragraphs, etc.

The most important thing, though, is to make it more unique. Don't just gather information from everywhere else and repeat the same things that everyone is saying. Try to write content where you actually have something new to say, because of your experience or because customers have asked something. You have a business, so you probably talk with people all the time, like customers and employees. There are ways to give it a more personal twist, and that's what makes it unique and more helpful than the next article."

Is keyword search volume less important than it used to be?

"I don't think it's less important, but I've always thought that keyword volume is a little dependent on who you are. If you're a small business selling a SaaS that's very expensive, you might get a keyword that has 100 searches per month, but those 100 people actually trust you because you're the expert, so they come to you. You can build your brand like that, and people will buy.

Even a small volume can still result in a good conversion rate, in the bigger picture. I'm not saying it's not important, but it depends on what niche you're in, what kind of business you are, and who you want to attract. The numbers can be a bit irrelevant."

Do you think that the SEO role is changing, and SEOs are having to become either more technical or more creative?

"I don't think SEO is changing. Everyone follows the rules when it comes to SEO, but Google has been saying the same thing since 2011. They are just trying to push more toward that now, and it's become more clear.

SEO is still a bit of both. You still need the technical. If you can do everything at the same time - you can write four articles every week that are great and creative, with unique media and schema all over your site - then go ahead and do it. I don't think that has changed. Anyone who can actually do that will still be doing it. I don't think it's about taking a specific direction between one or the other, Google is just making it more clear what you need to be doing."

Is Google sending everyone in the right direction or are there still techniques that work that Google wouldn't particularly recommend?

"There are some things that they don't want you to do, especially with technological advancements like AI. Their algorithms are becoming more and more advanced, though, so there are fewer opportunities to cheat.

I don't think AI content by itself is a good idea, but it can assist when you're a little bit stuck with getting content out. It can help you to get started with something and get what you have in your mind out there, but it needs to be an assistant, not full-on AI content generation.

I like writing as a hobby, but as a marketer, I struggle. I find that AI can be very helpful for giving me a little push to write the blog that I want to write, or something else. It can give you inspiration - there are tools using AI that will give you things like headlines, for example, so you can definitely get something creative from it. However, you always need to think about whether it's actually something new.

Don't just take everything it gives, and don't rely on it to write a creative piece for you. I haven't dived too much into AI, but if everyone is asking about the same content, how unique can it be? You will start to generate the same things over and over again, and you won't be offering a unique perspective."

What shouldn't SEOs be doing in 2023? What's seductive in terms of time, but ultimately counterproductive?

"A big part of what you shouldn't be doing is forgetting about the user, as I've said. We've also already talked about AI-generated content, and that's a big no-no for me as well. Use it as an assistant, but don't generate content for the sake of content. That won't be useful at the moment, especially with the helpful content update and since Google has always been against auto-generated content.

The thing that I have found hardest to pass on to my customers is the idea of creating helpful content for users: you need to be an expert on what you're doing and demonstrate the EAT factors of expertise, authority, and trust. Don't just get someone to write content and put the keywords in there if that person is not an expert, even if that content is unique. We need to know who the author is, so we can know who to trust. The person is important, but at least the brand behind it should be authoritative in that niche or on that topic.

Many of my tips would be the same as we've always had. Don't buy backlinks, don't buy content from people that are not experts on your content, etc. Don't do anything just because the rules say you have to - because there are no rules. There are some best practices that we believe are working, but nobody knows exactly what Google is doing. The one thing that Google has been clear about is the user. Focus on the user and give them helpful content. Why would we not be following the one rule that they're actually clear about?"

Olga Tsimaraki is a Marketing Consultant and COO at Zima Media, and you can find her at thebuddingmarketer.com.

Stay on top of UX best practices—Sara Fernández Carmona

Sara Fernández Carmona tells SEOs in 2023 that they need to embrace the term 'Search Experience Optimisation' and understand that SEO can no longer exist without UX.

Sara says: "As SEOs, we need to stay on top of UX best practices.

Rather than talking about Search Engine Optimisation, we should embrace the term Search Experience Optimisation (or SXO) which combines SEO and user experience. In fact, SEO shouldn't exist without UX anymore, and UX shouldn't exist without SEO either.

We are all familiar with Google's Core Web Vitals and performance metrics like LCP, FID, and CLS. They focus on user experience from a technical standpoint, but a website is more than that. It's a puzzle with many pieces. Things like UI design, accessibility, and inclusive design all make up the user experience, and we should be aware of them as SEOs.

We need to care about the look and feel, and about improvements that may not be considered a ranking factor, per se, but are still good for the user. If we are seeing that something is positive, from all the data that we have (quantitative and qualitative, from user testing, interviews, feedback from users, and also from colleagues) we should be prioritising those improvements, even if they are not a ranking factor."

What are some of the UX best practices that SEOs need to be aware of?

"It's important that you take cognitive biases into consideration. We all have them, so it's important that we are aware of them. There is a long list of cognitive biases, like the hindsight bias, the confirmation bias, refusing to listen to the opposite side, etc.

There are also different UX laws, like the Von Restorff Effect. There are so many UX and usability principles that you can find out about. You should also bear in mind all the research that UX teams do, like UX research and user testing. We tend to prioritise quantitative data, but qualitative data is also very important for making good decisions."

How do you measure the impact of qualitative versus quantitative data?

"When your teams are carrying out usability testing, it's important that you have access to all of that information. Whenever UX teams (or eventually ourselves) use platforms like Hotjar or Crazy Egg to understand how users navigate or scroll through your websites, you need to have access to this more descriptive data.

Also, you should get in touch with different teams (like customer service teams) that have access to your users, feedback, clients' feedback, etc. It's hard to measure because it's a relatively new field, and we tend to measure things quantitatively. When it comes to qualitative data, we often try to come up with numbers or percentages, and it's not always easy. However, it's very important that we take into account the feedback that we get from our users."

How do you avoid falling into the traps of cognitive biases, and how do you create content that appeals to a greater range of your target market?

"It's very important that you take into account the market that you're communicating to - your target market. For example, if you're writing a piece of content for a Canadian audience, you should be aware of all the cultural biases that will be relevant for that market. Localization plays a fundamental role both in SEO and UX.

We all have biases, and it can be difficult to fight them. Rather than fighting them, you should accept them, understand them, and try to avoid any kind of misunderstanding or cultural differences as much as you can. Try to make sure that everything is clear for that target audience - and that you're using the right words. If there's a word that means one thing in one market and another in a different market, you should try to avoid that as well.

Even seeing English written for a different market can turn off potential users, like phraseology that is specific to the US or the UK. You should try to avoid that kind of language and create localized content that feels targeted and natural."

Should every SEO be a Search Experience Optimiser or is there room in the SEO world for other activities, without having to worry about UX as well?

"It's not that we should all aim to become experts in UX, because most of us work with UX teams, at the end of the day. What really matters is that you make sure you are communicating with those teams, and you have access to their work and their research. If there's anything that needs clarification - something that they've worked on that you don't understand – then you need to be asking questions.

It's useful to know the basics and, luckily, there are many resources online that you can check - and most of them are free. You can access the Nielsen Norman Group, the UX Collective, the Interaction Design Foundation, and so many different organisations that share information and have courses as well. There is a lot of information to take in, and it's all going to help us as SEOs, and as SXOs as well."

What are some typical mistakes that UX teams make that have a negative impact on SEO? What can SEO teams do to make sure that doesn't happen?

"It does happen quite often where UX teams make changes in the UI. You might have some issues with the H1s and H2s - all the headings and subheadings - because they may use them just to make the font bigger. The overall structure of the content and the size of the images are also issues that come up quite often, where they are not properly optimised.

It's important that we make sure that both UX and SEO teams are aware of best practices, and that we communicate. At the end of the day, we're working towards the same goal so both teams need to be flexible. There will be disagreements along the way but, in the end, we should all be focusing on users, and making sure that we give them the best experience.

Another frequent mistake is removing content when adapting the desktop version of a page to mobile. For example, deleting information from e-commerce category pages just to make them look more mobile-friendly. You can have a different design to maximise UX, but the content should always be equivalent to the desktop site."

Should SEO and UX actually be just one team?

"No. I think that it's important for each team to keep their independence. There will be things that we work on that do not necessarily have an impact on everything both teams are doing. The SEO team may perform actions that are not that relevant to the UX team, for example. It is important, however, that the communication is always there, and that you have touch-point meetings on a regular basis."

Should UX be involved in the early stages of developing individual pieces of content, as well as the SEO team?

"Definitely. It's very important that UX is involved in content because UX also takes accessibility into consideration. It's important that you focus on readability in your articles - in the structure, the way you construct sentences, but also in the language that you use.

When we talk about accessibility, we are also talking about the words that we use to make sure that any user will understand what we're talking about. You need to avoid certain words that may be a little bit too technical for that audience, or that you explain what those words mean. UX can definitely help with content because it's about making sure that the content can be understood and easily consumed.

Usually, your SEO team will work on the content first and, once it is done, the UX team can provide some guidelines, check through it, and help out if there is anything that is not clear. UX cannot predict all the content that is going to be developed so it's easier to spot issues and fix them once the content has already been produced."

What shouldn't SEOs be doing in 2023? What's seductive in terms of time, but ultimately counterproductive?

"We should stop working in silos. It's very counterproductive for SEO success when teams don't communicate enough, so we need to make sure that we maintain communication with any relevant teams.

In this case, we've been talking about UX teams, but it could be marketing teams, content teams, engineering teams, or any team whose work could be affected by changes that we make.

Everybody should have visibility over what is being done and anything that we change, because it could affect them. You might not be aware that they're working on the same project, for example, or that your project could also have some implications for their team. Establish clear communication and stop working in silos, because we're all working towards the same goal."

Sara Fernández Carmona is an International SEO Consultant, and you can find her over at sara-fernandez.com.

Use user-focused research to stay ahead of search quality thresholds—Billie Geena Hyde

Billie Geena Hyde believes in using user-focused research to improve search quality thresholds in 2023 and make sure that what you are putting online site is fulfilling the needs of your users.

Billie says: "It's mega important to ensure whatever you're putting online meets the purpose of your users and is helpful, not counterproductive.

User-focused research has become more prevalent since the content update was announced in August 2022. It's a more important factor than ever before, and a quality indicator for Google when they're indexing. By including the user and putting them at the forefront, you'll rank better and convert more because you'll be providing a more focused, successful strategy."

How do you carry out user-focused research?

"When performing keyword research, you should add a few extra steps at the beginning. Let's say you've got a big list of keywords you're contemplating targeting, and you're nearly at a point where you're going to start mapping them to the pages of your site. You've got past the point of search volumes, you know the keyword difficulty and everything else you need to acknowledge. In this instance, you shouldn't map the keywords to the pages because that wouldn't be enough to ensure you're doing something helpful.

What you would need to do is manually go through all of those keywords and actually search them. You'd be surprised by how infrequently SEOs search for the keywords they want to target. It's important to ensure that those keywords are actually in line with what you offer, what your page offers, and what's there in search. You need to factor all of this in before you make a decision and start that mapping process.

By understanding the search landscape, you can create a more specific and factored-in strategy. You'll also start to appreciate that search volumes don't always matter because Google and other tools that monitor search volumes can't always provide a full set of every single search term and give search volumes for them.

Sometimes they'll show you a search term with zero search volume. If you do use tools to look at the traffic of the pages those terms rank for, you might find out that they do provide a lot of traffic. We can't just trust search volumes. You need to trust what's out there in the landscape and ensure your pages are in line. You should provide strong, helpful, useful content that's in line with what users are searching for. If you can do that, you'll be better positioned to hit the quality indicators that Google use. You'll rank higher and convert more by performing a few hours of extra research at the start."

What tools do you use to find traffic volume for allegedly zero-volume keywords? How do you convince stakeholders that you should be spending time attempting to rank for keywords with no volume?

"Ahrefs and Semrush are useful tools where you can search a term and see the traffic that's there rather than the search volumes. There might be some search terms where the tools are adamant there's no search volume, but if you click into them and look into the data they're actually bringing in thousands of clicks. Having that data will help convince stakeholders that something is worth trying to achieve.

However, that won't always be enough. Stakeholders will often see a zero search volume and, because they're not an SEO, they'll fail to acknowledge any potential benefit. It can become a bit of an uphill battle, but you should do that research, find something that feels like a good avenue to try, and experiment on 1-5 pages as a sampler. When that is bringing in organic traffic you can use this small-scale evidence as proof you're seeing results. You can then suggest making your campaign more widespread and investing more time into it. This is a useful approach because search volumes are becoming more obsolete by the day.

Having data and proof will always give you the tools that you need to convince somebody. If they're dead set against something, it can feel like you're never going to win, but it's always worth a try."

Do you value the importance of having conversations with your users to learn more about who they are?

"Absolutely. If you're working in-house you'll have great access to communication with customers. If your business is very community focused it's easy to reach out to people and get to know them a bit better. If you can do this it's definitely worth finding opportunities where you can. You might not know the nuances of communicating with users, but being able to sit down and talk to your audience is a great idea if you're agency based."

Do you advocate having one-on-one conversations with users as well?

"Absolutely. It's important to really understand your target market, which you can achieve by physically reaching out and having conversations with your user base.

Every business is different and the process of speaking with users may differ, but it's worth experimenting to configure a suitable approach. You might discover polls work best, one-on-one conversations, or even surveys. If you're agency based, it's harder to work with your client's customer base. You could have success with SaaS or B2B companies by reaching out to the client and requesting a sit-down conversation with their customer service team. You can then learn about the frustrations from the person that actually hears them and factor those learnings into the SEO process."

What's a specific example of something you've learned from a customer services team?

"One customer support team was getting complaints because the business made it possible for people to publish information on their website and share it for a cost. There were two processes to accomplish this, you could either phone up and quote word-by-word or process information online. The business was pushing for online availabilities, but the process ended up making the website so slow it would time out. Consequently, the information people submitted was not published.

However, because the payment was going through a third party, the business was not picking up on the issue. Customers would phone up to do this and say they'd been wasting lots of time, levying significant blame on the customer-facing salesperson. All the while, the rest of the company was left completely unaware because complaints weren't passed on and the content was later produced by hand. It was essentially a severe communication issue that highlighted big technical problems - things the SEOs could fix and signpost. Eventually, we were able to identify the issue via conversations and, had that not happened, it would have probably boiled over until it took to social media.

This issue influenced our content creation because we could create something user-focused from this pain point until things got resolved. We created a landing page and added an extra step to signpost a person's service and create a better user journey. While working on this we positively impacted conversions because instead of someone clicking the link, trying, and giving up, they'd get back to the landing page and find our contact number. Before this, the business had been keeping things secret. You can positively increase sales without fixing a problem by identifying it and doing something that actually helps the user."

What shouldn't SEOs be doing in 2023? What's seductive in terms of time, but ultimately counterproductive?

"The entire search landscape could change in the next year. If content becomes more helpful, the way things are crawled and indexed will change completely. Google will be able to find something that's significantly more beneficial to the user, and that's going to kill off people copying, pasting, running things through a paraphrasing tool, and publishing.

This approach is going to die out because the search isn't going to work that way anymore. With the new quality indicator, search is only going to get more advanced. It's going to get more human, so churning out rubbish won't lead you to the same results as in 2022.

Stop talking about what others do and talk about what you do well. Help your users."

Billie Geena Hyde is a Learning and Development Manager at SALT.agency and you can find her at salt.agency.

Be more human and integrated within the wider marketing strategy—Becky Simms

Becky Simms believes that by being more human you can have greater success as an SEO in 2023 and encourages you to consider the motivations of your users when developing your SEO strategy.

Becky says: "It's important to remember that the algorithm is chasing humans, not the other way around. Google is edging closer to how we search, interact with one another, ask questions, and help each other. By focusing more on the human side of a strategy, you can think about your audience first and understand the motivations behind their behaviour. By assessing what people are looking for, we can build a strategy that has a much greater chance of being successful."

Does being more human mean understanding the customer better or being a better human to other people in the marketing department?

"It's important to work closely with people across your department and avoid focusing too much on channels and silos. Your customer won't care about where they find the solution they're looking for. What they'll care about is finding it when they're looking for it - in the right place at the right time. It needs to be the right solution. As marketers, if we get hung up thinking that SEO is always the answer, we could easily miss that the customer isn't necessarily looking on Google at that time.

We can better understand the customer journey by visualising the user as a baton in a relay race. As a brand or business, it's your job to get hold of that baton in your ecosphere and have it with you as an awareness point where you've answered a question along the journey.

You need to find a way to keep hold of that baton, and every single point that the customer touches within your world. The more you can understand all of those touchpoints, the stronger your SEO will be. You can then appreciate where you need to be visible, where organic can play its role, and how it can work with other channels. You can understand touchpoints better by using methods like paid media or email marketing.

Success has lots to do with being a human in a marketing department and not being too focused on your niche."

Regarding being aware of other aspects of the customer journey, where does an SEO's role fit into the consideration phase?

"It is very much on a customer-by-customer basis. Suppose you're looking at a more holistic digital marketing strategy. In that case, you should begin with a customer piece to better understand who they are, their buying motivations, and what they care about. This approach works well from a B2B perspective because you'll start to focus on things that make a difference to the human that's going to buy it.

Once you've done this, you can go on the process of customer journey mapping. You can look at all of the potential touchpoints and ask what it is they're doing, where they are, and whether they're looking for reviews, to build confidence, etc. You can also work out the format of the content they're seeking - for example, long-form articles or videos.

TikTok is a great place for research because you can get an up close and personal look at the modern consumer. In this sense, it's important to broaden your research horizons and not limit your search to Google. Think about where your audience is spending their time and what it is they're doing. Take time to evaluate this, but be open to testing and refining to ensure you're getting things right."

Is TikTok only for those under a certain age bracket or does everybody use TikTok nowadays?

"You'll find lots of people of all ages there. It's a common misconception that TikTok is just for silly, fun things. The content viewers are shown there has a lot to do with what they're feeding the algorithm. If you so desire, TikTok can be used as a learning resource. Social platforms rarely used to offer this type of content, so it's evident the landscape is changing a lot."

If there are multiple touchpoints for getting traffic from SEO, how do you attribute its value?

"It's getting harder, especially with all the tracking challenges. GA4 is an emerging method that's better than Universal Analytics. As digital marketers, we've done ourselves a disservice by making everything so measurable. We're often enamoured with measuring and forget there is a massive brand and relationship piece that's integral to driving results. This is very difficult to measure at the top of the funnel, where we are inspiring with content.

Try to tie email in with the upper funnel as much as you can. You can do things like grabbing email addresses in exchange for some amazing content, providing you do things that make sense to the consumer. From this awareness content, you'll have another way of bringing them into your world and tagging when something is generated from SEO.

There are lots of routes for mapping and tracking, however, we as SEOs must collectively take our foot off the pedal and accept that awareness in a relationship is a big part of marketing. Failing to focus on this will cause sales to drop because you'll need to fuel people with the confidence to convert in the area you normally track closely."

What are your thoughts about how email and SEO can work together effectively?

"It's more about looking at things from the user journey perspective and deliberating whether they can work well together. Once you've passed the baton onto email you'll need to drive that person back. When we look at audiences and personas and try to determine motivations, we often look at how we can layer that into emails to see if we can bucket users into the personas we're trying to understand.

For example, if you've got a hypothesis of four or five personas, you can test out different messaging throughout the email. If it's box B they click on, and that's tied to persona B, you can begin to understand the type of messaging they prefer and the direction you need to lead them in. It has a lot to do with how you can drive the person through to conversion using email and SEO together."

Is the future of big marketing teams creating small teams within that department or is it more effective to keep those different channels working together?

"It's great to have pods that work together within the same department, structuring your team across the funnel. Introduce an 'awareness pod' where an SEO person can confidently make sense of their environment.

For example, they might say they're having great success with a group of keywords within awareness. However, they'll know the customer is not going to buy at this stage because it's awareness. You can then use a combination of email and paid to determine how you can push them through to conversion. If you've got them to this point but do nothing, your job will feel somewhat pointless. This would be similar to the first salesman touchpoint, where you manage to get someone on the phone and have a conversation with them but then fail to follow up. From a sales point of view, you wouldn't do this if you've had a little bite.

As an SEO person, you need to be saying that you're doing a great job and driving this traffic on these keywords. It's then important to look at things from an internal perspective and get help to ensure you're not being rude when you reengage with the customer. If you know a customer is weeks from making a decision, you should do everything you can to ensure you're still interacting with them."

What shouldn't SEOs be doing in 2023? What's seductive in terms of time, but ultimately counterproductive?

"Being too blinkered and assuming that SEO is the only answer. Often, people are so passionate that they get over-passionate and lose their influence within a team. If you find yourself in this position, others might think that you're failing to see the bigger picture.

There's a danger of being too focused on chasing the algorithm and chasing certain keywords while ignoring the overarching objective. Your ultimate job will be to drive sales, inquiries, revenue, etc. Keep your eye on the prize and ask whether your actions are a priority and will help you to meet your targets/goals. If you can't confidently say 'yes' then you need to reassess what you're doing."

Becky Simms is Founder and CEO at Reflect Digital and you can find her over at reflectdigital.co.uk.

Have a user-centric and holistic approach to all things web—Ulrika Viberg

Ulrika Viberg recommends focusing on what the user wants in 2023 and working together with traditional marketing, digital marketing, and the UX team to improve the customer experience through your SEO.

Ulrika says: "Be a user-centric, holistic SEO - together with the marketing department and the UX department. That is my number one tip."

What does a user-centric holistic approach mean in practice?

"If you look at the last couple of algorithm updates, Google has been pointing out that you need to be user-focused. They want to make the web more friendly and truthful. They are pushing for user-centric content that complies with the EAT update. It should be well-designed and accessible for people with hearing and sight impairments, as well as compliant with Core Web Vitals, mobile friendly, etc.

All of that translates to the fact that there needs to be a good user experience. You need to consider the user journey, or customer journey, and it has to be UX-friendly. SEOs working together with marketing departments and UX departments gives a holistic view of what is being created on your website. It makes you think: 'What does my user really want?' and 'What are they asking for?' rather than 'What is it that I want to tell them?'"

In a large marketing department, who tends to own the user journey? Is there one distinct, singular perspective on what a user journey is?

"No, there is not. There is an interpretation for each organisation or company. I work with a lot of larger companies, and they don't always have a clear user journey or customer journey in mind. That is something that I help them with. Usually, it's the CMO who is taking the lead, but everyone is involved.

I invite the whole marketing department, both traditional and digital marketing - but also the sales department, because they are very close to their customers, maybe more so than the marketing departments are. Then, we create the user journey or the customer journey.

Once they have it, and they have worked through it, it's something that needs to be talked about throughout the whole organization. Everyone becomes aware of it. It's a strategic document that they need to follow in everything they do."

When SEOs are having conversations with the UX team, what can they learn from each other?

"What SEOs can learn from the UX team is that they are very user-centric. Every second sentence they say is: 'What is the user expecting?' We, as SEOs, need to learn to think that way, and we need to create content and a strategic way of flowing through the website that focuses on the user's expectations. That builds into what kind of architecture we are recommending on the site. It has to translate into the user journey.

It's easier for the user to travel through a website and take in the information if it is designed from a user perspective. What are they expecting? That question translates into each and every individual page. You need to think about what the page is actually about. Look at search intent so that you understand what the user has searched for, what they are expecting to land on, and what kind of information they are expecting to see.

It's not only about the information, but also how you are presenting it. Are you presenting it in a way that encourages the user to do something after they have read this information? What is it that you want them to do? Here is where you bring in internal linking - in terms of calls to action and everything else. Maybe you have a semantic cluster that you want the user to walk through or get more information about. How do you make it easier for them?

Here is where the UX team will decide how to place things, where to place them, and what to call them. As SEOs, we're thinking about how we then add internal links, and where that will matter - both in terms of SEO, but also in terms of the user and what they would expect to do next. If they want more information, we need to provide them with that."

What can SEOs learn about user journeys from more traditional marketing departments?

"I have never worked with traditional marketing myself, but I've worked in departments who have done traditional marketing, and it's all about the understanding of the persona. Who are they?

Traditional marketing can teach SEOs how to paint up a persona and how to categorise that. How are your personas or your users treating information? What are they expecting to see, and how are they processing what they see in traditional media or traditional marketing efforts? We need to think about how we can pick that up and continue that journey into the digital space. They will certainly search for the things they have seen in traditional marketing campaigns."

If an SEO is in charge of conducting a training session for marketers that don't know a lot about SEO, what information is key to impart and what information should you not talk about?

"Try to tap into their domain. Talk using their keywords, so to speak, so that they can take it in. I use a lot of metaphors because, for someone who has never done SEO, it can be very theoretical and abstract. To help them understand what I'm talking about, I use metaphors and I try to describe the concepts using situations they understand and are familiar with.

SEO and marketing meet, and they overlap a lot when it comes to the user and what the user expects. All of those are also ranking signals. I tell them that these things that they work with are also important to us. The customer journey is also important for SEO, and I tell them how and why and so on.

I tend to leave out the technical parts because that usually confuses more than it helps. We tend to speak in lingo when we talk technical, and that is a good way to kill a conversation. We don't want that"

SEOs can be guilty of focusing on driving traffic, and not the whole user journey experience. How can SEOs do a better job of attracting repeat traffic or traffic at different stages of the user journey?

"I actually stopped just measuring traffic some time ago. It is still what we can influence the most but, if we take the next step and work a little bit more holistically, we can influence much more. We can recommend what the content should be and the internal linking, etc., so that we can make the user proceed in their decision-making. In this way, we can have a greater impact on goal completions and conversions.

By giving the user what they are expecting, we are also more likely to create a relationship between the user and the brand. People are lazy. If we have a good relationship with a brand that we once trusted, then we tend to go back to that brand when we want that service or product again. If we were not happy, we carry out a new search the next time the need arises, but if we were happy, then we would probably go back to that brand.

It's crucial to make the customers happy. That should be self-explanatory, but it's not always. SEOs can help with that by making recommendations for content, but also internal linking, menus, and how you walk through the website. Of course, it should also load fast and look nice, and not jump up and down or have lots of ads in the way, etc."

What are your thoughts on attribution and how you can attribute SEO to different touchpoints and channels? Are there any optimal models or pieces of software that you would recommend to show the information decision-makers need in terms of the value of different channels?

"We use contributing models or attribution modelling. You can build attribution models in Google Analytics, to see what channels provide the best traffic and where it was attributed.

In terms of what is currently missing, those models won't really show that. You would have to do heatmaps, etc. See how people are interacting with the page and actually look at the user. You could do some live testing with live users and ask them questions. You can also do that in smaller tests - they don't have to be super big or very costly. That's very useful to do. Then you will see, live, what the users are liking and how they are interpreting the pages that you want to test."

What shouldn't SEOs be doing in 2023? What's seductive in terms of time, but ultimately counterproductive?

"I would love it if SEOs would stop doing isolated keyword optimisation based on search volume. It is counterproductive for the user journey, and for decision-making as a whole.

It creates isolated touchdowns on single pages - and what are they doing then? Just trying to rank number one, or one to three, on a specific high-volume keyword is counterproductive by itself.

If, on the other hand, you create a cluster around that keyword and you think about something you want to do around that keyword, so that users feel that they found what they expected, then that is actually helpful. That would be the next level to go for."

Ulrika Viberg is Agency Owner and Senior SEO Consultant at Unikorn and you can find her at unikorn.se

What are people saying about you?—Miracle Inameti-Archibong

Miracle Inameti-Archibong informs SEOs in 2023 that SEO is becoming more about what people say about you and not what you say about yourself.

Miracle says: "In the past it was all about doing research, getting a bunch of keywords, and saying lovely things about your product/service. You optimised for keywords, considered the link engine and then ranked. Now, Google is so sophisticated it's become less about what you say to your customers and more about the feedback your customers give to Google on how you're performing. This will affect your rankings."

In what ways do customers give feedback to Google? How do they actually deliver this feedback?

"Reviews and also what they're saying about you on forums. Another feedback that's become increasingly important is the volume of 'brand + product' searches. There are different kinds of industries where an increasing number of brands with high demand and 'brand + product' searches usually rank higher. It's that kind of user demand/interest that's fielded into the algorithm."

What does treating SEO as a product mean?

"It's about paying a lot of attention to your brand, which is something that used to be the primary domain of marketing. SEO focuses on generic, but you have to pay attention to your brand. Treating SEO as a product means knowing your PR agency, and being involved in social at a product level when people are making changes, creating products, etc. You need to know what your competitors are doing and not treat SEO like a silo or a department of its own. Treat it as an online owner. The more you progress in your career, the more leadership responsibilities you'll have. Be the one to say 'I know we're creating this product, but if we don't put this in at the end that's going to affect our brand.'

Usually, all of these discussions are made way before the SEO team gets involved. The SEO team is presented with a topic that they now have to optimise and create visibility for. In 2023, the SEO will have to be in the conversation when new products are being created. SEOs have information on what competitors are doing online and what the landscape looks like. This is beginning to feed in.

It used to be that you could have your offline campaign drive everything to the SERP, but now competitors are searching social media and looking at reviews. There are so many other things fitting into that. You could be screaming about how you have the best online product in the world, but all the online chatter says your product is bad.

It's really interesting to see how the power dynamics are shifting and the conversations that SEOs are joining. VPs from SEO departments have crept in, because people are beginning to understand the power of online marketing. It's not like they didn't understand before, but it was just easier to push money into different above-the-line campaigns and guarantee certain results.

The lines are now getting blurred, especially as above the line is getting more expensive and receiving less visibility. People skip ads all the time, and they want brands that aren't constantly giving them the hard sell. Online marketing and visibility have been seen as cheaper, especially as ads continue to get more expensive. Competition is getting really tough and SEOs need to be involved for a successful outcome. You need to be involved at the core of what a product is. Do your research and get involved in those conversations if you want SEO to be successful."

What kind of questions should SEOs be asking product teams, and what should they say to product teams to try and influence what is included?

"The first thing is 'How does this translate in the online space?' It's good to talk about build because usually when the product team is talking to the developers, they're building something they know will work.

The first thing they'll want to do is put X into Y and get Z. They won't be thinking about how Z is displayed online when you put X into Y. If you don't get involved in those conversations about the build, then when they get to Z they'll come back to tell you whether something displays well or not. This will be in retrospect and can lead to the implementation of hacks which can be too expensive. The more you get involved in conversations, the more you can think about how this translates online - and how you're going to be able to display this.

As you're building a product, you can look at what the journey looks like and how you're going to be able to track the journey. What can you put in place that will make it easy to track the journey so you can get the data you need to make improvements? These are the kinds of conversations you need to be having. When you're talking to your marketing team about putting a product out, what is so unique about the product that you can market from an online perspective when creating content? Yes, you can look for generic keywords and find out what a product does, but if everyone is saying that (in the era of useful, helpful content) how is this helpful and how does this translate online?

It's interesting because you see above-the-line campaigns that focus on slogans, but they rarely translate online. Let's say you create a marketing campaign about biscuits and say 'biscuits make you happy'. That would be a lovely thing to take on during your above-the-line campaign, but it probably won't translate when you come back to the web. It's very unlikely that people will be searching for 'biscuits that make you happy'."

Should marketing and business departments be better arranged to ensure SEOs are offering input at the right time?

"SEOs should be given more seats at the senior table. We should start seeing more VPs from the SEO program. What usually happens is someone from PPC gets promoted to the directorate level and takes that top seat. However, you never see the SEO person become Head of Acquisition. We want to start seeing more SEOs in the head of acquisition roles."

Why don't we normally see this?

"SEO is less measurable. It's easy to say 'I spent 20k on PPC and got 40k parts.' With SEO, there are more correlations than causations. Because of that, it's not seen as a trusted medium. They know it makes money but it's only when it stops making money that everyone panics. While it's making money, everyone downplays the 'dark art' of SEO.

It's not something that's easily understood, especially when SEO gets simplified into things like 'SEO is just about creating content.' SEO is not easily measurable and when it's working people tend to ignore it and simplify the SEO department by saying 'They're just content creators.' It's a difficult sell. With other departments, like PPC, it's easy to say you've put X amount in and received X back - where the more you spend the more information Google gives you. You hear Google inviting PPC managers to the headquarters, they even pull reports for PPC. No one does that for SEO. SEOs don't get the prime seat at the table until something isn't working. The oversimplification and lack of direct measurement in SEO are real. However, more and more people are starting to understand the perils of not doing SEO. Hopefully, this will give us a better seat at the table."

SEO is getting even harder to measure now. How can you measure what people are saying about you online?

"Those are not things that are easy to track using normal tools like Google Search Console, because they don't update in real time. It's mostly about getting really good data from people. Get people with really good data insights who can scrape, measure, and build tools that will bring all of this data together. Create really exciting dashboards that can help you identify trends, uplift campaigns, and know exactly where it's coming from. It has a lot to do with being able to filter.

Data is becoming increasingly important to SEO. Everyone is trying to crack the nail on data, because we're getting less and less from all the Google tools. We need to be able to scrape things like social media, understand what trends are there when you launch campaigns, and make sure you have responses in there as quickly as possible. These are the kind of things that will be really effective now.

Make sure you're in the SERP when someone searches for 'your brand + product'. It's about understanding those brand results for key products and making sure you have an answer for everything. Ensure the right things are appearing. Have those difficult conversations and identify when something isn't an SEO problem. Communicate when you've done everything from an SEO perspective, but the product is rubbish. As much as you could shout and say 'This biscuit is going to make you happy!', if it doesn't, you're going to get trashed online. SEOs can't save this - even though they used to be able to years ago. Previously, you could just build links to rank number one. Google didn't care as much, but now there are so many elements to the algorithm."

If people talk about you online and you get nofollow links from social media, is there any traditional SEO value in that? Will your perceived authority increase as a result of brand mentions, social media, and nofollow links?

"Yes. You might not be able to see that there is a direct benefit, but you could definitely say there's a correlation. A brand might launch a product or campaign that's started to trend on social media even though Google doesn't index on social media. However, the rankings could still increase and as soon as the hype dies down the product could drop. There's always a correlation between things. Who knows what came first but if something is trending people will search more.

Google's whole marketing approach is that they want to give the users what the users want. If the users are searching for you and they're not clicking on the competitor, it makes sense for you to rank number one. All of these factors have a correlating effect on the fact that if the user demand for you goes up the product demand goes up.

There were lots of independent providers of medical services doing really well in the SERP during the pandemic. They were doing better than other, bigger competitors that were not providing personalised services. That was because of an increase in demand and people looking for those services and saying great things about them. This was driven by people not being able to access GP services and the presence of alternate services offering a GP appointment on the same day. The big services were still operating on old models, so smaller GP services started to kill it in the SERPs. There's always a correlating factor. They weren't even doing any outreach, but just because of the situation at the time - the surge in people searching for those services - they started to see rankings and their 'brand + product' search grew exponentially. It was interesting to see these companies' brand searches grow alongside their generic rankings. As demand for providers went down in terms of brand search, their generic rankings also dropped."

Do SEOs need to do a better job of learning from traditional PR, especially the measure of brand exposure based on perceived opportunities? Should SEOs not shout about the impact SEO can have on brand uplift as much as they do?

"Yes, but it's a difficult space - especially now we're moving away from traditional link building. Most companies use PR agencies that take credit for securing coverage. It's all about who gets the credit for that: is it the PR agency or the SEO department? We all know that it's valuable and that's how traditional PR has worked. But if it was the SEO team who secured the link, you should by all means scream and shout about it. Do a dance, and really track and measure. Lots of people are moving away from old school link building and are now working with big PR agencies that know how to get better coverage."

What shouldn't SEOs be doing in 2023? What's seductive in terms of time, but ultimately counterproductive?

"The Google helpful content update was a godsend because it destroyed the content landscape. You often see the same page titles, and it's difficult to distinguish what content is good and what's bad. The art of doing broad keyword research and writing about something because your competitor is writing about it is what needs to stop.

Offering no unique perspective is pointless, and it's an approach that will be eradicated. SEO is not just about content creation - we need to be thinking about new ways to add value. If you have nothing unique to say, it's not worth adding to the millions and millions of pieces of duplicate content out there. It'll be interesting to see how Google polices this as a big brand with a big authority kind of view.

Hopefully, the helpful content update will kill the myriad of trashy, same-title types of content. People will write things from a unique perspective instead of just because a competitor has a page about something on their site. SEO is not just about content creation so we should be looking for new ways to add value."

Miracle Inameti-Archibong is Head of SEO at John Lewis Finance and you can find her at miracleinametiarchibong.com.

10 LINKS

Reap the full impact of link acquisition by having a sound site—Natalie Arney

Natalie Arney suggests that SEOs in 2023 should be reinforcing the three pillars of tech, content, and links, and getting those pillars working in tandem to make sure your website is as sound as possible.

Natalie says: "My number one SEO tip for 2023 is that, in order to reap the best benefits from a link acquisition campaign, you need to ensure that your site is as sound as possible."

What does having a sound site actually mean?

"A lot of people think about a site being technically sound, but it's not just about having good technical SEO. We need to think about the three pillars of SEO constantly working in tandem with each other. That means tech, content, and links working together. You've got to have a good technical structure, your content needs to be helpful and of good quality, and you've obviously got the links side as well."

The first pillar you describe is tech, so what are the tech areas that typically trip websites up at the moment?

"It's a mixture. In this last year, Google has admitted that their indexation - and their reporting of indexation - isn't as great as it should be, so we know there's an issue around that.

It is really important that we make sure our sites are crawlable, and the content is crawlable. This is especially true as we move towards a more JavaScript-savvy web. There are a lot of things that Google can read and see when you're looking at things like a JavaScript site. Depending on the platform that you're using, however, you've got to have a belt and braces approach.

If there is content on your site that can't be crawled - if there's JavaScript that is not being read, or if search engines are struggling to read that content for some reason or another - then you need to be solving those issues."

How do you check that a site is crawlable?

"There are many ways to check. I use a lot of fetch and render tools. There are some really great ones out there, and they let you look and see what's rendering in terms of JavaScript versus HTML. You can also, obviously, use Google Search Console.

As I previously mentioned, there have been issues this year with regard to Search Console's reporting of the crawlability and indexation of websites. However, you can bypass Google and use tools to test the site yourself. Google is only part of the story.

Use the tools that you can - whether that's a crawling tool, a fetching and rendering tool, or another search engine console like Bing or Yandex. These alternate viewpoints can help you to predict what Google may or may not be able to see."

What crawling tool do you like, at the moment?

"My two main crawling tools are Screaming Frog and Sitebulb. I know that they're rivals and everyone's always comparing the two, but I use them in tandem. I like the Sitebulb interface, but Screaming Frog can help pick up certain elements as well. I want to have all my bases covered, and I don't like missing things. Every now and then, one tool might pick something up that another tool might not.

If the two tools disagree, that's where I go in and have a look manually, depending on what the issue is. That includes having a look at the code on the site, having a look server side, and delving deeper to see exactly what the issue might be. There are additional tools that you can use to double-check -like ContentKing, Lumar (formally Deepcrawl), etc. - however, it is important to delve in and see for yourself, so that you can pick things up in the code.

There are also plugins that you can use in Chrome, and additional tools besides, but it really does depend on the issue and what the crawling tools are disagreeing on. When it's a page title, a meta description, an H1 issue, or a duplicate content issue, then it's a lot easier to look for than a piece of code or script that's not firing properly."

In terms of the second pillar, content, what are the issues that you're seeing on websites at the moment?

"I'm seeing a lot of different issues. One thing that's common is in relation to tech. When the content is not actually being indexed itself, it could be a technical issue, or it could be that it is just poor quality and it doesn't answer the query or the intent of the user. Making sure that you are addressing the query, and the intent of the query, is incredibly important.

Thanks to recent content updates, a lot of sites are trying to create content to show expertise, but not in the best way. They think that they're showing expertise and understanding of a topic or a subject, but it's a little off the mark.

Missing out on the most popular questions that people ask about a topic is a big problem. Make sure that those questions are answered. It might seem obvious to someone who's on the client side or someone who's an SEO or content writer, but you need to remember that those questions are there, and your users should be given the answers to them.

When you're creating a piece of content, you can't make any assumptions about what people are going to know about the subject. Not everyone has the same specialism, and not everyone has the same understanding. We need to be casting a wide net."

Do you use a tool to help categorise intent or is determining intent a manual process?

"I use a combination of tools and manual efforts. Whether it's an in-depth, massive keyword research document, or whether it's researching the top 5 or 10 keywords for a piece of content, I use a combination of tools, depending on what the client has access to and what I have access to.

Semrush has intent classification in their keyword tool, but I also like using Keyword Insights. It lets you upload keywords, categorise them, and cluster them, but also get intent - and it takes the intent from the SERP. You can put in a small number of keywords, or you can add keywords in bulk, and then categorise those keywords by their intent.

On the manual side, it's about speaking with the client or with your internal team, and making sure that they're aware of the intent of the keywords you're targeting and the content that you're creating. You need to determine who a piece of content is for and what they are going to do with that piece of content. Are they seeking information at the top of a funnel or is this bottom-of-funnel conversion-point content?

Really discuss this with the client and your internal team. We've all been there, where you've created a piece of content, and someone has said, 'Why have you put that on the website?'. As a consultant, when I come in and look at a site's content, I am often trying to decide whether I keep that content or throw it away. Why did you decide to create that content? What do you want the user to do with it? Do you want them to read it and understand it? Do you want them to go on and convert? Or have you just created that content just to acquire traffic to the site? That's where you're addressing intent."

How do you put a piece of content together? What should it look like and how long it should be?

"Looking at what's already ranking is always a good idea, but it is a bit of a mixture of things. You need to decide on the intent of the piece of content, what makes sense, and what the reader may want to do with that content.

If you want to create a massive guide, for example, you're targeting a lot of informational terms. However, if you're looking for a conversion piece of content, you may want something short and sharp that answers the user's question and has a really nice, clean call to action. It should tie in with what your CRO team want to do in terms of conversions as well, so that you are supporting one another in that journey.

For a lot of conversion content, you don't want to be creating a massive piece that may either confuse the user or provide them with too much information. The intent is completely off. It really does depend on what stage of the funnel you're at, and the whole idea of that content in the first place.

Thinking about the 'why' is so important. You don't want to write a 3,000-word guide for someone that just wants a concise bit of information when they're ready to convert. If you're looking at an eCommerce site, you want a brief product description and a few FAQ questions on a PDP. It's about making sure that you have the right intent for not just the keyword, but the actual purpose of the content as well."

The third pillar you describe is links. What links work now, and what links don't work?

"It's difficult because it is always changing. A lot of the time, it depends on the query and the type of content that you want to link to. If you're doing a brand activation PR piece, then the type of sites that are going to be linking to your page will be very different from those you would be getting for a really helpful guide that might be linked to from academic publications.

It really does vary but, when you're building links, intent is key. Do you want to reach mass markets through top-level publications like daily newspapers? Do you want more niche publications? Do you want coverage and sourcing from more academic fields or specialist sites?

Obviously, there are benefits to getting all of those different types of links, and having a varied backlink profile is really important, but it's about how you create content to acquire those links. You need to make sure that they are relevant to your brand, to the piece of content or campaign that you're trying to outreach, but also to the topics that you're going to be writing about.

I hate saying it depends but, at the same time, there's a lot of variety in terms of publishers, campaigns, and pieces of content. There are the publishers themselves, the niches that those publications are in, and so much more. Targeting the right people and the right publications, with the right content and the right campaigns, is key."

What shouldn't SEOs be doing in 2023? What's seductive in terms of time, but ultimately counterproductive?

"Stop spending so much time chasing algorithms, because Google says that the algorithm updates day-to-day so we shouldn't be doing that day-to-day. Also, stop chasing keywords and the rankings of keywords.

Just because a keyword's ranking increases or decreases in a week or in a month doesn't mean that you're not doing well - or that you should completely change course in terms of what should and shouldn't be done. What's important is making sure that you monitor relevant traffic alongside that keyword ranking.

I don't mean that you shouldn't monitor your keyword ranking at all, just don't spend hours and hours every day looking at the fluctuation of specific keywords and trying to find the reasoning behind it. You're better off spending that time actually getting dev fixes actioned, getting pieces of content briefed, or outreaching to specific publications and acquiring links."

Natalie Arney is a Freelance SEO Consultant and you can find her at nataliearney.com.

Don't let the state of your site hold back your link building strategy—Bibi Raven

Bibi Raven warns SEOs in 2023 to not limit yourself by feeling trapped in your link building strategy and reveals some of the key opportunities that you may be missing out on by focusing on just one avenue.

Bibi says: "This applies to all companies, but is especially applicable to those that sell physical products in the real world. Many retail chains have experienced lots of leads coming in from SEO, but not so many from investing in a solid link building strategy.

In the aftermath of international lockdowns and general uncertainty, you'll want your eCommerce components to become a solid stream of income. Link building is a great starting point, where you can experiment with different tactics until you get it right. Too often companies experiment and get stuck on one type, whether that's PR stunts, HARO, guest posts, or press releases.

The current state of your site will dictate your link building tactics. For example, if you don't have enough content or your site looks too commercial/unauthentic, your link building tactics will be limited. While you're working on SEO and sales-oriented copy, you should start experimenting with linkable assets right away.

One of the most common misconceptions about linkable assets is that lots of companies think they need to be epic - with beautiful graphics, really controversial topics, etc. Though 'epic' definitely has a place, there's no harm in starting with a very low level and progressing naturally from there. For instance, you could do statistics or foundational pieces that tell you about the definition of a certain thing. Because these pieces aren't commercial, it will make it very easy to build links in this area. However, these pieces can also not connect at all, which means you'd be sensible to start experimenting right away.

While you're dipping into link building, keep reverse engineering what's working really well in terms of picking up links. You can then start producing similar pieces or something else inspired by those pieces."

What do you mean by 'the state of your site'? Are you talking about poorer states of your content per technology, stats, stacks, etc.?

"There are many retail chains with huge eCommerce components that need fixing. Attempting to do so can drain significant time and resources, all while the company's blog remains hidden, minimal in terms of layout, and dictated by the eCommerce platform in operation. This approach is fine in the beginning - because you can always build links to sites - but it's important to start improving these right away. That way, you'll be able to create more assets in the future that are easier to build links to - and bigger, passive things.

Often retail chains are beaten at their own game, such as by their affiliate partners/sites. It's important not to rely solely on one link building tactic just because it works now. At some point, you'll get behind in terms of content and have to make additional efforts to recover your position."

Do big brands get beaten by affiliates because they do a terrible job at telling Google who the true entity is and a bad job at linking?

"It's a combination, but the entity thing is really interesting as well. Lots of big companies skip the basic stuff because they want to sell so hard that they start focusing their content on the product itself. If you have a product with specific ingredients in it, you should instead focus on building out a cluster of content that focuses completely on said ingredients.

Affiliate sites often focus on the low-hanging fruit - for example, long-tails. They completely dominate those topics then start vacuuming up everything around it that's related to it."

What kind of things are SEO sites doing better today than they used to?

"One thing they're doing better is targeting keywords that are at the top of the funnel. Companies are targeting those more than ever and a lot of them are cleaning up their content structure and internal linking."

What are some SEO mistakes that eCommerce sites are still making but are yet to rectify?

"Content and link building - specifically the tendency to focus on the big dogs. For example, strategies aimed to win links from Forbes, basically links from huge, generic brand sites. In doing so, they lose sight of relevancy. Getting links from real, authentic, smaller authority sites on specific topics can help."

In terms of the core competency of link building and content generation, what changes have you seen recently? Are there any tactics that are working more effectively now as opposed to a couple of years ago?

"Embracing a personal style of link building is a great way to resonate with different target audiences. Focusing on creative outreach can have a lot to do with being more personally relatable, where incorporating humour like puns and jokes is a fantastic approach. Take inspiration from The Charm Offensive with Jon Buchan. His jokes are great as a starting point for your own templates, yet everybody tends to copy his style.

Ultimately, it's best to not rely too much on one style of doing things and instead embrace a multi-faceted approach. Use what's out there, but inject your own uniqueness into it."

What about the types of links that are most impactful nowadays, have they changed at all?

"It's difficult to identify these because, when building a variety of backlinks for clients, it can be difficult to pinpoint which ones are working well and which aren't. Guest posts seem to still be working well, but when you research competitors you're likely to find their worst links are still working too. To say it's confusing at the best of times would be an understatement."

With guest posts, do you want to incorporate a link within the body of the text or do author bio links work okay?

"Most clients will say they're not particularly keen on author bio links. You're probably better off focusing on in-content links because there's a whole context around them and people will be more inclined to click on them. However, you'd be wise to accept an author bio link from a great site."

Do you also try to add links to other entities in the industry to demonstrate where the website you want to build a link to sits?

"External links? Absolutely. On the client side, certainly, but also in guest posts and other content. It always makes sense to link out to other sites - though maybe not always to direct competitors."

Do you use second-tier links as part of your active strategy?

"No, they're too complicated, for me at least! It's difficult to think more than two steps ahead, so second tiers have a habit of being brain-busting. However, there is evidence to say they work."

Should you not try to get too clever and simply build links to your sites from relevant, authoritative websites?

"Yes. You should start with link building practices that fit your personality and lifestyle well. It's like that episode from Authority Hackers where you have to think about how things affect you. If you're risk averse and you don't like looking over your shoulder, you should probably be avoiding black hat tactics and, instead, focus on getting ahead of the game. However, it is useful to see what everybody else is doing to determine whether you're likely to get hits.

These tactics can be great as a starting point, but it's better to fine-tune your approach so it better fits your personality."

If you've published a great piece of original content, can you use links as a launch strategy, where you try to build links for the first month or so and then leave your content to organically obtain links?

"This is where a combination of link building tactics can work well. Lots of people build linkable assets that they think will attract all the passive things in the world. Unfortunately, what they fail to realise is that this is unlikely to be successful - because the domain won't be strong enough yet or won't rank for relevant keywords. What you can do is boost that piece of content with a couple of buildings so it gets picked up and starts getting passive links."

Does the content have to be exceptional for this tactic to be successful?

"Not always. If your content isn't up to scratch you can just reverse engineer. You can look at a content explorer like BuzzSumo and also use Ahrefs. Instead of using a topic that's relevant to the client, you can use a word that indicates the type of content. For instance, 'how many', 'why', 'the worst', 'the best', 'stats', etc. You can then filter the amount of referring domains, the amount of paid traffics, or the number of social shares. You can start seeing what kind of pieces worked well, how you can apply them to your niche, or whether they're already in your niche.

We once got a link from a US magazine surrounding Jennifer Lopez's engagement ring. We were doing lots of content ideation for a client and did some foundational pieces around gemstones. One of those gemstones was mentioned in the article and they quoted clients. All of this happened via content that wasn't even groundbreaking, it was merely a Wikipedia-style article about the origin, meaning, and benefits of a specific gemstone."

Concerning link building, do you look into competitors, see what links they've generated and try to replicate the same links?

"Yes - competitors, backlink sizes, etc. are certainly worthwhile because they'll give you inspiration for angles you can use on your journey. It's difficult because everybody is picking up so many links these days, especially spammy ones. It's tough to wade through and see the kinds of strategies people are using."

What shouldn't SEOs be doing in 2023? What's seductive in terms of time, but ultimately counterproductive?

"Though reverse engineering and getting inspiration were mentioned earlier, that doesn't mean to say you need to copy everything. Once somebody publishes a template somewhere for an email or link building tactic, everybody tends to copy it exactly.

You should really stop just copying people, because this is a tactic that'll die out very soon. Learn from the best, but be unique."

Bibi Raven, also known as Bibi the Link Builder, is the Founder of BibiBuzz and you can find her at bibibuzz.com.

Diversify your tactics and create a network for link building—Debbie Chew

Debbie highlights effective link building as the key area for 2023 but also cautions against ignoring the other aspects of SEO, like content and technical SEO.

Debbie says: "Link building will be all about diversifying your tactics and building relationships."

What link building tactics are most effective at the moment?

"A lot of people are focusing their efforts on things like guest posting. There are a lot of great things about guest posting. You can have control over the content that you write, the pages that you link to, and the anchor text that you use. Sometimes, even with one guest post, you may get three or even more links to your website, which is awesome.

On the other hand, guest posting can be a bit of a numbers game, since you're sending a bunch of emails out to people. Some people are not fond of these emails, especially if they don't advertise guest posting. Plus, if they are a highly authoritative site, they might not be open to letting people create guest posts and then link to their sites because they want to protect their link equity.

Therefore, instead of just focusing on guest posting, you could look at other tactics, some of which are higher risk. Guest posting is a lower risk, medium-low reward. There are also other tactics out there, like creating a research report. Assume there is a topic I am interested in, and I do a study

- maybe a poll. I might learn some interesting statistics or data points about this topic and share that with journalists or content writers. That will be something much more valuable for them that they want to link to. That's what I would recommend, in terms of more long-term, high-risk, high-reward tactics."

Would you recommend trying to build relationships with top journalists in your area and giving out your unique content?

"Distributing it to as many places as possible is better. It's possible that many journalists are interested in reporting that one study that you do. Don't limit yourself. If possible, try to find statistics or uncovered data that will be interesting to a large audience - and widen your net. You can approach even more journalists rather than remaining very specific to your product."

What are some more effective ways to start building relationships if you don't know any journalists or top writers personally?

"For journalists, it's about understanding what they cover by reading the actual posts they write, and then following and understanding what types of topics they want to cover. That way, you know exactly whether or not your report matches their interests.

Also, aside from just building a relationship with journalists, it is easier to build relationships with your product or service partners. Say you have an app which you integrate with. You can talk to them and see if you can amplify each other. That way, you can write guest posts on their site, and they can write on yours. In the future, if you produce a valuable report, they can also share it. Then you're not only just getting a link from the guest post, but you're building that relationship to increase the number of links, mentions, and interactivity with your partners.

Another way to build relationships with journalists is using a service called HARO, which stands for Help a Reporter Out. If a journalist is looking for a subject matter expert to give a quote on a topic, they'll post a request on HARO. A subject matter expert can then submit a quote and potentially get a link and build a relationship. These two tactics are key to helping you maintain that relationship with journalists."

Is it also important that you try and personalise your outreaches, to begin with?

"Yes. So many people send emails, and it can be pretty obvious that they haven't even looked at your website or thought about how you can practically work together. If you just raise the bar slightly by demonstrating that you're reading their content, they're much more likely to listen to what you have to say."

If you don't have the data yourself, as an organisation, can you partner with a data provider, and then both of you could feature within whatever report you're creating?

"There was an example of this a few months ago, where Zoom partnered with Survey Monkey to do a pretty big survey related to remote work. Now, that's a partnership that they can leverage. They published the report on Survey Monkey and Zoom's domains and got links and press mentions. With this approach, you can work with someone potentially bigger than you and get people interested - especially journalists."

What gives you the best chance of generating links back to your site? Is it possible to get a keyword-rich link as part of this?

"It depends. I worked on a research study earlier this year for Dialpad that was on the state of video conferencing. We were able to get links. However, sometimes, after publishing a report, they might link to the homepage and mention Dialpad but not link to the report directly. Yet, I'd want people to get to the report and find it. In those cases, I might reach out and ask them to link directly to the actual blog post. That way, people can get there without getting lost.

You shouldn't necessarily fret over anchor texts because it steps more into spammy link building. You want the writer to decide on what that anchor text might be. For the destination URL, try your best to get them to link directly to that page instead of something like your homepage."

What are your thoughts on Google's awareness of social media links from social media? Is there any SEO value even when the links are nofollow?

"The value in that is the visibility that you get on social. More people knowing that your content exists will open more doors. If a journalist is following a publication, they share a report, and many people are linking to it on Twitter, the journalist might be compelled to write their own posts about it - maybe from a different angle. It's hard to say if Google counts those links because they are nofollow, but they open many doors for more link opportunities."

Do you try to keep conversations going with thought leaders with journalists on an ongoing basis? What are the best ways to keep these relationships warm?

"You can use Google Sheets to stay organised. It works most of the time, since you can group journalists according to the topics they do. Then, when you go back to the sheet and do a Ctrl-F, find the specific topic that these journalists cover, and then reach out to them when there's something relevant.

Basically, anything that you can use to organise your contact list works. Then, if you get people that like your work and ask you to inform them of future publications, you can annotate that on your list. When the need arises, it will also be easy for them to mention your report and copy and paste statistics and the link into whatever they want to write. That's how I usually approach it."

Is there a link building technique that used to work quite well but doesn't anymore?

"People who are trying to do the skyscraper technique. Basically, you find something link-worthy and create another that's maybe 10% better than what's out there. Then, you go back and look at who linked to them, reach out to them and say, 'Hey, I created something much better than what you linked to. Can you please link to mine?'

Such emails don't add that much value because no one wants to spend time going into their CMS and updating that content. With link building, you need to consider what value you will give to the person you're reaching out to."

Would it be a better long-term approach to build relationships with up-and-coming bloggers within your niche who are more open to having conversations and might be more authoritative in a couple of years?

"Definitely. You should also be looking at people who edit the content on different blogs. If there is a new editor that just got hired, you could send them a congratulatory message and hint that you are open to collaboration in the future. That's potentially one way you can try to build a relationship without being too creepy."

What shouldn't SEOs be doing in 2023? What is seductive in terms of time, but ultimately counterproductive?

"When it comes to SEO, many teams might focus on content. Yet, there are three pillars of SEO: content, links, and technical SEO. All three of these are essential; you cannot only focus on one thing. Let's say I create an awesome piece of content that takes forever to load. That's not going to be a great user experience, and Google will probably not rank your page well for whatever keywords you are targeting.

Let's also say I have good content and my pages load fast, but there aren't many links to my site. Links show Google that you are a trusted authority on the topic you are writing about. If you don't have a bunch of links, then Google might be a bit sceptical about sharing your content. It is important to not only focus on one thing - but all three areas of SEO."

Debbie Chew is the SEO Manager at Dialpad, and you can find her over at debbieychew.com.

Focus on accuracy and work precisely—Andor Palau

Andor Palau encourages SEOs in 2023 to worry less about the next shiny object and focus more on accuracy: work on the details of what you do and be accurate in your processes, because there is less and less room for error as time goes on.

Andor says: "My number one tip is accuracy. That may sound a little weird because it's not talking about the next shiny object or any specific tactics – I'm talking about a necessary habit.

All SEO consultants, or people in agencies, can probably understand this idea because, when you do a lot of analysis and audits, you see a lot of self-made issues which shouldn't be there in the first place.

When we talk about accuracy, we're talking about choosing the right keywords for the right landing pages, so that the targeting is better, and the landing page better fits the user intent. We're talking about internal linking -

not creating broken links or broken URLs, and using the right anchor text. We're also talking about structured data - how it's implemented, what information is needed, and so on. These are all problems in SEO.

When you see websites that are dealing with performance issues, for shorter or longer time periods, there is rarely one smoking gun. There is usually a collection of things going wrong. This is why working on details and being accurate in your processes is so important.

Google is getting more and more sophisticated, and search is getting more and more sophisticated, so there is less room for error. We need to become more aware of the fact that it's not a game anymore, and we need to work really precisely on things."

What inaccuracies do you see in internal linking?

"Internal linking is a very good topic because it is something that is totally in your hands, so you can influence 100% of what you are doing there. It starts with using the right anchor texts.

We know the anchor text is passing signals, and the better the anchor text is, the better the signals are. Check which anchor text you are using. Are you using non-descriptive anchor texts for important keywords or important landing pages? Try to improve the situation there."

Should you be using keyword-rich anchor text all the time?

"In internal linking, there's no penalty for having exact match anchor texts. Try to use an anchor text that is descriptive, and it makes sense to have an eye on that.

SEOs often use one specific anchor text, or a collection of anchor texts, for topic optimisation on a landing page. Don't use the same anchor text for 20 different pages. That's also not what we want to have in SEO.

All of this is down to accuracy: simply checking the list of anchor texts. With whatever crawler you're using, you can sort the anchor texts and see if they are on different target pages. Then you can go through that.

We can also talk about broken links and broken landing pages. If you have a massive site, with several hundred thousand pages, are you sure that you are not creating URLs with no items, for example? For shops, marketplaces, or classifiers there are some mechanisms that generate internal links which are totally redundant. You can check for all of these kinds of things."

You've used the phrase 'signal inheritance' before. What do you mean by accurate signal inheritance?

"Signal inheritance is connected to internal linking. We know that internal linking has three tasks. The first task is accessibility, the second is prioritisation, and the third is signal inheritance. When we talk about signal inheritance, we are mostly talking about anchor text, and using descriptive anchor text to make sure that you have clear lines of signals."

If you've got two or three pages that could potentially rank for a target keyword phrase, how do you decide which page should be your target landing page?

"There are several things to check. Which is performing the best right now? Which has the most external links? Which is driving the most (or the best) conversions right now?

I would look at a collection of signals. If you think that there is no transformer, and all of your landing pages are actually targeting the same intent and the same group of keywords, then you just have to choose one and go with that. Then, you can combine the other ones. It's as simple as that."

What are some common mistakes that happen with structured data?

"When you look at the documentation, there are some expectations from Google in terms of how information is provided, and not misusing structured data for other things. When you want to implement something, you really need to check the implementation documentation to make sure that you're using it right.

I actually just received some information from someone else about a manual action based on the misuse of structured data in job postings. Job postings is one area where Google has a lot of strict rules. It's important to really check the documentation and have an eye on that. Also, check that you use the right URLs for your structured data.

Another common error is with FAQs. Sometimes, folding FAQ elements are automatically combined with structured data, but you are only allowed to use that data once on a page. If you use these elements three times on your page then you have three times the structured data, and Google will show that as an error. Things like that are very common when we talk about structured data and accuracy."

How do you identify which internal links aren't optimised or accurate in terms of the text that you used?

"Again, it's about taking those lists from your crawls and actually going through them. I'm an ambassador for Oncrawl, so I'm using that, but most tools will easily get you that data. Whether it's Screaming Frog, Sitebulb, etc., all crawlers should be able to do that to some degree. Then you can easily go through the list."

Is there a process that SEOs can follow to ensure that they're more accurate in the future?

"I'm a huge fan of checklists as part of the process. Making checklists for almost everything you're doing is very important. We often only talk about checklists when we talk about migrations but, depending on the team setup and how many people are in your team, it is important to have these kinds of checklists and processes.

Errors often happen when knowledge is not passed on to the next person in the right way. You can catch those errors by having a really good structure, good processes, and a good checklist. That's something I would definitely spend some time on. The bigger the team, the more important it is.

In some ways, accuracy is also a mindset. You really need to be willing to make those checks again and again and again. If you have tickets - something was developed, or a change should go live - then there should be a process. There should be checklists and there should be at least two people looking at those changes. There should be processes that are clear, like 'no rollouts on a Friday', for example. All of these things can make sure that accuracy is increasing on the site."

What kind of impact can accurate internal linking have? If you optimise all of your internal links for a target phrase, would that affect your rankings?

"Some non-descriptive anchor texts will have less of an impact than others. What happens quite often is that anchor texts with different meanings are used, or a different query, so the anchor text does not match the intent of the page. These are bigger problems than having very generic 'home' or 'click here' links.

In the end, if you're totally happy with the performance of that URL, feel free not to change anything. If, however, you want to carry out every possible optimisation, then I would definitely check the anchor text again.

As we said at the very beginning, it is often not just one thing. When it happens with one URL out of a hundred URLs, you probably won't see that big of an impact. When you're optimising several thousand URLs on your domain, then this can really impact your rankings."

What shouldn't SEOs be doing in 2023? What's seductive in terms of time, but ultimately counterproductive?

"One thing I have in mind is not to lose your focus. I've been an SEO myself for more than a decade. I know we all love to work on several things, and new things are always coming up - the next thing you want to check, the next thing you want to improve, etc. – even though you already have a list.

I try to focus on three or four things, work on them for a long time, and make sure that I really get an improvement there. Take a few things all the way to the end rather than starting a hundred things and not finishing anything. Choose two or three topics for a year (or a quarter, whatever your timeframe is) and work on that, but work on that with a focus.

Another thing you shouldn't do is overanalyse without testing. Be aware of the fact that, sometimes, you simply have to test things. Put it online and see what happens. If your assumption wasn't right, then you can roll back, but we tend to overanalyse and not act. SEO is still about getting things online, getting things changed, and seeing what happens.

From the company side, you shouldn't underestimate the value of SEO. Companies should invest more into it. I often see companies hiring SEOs, but they only get one tool and expect them to do proper SEO with that. We all know that having one tool for SEO is not enough. You don't hire someone to repair your car and give them one tool. Companies need to have the awareness that SEO needs investment. It means having a budget for research and development, having a budget to hire the right people, having the budget for the right tools, and also having the freedom to test things."

Andor Palau is an International SEO Consultant and you can find him over at andorpalau.com.

Optimise your internal links—Jan-Willem Bobbink

Jan-Willem Bobbink believes that, in 2023, SEOs should be spending more time optimising your internal links and thinking about best practices where 95% of websites could see significant benefits.

Jan says: "It might be surprising, but internal link optimisation is my number one focus. It's not something new and it's completely different from what others are doing, but internal link optimisation is the most underutilised tactic in SEO.

This is because it's difficult to measure. Many smart people have thought about building specific models to determine the possible impact of changing internal linking, but there have always been issues. It's not as straightforward as you think. It's not only the internal linking you need to take into account but also the external linking that is flowing in as well.

Most SEO tactics nowadays talk about content. It's really easy to come up with a rule like 'Every page needs to have three hundred words' or 'Every page needs to have a specific Core Web Vitals score.' Internal link optimisation is a bit more advanced and actually doing it can be a bit boring, because you don't see the immediate impact.

Even though it's difficult, 95% of websites would benefit a lot from simply thinking about best practices. You don't need fancy models or before/after comparisons – there are lots of low-hanging fruits available for all domains. It's less important for a small blog or a big Amazon-like webstore but, for everything in between, internal linking can be really powerful when it's done right."

What's the best way of viewing your current internal link graph?

"The first thing to take into account is that Google looks at the specific positions of links differently. There's a difference between a link in a header or in a footer, compared to a link within a piece of content.

You can take a look at the patterns that are found using a Random Surfer Model. This kind of model was written by Google engineers, and it demonstrates how some links within a webpage have a higher probability to be clicked than others. Using those probability scores, you can assign a value to specific links. Based on that information, it makes sense that a link that's directly visible when a user reads a piece of content will be clicked more often than a link that's hidden at the bottom of a long page.

It's important to see that difference first, before you start analysing anything. Once you understand that, have a look at which pages are mostly linked from the main navigation elements. Check what's in the header, check what's in the footer, and check if those pages also have links from within the content.

Most of the available crawlers nowadays (like Screaming Frog) will check which part of the website your links are located in. If you do a basic crawl, you will already have the data available, but you should be manually looking at your page as well. Where are the main navigation elements? Where are internal links? Do you have any widgets that crosslink?

Once you have that data available, combine it with your data from Search Console. Screaming Frog has a straightforward connection with the API, so it's easy to ingest data and combine it with the internal link data you have already collected.

A really concrete tip, and one of the easiest wins to get, is to check for pages that are currently ranking in positions 5 to 20 and don't have any internal links - or have a low number of internal links compared to your overall link graph. If you can see that your top-ranking pages have 10 links on average, and your lower-linking pages have only 4 or 5 of those, you may want to move around a number of links and push more value towards lower-ranking pages.

Another quick win is to look at pages that have no links at all. Use a crawl source like the XML sitemap - which usually contains all the URLs of your website - and check if there are pages without links. Bigger websites, where some of the internal linking is automated, usually don't have this problem. However, marketers will often create specific landing pages targeting specific keywords and they forget about actually linking that page in order to win a useful spot. That leaves pages that have no links at all, but have a lot of SEO potential due to other factors like the content on the page or the relevancy to specific keywords.

I have another tip that is particularly relevant if the domain has a top-down structure. A webstore, for example, usually has a homepage that links to categories, that link to subcategories, and then to product pages. You have a structure like a pyramid, -and Google needs to go through that structure from top to bottom for every product page to be discovered.

Think about how you can crosslink to the lowest level within the pyramid. How can you crosslink product pages, for example? Think about adding widgets for best-selling products, or biggest discounts, or widgets that generate useful links for users like 'often sold with'. By doing that, you get much better coverage to allow Google to find all your product pages."

How do you determine which pages to target and whether a page is likely to perform better if you build more internal links to it?

"It's always important to balance it out. Removing a link to a top-ranking page and directing that value towards another page may actually decrease the rankings of that currently top-performing page. It's a balancing act.

If a page has 100 links and another only has 2 links, then it probably won't matter for the higher-ranking page if you bring it down to 99 internal links but, in terms of percentages, the other page will get a much bigger increase in link value. One page will only lose 1%, but the other will increase by 50% compared to the previous situation.

I usually try to visualize it. There are a number of software tools available (usually based on the old PageRank algorithms) that can visualize the size and impact of making internal link changes. You can compare your link graph before and after the changes and then see what the actual internal PageRank values are before and after. Then you can see whether you are taking a risk by making those changes - like removing too much internal link flow from the top-ranking pages.

These kinds of changes can easily be reversed. There may be a risk but if it doesn't work, and rankings don't improve, you go back to the original situation. It's not a one-directional change you are making; it's a constant change.

You should also consider seasonality in this. Maybe during the summer you want to link to swimwear and in the winter you want to link to jackets. Even throughout the year, you may want to balance it out."

When would you want to ensure that a page isn't indexed and how could you do that at scale?

"I would consider crawling. Firstly, you have the crawling and then the indexing. For the average website, crawling isn't really a problem. Google spends enough time on your website to find all the pages and then decides, on the individual page level, what to do with each page. Let's say you're an Amazon, however. Google can't update and crawl every page every day. They need to make a choice.

If you have 5,000 new blogs posted every day on your content network, it would be wise to create widgets that guide Google to the latest and freshest content. The same goes for the most recently uploaded products. You can help Google to prioritise their crawling by adding or removing internal links. This usually works best if you have a section of the website that you don't want to be crawled and indexed.

First of all, make sure that Google doesn't end up there. Hide the links. You can use JavaScript to create a link that's usable by a real user but not by Googlebot, so you can make sure that Googlebot can't actually see the link behind the script.

If Google is on the page (either through external links or other ways) then see if you want to canonicalise it or noindex it. That's a choice that really depends on the overall model of the website. If it's a product that's temporarily not available, a noindex would do - because when Google comes by and the product is available again, the noindex is gone.

What you see with canonicals is that the whole value, and the history of searching that URL, will be transferred from one page to another. Over time, Google starts crawling the URL that has the canonical on it less than a URL with noindex on it. It depends on the page but, overall, noindex is the safest option and canonical should only be used if you're really sure that the page will never have any SEO value or purpose at all."

What shouldn't SEOs be doing in 2023? What's seductive in terms of time, but ultimately counterproductive?

"99% of link building activity has so much time and money spent on it, but it doesn't deliver any value. Link building used to be really effective, if done right, but Google has become quite effective at determining which links are there for a genuine reason and which links are being placed mainly because SEOs think they should be there.

Consider blog networks - where every individual blog post contains external links. It's really easy for Google to detect that really aggressive linking is taking place, and therefore it usually only has a short-term impact. I've seen clients spend thousands of dollars buying links and the impact was basically zero. The agency that sold the links might have made up a nice story about there being an impact, but there were so many other factors that also changed that it's really difficult to point it back to those individual links.

The majority of the links currently being placed with the idea of pushing SEO rankings are useless. Google has so much data about what a real link is, and what is useful for the user.

We talked earlier about the Random Surfer Model, and the same principle can be applied to external links. Check if the domain where you're getting a link from is ranking itself. Is there any actual organic traffic going through that domain? In most cases, the websites that offer the links don't rank at all anymore.

Be really critical of what you're doing in terms of link building, because there are still valuable links to be obtained but the number of crappy links being placed is much higher.

You really need to be doing quality link building, especially if the competition is fierce. Everybody is able to create quality content – in-depth content and content that aligns with the user intention – and the technical quality of websites is usually above average in competitive niches, so the only deciding factor that's left is link building.

It's not about the numbers - it's about the quality and the relevancy. You need to spend a decent amount of time and effort actually getting those high-quality links. It's also not about the scale. People still see link building as something you have to do on a site, so they buy full packages or they close deals getting 10 links a month for a specific amount of time for a specific amount of money, and never check if the links actually sent through any referral traffic, or had the right metrics."

Jan-Willem Bobbink is a Freelance SEO Consultant and you can find him at notprovided.eu.

Use an API for intelligent internal link building—Christina Ehrensberger

Christina Ehrensberger encourages SEOs to use an internal linking API to power the logic behind the internal linking modules within your site in 2023.

Christina says: "This API recommends internal links either at random or based on relevance/recency. It's easy to integrate and you can ensure that traffic is recirculated throughout the site.

Using an API of this nature will position you for the best SEO outcome possible. We often encounter sites with suboptimal internal linking strategies. They might have pages with numerous internal links and some that have none. For example, on some pages, 20% of URLs get 80% of all internal links and on other pages, 80% of URLs get 20% of all links. This API helps us resolve a lot of issues on sites."

Will the API select a link and then that link will be permanent on the page or is it a case of rotating the links on the pages?

"It rotates them."

Is that a concern from Google's perspective, if they see links being there one moment and not there the next?

"No. The API does this intelligently and the links are constantly being refined and optimised. The links that are returned by the API have feedback loops and check data from Google Search Console as clicks and impressions. They estimate where the links will be most effective. The links don't constantly rotate, but it's an intelligent way of placing the links."

If links point to a page and that page isn't ranking, might the API decide that there's another page that's more likely to rank for that particular keyword phrase and select that page instead?

"Yes. We see that some pages, for example, have a limited number of internal links. This can be problematic because it can affect the discoverability of pages for users. We know that Google navigates the site and finds the content with the links and navigates it. An effective API can help ensure that all pages within a site have a sufficient amount of inbound links so that the overall equity and traffic flow is passed to all pages of the site."

When automating things like this, is one of the challenges the position and contextual nature of the links of the page?

"The links are inserted in the form of different modules that can, for example, be put at the bottom of the site or on the side navigation. You can place them wherever you want. The design can also be more than just text, and it can have thumbnail images in place. For example, if it's articles you can place similar articles and different links, and then interlink the content."

Regarding the size of a website, what would be the minimum number of pages that would make this approach worthwhile?

"We recommend you have at least 100 pages because, otherwise, it might not be worth it. If anyone is interested in using this particular API, you can contact the Graphite agency and get a subscription. The API is priced based on the number of pages the site has. You can reach out to il-api@graphitehq.com to get a quote."

Is this more relevant for certain languages or can it be used in any country around the world?

"Yes, we just launched a multi-lingual support for the API. It can be implemented in different languages."

How do you measure the ROI of spending money on link building? Are you able to measure things like the increased amount of traffic through the API and conversions you're getting as a result of the links being built?

"Yes. Usually, we generate an impact report and you can measure the success very well. For example, we check URL clicks, impressions, average position, CTR, and various other metrics. We look at what has changed since the API was implemented in a specific section. We have seen magnificent results from different clients; there is one that implemented eight APIs. They went on to experience continuous growth in the sections the APIs were implemented. They received a 95% increase in URL clicks where the API was active, and had another section that jumped 105% in URL clicks."

Is there any limit to the number of calls that an API can make with Google Search Console, for example, to get the data that it requires?

"Yes. We do have a limit request."

Are there any other sources that you take data from to deliver the optimum quality of links on an automated basis?

"Yes, we can. For example, we can interlink specific silos. This can be done with category pages that have similar topics. There are several different ways to implement the API."

Is it possible to do this on a manual basis instead, so you can select everything yourself and get better quality results?

"There's no way you could realistically do this selection of links manually. With the presence of AI and these kinds of APIs, we can automate the process and place links in a way that we weren't able to do before. This improves web pages so that they are crawled faster and more frequently. There are lots of benefits that lead to an improvement in page rankings.

The internal links are relevant to the content the page has and will also drive better on-page engagement. Maybe someone could be analysing all pages and links manually and placing the links themselves, but doing it in an automated way is much easier, faster, and more efficient."

It's important to ensure that search engines don't perceive this as automated internal link generation. Do you want to ensure that content provides as good of a user experience as possible and retains highly relevant links to the users visiting each page?

"This API actually helps you to give a better user experience in many ways. For example, it helps you avoid orphan pages or sites that might not be linking to any crawl points. These are usually sites that get a high amount of traffic, like a home page. When a page is not internally linked correctly to these crawl points, or just overall, it will be a missed opportunity.

We're not inventing new links or performing any negative link building actions, we're just resurfacing existing information and making it easier for search engines and users to discover those pages. We focus a lot on the user experience - providing the data and endpoints to clients and incorporating images, thumbnails, and more to ensure that the user experience is preserved. It's just that the links are smart."

What shouldn't SEOs be doing in 2023? What's seductive in terms of time, but ultimately counterproductive?

"Everyone who does SEO should focus on the user and the user experience. Many clients today are asking about optimising for robots and SEO. Many perceive SEO as a one-time thing and move forward, but SEO never stops. It constantly changes and SEO is all about the user. If you don't understand this, you won't have much success in 2023."

Christina Ehrensberger is Growth Leader at Graphite and you can find her over at consultina.com.mx. She is also a Co-Founder of Latinas en SEO, a community that focuses on closing the gender gap in SEO in Latin America.

11 LOCAL SEO

Optimise the 'heck' out of your Google Business Profile—Greg Gifford

Greg Gifford espouses the value of your Google Business Profile and explains why, for many SEOs in 2023, that profile should be the cornerstone of everything you are doing in Local SEO – so it needs to be thoroughly optimised.

Greg Gifford says: "If you do face-to-face business with customers at a brick and mortar store OR you serve customers face-to-face at their location (like a plumber or electrician), then you absolutely need Local SEO. If any of your important queries display a map pack, you may need it even if you don't do face-to-face business with customers. Basically, if Google thinks a search query has local intent, it will use its local algorithm, and you need to be doing Local SEO.

Keep in mind - if you don't have a physical storefront and you don't do face-to-face business with customers in a local area, you're not eligible for a Google Business Profile.

For those who are eligible, your Google Business Profile is basically the cornerstone of Local SEO. It's what allows you to show up in the Map Pack or Google Maps. It's hugely important for that proximity factor in

Google's local algorithm. You need to fill out everything you can and maximize your opportunity for showing up in local searches by optimizing the heck out of your Google Business Profile."

What does optimising the heck out of your Google Business Profile look like in 2023?

"Lots of people will still add additional keywords to the business name, which is really against the rules and can get you suspended. You should instead include your actual business name, local area code phone number, and correct address. You should then select all of the appropriate categories. Though there are ten slots for categories, that doesn't mean you'll have to fill out all ten. Just pick everything that applies to what you do. This will probably be at least three or four for most businesses.

There's a great list at PlePer.com - where there's an interactive list of all the GBP categories. You can enter a category and it will show you all the other categories that are commonly selected alongside that category. You can also use the GMBspy Chrome plugin to see which categories your competitors have chosen.

It's all about picking the correct categories and being strategic about which category you pick first. That primary category will carry a lot more weight in the algorithm. You should upload a tonne of photos because the more good photos you have, the more likely you'll be to get clickthroughs. You should write a killer description and pick all the business attributes that apply to what you're doing. If you're in a vertical that gets specific rules - for example, hotels or car dealerships - you can do some things that other people can't do. You must ensure you're doing everything you can for your particular vertical. This will include putting preloaded questions into the Q&A section and answering those questions. You should monitor the Q&A section and make sure that the owner's answers are always the ones with the most thumbs up. They will then appear as the primary answers.

You need to be doing Google Posts on a regular basis. Google Posts used to be a once-a-week kind of thing because they would disappear after seven days. Now they last for six months, so you don't necessarily have to do them weekly. A lot of people do Posts incorrectly and approach them like social media. You really need to treat each Post like a free ad that appears in your profile. That's why you need to write something compelling there.

Look at your Google Business Profile like a novice. If you've got your blinders on and assume you know everything about your business, take those blinders off and look at your profile from an amateur perspective. If you were someone who knows absolutely nothing about the business, could you find what you need? Is all of the pertinent information there that you would want to see as a customer? If you do all of these things, your profile will be more likely to show up often in searches and you'll get more business from local customers."

What about reviews and customer photos, are these tied into your Google Business Profile?

"This gets confusing for a lot of businesses. People can leave a photo along with their review, or they can take a photo and tag the business. This will show up in the public group of photos for that business. Because many businesses don't do much with photos, customer photos are often the only things that show up when people go to look. You want to control that customer experience and upload high-quality, professionally-shot photos that have a bit of an edge - and in most cases, those will show up more often than mobile phone photos.

You have to be proactive with your reputation management. You want to have lots of awesome reviews, so you need to be sure to ask every single customer to leave a review. Make it easier for customers to leave a review and then monitor those reviews. Post responses as quickly as possible for both positive and negative reviews. When you're responding to negative reviews, remember that your response is not for the person that left the bad review. You should be dealing with that person offline in the real world to fix the situation. Your response to the negative review is for every potential future customer that's going to look at your reviews and see how you handled that situation."

Has the way your profile is claimed changed? Ten years ago you'd receive a postcard, is it still done the same way?

"Though it's crazy to think about, this is still the primary verification method. When you request a postcard, that code is only valid for thirty days. The postcard has to come from Google in the US, so it will need to be sent overseas. If mail is delayed, you might end up receiving your postcard late and having nowhere to enter it because the code has expired.

Google is testing some new verification methods though. Hopefully, they'll end up getting rid of the postcard, but who knows what they're planning. There are now two ways to do video verification - if they're offered (your vertical will play a huge role in the verification method you're offered). However, you can't request either method - you can only use what Google offers to you. If asked, you can do a live call that's scheduled on your phone. Somebody at the Google verification team will call you via video and you can show them the things they need to see to know you're legitimate.

Sometimes, Google offers the chance to record a video and upload it. In that case, you'll have to prove you're located where you say you are. You'll have to show the inside of your business too, and show some sort of access that the general public wouldn't have. If you didn't have to verify your location and specific access, any random person could steal those listings away. Google wants to make sure you have access to the building and show you're in the office logging onto your computer. You would need to show something that some random person couldn't do to prove your legitimacy.

Video will hopefully replace postcards someday because it's much more efficient and faster. Right now it takes 12 - 14 business days for a postcard to arrive, which could easily be delayed and leave you not being able to do anything. It's much better if you can do instant verification via call."

It's important to establish a wonderful Knowledge Panel and have a great Business Profile that can feed into that. Which elements does Google typically take?

"That's the really cool thing about the Google Business Profile experience. You literally have a direct interface to Google's Knowledge Graph and the information Google has about your business. Lots of people get confused and think it's feeding the Knowledge Panel, but if you're a local business you won't really have a Knowledge Panel. You'll have a Google Business Profile panel that feeds all of the pertinent information into the Knowledge Graph. It'll pull things like business name, address, and map pin location.

Often, people don't check the actual location of the pin and it may not be accurate to what your address is. Sometimes in crowded urban areas, it can be a little bit off. All of your business hours and attributes will get pulled in. That's another reason why it's important to be very diligent and fill everything out correctly."

The Google My Business App was replaced in 2022 by Google Search and Google Maps. What does this mean, practically, for businesses?

"Lots of people freaked out when they got the email saying the Google My Business app is on its way out. Everybody assumed their Google My Business profile was going too but, in reality, they were just renaming it as Google Business Profile. Also, Google has fully rolled out the in-search editing experience - so there's no more Google My Business dashboard.

Basically, you'll have your panel pop up and there's a link that you can click to edit your information. You can then edit all of your elements right there in the search experience, as opposed to on the old dashboard or app. Now, if you've got multiple locations for your business or if you're an agency or freelancer working for multiple clients (providing you've got more than one), you'll still be able to go to that old-school dashboard. This is easier than having to look up multiple businesses and edit there. When you click on a business in the list, you'll be taken to the in-search editing experience. Since it's new, many people are freaking out because it's a different experience than they're used to."

If you work in a big enterprise with lots of different physical locations, has this changed the way that services like these work?

"All of the services still work the same way, because they all have a direct API into the backend of Google Business Profiles. All the services still work. If you're using Yext or any reputation management platform, it'll allow you to edit your Google Business Profile information."

What's next for Google Business Profiles? Is there anything that's likely to change what SEOs should be looking at to get ahead of the competition?

"Within the car dealership industry, something called Cars for Sale has been introduced. This allows dealers to have an inventory feed and display their inventory in their Google Business Profile. This is only available in the United States, but most US dealers are getting involved as they continue to iron out the bugs.

Hopefully, they'll roll this out to the rest of the world and something similar will be available for all industries. Google is investing more in the editing experience in search results. We're going to see more functionality and more features there as things go on. Other than that, there's not really anything big upcoming."

Should you try to make your feed as friendly as possible for search engines? Then, if a service like Google Business Profile supports that information, you can immediately take advantage of it in the future?

"For sure. Any marketers reading this will appreciate the fact that many business owners don't pay attention to what's going on with Google. It's worth paying attention to the Google Business Profile side of things at the very least. Then, if something new does come out, you can take advantage of it.

There were lots of updates during the COVID lockdowns to help businesses that were struggling to stay open. Google released additional attributes like curbside pickup, senior-only hours, brunch hours, and other things that didn't exist beforehand. There are still lots of businesses out there that don't know about these things. Most business owners or managers go in and set up a Business Profile but never really go back and do anything there. Pay attention to all the features that are available. If you're not paying attention to whatever updates might be coming from Google, at least log into the editing interface once a month to see if there is something new that wasn't there before.

Take advantage of everything you can, because your Google Business Profile will be your new homepage. It'll be your first impression with customers. People don't have to go to your website to get your phone number, address, pictures, and testimonials. They can do all of that right there, through your Google Business Profile in the search results. That's why it's important to do everything you can to stand out from the rest."

What shouldn't SEOs be doing in 2023? What's seductive in terms of time, but ultimately counterproductive?

"People deliver horrible SEO reports - reports that include everything that possibly matters without considering whether it matters to clients. If clients come to you with a problem and decide that you are the solution to that problem, the solution needs to be reflected in the report. Just because we monitor what we're doing on the SEO side doesn't mean it'll matter to the client or the client's bottom line.

We need to simplify our reports and stop overloading clients with thirty pages of meaningless data. We need to pay attention and deliver reports that are easy to understand and that tell a story with the data. We can customise those reports for clients. We don't do the same SEO for every client, so we shouldn't give the same report to every client.

Another big pet peeve of mine is content marketing. It continues to grow and has taken on a life of its own. Everything is content, content, content - but you can't just write content and expect to do better in search results. You've got to create helpful content and remember that if you want to show up in a search result when someone types in a particular phrase, you need to have a page about that concept on your website.

People are still covering multiple concepts within blog posts, pages, and product pages rather than honing in on a specific issue. Keep it to one concept per page as part of your SEO strategy. You don't have to write the best answer on the internet, but you do need the best answer in the local area to the question that the potential customer is asking. Writing the best answer usually means answering that initial question but also thinking ahead and answering possible subsequent questions. This will be hard to do in the short format most small businesses use for blog posts and pages of content. You're not going to show up well with a few hundred words because you won't be writing the best answer in your local area.

With content marketing, people continually focus on producing more content. The biggest problem is that they skip the necessary keyword research to figure out what they should be writing about. Always look at the question you're trying to answer and the problem you're trying to solve. This is the first step, then you can plan your content, and create and publish it. You can then optimise your content accordingly.

Don't just pay for content and risk it not performing well. Don't just churn it out for the sake of churning it out. Content is important, but it's only a small piece of the massive puzzle. If you've got 5 puzzle pieces from a 1,000-piece puzzle, you're not going to solve the problem. You need the whole thing."

Greg Gifford is the Vice President of Search at SearchLab Digital and you can find him over at searchlabdigital.com.

UTM tag up everything in your Google Business Profile—Claire Carlile

Claire Carlile says that, if you're a local business and you have access to a Google Business Profile, you should Urchin Tracking Module (UTM) tag up all of the links from your business profile.

Claire says: "The key elements of UTM are source, medium, content, and campaign."

What does source mean?

"UTM tagging can seem overly complicated but it's highly important to digital marketers. There isn't a one-size-fits-all approach to UTM tagging; it largely depends on who's managing the data in your organisation.

If you just think of UTM tags as tracking codes that we add to the end of our external links that tell us more about where that traffic came from and how it got to our websites. So when someone clicks on a UTM tagged URL, details of the source, the medium, and the campaign that that website visit comes from get transferred over into Google Analytics.

Imagine that the source is where the journey started, and the medium is the method of transport.

Whatever you set up with your UTM tags you need to make sure that you set up plays nicely with what your colleagues are doing internally.."

Is it best to start off with the end in mind and look at the data you're getting as a result of tagging correctly?

"Yes. You can create a very simple framework, but it's important not to implement it before you've checked with higher-ups in your organisation. This will avoid your practices clashing with what's already occurring – for example, if your UTM tagging starts 'stealing' traffic from the organic channel.

Tagging links from your Business Profile gives you a chance to show a return on your time and effort. You can then ensure you know which parts of Google Business Profile are giving returns. This is important because, when someone clicks on a link from a Google Business Profile, there are lots of things visitors can achieve which won't send them through to your website. Apart from measuring all the things they can do without going to your website, you'll have plenty of opportunities to link there.

Without adding UTM tagging, the traffic from the Google Business Profile will end up in the organic bucket. There, you won't be able to tell the difference between organic traffic from the local organic results and organic traffic from the local finder or 3-pack. Lots of apps and some browsers will strip out any referral information by the time it gets into Google Analytics. Therefore, traffic from lots of places will end up in the direct bucket. By adding UTM tags, you'll be able to demonstrate ROI and you'll be able to dig into which parts of the Google Business Profile drive traffic and conversions."

How much traffic is available directly from the Google Business Profile?

"It depends on your business type, but potentially loads. Let's consider branded traffic. If someone searches for your business name and your Google Business Profile shows up for that search, that'll be the first thing they see. They might not need to go through to your website - they'll navigate from there, take your phone number, look at your photos, browse your services, read reviews, make an appointment, upload photos, etc. There are many things that can take place in the Business Profile - but there are also plenty of opportunities to drive somebody through to your website.

This could be via a website link, appointment link, menu URL, a Google Post and any other external link for which your business profile is eligible. There will be multiple opportunities to move people to the useful page on your website. As soon as you tag these URLs, you'll be able to see what percentage of traffic and revenue was driven by the Google Business Profile. Until you do this, it'll be difficult to measure where your traffic is coming from in terms of the Business Profile - and you won't be able to identify the contribution.

All of these things take time and effort: to optimise listings for conversion, have great photos, reply to reviews, etc. If you suggest initiating some of these things, you should have a test set up that you can roll out initially to see what the return is. For example, if you have a Google post schedule or want to add products, you can capably prove and demonstrate return via tests. You can then roll out your strategy across multiple locations. It's great to do some A/B or multivariate testing as a way to measure whether it's worth investing in and curating your Business Profile."

Will Google or anyone else use these UTM links elsewhere, and make it tricky for you to attribute exactly where the traffic is coming from?

"This is something you can monitor via malformed URLs that have somehow snuck in. You can trace where they come from and ask them to be updated, but this will be few and far between.

For example, Airbnb scraped content from business profiles for accommodations and attractions. They then used that UTM-tagged URL in the content, and that was causing issues. By spotting this internally, they were able to strip out those UTM tags as a solution. If anyone did copy and paste the URL from your browser bar after opening a link via a Google Business Profile, they could add that to their link - and that would give you incorrect information. It's worth using tools to check your analytics and backlinks."

Some SEOs are not clear about the difference between 'source' and 'medium' tags, do you see that as an issue in people tracking?

"Yes. This underlines the importance of consistency and having a plan in place. 'Source' and 'medium' are the two things that get muddled the most. If you get them wrong, your traffic will end up in the 'other' bucket - something you really don't want, from an analytics perspective. The best way to look at it is to think of the UTM-tagged link as a journey from one place to the other.

Think about the source as the place where it started and the medium as the method of transport. I'd suggest using 'google' as the source and 'organic' as the medium. Then you can use the 'campaign' and 'ad content fields' to help you work out which part of the Business Profile it came from.

If you're using a third party tool for managing GBP then check how it tags your URLs. Make sure that the source, medium, and campaign fields are consistent with the way you'd like your GBP traffic to be bucketed in GA. If your GBP campaign data gets borked because of bad UTM tagging you'll be able to fix this by taking it out of Google Analytics and using CASE statements in Looker studio.

Before you get going, spend some time thinking about how you're going to do it, how it's going to be consistent, and how it's going to play nicely with other data that comes into analytics."

What's the free resource people can use to form the UTM URL?

"Search for 'UTM tagging' plus 'Google Business Profiles' or 'GMB' and you'll find *Claire's Complete Guide To UTM Tagging for Google My Business*. This will take you to a post that tells you all about UTM tagging, why you should do it, how to do it, and more. It also links to a free Google Sheet - where you can drop in URLs and it'll auto-generate those UTM tag URLs for you."

Where do you look to determine how successful your campaign is?

"I'd recommend using a GBP connector to pull your data into Looker Studio, this can show actions taken on your business profile. You can pull in relevant conversions from GA, and also visibility data from GSC."

The Google My Business app was replaced in 2022 by Google Search and Google Maps. Does this have any practical implementation for Local SEO?

"Yes. The Google My Business app was useful for uploading photos and responding to reviews. Rather than being replaced when it fell out of use, everything just went over to Google Maps and search. It's always interesting when functionality has to move between different interfaces. Also, teaching clients how to do the things that keep changing is part of the joy that keeps us in business."

What shouldn't SEOs be doing in 2023? What's seductive in terms of time, but ultimately counterproductive?

"Anything that opposes our innate focus on measurement and why we use it. You shouldn't just attach yourself to anything that's bright and shiny. Avoid implementing something without understanding why you're doing it or what it'll do for your bottom line. Make sure that you have a business use case for anything that you decide to do.

If you apply something new, make sure that there is some sort of hypothesis framework attached to it. Think about what you're doing and what you think it might do. You can then measure the results afterwards."

Claire Carlile is a local search expert for BrightLocal at brightlocal.com and you can find her over at clairecarlilemarketing.com.

Optimise for augmented reality with location schema—Dixon Jones

Dixon Jones brings awareness to emerging opportunities in the augmented reality space for SEOs in 2023, and highlights the importance of being ready for the future in this space.

Dixon says: "Now is the time to start thinking about how to optimise for augmented reality".

What qualifies as augmented reality?

"Pokémon Go is a good example, but it's not particularly good for SEO. Augmented reality involves using a device to literally look at a location through a camera lens. You can then augment further information onto that - for example, looking at a flower and the augmented reality telling you its name and characteristics. The future will see us pointing a device at something and uncovering considerable information about it. Let's say you're travelling past Wembley Stadium and wonder what's going on there next week. You could point your camera at the stadium and get information about what events are scheduled.

It's worth carrying out some specific SEO now if you know it will have an effect when augmented reality becomes more prevalent. Location schema is useful for certain types of businesses, although not so much if you're a virtual business. If you work at a restaurant, you could use location schema to inform customers about the kinds of food you offer. You'd also have information tied to the location of the restaurant, meaning people could extract insight into the food you serve or when you have a special event coming up.

Augmented reality could then soak up that schema and use it within Google Lens. However, it's important not to limit your scope to Google Lens because there will be other similar technologies that emerge later down the line. With this being said, there are some real things that we can do now as SEOs, to position ourselves for augmented reality."

Should we make sure our websites are marked up in a way that makes it easy for search engines and discovery bots to work out who we are, and make them confident that they should be including your data?

"Yes. There are many different schemas built to help industries define things - with a view to a machine somewhere using this as part of its database. For example, it could help filter through a particular industry, product, video, etc. We're yet to scratch the surface of schema. Lots of modern conventions try to automate schema for you, but these only tackle simple tasks and often fail to take tomorrow's technologies into account. If you're featuring more than one video on a page, for example, video schema will be completely useless - because it can't refer to multiple videos on a single page.

It's important to appreciate that schema is a little murky for SEO. People have started to use schema stuffing as a new version of keyword stuffing. You need to be laser targeted if you're going to benefit because people won't always go to 'Google.com' to find the information. It could easily be someone pointing a phone at a shop and picking up reviews that way. Our ways of 'searching' will start to transcend and become more embedded in augmented reality. What you can do is help inform users to decide what they want to do and where they want to go. Your ultimate goal is to make sure that the right customers come into your establishment."

Is there ever a situation where a commercial website doesn't need any schema or should there be schema on every single commercial website?

"No website has to have a schema; search engines can glean some things naturally. Just because you say your website is about 'airfares' doesn't make your website any more about 'airfares' than the next website. All this does is clarify that information. If you're starting to conceptualise things in a location-based setting - for example, you're the only establishment in a given area - prospective customers could pan their camera around and see where you are, who you are, etc. This would save them the time and effort of looking at an old poster that's out of date or browsing to access information online. It's interesting to think about how augmented reality is going to propagate and the schema that will help augmented reality clarify your business.

Information from Google Business Profile can be embedded straight into your schema, meaning you won't need a Google Business Profile type of portal if you use schema properly. That's something that would get embedded into a Lens when someone is looking at your establishment."

Is schema something you have to check quarterly to see if new ones have become available?

"That depends on the schema you're using. If you're talking about products and pricing (product schema) it'll have the pricing of your product in there. As your pricing changes, your schema should change to reflect that. It's not so much that the underlying schema will change - it's the data it needs to be populated with that will need to be more dynamic going forward.

Other schemas are much more static - for example, the name of your organisation, registered address, etc. Schema.org is a very living, open kind of document - with lots of people editing and coming up with new types of schema that take time to be recognised by a large search engine. Other stuff is obvious and ubiquitous, so it's valuable to go through and use what you can.

There are tools to help you WYSIWYG it, but SEOs are just setting up a schema for the home page of a website or on every single page. This is the equivalent of hitting a very finely tuned pin with a big mallet. Each page should be crafted in the same way that people craft content."

What shouldn't SEOs be doing in 2023? What's seductive in terms of time, but ultimately counterproductive?

"People shouldn't be trying to get more visitors specifically around a certain keyword. In 2023, people should stop using keyword search query volume to try and configure their keyword marketing strategy. The number of people that type in a keyword rarely bares relation to the number of people who are interested in buying a product.

For example, most people who type in the word 'horseshoe' are looking for a pub with that term in its name, not a farrier. There is a huge contextual difference between the number of people typing the word 'horseshoe' and the number of people looking to make a horseshoe for a horse. In fact, according to Knowledge Graph, people are more likely to be looking for the game 'Horseshoes'.

For years, SEOs have been saying that user intent is all about whether a keyword is transactional, navigational, commercial, etc, but it's not. Unless you've got the verb someone has typed in, you won't have any idea.

If somebody types in 'house', it's very different if they type in 'buy a house' than if they type in 'decorate a house'. These are extremely different ideas. Often things are semantically very close but very different ideas. We need to get away from using a list of keywords and the search volume in a given country to plan our world. Life has to be more about answering the full query of the user."

Dixon Jones is CEO of inLinks and a brand ambassador for Majestic. You can find him over at dixonjones.com.

12 INTEGRATE

If your SEO is not in place, any dollars you put in on your paid media campaigns won't work—William Álvarez

William Álvarez believes that SEOs in 2023 should invest in SEO as preparation for what's ahead rather than a reactionary tool, and businesses should utilise an omnichannel approach instead of funnelling their budget into isolated paid campaigns.

William says: "Now, and in the future, SEOs need to focus on how we communicate across different channels. An omnichannel approach will be important. Any media dollars you put into your strategy will fail if SEO is not performing as it should."

Is SEO the first channel?

"SEO is the first channel if you consider it a preparation for what's ahead of the media plan, rather than a reactive approach. That way, you will see better outcomes.

Clients typically fall into different challenges - how to sell, getting rid of bad reviews, driving more visits to the store, etc. Then, they start spending more on immediate paid media channels. That fails because Google has become more sophisticated regarding what they expect websites to offer their visitors. This makes the cost much higher when your content, user experience, and page performance are not where they should be.

In the past, we discussed those issues in isolation, and we could tackle them through SEO. If you had an SEO foundation from the beginning, the rest of the channels would perform better because they see the results of those efforts."

If you're doing paid marketing, what pages should you be targeting?

"There are many approaches there. From a quality perspective, you will be doubling your work if you are targeting two pages instead of having one landing page that covers all the requirements of paid search.

Instead, you could consolidate your efforts in one single landing place that accomplishes everything. You would then have the data you need to better inform the strategy, rather than having different landing pages in isolation. That works especially if you're tackling or targeting similar products or the same product."

What if the paid search team doesn't want something the other team wants, like header navigation, one call to action, etc.?

"That is usually the case with certain strategies. However, the recent requirements of Google and large eCommerce platforms - like Walmart and Amazon - have to do with offering more information. The simplicity of just having a 'buy' button, a key message, and a headline is not applicable anymore. There must be other elements essential to users for them to become customers.

Offering more validation from the tools and more support from testimonials will have a better impact on the quality scores of the landing page. It will result in lower-cost, positive performance on organic search and, of course, good performance on that channel you're paying for. It also helps with programming and email marketing efforts.

When you are using SEO as the main driver for traffic, you're also facilitating the collection of first-hand data from the users. This data is tremendously important for brands today. There were some challenges in acquiring consumers in the past, when we used tools like Google and Facebook, etc. That approach is shifting, little by little, and brand results have been incredible."

If you have a single call to action and people don't find the answer they are looking for immediately, they are less likely to come back, but if you provide other options and a great brand experience are they more likely to return?

"If you pay attention to what Google, in particular, has been doing with their paid products - you'll see that they've been learning from our wars on organic search. They accommodate that in their algorithms and in how they score their paid campaigns through the use of site links that provide more information. They learned from us that it is beneficial to put this information in paid search.

The ability to use answers that inform certain queries on organic is something they are considering more for paid search campaigns now as well. There's proof that there are more elements from organic search that worked well on paid media than elements that worked on paid media that are coming into search. We have been able to contribute more as an industry, which is helping other channels as well."

What aspects of SEO do you need to get in place before focusing on paid media?

"SERPs are quite diverse today, and they look more like an interactive magazine. If you want to secure visibility, you'll see that there are elements like video, direct answers, and rich snippets. That makes it impossible to track quarterly changes because Google brings a new format every day, and they're running many experiments. There are interesting visual elements, where you must identify the right types of elements to produce to gain space across the board.

If we learn from that, we'll understand the content landscape better, and immediately trigger content types and formats that can produce greater visibility.

With Google, it's now a game where, if you can't produce content in any of the emerging formats they offer (like Google discover), you are behind. You need to learn continuously. That also comes from knowing what's happening on paid media channels, and how you can inform those paid media channels about what you're doing in terms of SEO. You should be telling them what content is successful and what converts well, and they can use this information to inform creation in the channels where you have to pay to perform.

It's about content and how you make it more dynamic and adaptable. We have seen many brands that have become great content producers. On the other hand, those still lacking in resources are not participating in this content game. You need to have a good and solid content framework in place to have a presence on the Google of today."

What can SEOs learn from paid search?

"The dynamic aspect of paid search makes it easier to test and make page changes. Some areas of the business can have legal and compliance implications, which means that they cannot immediately implement learnings from paid search. Plus, it can take us much longer cycles to validate these things, get approval, and bring it live on the website.

Paid search helps with that because they can change a lot without scrutiny on what's being put up on the website. That works well as a proxy to ensure that what we want to produce for the long term will not change so frequently."

How would collaboration with paid search in that way work in practice?

"It depends. One example is the use of images for jewellery. Recently, we started testing different models for luxury jewellery. We discovered, after optimisation, that audiences were responding in different ways to the different images of models wearing the pieces. We could then inform the organic search about the images that were getting the most positive responses. The ones with low approval were ditched and replaced on the paid campaign, both on Google and the Google Merchant Centre.

In the end, we produced better images with higher click-through rates and conversions, which could work as permanent placements on the landing pages for organic search.

Content marketers generally pick images based on what looks nice, but don't necessarily think it impacts ongoing conversion rates. If you're selling a phone, you might have six different angles but never consider which side the viewers want to see. We don't test that on organic search."

What shouldn't SEOs be doing in 2023? What is seductive in terms of time, but ultimately counterproductive?

"We know that SEO today differs from what we did 10-15 years ago. Now, the way Google is scoring content has a major impact. They have become more strict and more sophisticated with their use of Artificial Intelligence to weed out everything that is not unique, high quality, or doesn't represent the business well.

For instance, if you're using and reusing images from the same database - you're not showing interest in increasing the authority and quality of your content pages. The same applies if you're using content brokers, churning out content en-masse just to fill up pages. All that will fail.

That is why we are seeing better results today in businesses that have become more aware of the importance of hiring the right talent to produce the right content. SEOs will have to react to the trend and start finding ways to bring content that answers user questions in a personalised way.

Some consultants still advise clients to check out the SERPS and produce something better. We should stop doing that; it is basically using shortcuts just to fill out your pages. This strategy will not work anymore because the latest Google algorithm update is tackling that."

William Álvarez is the director of Organic Search at Catalyst Digital, and you can find him over at catalystdigital.com.

Use knowledge from Google Ads to boost your SEO (and vice versa)—Krzysztof Marzec

Krzysztof Marzec believes SEOs in 2023 should be taking advantage of the knowledge, you can gain from Google Ads to improve your SEO efforts, and vice versa.

Krzysztof says: "By using data from SEO, you can achieve better results in Google Ad campaigns and the opposite is also true."

What information can we get from Google Ads that will help with SEO?

"Keywords. In SEO, you can't check the results of keywords, because Google Analytics is asked not to provide it. You might only be able to check the landing page and how it works toward your ROI. In Google Ads, you can test exact keywords. If you're fighting for a few keywords and go after them, you might find that those keywords don't work. Without Google Ads, we'd all be using content links to fight for the same keywords - but end up getting no sales from them.

If data shows that a keyword is working in Google Ads, it will usually work in SEO too. If you have thousands of clicks in Google Ads and a very low conversation rate, you'll probably get the same low rates in SEO.

The next step is all about user intent in SEO keywords. When you put content out to users on the Google SERP, you'll experience different click-through rates (CTRs). You can test them in Google Ads and use side links as a content extension for ads, callouts, and headlines. In Google Ads, you'll get results in real-time and you can know which elements give the best CTRs. You can take this data and use it to improve titles, descriptions, etc. You can also put new content on your landing page. With the knowledge that something works in Google Ads, putting it in your content can make people stay on your landing page longer. It's worth testing something in Google Ads for some time and then implementing it in SEO if it's successful.

Dynamic Search Ads (DSA) are a great way of searching for new keywords for SEO. It works because Google tries to match your keywords with your landing pages based on its algorithms. You can use Google information to configure which keywords go to which landing pages as part of your long-tail strategy. This is a great way to implement data from Google Ads but also, in reverse, you'll find better results in DSA campaigns and Google Shopping when landing pages are optimized by SEO.

Incorporate more common keywords that will extend the reach of your campaign. You can also optimize the landing page speed to improve your Ads campaign. Collaborating with someone who's working on a Google Ads campaign will also provide a lot of benefits. You should test ideas before implementing content strategy in SEO, for example, to ensure you're doing things that will result in sales/conversions."

Should the ultimate goal be to stop paid campaigns and focus on getting to page one organically? Should you optimize as efficiently as possible with the data gleaned from PPC and then switch it off?

"No. What's more important is establishing synergy with clients. You won't find every keyword accessible in SEO because they are expensive to get. Being in the Google Ads and organic search results is better for clicks and therefore conversion rates. Google Ads campaigns can be used as leverage for more budget, leads, etc.

With a good strategy, you can do SEO on a fundamental level. If a crisis hits and you can no longer use Google Ads, this could be a blessing in disguise for greater focus on getting your SEO strategy in place. You could do nothing new with no budget and still get leads from organic.

Have a baseline of sales leads from SEO and try to improve this with Google Ads. It's not a case of doing one meeting and trying to implement data - you have to check the data. With Google Ads, the best ads will only be suitable for specific periods. After months, competitors change copy and you may find your ad is no good anymore. If this happens, you should implement changes in titles, descriptions, blog posts, etc. Be careful not to make title changes site-wide because it can take months to change the whole title structure on a big site."

How is this kind of keyword data better compared with when SEO was confined elsewhere?

"You can go to Google Analytics and try to check the viewers that you don't have any data for. For example, you can check the landing page and see whether you have a page about SEO audits and surveys. If you put both of these terms in Google Ads and SEO, you can fight for the relevant keywords.

Some keywords can be very expensive because they'll be industry keywords, but you can use Google Ads to see what the actual conversion rate might be – which is very useful when it comes to SEO audits. People often fight for SEO keywords but fail because the conversion rate is so low, not just because the keywords are expensive.

Many people look for tools to do things for them rather than find an agency. It would help if you learned how to determine whether a sales keyword is wrong by spending money on Google Ads and devising an SEO strategy. If you check the landing page, you'll get a bunch of brand-new keywords that will up your conversion rate a lot.

Trying to extrapolate data by analysing landing pages in Google Analytics is not a good idea when you have brand keywords involved. You can use data to tell clients not to go for common keywords on the entry-level side of eCommerce. You can also show a big store that they can work for keywords they're likely to sell for if the attribution suggests so. They might then go with the campaign in SEO and experience great sales. When you can't show data in SEO, you can show it in Google Ads."

What can Google Ads learn from SEO?

"Many Google Ads specialists don't use their knowledge to say when a page is wrong. They could work out when to update, improve usability, and speed things up if they did. Specialists tend to stick to the interface of Google Ads; SEO will tell you when something is wrong or when you need more keywords.

For example, if you have a shop with no keywords and specify further information about your products, these descriptive keywords will work great for SEO and improve shopping ads. Many keywords will often be missing from titles that fail to describe products in more detail. When these are expanded, Google will have more content to find new keywords to market a product for DSA and shopping ads combined. If you
spend time expanding on the description of product titles, you'll achieve more and more reach. Then you won't just be refreshing some old common keywords, but long-tail precision ones - like the exact colour of a product. Specific descriptions will have better conversions than common words.

The optimisation is focused on sales. If you look at quality scoring in Google Ads, you'll find there are three pillars: expected CTR, relevance, and landing page experience. If you assign a keyword to your campaign and your landing page gets 5/10, you'll know something is wrong. You could try to optimize for a week and still be at 5/10. In this case, you could try to improve your campaign but also improve in terms of technical SEO.

There are human behaviour and algorithm-based elements to consider. If you improve the algorithm-based side of things, you'll be better off in terms of PPCs. Analyse aspects of the quality score and focus on where you can do better in the Google Ads interface and on-page. Expand your knowledge and what you know about the page. Testing new landing pages is hard in Analytics but easier in Google Ads. You can do these tests Ads to work out whether you should implement changes across your whole site."

Should search marketing teams, SEOs, and paid search experts interact together all the time?

"Yes, they should definitely interact. In a situation where one agency is doing SEO and the second is doing PPC strategies for your company - they should all communicate to unite toward the common goal of client success."

What shouldn't SEOs be doing in 2023? What's seductive in terms of time, but ultimately counterproductive?

"The business structure of agencies and specialists is usually geared toward making big sales. However, selling content by quantity over quality can be counterproductive. Internal content often only focuses on results like the number of keywords and users in Google Analytics. When you delve deeper into those results and ask for data, you might find your campaign has been unsuccessful.

It's easy to write an article that attracts users by incorporating keywords from a keyword planner, but will it sell more? In Google Analytics, we can do exact reports to check the traffic on a new landing page and whether it led to long or short-term sales. You can use this information to embrace the importance of not focusing on all keywords purely based on volume data.

It would be best to think about the real people who type those keywords in to buy your stuff after reading your content. Learn that investing in SEO is suitable for the long term. Planning to sell X amount of content over some time is a bad strategy, and you might experience empty traffic in sales. When you pay for content, you always have to check the results. The best way to benchmark is on conversion rates/value. Sometimes you'll sell big stuff and have big merging profits, but if you don't look at your analytics, you'll probably pay for content that doesn't sell at all."

Krzysztof Marzec is CEO at DevaGroup and you can find him at devagroup.com.

Harmonize all channels and ranking signals into one repeatable formula—Joseph Khan

Joseph Khan stresses the importance of having all of your social media and marketing channels in alignment in 2023 – before you think about getting your content out there.

Joseph says: "Get your channels in alignment before you launch your SEO-prepared content. That'll make a massive difference in 2023".

How does social media impact SEO?

"Social media is the new backlinking juice, because of the expertise, authority, and trust algorithm. Today, Google wants to see the spread as opposed to focusing on one link from one person. Google doesn't care about one person anymore - so focusing on getting a single link from CNN won't work because there need to be lots of people that are thinking in alignment. You can achieve this by casting your net wide and having all of your channels in harmony with whatever you're trying to create. Create all the harmonies and channels around your post, and launch out to the market for shares and engagement.

Schema is an essential part of this harmony because Google connects everything and sees all. If you don't have all the connections, one backlink isn't going to help you. Your content can take over the market without having a single backlink, but with the connecting web in place and through viral engagement. If you can get people to share your content, you'll get people talking about it. By achieving this, you can move up in the search engine because you've cast your net wide.

Going forward, the new algorithms will probably be based on the user intent and the user web: what they're doing, what they're connected to, and what they're interested in. They're going to care more about that heart than any backlink to CNN. The future of SEO will have more to do with social markings than backlinks."

Are you saying that dofollow and nofollow don't matter as much anymore?

"Yes. Google has even acknowledged that they don't matter as much. They would rather you do the right thing than just do THE thing. If it's a sponsored link, they want you to mark it. If it's somebody you don't know or trust, they want you to mark it. They don't care what it is; they just want you to be honest so they know whether they can mark it in their database.

All links count, all connections count, and all harmonies count. Something you think is counting for you could even be counting against you. However, if it's not topically relevant or clear on the intentions of what it's designed for, Google's advancing AI is more likely to detect it.

Before, you could fake it - but Google is getting smarter. They know when the user isn't going to appreciate something or if it looks like link bait. It's important to create engaging content, that matches what the user wants and the searcher intent. If we're marketers trying to make money in business, isn't this what we're trying to achieve? Sell people products that they want and that meet their needs. That's what we need to do in SEO too: interconnect our channels and make sure everything is in harmony."

When harmonising your channels, how would you approach devising a launch campaign? Should you publish on social media, split your content up, or pay to promote?

"These channels are not one-size-fits-all, which is why it's important to harmonize them. You can then see what works, what fits your niche and your topic, and whether you're advertising or doing an influencer campaign. As a general rule of thumb: if you have a blog/article you should multipurpose that content. You can even take a video, create some infographics from it, and share those on a separate website. You should focus on creating multiple pieces of content from a single article.

Let's say you've got an excellent SEO-driven article with great link ads. What you could do to further your aspirations is take the article, and the images within the article, and turn them into social posts. All the H2s and H3s could become social posts. There are several AI tools in existence that can take a YouTube video and automatically create 50 Twitter posts from it.

You can take an article you want to reach number one tomorrow, harmonise it, and create several additional articles and smaller videos from it. You can challenge and have some fun with it since some concepts will stick and others won't. If they match the user intent you can get them there quickly by getting all your social channels to fire on that content.

Write a blog post, turn that into a YouTube video, and turn that YouTube video into three or four smaller videos that get posted on Twitter. Turn that into a Facebook post, then turn that into a LinkedIn post. Take this new content and share it. Communicate the new content you're releasing with the Google Search Console and index. Once it's in your sitemap that's been updated in Google, you can launch your social media automation. Your YouTube video about the content, linking back to that video, will then get posted. Your social media posts get a little piece that's a snippet out of that article. They then get posted on Facebook, Twitter, etc. as part of an effective content repurposing strategy.

All of these things should be monitored for engagement. As soon as something gets a bite from the fish, you should go in and attack immediately. Any bites that are attacked immediately can harmonise, go viral, and can get interacted with. As soon as there is interaction, Google's warning signs will indicate it's a great piece of content that needs to be indexed as soon as possible.

You can leverage tools like Hootsuite to harmonise with your content. Do your SEO-driven surfer content but maintain your social as harmonising channels to launch with. If you want to launch against me with a backlink - you're taking on an army.

Start with the written content because you'll be writing it with NLP words, headers, etc. before constructing a video. This is important because Google is going to look at that video for content, headers, topics, and words. You should do all your keyword research beforehand rather than doing the video first. Make sure all the compelling things are in that research and then do your video off the back of that. If you want your video to rank number one, you should do the research upfront and then put resonant content in your video.

When sharing on social media you can use different hashtags, different graphics, and different calls to action. If your written content is keyword-driven your videos will reach a vaster audience. With Twitter, tools can inform you about when you are getting more than two interactions on a post and then retweet it, for example. You won't be retweeting anything that doesn't get engagement so you won't be causing red flags for the algorithm. Tools are automated to inform you on how you can update your content. When things are automated, you can send out the right messages because you won't just be blasting the same thing out to everybody. An automated tool will make your life much easier because, when you launch out, it'll tailor your approach to specific social media platforms."

How do you decide on the keyword that you're going to target for that written piece of content?

"Start everything with Google itself. Put yourself in the shoes of the searcher. Picture what they're looking for, what they're trying to solve, what their pain points are, who they are, etc.

For example, if they're looking for a tent or have a camping event coming up, you'll know to write about tents. However, it's important to consider who the searcher is and what they're searching for. When you look into Google to see what's there, you can see if there are things that match the content you're going to write. Address searcher intent from the start. You can assess whether what you're seeing on Google is exactly what the searcher is looking for. If the answer is 'no', you should start over with intent and appreciate you might not understand the SERP.

Alternatively, you might not understand the person. In this case, you could interview someone within your market and pose questions from a customer perspective. For example, you could ask what they're searching for when looking for a tent. If what you're finding isn't what you originally thought, go to the target, ask them directly what they'd type in, and verify if it's correct. When you target this as your seed word the SEO will start working. Begin with your seed word and match the server intent to the content you're about to create.

If you start with that seed word, you can look and see the topically relevant NLPs. You can decipher the appealing parts and write content around what is going to relate to the searcher. You can then get ranked and related to the searcher of that content. Start with Google, make sure that matches the searcher intent, and then start looking up all the relevant keywords. Once you've done that, you can start using tools like SurferSEO, Scalenut and SERPStat to capture the right keywords. You can then hire a writer and match the brief you're looking for, use AI, or even write the content yourself.

Ultimately, everything starts with the searcher intent."

What shouldn't SEOs be doing in 2023? What's seductive in terms of time, but ultimately counterproductive?

"Lots of people in business focus too much on the numbers. Focusing on the number of users isn't important, nor is having your KPI rank number one for a given keyword. You should contemplate whether the keyword matches the intent of the searcher. Focus on the intentions over the numbers. Clicks don't count as much as the intention and are not as powerful.

Say, for example, you get 100 clicks. You should ponder whether it was 100 clicks of people who actually care or was it just 100 clicks. Ultimately, the numbers are irrelevant. What matters is what the numbers represent. What's important is the intention, the conversion, or what's behind it."

Joseph Khan is an SEO and Digital Marketing Expert and you can find him over at humjam.com.

12 Integrate

13 THINK OUTSIDE THE BOX

Think about search engines other than Google—Eli Schwartz

Eli Schwartz tells SEOs that you need to think beyond Google as the only search engine that matters in 2023 and open up your horizons by focusing on the user and not the algorithm.

Eli says: "In 2023, it's time for SEOs to stop thinking of SEO for Google and its algorithms - or about finding loopholes in those algorithms. You need to remember that there are broader search engines like Baidu, Bing, Apple, and Amazon.

If you focus on the user, you can be agnostic to the search engine - because they are all about people looking for things or pulling for information. If you focus on Google and the algorithm, and Google suddenly stops being the most popular search engine or changes its algorithm, you could lose traffic. However, if you focus on the user looking for information – the person typing a query into any search engine - you're guaranteed to find that user somehow."

Is Google showing signs of not becoming the most popular search engine or should SEOs be considering other search engines anyway?

"It's interesting that, for the first time, Google has mentioned a competitor. Early in the year, they said they were concerned about TikTok. Although TikTok is not their competition yet, it is really popular. It is the first app people go to on their phones. They could launch a search engine that takes advantage of the fact that the user is already there and watching videos, and that user might want other information - like where to find a doctor, what time the Super Bowl is, etc.

Such an instance is the only sign that Google could lose its dominance. Regardless, if you focus on the user instead of search engines, both the user and your website wins."

Is TikTok just about discovery and top-of-funnel, or is it something people natively use as a search engine?

"Currently, people are using it as a search engine to find videos. That is how the behaviour changes. However, it could be a less obvious search competitor to Google. The closest search competitors to Google could be Amazon, Facebook, and Apple - where people are already going and starting their internet journey.

With Amazon, for example, you are already shopping. Could Amazon now try to provide you with more information besides shopping? Many people observe that Google's advantage is that they have several decades of experience fighting spam, which could mean they are still the best search engine."

Is it possible to track a user journey across multiple search engines, where they might discover you through TikTok, and then subscribe on YouTube before visiting your website to make a purchase?

"Probably not. That is why, if people are doing those kinds of things, you should focus on that. Currently, TikTok does not have a crawler but that could change very quickly. It is already such a big company and it makes a lot of money, so they could just buy a search engine. They could purchase that crawler already in action on your site, and your website can now become a part of ByteDance and TikTok."

How do you find out that users are finding you in this way?

"It is mainly through one-on-one research, but it's also via something that is not often done, which is mapping out the user journey. For example, some businesses thrive on referrals. They might wonder whether they should put effort into SEO if all their customers come from word of mouth. It depends on the nature of your business and how you expect to find customers. That factor determines where you put effort.

Many SEOs focus on queries related to the business and use that as a basis to create content. Instead, they could be questioning whether those queries would translate into users.

The other side of this is related to interviews. If it is impossible to map out the user journey, then interviewing customers would do the trick. You would find potential customers and ask questions like, 'How would you go about finding that kind of business?'"

It is a lot more difficult nowadays to get easy organic traffic from any search engine. Do you advocate building an ongoing content strategy before allowing yourself to rank on alternate search engines?

"Content strategy is critical, and that is the missing link for many people in digital marketing. It consists of many tactics: planning relevant content, how users will find it, and so forth. For example, if you're launching a podcast, who will listen to it? Where are your listeners going to find you? You cannot just jam it with keywords because many sites and podcasts are competing with you today. You can't naturally expect that, just because you use those keywords, you're going to win.

Yet, if you have a strategy, you know which user base you want to appeal to and which keywords they are likely to use. If they stumble upon you, they will refer other users because your podcast is perfect for what they're looking for. That strategy is figuring out how to build all that together."

Do you feel you must blend your SEO strategy with other digital channels? Should you integrate organic search and paid in your strategy as well?

"That is part of the strategy, where you want to consider how all your channels work together. When you think about the customer journey flow, it's also about knowing where SEO fits in that funnel. In most cases, SEO will be at the top of the funnel. You want to carry people through that funnel so they convert. That is likely going to be paid traffic. Therefore, top-of-funnel might be very broad.

Now, you've introduced them to your business, service, and information. As they move closer to the bottom of the funnel, those might be some specific keywords which are expensive and competitive. You, therefore, need to figure out how to retarget them and try to convert them. However, it shouldn't be a one-off. You should understand that you are ranking for a keyword, which might take a while. It would also require you to know the stage of the buyer journey that the users are on."

Are there other specific things you need to do to your site to optimise effectively for different search engines?

"There aren't specific things you can do because most search engines are similar. You don't necessarily want to create a Yandex and Bing strategy specifically because it will cost your Google strategy. The idea of search engines becoming fragmented is good - where everyone is gaining market share - because you can no longer have a single search engine strategy. That could become an SEO trap. You need an organic user strategy to acquire that audience from any search engine. You'll want to build the best content, links, and visibility.

Another interesting thing is that, when using other search engines, many people do not realise that it is not Google. That points to the fact that people really are platform-agnostic. The search engine doesn't matter, provided they get the right results. Google results might always be the best, but other engines are not terrible, either."

What does a fragmented search environment mean for analytics? Can you pull your data from different search engines into one or two pieces of software?

"There probably aren't any tools that are pulling all that information right now. Currently, most people do not know that Bing has a Webmaster Tool just like Google Search Console. Yet, to set up Bing Webmaster Tools, they allow you to verify your site and pull in all your Google Search Console data. The same is the case with Yandex. Again, most people are not paying any attention to this. They are only paying attention to Google.

In a fragmented world, you probably need to use a tool that pulls it together. You will find differences between each search engine, which is good - it means you're focusing on the user. Then, you can no longer opt for your URLs to only show up on Google. You need to look at how to please users outside of traditional search, considering what would appeal to them."

If you focus on your users and know who your users are, then you're certainly going down the right path for 2023, right?

"It is the most cliché thing, but true. If you look at a lot of the content that people put out around focusing on users, it always ends with 'using this keyword', as well. Instead, if the users aren't buying - for example, if you are selling a B2B tool, where a CRO needs to buy it, and they're never going to use organic search - then don't focus on the organic search. On the other hand, if you're focusing on something people only use on their phones, you need a mobile-only strategy.

The main idea is that users are the absolute king/queen when it comes to this. Therefore, you're building your entire strategy around what they need and where they will find you, irrespective of what the algorithm says."

What shouldn't SEOs be doing in 2023? What is seductive in terms of time, but ultimately counterproductive?

"People should stop saying 'it depends', which means, 'I don't know the answer'. Imagine you go to a doctor and ask them whether you will die, and they say, 'it depends'. You then go to another doctor, and they say, 'No, you're not going to die, you'll be fine.' That is the same thing here.

Many SEOs fall into this trap and end up being side-lined. Instead of saying 'it depends', say, 'It is a great opportunity for us to learn. Let us run an experiment. I do not actually know what will happen because I'm not Google.' Then, suggest the most logical route - whether it is changing the title tag or launching 1,000 new pages. You can always go back two weeks later and learn something new."

Eli Schwartz is a Growth Advisor, and you can find him at elischwartz.co.

Prepare your images for visual search—Crystal Carter

Crystal Carter believes SEOs should focus more on the visual side of search and promoting the overall brand in 2023, rather than dwelling on keywords.

Crystal says: "My number one SEO tip for 2023 is to prepare your images for visual search."

Which search engine are we talking about; Pinterest, Google image search something else?

"Visual search has evolved quite significantly during the course of 2022. I expect that, in 2023, it will evolve even further.

Preparing for visual search doesn't mean preparing for image search because many people think it is the same thing. image search is just a valuable part of the former, and image search SEO tactics are a valuable part of visual search optimisation, but they do different things.

For example, if you are preparing a photo of a loaf of bread for image search, you will be entering image search attributes, like alt tags, file titles, file size, etc. Those will help users find you if they enter the text you've attached - or some text similar to some of the cues you've added to your image attributes.

Visual search is about images, visuals, recognition, and image recognition. Essentially, someone would take a photo of a loaf of bread, and Google will use their various tools and image recognition abilities to understand that image. You might take a picture of a loaf of bread, and they might say 'this is a baguette', 'sourdough', or 'a pretzel'. Their visual search recognition tools can parse different information about that image to give the user even more holistic information in ways that would be impossible to type out if you were doing so manually. Sometimes, you're looking at something, you don't know what it's called and can't search for it with words, so you have to describe it.

Visual search allows users to understand the world without necessarily knowing what a thing is called. Search engines can also return not just images but any kind of content. You might get back a video, a Featured Snippet, or whatever is appropriate for that particular query. Sometimes it's shopping information as well.

You need to consider your standard with image optimisation when preparing your images, but also think about other elements. Remember that Google cannot understand text backwards - not currently, anyway. If you have images with text in them, ensure the camera can understand them the right way around.

Another thing is that Google can understand entities that include many things. For example, a bicycle can include more abstract things like sunsets or mountains, so it also helps to consider those. If it was a loaf of bread, you might want to show a chopping board, knife, or butter, which would help Google understand that this is a loaf of bread.

Particularly for brands, you should include your logo, where appropriate, when preparing images. Google can also understand your logo, particularly if your brand is entered into the Knowledge Graph. So, for instance, if you have a Wikipedia page, ensure that your logo matches what's on your structured data and in your Google Merchant Centre information. That way, when people take photos of your products and search, they can find them based on your logo and any images you have."

Is image search when the user is looking for images in search engines, while visual search is a user using their own image to find results?

"When you consider what you see with Google Lens - which is the primary driver for this - you would take the photo and have the option to see visual matches of similar things. You need to consider the types of images people use to interact with your brand, when thinking about your brand and the kinds of images you should have on your website.

For example, there's a photo of me next to the Space Shuttle at the California Science Centre, which is the same photo they have on their homepage. They know that everybody walks in and wants a picture with the space shuttle, and those are the kind of pictures that people take. They have that on their website so that people enter that photo, and it's the same photo on their Knowledge Graph and website. When people are looking for that visual or that place, they can find it quickly - because NASA has prepared themselves for visual search."

What type of business could get a lot of value for optimising for a visual search? How would you go about doing it?

"It applies to many businesses. A small business that I have looked at, a girly salon, created a unique image distinct to them. One of the things they did was create a highly Instagrammable space with lots of flowers, and put that on their Google Business Profile and website. When users enter the pictures that they take in that space, you can search with those photos - using Google Lens, the Bing tool, and Pinterest. If you enter that image into Google Search, Google knows that the business is connected to that image, because they also added it to their website.

That's something that can apply to many different businesses. Even if you're a small business, many people will already be taking photos of your lattes or tiramisu. Also, Google is using Google Business Profile photos for their visual search to return visual search results. They now have an option called 'near me' where, if you take a picture of something, they can scan it across all their Google Business Profile photos and show the user how far away the business is.

This applies to businesses of all sizes. If you are a large business, then visual search is important when you're thinking about things like sponsorships. For smaller companies, it can enhance brand visibility locally.

Google can use visual recognition to create search results and increase brand fit and visibility. It's important to consider how your brand is visible and how those images can affect your ranking in the SERPs. It might not even be on your website, but it will impact your overall brand visibility - which is really important."

How can you optimise your site to give it a better opportunity to display for those visual results?

"All of the standard image optimisation stuff still applies; ensure you've got unstructured data for your images with all text and captions. But also, think about which images you include and which are most likely to align with what people will be searching for.

If you know that you have visual brand representations going out in the world, make sure they have space on your website. For instance, if your van is marked up and you spent all that time on getting a custom wrap on your van - make sure it's on your website too, so that people can see what you're doing. While you're at it, there is an opportunity to think about galleries and provide the context. That adds value in several ways, even for visual search.

Regarding visual search, it's also about the content you include and ensuring that your content is backed up by the research of the kinds of images people are taking. Ensure you're including images similar to what people will be searching for. If you're not sure what types of content you should be including, then it's worth having a look at what images people are tagging you in on social media, Tripadvisor, Google Business Profile, Facebook, etc.

If you don't have a customer-facing business, it might be that people are often interacting with your team. It might be worth getting people badges that say your name on them, or have the logo you can wear when you go out on company business. That way, people can find you when they need to find you. For such businesses, it can be effective (in terms of conversion rates) to create team profile pages. It helps when people are looking for a specific person and are reassured that they found the right one.

A little task for SEOs here: if you've got a brand that can take advantage of visual search, get photos of your brand doing something exciting and different, that could take advantage of visual search. Tweet that @majestic and also @Crystalontheweb, then include the hashtag #SEOin2023. Tell us what you're doing. We'd love to take a look at it."

What shouldn't SEOs be doing in 2023? What's seductive in terms of time, but ultimately counterproductive?

"It's time to release the grip that we have on keywords. Keywords are super important, but I think they're more of a guide. It's important to know what people are thinking about. It's also essential to do keyword research around the brand but I think that, historically, people have hammered in some of the keywords, and they are the same everywhere.

When we think about Natural Language Processing, which is one of the ways that Google understands search, we need to speak in natural language. That includes keywords, but more as a topic and less as a literal thing.

It would be great to see people thinking more holistically about keywords and how they work with ideas, entities, and a brand overall - and to be just a little less literal about them where possible."

Crystal Carter is Head of SEO Communications at Wix, and you can find her over at wix.com/seo/learn.

Get started with Web Stories—Mufaddal Sadriwala

Mufaddal Sadriwala is betting on Web Stories in 2023 and encourages all SEOs to start understanding the basics of how to create them, why they are important, and where they can be visible.

Mufaddal says: "My number one tip is all about Web Stories (formerly known as AMP Stories). That is going to be a huge thing in the near future, in my opinion - for Google and for the users as well. It is going to improve a lot in 2023 and, obviously, further down the line. I would recommend all brands, and all SEO consultants, start some of the basics around them."

If an SEO hasn't heard of them before, what are the advantages of Web Stories, and what target markets and businesses is it best suited for?

"We all know about Instagram Stories and social media Stories. A Web Story is the same as the Story that goes on Instagram and other social media platforms - the difference is that it has been added to your website. You also have a shareable URL, which you can send out to anyone who is wanting to view your Story on your website, and on any other platform too. You have more control over your Story, and you can track them in web analytics tools like Google Analytics or Adobe.

The best part about this is that your Stories can be featured on Google Discover. If you're putting out a Story, Google will index it and it can feature on the Discover playlist feed on the Google Search app (currently, the Web Stories carousel on Google Discover is only available in the United States, India, and Brazil). Google has all the data about our browsing history, our search history, the websites that we have visited, etc. - and it will display your Story to the users that it feels are relevant.

If I'm a sports enthusiast that's into soccer, and I have done a lot of searches in the past about the players, scores, and everything about the matches that are coming up in the future, Google will identify that I'm a soccer fan. If a sports or news website puts up a Story around Ronaldo or Messi, then Google might start showing that Story in my Google Discover feed.

Another great thing about Web Stories is that Google has recently started featuring them in the search results. All the shifts that we are seeing in terms of higher visual content consumption happening across platforms are also reflected in Google search. Google is realising that, so they're putting out Web Stories in the search results as well. If someone is searching for a very visual-heavy search, Web Stories will show up, along with the image and video snippets."

Google Discover is a relatively new concept. What is it exactly?

"Discover is a machine learning-generated feed. It features content from across the web - not just Web Stories, but other content like articles too. It shows content dependent on the user's preferences and personalization. It takes into account your browsing history, search history, the kind of content that you consume, etc., to determine what will appear on your Discover feed.

It's like your Instagram feed. Based on the type of content that you engage with on social media and the accounts that you engage with, the algorithm pushes those kinds of content to you. Google Discover works in more or less the same way. It shows websites, articles, or Stories in your Discover feed - depending on what you have been looking for, what your interests are, your location, and things like that. A lot of factors are taken into account.

What Google shows to the user is much more accurate, and much more relevant, because Google has the most data about what we have been searching for. It's not just your Web Stories that can be featured on Discover, it's your articles too, but Stories are more visually appealing, so I'm putting my bet on that."

How can you publish Web Stories on your website, and what does that look like, technically?

"There are two ways that you can create Web Stories on your website. The first is that Google has created a plugin, which is specifically for WordPress websites. If your website is not on WordPress, you can buy a subdomain (i.e. 'webstories.thedomain.com') and install WordPress on that subdomain. Then, you can start creating Web Stories using that plugin, which is very easy and very user-friendly.

It's just drag-and-drop. It works in the same way that you create presentations: you have a couple of slides, you can add images, you can add text, you can visualise it, and you can create a design and make it beautiful. You have all the control at the click of a button. People who have used WordPress know how easy it is to create content using the platform.

That's one way of doing it. The other way that Google lays down, if you have to code it yourself, is that you can use AMP as a technology to create Web Stories. For that, you will need the help of a developer. The way that works is that you have to decide upon the slides that will go into that story, and then check with a developer, and get that as a hard-coded page. That can then become a Web Story attached to the URL, or to the website where you're publishing it."

What is the best practice in terms of format for a Web Story?

"Web Stories should be more in the listicle format, and they should be more on the visual side of things. One of the ways that I started doing Web Stories was that I figured out all the best-performing textual content that I had on my website (blog content, articles, etc.), and I turned them into Stories. Not just copying and pasting things from there, but figuring out the top 10 or 20 articles, deciding how many slides I needed to create, and then adding more media to that - more images, audio, videos, etc.

Web Stories should be very visually appealing. It's not like your usual text content, like your articles or the long-form content that you have. You want to be putting information out in a visual way, rather than just adding a block of text."

Is video supported on Web Stories?

"Yes, you can add video. It supports video, it supports GIFs, it supports animation, and you can also add audio. The great thing is that you can also add a call to action at the end of the Web Story, or even in between any of the slides that you are looking at.

If you're wanting users to subscribe to your newsletters, to read more about the story that you've created in a textual format, or to buy your product, then you can add a call to action. Let's say you have created a Web Story on '10 Wedding Dresses for Brides to Consider'. You can actually add a link to each of the slides for each of the dresses that you're talking about. Then, people can explore the product and also make a purchase accordingly.

Everything is possible with Web Stories. You can add a link, you can add a call to action, you can get more subscribers, and you can also promote your advertising now. For every 10 slides of Web Stories, you can also add one slide of ad in between. You can integrate your ad platform and your ad can start showing up in your Web Stories. Google is looking at it as a long-term thing. They are putting their best technology forward and improving it on a daily basis."

What does analytics look like for Web Stories?

"When you create a web story it generates a unique URL, just like you have for articles and long-form content. You can measure the traffic and the impact of it by putting the URL as a filter in Analytics and Search Console. You will get to know what type of users, what countries, how many, etc.

You don't need a specific analytics tool for Web Stories - it's like analysing traffic or performance for any other URL. You have the URL, and you can put that as a filter in any of the tools that you're using to analyse the performance or the traffic. It will give you all the same information, like gender, demographics, locations, languages, etc.

In AMP HTML you had to create a separate GA code but, for Web Stories, you don't have to do anything like that. It's just like a normal Analytics code."

What shouldn't SEOs be doing in 2023? What's seductive in terms of time, but ultimately counterproductive?

"As SEOs, we should stop looking at SEO from a narrow perspective - 'This is my on-page. This is my off-page. This is link building. This is technical. This is my job.' Also, stop looking at SEO in silos. We should look at SEO from a broader perspective and consider how it fits into the marketing budget. Where does it fit in the product market? What value can we add as SEOs? Where do we stand in the bigger picture for the brand, for the marketing team, and for the product?

We need to think about how we can contribute beyond just the SEO changes that we are recommending. Web Stories is one example of that. If you're using Stories, a marketing strategy can go much further. Let's say the social media team is creating a campaign for IG, Facebook, etc. We can recommend a strategy and use that in our Web Stories as well. Whenever stories are going on Instagram, we can also utilise that and put it up on our Web Stories as well. The performance that is being measured on these social media platforms can act as a test for Discover, and it can feature on Google search results as well.

Stop looking at SEO as just an SEO thing. Start looking at it with a more holistic approach. Look at what we can do better, how we can work with each other, how we can work cross-functionally with other departments, and how we can make our product, our website, and our brand better.

Another piece of advice is that I've seen a lot of agencies still talking about obsolete techniques, like social bookmarking and directory submissions.

These kinds of techniques have really been obsolete for the last 10 years now, but I still see them in the decks that are pitched to clients. It's high time to stop talking about these techniques and start looking at SEO from a more holistic approach. Look at the bigger picture, rather than just looking at on-page, off-page, and the technical side of things."

Mufaddal Sadriwala is SEO Manager at Assembly Global and you can find him over at mufaddal.digital.

Use Edge/CDN to stitch together and publish content across any website—Nick Wilsdon

Nick Wilsdon is a strong proponent of utilising the edge in 2023. He explains how it works, the opportunities that it presents for changing the experience and delivery of your content, and how you can utilise it to make anything that you dream of possible.

Nick says: "My number one tip this year is a continuation of last year's tip - it's to better understand the edge platform for deployments. That's where you're deploying content or stitching content together. You need to understand edge as a way to change the content and experiences that you're delivering to your users."

What do you mean by stitching together and publishing content on the edge?

"Edge is a CDN (or Content Delivery Network) platform. This can be Akamai, Fastly, Cloudflare, etc. These are the platforms that deliver your content to the end user, no matter where they are. We've been using these platforms for many years now to successfully deliver content - not only locally, but faster – and we have essentially been doing this for performance. Now, these platforms have become more and more advanced, and their computational power has become more advanced.

This relates to Moore's law, which we'll all know as geeks. The CPUs have become better and the memory's better, so these platforms can now handle much more complicated requests. We first started using edge to do requests that happened in the header, like redirections. Now, as the capacity of the edge servers and the edge nodes has increased, we can start to do more complicated things.

One of the things we can do is take the request, take the entire page, and unpack it and change it. We can pull in different content from other places, and we can essentially change the entire page that the user then receives, and then deliver it on to them. Your edge platform can be doing anything that you could dream of - in terms of changing that content request and serving it to the end user - which is incredibly exciting for everyone who's working in the edge area."

Can you take an original piece of content published on a web server, pull it apart, and then insert personalised content in there?

"Absolutely you can insert personalised content, but even just generalised content. Let's say we have an eCommerce site. For years, SEO teams have talked and dreamed about getting more content onto product-level pages, but the pushback has been from the dev team. The dev team has said, 'No, we can't change the template, we've got a long backlog, we can't do this.' If we come in on the edge, we can take those product-level page requests, we can inject blocks of content onto those pages, and then serve it to the end user. By the end user here I mean the user, but I also mean Googlebot - because Googlebot and other search engines will see this as the request.

We could be using the edge to insert the content that we always dreamed about, to rearrange the nav menu in the way that we'd always wanted, or to just completely rearrange the page in any way that we wanted to. This could be a permanent change that we are making for our end users (or for Google) or this could be a test that we are running over a period of time. Maybe we wanted to change the nav over a six-month period for the entire website. The edge platform is a way that we could do this."

For an eCommerce store that has some kind of seasonal offering that you want to give greater emphasis from the navbar, would this be a quicker way of doing that than your existing system?

"It could definitely get you out of that kind of problem. Say you wanted to insert a whole different set of links into the nav for Black Friday – the edge would be a way to do that. It is a whole development platform, essentially.

If you think about your origin server, the edge is an entirely new layer that you can do this development on. As you make those changes, and that development, it then gets served to Googlebot or the user as the actual request. It's a second chance for us to change the page that doesn't involve the origin server."

When and where is the edge most useful? Is it for presenting a slightly different message to users at different stages of the buyer journey?

"It can definitely be used for that. You're touching on personalisation, and you do have those options with the edge. You can serve different content to different users, different groups, or even to people in different locales. Some of this could have a huge advantage for SEO. We do kind of veer away from SEO when we go down this path, though, because it's more about personalisation.

For us, part of the personalization process that we've always been interested in is: how do we personalise for Googlebot? For this question, the intersection between SEO and edge has been particularly interesting.

Googlebot is a user of our site and, historically, we've always been quite worried about that. We don't want to present something completely different to Googlebot than we present to our normal users, because that would be cloaking. There can, however, be circumstances where it's advantageous for us to fix a certain problem for Googlebot that we couldn't justify fixing in our normal development workflow. There are things that we might choose to do for Googlebot that could be advantageous to that crawling and indexing of the site."

Does Googlebot ever know that any of this content has been stitched together?

"No, Googlebot will always see the end result. Even in the future, Googlebot has no way of detecting that this request has happened on the edge server.

However, all the usual rules apply. You have simply got another opportunity to change requests, which is the same as changing it on the origin server. You still have to consider what you're doing for your users, what would be considered cloaking, etc.

That's where the whole area of personalised content has become much more complex over recent years. We want to give a personalised experience to different users, but we also want to be able to control the experience that Googlebot has - because that is the experience that gets indexed and ranked. There is a grey area there, but the rules haven't changed. The edge is just another means of deployment, or another way to change the request."

What are the benefits of using the edge to control and edit content instead of a conventional CMS? Is it generally faster and does it help SEOs that are dealing with old CMSs that don't have the same functionality as modern CMSs?

"All of the above. You may also find that there are blockers in terms of development, and the dev teams that you have on the origin server. They may have a very long list of backlog items that they're working through. You may find that you're dealing with multiple CMSs, which we often do as SEOs. We find that we have more than one CMS, or we're mid-migration - and having a layer that goes over all of these CMSs can be a huge advantage. You can start to make changes that affect every single request.

You may have legacy CMSs (I've worked with clients that still have Perl CMSs, for example) that you simply can't do anything on. The ability to add SEO functionality to old, legacy parts of the site, as you upgrade them or move them across, is fantastic. There are lots of advantages to doing this.

A lot of the advantages for SEOs are ways to get around blockers, but there are also advantages that are particularly pertinent right now, with the macroeconomic climate that we're in. We know that a recession is around the corner, teams are under pressure, and we're asking to do more with less, which always happens.

The edge is one way of getting around this. You're using architecture that's already being bought by the company. They're looking to leverage that expenditure, and it has usually been brought in because it helps you deal with security, bot management, content delivery, or even performance. Leveraging that existing spend is very attractive to senior management. Also, you have the ability to do this without any additional software or platforms. You're adding things to a platform that is fully covered by your security policies. You don't have to worry about any kind of performance impact, because this is how your content is served. You're not going to take these requests off to a third party, or a third-party platform. You're serving them through the CDN that you already have set up.

There are a lot of reasons why people are doing development in the edge environment, because they see it as an extension of what they can do on the origin server. You can develop in both the origin server and on the edge.

You can also deploy very quickly because you don't have to worry about all the interconnecting parts, the politics, or anything else. You can fix something on the edge in a three to six-month period that may take years, or be so blocked that you can't possibly see a solution.

You may want to do that permanently, or you may want to do it as a test. We talked about changing the navbar, and the SEO team could have the hypothesis that if you had more control over the navbar - you were more reactive, and you could start to put links on there quicker - then that would help your SEO. The dev team might have fed back and said that it's impossible to have that kind of control over the nav. You can then implement a quick nav change on the edge, and the SEO to improve that by having additional control over adding and removing links. That can then benefit SEO in all those different areas. You can choose, then, whether you keep that functionality on the edge, or say that this functionality needs to be implemented on the origin server because you have made the business case for it.

You've proved why you needed it and you've shown real-world results, so you can say why it should be prioritised in the dev queue. It's a very powerful additional tool to get things moving within a company. With the macroeconomic climate that we're in, companies are looking at being able to make these changes faster, and the edge is a really good way to be more agile."

Are there any cutting-edge edge/CDN developments that SEOs can take advantage of in 2023?

"It's hard to know that they're happening because you can't actually detect them on the edge. Large companies and large brands are doing more work on the edge than ever, and they're all very interested in this area, but it's hard to point to many specific examples.

It's very interesting work for SEOs. There's never been so much opportunity to make large-scale differences for the brands that we work on. In my work now, as an edge architect, I'm largely brought in to solve the unsolvable - which is my remit in a lot of the work that I do.

One of the advantages of being a smaller firm was always that they were more nimble and able to make changes quickly but, with the edge, enterprises are catching up. This will particularly help large enterprises because they are slow. They have so much politics, development, multi-CMSs, etc., and everything that happens in enterprise creates these blockers. The edge is particularly interesting to them.

However, companies of any size can benefit from it as well. Cloudflare (which is one of the leading CDNs) is essentially free for any company, and there are an increasing number of people producing scripts that can run on the edge. I think Torque (my company) even got the Majestic tags and functionality working through Cloudflare, which we released on the Majestic blog. You're going to find a lot of people making things work in that environment, which can benefit every company of every size."

What shouldn't SEOs be doing in 2023? What's seductive in terms of time, but ultimately counterproductive?

"I'm going to say AI content. The reason I'm saying that is because I've actually worked a lot with AI content. We produce it, and it is even one way of deploying the edge. You can create content through the AI content production process, and then use the edge to insert that into certain pages to get it working for Google and users.

What I've learned from that, however, is that AI content is complex and if garbage goes in, garbage comes out. A lot of people are looking at AI content and thinking that it's very easy, because you can simply produce content, so it's going to reduce the costs that you spend on writers. I would disagree with that quite strongly. To get good quality AI content, it's going to move the emphasis from writers to editors. It can produce something that's very high quality, and grammatically accurate, but it does need an extra bit of work and workflow to keep the quality up.

AI content is very interesting, and it's going to be increasingly interesting in terms of producing text and content for SEOs over the next few years, but it's not a shortcut. It's going to involve you reallocating those resources into workflow. What's the thinking behind it? What's the quality of it? What's the meaning of it? What's the intent behind it? Don't fall into the trap of thinking that you're going to cut costs dramatically by producing everything with AI."

Nick Wilsdon is the CEO and Founder of Torque. You can find him over at torquepartnership.com.

The future of technical SEO is SEO on the edge—Barry Adams

Barry Adams feels that, in 2023, SEOs need to start seriously looking at doing SEO on the edge and explains how you can take advantage of the power of the CDN.

Barry says: "We all know and love CDNs; platforms like Cloudflare can help our websites perform better. The beauty of CDNs is that you can ensure your international users connect to a version of your website hosted close to their location. CDNs are a great way to avoid communicating over the internet via servers located on the other side of the planet.

SEO on the edge involves leveraging the power of the CDN. By utilising advanced, expansive features, you can adjust your website on the CDN rather than on your own servers.

The cached copy will contain web pages that the host can manipulate when implementing SEO practices like redirects, canonical tags, hreflang tags, schema markup, etc. Why would you want to do this on a CDN? Primarily because it makes it easier to test things rather than entering a busy developer's queue on your own server. It's a great mechanism for testing changes on a limited set of web pages - for example, a set of category pages on an eCommerce website.

The ability to perform split testing for SEO can elevate your technical SEO to new heights. You can also experiment and see which things actually work under your specific conditions. You can then avoid a potentially lengthy and expensive development project for an untested and untried implementation.

It's exciting to see how edge SEO will continue to evolve over the next few years. As a concept that's been around for at least five years, it's starting to reach a level of maturity and is ready for the limelight."

Is Cloudflare the best CDN for this?

"Yes. Cloudflare is at the cutting edge of edge SEO. Its features and capabilities are second to none, and to top it all off you can sign up for free and benefit from testing things at no extra cost. This is something that you can't accomplish on other CDNs, but with Cloudflare, you'll have a chance to confirm the definition of SEO on the edge free of charge."

Is it just about executing Javascript onto a CDN or can you execute other technologies?

"It doesn't have to be Javascript at all. The beauty of using Cloudflare and SEO on the edge is that you could manipulate web pages with the Google Tag Manager container, for example. The downside is that it requires client-side JavaScript code to be executed because Google doesn't index pages consistently with Cloudflare.

Though the code itself can be run in Javascript, it will run on the CDN instead of the client side. This means that changes to those web pages are made server-side and on Googlebot. Your end users will see the completely rendered, changed page instantly - in all HTML and CSS pages. It doesn't rely on any client-side JavaScript for those changes to be revealed to Googlebot, which means it's much easier, more thorough, and more reliable to implement SEO changes than with Google Tag Manager containers.

There are quite a few websites that use multiple CDNs depending on where the user happens to be in the world. In these instances, there will be some kind of layering of the CDN sequence that the page loading has to go through to ensure the most up-to-date versions of web pages load. This is one of the downsides or risk factors when manipulating web pages on the edge."

Do you need to know exactly where in the technology stack it's happening and keep very close documentation of what you're changing?

"On the edge, in the CDN, you'll need to build a very robust internal process - where you use the CDN to do certain things and document them extensively. The ultimate aim will be to implement it on your actual technology, on your actual live server where the CDN takes its root copy from. You'll want to avoid scenarios where changes suddenly disappear from one day to the next.

Your live web server gets updated with a new set of production codes and, if you operate effectively, the CDN caches to make way for this production code. However, sometimes changes on the edge won't be taken over by the new version and there are lots of other risks you can be subjected to. It's not just something you can jump into willy-nilly and think 'let's go and try this stuff out!'. There are actual providers to help with this, including SearchPilot which has a Meta-CMS that does it on the edge.

There are also new providers emerging with platforms to do A/B split testing for SEO on edge. Other platforms have emerged to help you automate this process and make sure it becomes part of a robust strategy. The goal is to prevent creating huge gaps between the website and your end users. Googlebot sees the website as if it exists on your own live server. When doing SEO on edge, arguably the biggest risk of all is creating a fork of your website on the edge. This could easily diverge too much from your actual website or what your life server is like."

Is there a recommended minimum size or genre of website that SEO on the edge is most suitable for?

"You can do it on any website of any size and any scope. Having said that, if you have a very simple brochure website that runs on a simple CMS like WordPress, doing SEO on edge is probably a bit overkill - because it'll be easier to do it directly on your website.

However, the more complex your website is the more advantages you can get from doing SEO on the edge. Generally speaking, for those sorts of websites, making major changes to your life site can seem high risk, expensive, and very time-consuming. That's why making changes on the CDN is so advantageous. You can bypass all those obstacles and get it done fairly quickly under limited circumstances so you don't risk the success of your entire web page when making changes."

If you're working on a site and implementing SEO on the edge for the first time, what are some of the potential biggest initial wins?

"One of the easiest, most impactful things to implement is automatic redirects. As things currently stand, managing redirects of large websites can be a daunting, difficult task that's not worth the enormous amount of time and effort. This is especially true when you're dealing with a large-scale website that potentially has millions of disconnects. On the edge, you can fairly easily write simple scripts that map redirects almost entirely automatically. In doing so, you can make sure that your end users never end up on pages that previously existed but don't anymore.

At scale, redirect mapping - especially if you do site migrations - is one of the most difficult and time-consuming processes. However, on the edge, it probably makes life a bit easier, as is also true when implementing hreflang tags. It's one of those things that can be very difficult to build on, but can be done in a relatively straightforward fashion on the edge when updating your schema markup.

If you have additional attributes you want to add to your schema markup but you're not sure of whether you should do it across the entire website or on the edge, just do it for one section of your website and see what happens. These types of practical implementations are the best and simplest ways to get started."

How would you start using the edge for SEO testing? What elements would you tend to test initially?

"Well, there's almost no limit to what you can test. This is one of the advantages of using SearchPilot because they have a newsletter where they regularly write about case studies of clients that run tests and see what happens. The outcomes can be quite counterintuitive. One of the tests they ran involved using emojis in titles, or listing prices in meta descriptions to see whether or not Google picked those up. The beauty of doing these tests on the edge is that you can just pick one category of your website and make the change for just that category without having to worry about how it performs compared to the rest of your website.

By doing this, you can fairly effectively isolate the particular change you've made and see what the actual impacts are. This is something you wouldn't typically be able to do because, if you build out across a whole site, you'll see that websites are complicated and yours might have different levels of topical authority for different product categories. In this situation, you can very easily get lost thinking about what is causation and what is correlation. With SEO on the edge, you can find a tighter connection between the changes you make and the impacts they have.

Often, we implement these things on websites because they are the best SEO practices. However, just because that's assumed doesn't mean these approaches are guaranteed to improve your traffic and rankings. That's why performing an initial test is a smart thing to do. It's better to do a test before you implement it across your entire website. It will enable you to undermine a certain practice by testing its effectiveness. You can then gather data and do a proper test on a significant number of pages to see whether they get more traffic and rankings. Let your test run for a couple of weeks or a couple of months before seeing what the actual impact is. You can then implement that change wholesale across your entire website."

It can be scary to think about potentially incorporating a price or an offer somewhere in the SERP because you won't be in full control over getting rid of them if that particular offer finishes. Should that be a concern?

"It's a concern because Google has a mind of its own. The SERP snippets that Google shows don't always necessarily reflect what the webpage itself says. Google is increasingly deciding for itself what to show there, so the best thing you can do is send strong signals to Google. This is what you'll want to show, but that doesn't mean to say it will be too much of a concern providing you back things up with structured data.

Google tends to show accurate data as part of its accurate search results. Legal restrictions often bind websites to display accurate content. It would be wise to avoid experimenting with inaccurate information on your web page. Google has a habit of overwriting your snippets in search results with its own copy that may not be an accurate representation of events."

What shouldn't SEOs be doing in 2023? What's seductive in terms of time, but ultimately counterproductive?

"It's very seductive to focus on the volume of content you produce. Many companies tend to put more articles out and try to cast their net as broadly as possible to capture traffic with what can honestly be considered low-quality content. Just having a content calendar and saying we're going to write X amount of articles with certain keywords, yet failing to consider the value of that content, is a seductive strategy. The intent of the search for your content is supposed to fulfil the quality of the content you deliver.

It's best to have different industry conversations with your clients, and with websites in general, to sway from the 'X amount of words, X amount of articles, and X amount of links' approach. What's more important is to focus on the value add you've brought to a website via the quality you've delivered to your audience. By doing so, you'll be positioned to positively contribute toward the business goals of your organisation.

Things should be less output-based and more value-based. When it comes to generating content for websites, you should put more effort into the individual pieces of content you can be truly proud of. You should genuinely feel like your article deserves to be a top-ranked result in Google because it fulfils the needs of the searcher when they enter specific queries."

Barry Adams is an SEO Consultant at Polemic Digital and you can find him over at polemicdigital.com.

Start utilising Google Cloud's publicly-available APIs to help you execute SEO—Lazarina Stoy

Lazarina Stoy highlights the virtues of Google Cloud's many different APIs as a way for SEOs in 2023 to build on your analysis and better understand the work that you are doing.

Lazarina says: "Start utilising Google Cloud's publicly available APIs to help you execute SEO. Google Cloud - and other giants like AWS and Microsoft as well - have a bunch of APIs that can be used by SEOs as part of our role.

To name just a few within the Google Cloud ecosystem: you have Natural Language API, Speech-to-Text API, Vision API (which is quite popular for captioning), Translation API (that can be very useful when you're working with large-scale, internationalisation products), and Knowledge Graph API that we should be incorporating into what we do.

All of these can provide an additional layer to the work that you are doing and to the analysis that you are conducting, that will help you to better understand your work."

At cloud.google.com/apis you find many different APIs that are available for SEOs to use. Why is Google giving us access to all of these?

"Profit is the first reason; they are making money out of it. They're not 100% free. Personally, I feel like it makes your life a lot easier if you know how to utilise them in different tasks.

It would be interesting to also know how these APIs are used in some of Google's other products. We know that these APIs have not been developed with the sole purpose of being released to the public, and at least some have definitely been developed as part of another product.

The Google Translate API has been released but, originally, it was used as part of Google Translate. The entity recognition Knowledge Graph is being used in search and the Vision API is being used in image search as well, as well as a bunch of other products that Google has.

It's very interesting to see how your content, or maybe your website, looks from the point of view of the systems that Google is using. It helps you to understand how they see your website a little bit better - if they are using these APIs in the same form that they are being released."

Should every SEO be aware of this and understand how these APIs actually work?

"'Everyone' is a very optimistic scenario, but yes. The reason why I am an advocate of everyone experimenting with them is because I think they give an additional layer of understanding of what is happening. It's a very good perspective for seeing how your website looks from the point of view of a model or a system.

Also, these APIs have been developed by a massive organisation with a very big budget, and by the best researchers in the world. They are very advanced for what you get out of the box as a working model. It's very easy to create custom reports, based on a certain use case that you have in SEO.

There are a number of different use cases for entity identification, for instance. Typically, it would be very hard to carry out entity recognition yourself - if you're just starting to code that algorithm or you're using an underdeveloped API. It's much easier to start with something that has been developed by a corporation like Google or Amazon because they provide you with the code to start with, and they provide you with different use cases for different platforms. You can use this in Python or using Apps Script in Google Sheets, you name it.

You can also apply the API to different things like internal link work, identifying anchor text opportunities, SERP analysis, content analysis, and much more. That's just a few examples of many."

Which API would you use to identify anchor text and links?

"The Google Cloud Natural Language API allows you to identify entities and also do sentiment analysis and text annotations. It is very useful for content analysis, SERP analysis, internal link opportunity identification, and anchor text identification. On its own, it can only identify entities but, as SEOs, we collect a large amount of data.

You can export the report from this API and pair it with crawl data and with search volume data, and you can build a very interesting picture of the correlations between different data points. From that, you can come up with a lot of scenarios about what you're doing day-to-day."

Why do SEOs need to be using these APIs directly? Are SEO tools and platforms not using these APIs themselves?

"I hope that they start incorporating some of these APIs at some point, but the cost is obviously a barrier to having this implemented. I also think that being able to push this to production for a live system or tool might be a little bit complex and may take more time.

The time barrier is a big one. These deployments even take a long time at Google. Daniel Waisberg recently spoke at BrightonSEO, and he walked us through the process of releasing a Google API. It takes about a year, and that's for an API that was already available to them. It's a lot slower to wait for a tool to integrate that API.

It's important to understand that you can start using these APIs without having any coding experience. There are Google Sheets templates available for almost all of them and you can quickly incorporate a very advanced level of understanding and analysis to your reports - and your day-to-day work."

Why should SEOs choose to use Google's Speech-to-Text API?

"From my personal testing, Google's Speech-to-text API has been a lot more precise at recognising speech. They also do more as well. Let's say that you have 500 YouTube videos as an SEO. If that content exists in video form, there's a good opportunity to have that published in a textual form on your website as well. Having a transcript for that - or converting it to a blog post - is a very easy way to repurpose that content, depending on the type of content that it is.

It's very common to have Speech-to-Text problems in that kind of scenario, and having an API that actually understands sentences and the complex concepts that might be mentioned in those videos is very rare. It's even more rare to have proper punctuation being put into the sentences that are being transcribed.

If you have this problem, and you're working with a client like that, it's obviously important to find an API that does all of these things:

understands text, understands complex entities, and understands punctuation - and uses those to the best of its ability. Google's Speech-to-Text API is good at solving all three problems."

Is this more relevant for larger, enterprise websites with thousands of pages than it is for smaller websites with fewer videos and fewer tests to carry out?

"I would argue that these APIs are especially useful if you have a smaller website because you probably have a very limited budget as well. The budget that you would need in order to commission someone to transcribe your videos would be quite big in comparison to having an automated API do that for you with a click of a button.

There's a common misconception that using advanced, technical APIs and machine learning is something that should only be done for large-scale enterprise organisations. Actually, it is even more useful for people that don't have the budget. Just five videos could be costing you the budget of a full PPC campaign, or maybe even publishing five new content pieces. You've taken that budget and given it to someone transcribing videos.

It's all about removing the barriers to how difficult people perceive it to be. People think that machine learning with APIs is challenging, but once you know that everything can be executed fairly easily then it can replace a very large chunk of your budget - even if you're in a smaller organisation."

If someone hasn't worked with APIs before, is there a lot of technical knowledge required? Are there things like plugins available for popular CMSs, to get things up and running quickly?

"I give a lot of props to Google Cloud in terms of the documentation that they provide for all of their APIs. They not only provide documentation on how to get started, but they also provide documentation in different languages. One of the languages is Apps Script, which allows you to build custom functions in Google Sheets. Once it's been built, the only thing that you need to replace is your API key.

I don't know which CMSs have managed to make these APIs readily available yet, but Google themselves have already done so. You just have to copy-paste the code from the Apps Script that is on their website, provide your API key after you have registered, and then you can start using it in the data that you already have in Google Sheets. There's not really anything further that you need to do – it's literally as simple as one or two steps."

What shouldn't SEOs be doing in 2023? What's seductive in terms of time, but ultimately counterproductive?

"Stop keyword stuffing and optimising content based on a singular keyword. We have very much moved past keyword-based optimisations - in terms of content and also in terms of how we should be tracking the performance of the content that we write."

Is it okay to have a core target keyword on a page, but then write naturally around that particular topic with a view to ranking for as many related keywords as possible?

"You just need to focus more on what the topic is covering, even if it doesn't include the keyword that you're writing for. A lot of SEOs still get really hung up on the concept of keywords in their strategies and research, without incorporating the topics, subtopics, and other keywords and entities that make that content come to life.

Your research shouldn't just include the main keyword or a related keyword, it should also include the questions that people ask and anything else that makes a website or piece of content an authority on a topic.

That kind of research can go both ways. It can be something that is used to identify an opportunity in a marketplace, but it can also be used to identify a place where you shouldn't create content as well. It's important to start doing that type of research, as opposed to collecting keywords and optimising based on just one of them."

Lazarina Stoy is SEO and Data Science Manager at Intrepid Digital, and you can find her over at lazarinastoy.com.

Get your head around the wide-ranging nature of AI—Bastian Grimm

Bastian Grimm informs SEOs that you can no longer be ignorant about the way AI and machine learning are impacting the online environment in 2023. You need to start understanding now if you want to stay in front of the pack.

Bastian says: "It's vital to embrace the broad minefield that is AI and machine learning. Fundamentally, this is an area that Google is investing lots into. It's important to understand the landscape because you can't optimise for something that you don't understand. From an SEO standpoint, it's a crucial driving topic for 2023 and beyond. That's why it's so important to get to grips with things now rather than being behind the curve."

Are you talking about it from the perspective of Google using AI to better determine what content to rank?

"Yes. It's an extremely wide area and AI in itself has different use cases. There are a bunch of tools out there where you can start inputting information around an article topic, for example, and receive insight. Whether you get great insight back or not is another question. This is a more hands-on use case, but when you zoom out you'll see that most SEOs tend to like patterns and ranking factors.

AI in itself is a wider area, so Google is probably using it for research left, right, and centre. Its goal is to see where machine learning AI or AI support could make a difference in terms of better search results. It could then determine the content quality on a page and potentially be used to create content. It could also be used to decipher which content has been created by AI and what shouldn't be ranking altogether. The future of AI is looking bright but, very soon, we're likely to see parts of these implementations driving some of the rankings."

Is Google using AI to determine what content is AI?

"Interestingly, yes. That's the nature of the beast. You have this kind of 'black box' situation where people often struggle to understand what that really is and what's happening behind the scenes. A lot of the current stuff we're seeing is part of a machine learning algorithm, or multiple algorithms that work in unison to spit something out. We're at a stage where the result of that is very much determined and driven by how good the training data is.
We talk a lot about English language stuff, but if you look beyond that we're not quite there yet. The English language is one thing but beyond that, and even in other European countries, there is much smaller training data available. The output of that is way less in terms of quality, which is something to keep in mind.

If you're talking about whether Google is there or not, this will probably only apply to the English search results. This is one of the reasons why, when you look at some of the recent announcements/updates, they tend to roll out in the English language markets first. Sometimes they're rolled out in English exclusively because the corpus of data is much bigger than what's available in other languages."

Do you mean every country that uses the English language worldwide or perhaps just the US?

"Historically, Google has always rolled out in the US first. Right now, there are certain localisation aspects between the UK and the US. You could say the English language in general, even though there are different variations of it. Google masters English quite well but if it gets to more complicated stuff, or there's less training data available, they might not roll things out in those different markets. That also means that machine learning can only do so much.

We need to move beyond that and develop a system that has some sort of intelligence to it. Once you have a system that isn't relying on a limited corpus of training data it will be able to train itself. That's why most people confuse the 'machine-supervised learning' versus 'What is Artificial Intelligence?' conversation. It's often an oversimplification to call something AI when really it's just a multitude of trained algorithms."

Would you say that Google is actively using machine learning at the moment but they're not using AI yet?

"Yes. That's one thing that has changed historically, especially on the search quality side. They were previously very much against using machine learning in any way, shape, or form. That was a couple of years ago, but today's visual platforms have many machine learning algorithms in place. For example, the recommendations we receive on YouTube. These are essentially all based on machine learning.

With AI, it's a thin line, because it's hard to judge. There's been a lot of discussion around AI becoming this machine that has certain feelings. Google is using machine learning but not AI as much. There is an acceleration curve of the progress we're making. Let's look at how the role of the SEO has changed over the past five years vs what will happen over the next five years. With higher computing power and more data and capabilities to process that data, we'll probably start seeing much faster progress."

What precisely is Google looking at within the content to decide upon the quality and map intent to that? What do SEOs need to do about that?

"Historically there's been a huge struggle between eCommerce businesses that want to sell products. They have to sell their products and have product descriptions around the items they're trying to sell. However, often the decision has been formed much earlier, when someone is in an informational stage.

Let's say you're looking for a washing machine. Perhaps you have a bigger family now and want to know what type of washing machine you need. This is part of the informational journey. The question is, what do you really want when you search for a term like 'washing machine'? Is that a purchase query or is it the information stage or somewhere in between? Conventionally you'd go to a local store seeking comparisons or recommendations. You could then attain search query refinement. Unfortunately, you won't have the opportunity to have a dialogue with someone when you enter a search query.

That's why Google is moving into this 'user journey' situation, rather than having one single input/output without understanding the context or meaning around it. From that perspective, what they're looking for is to find results that can answer or support the user no matter what stage they're in. It could be a piece of content that you get from a specific shop when the person is still in the informational stage of the journey. People might seek this comparison because they want to figure out which is the right product for them. You might then prefer to get a table or listing of different types of machines. You might want a single recommendation being shown.

Fundamentally, what Google is trying its hardest to understand is which companies or domains can help in all the different stages. This might not be true for every vertical but it's especially relevant in eCommerce - where you have different types of queries supporting each other in a really important way.

Regarding holistic content, no matter how generic or specific the query is, Google's biggest goal is to understand where someone is in the customer journey, and then serve the respective content. This could be very different when you search 'washing machine' vs when I search 'washing machine'. The big thing is that the more data you have, the more machine learning you can apply - and the more factors you can get in. This is a crucial thing for Google to understand.

Let's use searching for a new Audi car as an example. If you look at search results, historically there were times when they got a whole ton of brand rankings for their home and career opportunities pages. If you look at these generic search results today they've changed so much, because Google has got better at understanding what a proper selection looks like. For example, the searcher has an interest in driving an RS3 so we'll serve this model page, not one that speaks about working at Audi because that's not what the searcher wants.

If you turn it around and look at what SEOs do, it's all about creating content that's informing these different types of decisions and supporting different types of journeys. This is a big reason why there's not one single answer to how long content should be. In previous years this has been determined by metrics - which aren't reflective. The direction of content will be dependent on the topic and the amount of information that you can provide as a site. You should look at what kind of information you really need because, if it's simplified information that can be served through structured data or with a single input-output answer, Google is going to do that themselves anyway. If you want to know how tall a certain building is, you can get that answer straight away. The biggest stuff that Google can't answer straight away is where you need to build content that supports the entire journey. You need to support the entire process and serve the correct intent as an authoritative source."

How do you become the trusted resource on a particular topic?

"Focus on EAT to become a trustworthy general entity. The entity could be a person or a multitude of people. This is a broad topic, but you need to build up a reputation over time because it isn't something you can achieve overnight."

Has machine learning radically impacted the way that authority is built?

"No, I wouldn't necessarily say so. What it certainly does is help us understand if someone is, in fact, an authority because you can start mapping things out. If you're in the pharmaceutical context, for example, it would be easy for Google to take a certain set of training data that's solely related to prescription information for certain types of drugs. You could process that and - based on the specific corpus for a vertical like pharmaceutical - you'd know what a pharmaceutical site looks like, structure-wise.

It would be much easier for a machine to understand if it's a typical site or whether someone is just writing about certain drugs for rankings. With machine learning, you can have verticalized approaches to using different types of data and therefore come to different conclusions as to what a specific authority in the pharmaceutical company looks like. Appeasing machine learning certainly helps but, generally speaking, becoming an authority doesn't happen overnight. You need to invest in content reputation, citations, linking, etc. These things are still there but the process takes time."

What shouldn't SEOs be doing in 2023? What's seductive in terms of time, but ultimately counterproductive?

"There's still a lot of old-fashioned tactics out there. For example, auto-generated linking and these types of things. These outdated approaches have been dead for years, so let's put them to rest. The general mindset you see is a desire to chase different types of patterns or isolated ranking factors that might only move the needle by 1%. This is something that people need to stop obsessing about because that's not how search works anymore. If you have machines informing decisions based on a broad variety of data, yes you might move the needle by 1%, but the question is: is that really worth your time?

Don't obsess over individual isolated ranking factors as much as you've probably done in the past. Yes, you'll still need proper page titles but not only because they are a ranking factor. You need them because they make a difference in terms of CTR. They inform what that destination page is all about and could use an internal link, anchor text, etc. Don't obsess over individual things and ensure your overall approach is as comprehensive as possible. Build a site that has meaning and is informing decisions along the user journey. Stop obsessing over isolated ranking factors."

Bastian Grimm is CEO and Co-Founder at Peak Ace and you can find him at pa.ag.

14 ANALYTICS & TESTING

Understand your data—Rasida Begum

Rasida Begum believes that by better understanding your data, you'll be more successful as an SEO in 2023. Start looking at how your data can be compared and delve deeper below the surface.

Rasida says: "Many successful eCommerce brands miss or have a gap in understanding SEO performance by content group. To accomplish this, you must understand how your product pages are performing versus category pages and assess which part is brand and which part is non-brand. Instead, people focus on a very top-line view looking at seasonality and analysing data on a page-by-page basis. Doing so limits how you view your performance and what you're able to feed into your strategy."

How do you break down your different categories of pages? What other categories of pages are worth focusing on?

"The easiest way to break this down is by looking at the URL pattern in terms of setup. Lots of problems can derive from not having the correct setup. It'll be great If you have the skill set to execute the setup in conjunction with the data team. 90% of eCommerce sites are product pages, meaning your product pages must be good. The remaining 10% will be your homepage, category, content, or editorial, which will become focal points as you move forward. Editorial will be on an association basis in terms of looking at your brand and branding. If you're looking at editorial content you should avoid assessing it from a revenue perspective."

What makes a great product page in terms of volume, type, calls to action, and other elements of SEO?

"A good product page can be generated from working closely with your copywriting team. It's important to establish a close relationship with the copy that's being produced and understand the tone of voice, brand, etc. You should also look at the search element and determine what a user would look for if they wanted product X. This could also feed into the metadata logic, assessing what order the brand is appearing in, the product total, and whether you're naming things in line with what people are looking for.

You should avoid using terms that only resonate with a small number of people. Never assume that everyone will understand what you're talking about, especially when you're using niche terms. Take a step back and work with your copywriting team, better understand your brand, tell a story, and use data to target users who are looking for your product so you can show up and be associated."

Has Google changed the way it's using metadata?

"Regarding how you're creating metadata, a lot of the time there'll be a logic in your CMS and it'll just pull it from your product entry. You should look at whether this is automated and whether you can play around with that, improve the click-through rate, etc. It'll all be about understanding what's happening in the process and testing to determine whether you can improve something.

If things don't go as planned, you can apply your learnings going forward as part of a nice cycle to follow. It's worth running tests on product pages every six weeks, not in terms of changes but in measuring performance. Six weeks gives you enough time to do post and pre-work one week to see if results fluctuate. When you're working in eCommerce, there's so much seasonality. You can experiment with shorter periods but there are too many variables that could influence that. Six weeks gives you enough data to understand whether an initiative works. If so, you can roll it out to the rest of the pages. If not, you can put a pause on the strategy."

What's an example of some analysis that produced a result you didn't really anticipate, but that people can learn from?

"Making a simple change to a homepage meta title. This involved editing the title to incorporate express shipping as a USP. The changes were nothing out of the ordinary. The title had never been changed before, so it was worth experimenting with. We wanted to test the content ordering to see if the order of the message would be displayed in the meta title.

In eCommerce, shipping is one of the biggest factors that determine whether a visitor converts or not. Because of shipping, people often decide to go to a competitor at the last minute. A week after going live with the new title, our clicks were up 80%, and six weeks later up by 160%. These results remained steady for the whole year, which was incredible because all we did was add 'express shipping' in our meta title. From this, the homepage increased in click-through rate and kept bringing in those clicks for more than a year."

How can you isolate that it's definitely those particular keywords or phraseology that has made the difference? Are you able to do split testing or do you have to run it and compare results before and after?

"We measured about 12 to 16 months of data and then looked at the 30 days prior to that. No other changes took place on the site and there was no seasonality that we saw across the other marketing channels. Everything was really steady. The only change that had been made was this one, and it aligned exactly with when it went live. Of course, there will be external variables, but we isolated it as much as possible and looked at any wider impact it could have had."

What software are you using to analyse? Are you just looking in Search Console or something else?

"Keep it simple with tests and analyses. These won't need to be overcomplicated. It's great to do split tests using an algorithm; look at 100 pages and compare them to another 100 pages for likeness. This can be a useful approach if you have the budget, team, or people to justify spending lots of time on this.

Look closely at what you have and what you can do. Use really simple tests, addressing the pre and post to look at external variables. You can then use the Search Console and GA to understand how it's impacting KPIs like revenue. You can then look at how it's impacting traffic."

Where does SEO fit into editorial or is editorial more of a brand play?

"Editorial is interesting because, depending on your industry, there might be millions and millions invested into it. They'll often be significantly more invested in this than marketing, so it plays a role in terms of branding. When you're producing content online, you want to be reaching an audience so people can see the content you're producing. That way you'll be making use of the investment and will be more likely to see a return. However, when working for a brand it can be very difficult to gain any commercial value through content. You won't only be competing with other eCommerce brands but also large entities with huge marketing/editorial budgets. If you're unable to have a clear focus it can become difficult to get a return.

It'll be more about the brand and using it through email, on-site, and on social media. If you're looking to establish a hierarchy, and your product pages and sites are doing well, then you can look into editorial. If your site is not doing well, you should avoid investing your money there and instead look at the more transactional pages."

What's the importance of writing everything down from the previous year that didn't work before forming your strategy for the coming year?

"As SEOs, we all experience the same problems. For example: not having enough tech or people not listening to you in the business to get budget sign-off. In the midst of this, it's easy to become so overwhelmed with everything that you forget to reflect on something you've done that you probably shouldn't repeat. You should focus on getting support from your team or manager to understand how you can do something better.

Marketing SEO doesn't need to be overcomplicated. It's about narrowing down to the things that will make a difference. That could be the way you communicate: whether you need stakeholder buy-in, who to speak with, whether you've got enough exposure, etc. These are questions you must constantly ask yourself - and get help. Asking for help means you're good at your job and willing to embrace feedback to improve. That's why writing down and reflecting is so important."

How long do SEO strategies normally last and how often do you revisit and hone them?

"That largely depends on your business cycle. A lot of the time it's annual, but in terms of longevity of your strategy, you should be looking closer to two, three, or four years ahead. When you assess performance at the end of the year, you should look at things to determine what works, what doesn't, and what you should continue to do going forward.

Should you keep optimising content or carry on working with teams to better understand where you need to focus your time? It's like having an ongoing strategy that's open to yearly changes. We're operating in fast-evolving markets where it's important to adjust your strategy in line with changing market conditions. If your business vision has changed, then your strategy will need to change."

What shouldn't SEOs be doing in 2023? What's seductive in terms of time, but ultimately counterproductive?

"Though it's good to understand how algorithm changes impact your site, you shouldn't get lost in this. You could end up thinking about the algorithms, creating panic and assuming you must change everything.

First, you need to truly understand what's happened and how it's impacted you. How big is the issue and to what extent has it impacted your commercial KPIs? If it hasn't, then it's not worth paying much attention to. Focus on vision, strategy, where you want your brand to be, and the story you're telling. This will save you from panicking at the prospect of algorithm updates. If you can move away from this and focus more on the long term, when something happens, you can assess the risk and change your vision."

Rasida Begum is Product Manager of Search and SEO at Yell and you can find her by searching 'Rasida Begum' on LinkedIn.

Don't be afraid of ranking volatility—Adriana Stein

Adriana Stein states that because the Google algorithm is always changing, SEOs should not rely as much on those signals in 2023 but focus on establishing themselves as trustworthy sources.

Adriana says: "Basically, do not freak out about ranking volatility. It's a common issue, especially with Google algorithm updates. Ranking volatility is where we sometimes see a massive drop in page rankings. It simply means your keyword rank is not stable, but always changing. There is no need to panic. Instead, there are ways of handling that more methodically than just rushing to create new content."

What do you mean when you say 'Google is A/B Testing results'?

"Google constantly tests results to provide the best information to the user one that matches the query's search intent and provides the best possible content.

Everyone is doing SEO nowadays, which is great because it is powerful and valuable, especially with a good strategy. However, that means that even if you get a number one spot, it is not guaranteed that you will hold it for more than 24 hours. It is still normal, though, and that's nothing to worry about."

Previously, one could get keyword rankings for two years. Do you think that's not possible anymore?

"In today's SEO world, it's just not wise or logical to look at keyword rankings as static. That especially applies when you have an 'agency and client'-type relationship. It requires you to look at things from a wider perspective in describing our keywords, ranking, and SEO progress. That gives you a lot more of an accurate picture because there are so many changes all the time - in content, new competitors, behavioural changes, etc.

Recently, a LinkedIn post highlighted how the SERPs based on the search query 'King Charles' have changed. Before, that term would have mostly been referring to a dog. Now, we have a very different definition of 'King Charles'. The number one article for 'King Charles' is probably no longer number one, because that search behaviour has entirely changed."

If Google discovers a new web page from a competitor of yours, does it want to test it in the same position as your page just to see if there's a difference in click-through rate? Is it also trying other things, like changing meta descriptions and titles to see if there's a difference?

"It is testing all of that in tandem - and every minute detail as well. Nowadays, and into 2023, you must consider SEO a holistic process, not just about getting your keyword rankings in the SERPs. It's also about who actually clicks on your content and what they do once they're on your website. Has it been helpful for them or do they just find it annoying or frustrating and then leave?

Many of the updates Google implemented last year had to do with Core Web Vitals and content quality, especially in terms of page design and page structure. This year, they've focused on helpful content. If you can look at it as this holistic process, that's the best way to really track your SEO strategy - because that's how Google is looking at it.

It's changing all the time. Google tests about 80% of your metadata and changes much of it, like titles, meta descriptions, etc. If you have written it in a way that's effective and accurate, Google keeps it fantastic, which is also good for the user. Don't be afraid if they're replacing it, though, because they're probably trying to show what is the most helpful for the reader to get that click-through rate.

Then, they also look at how the reader behaves on that page. Suppose a website has a very good keyword ranking for something that matches the user query, yet the content is bad quality, or the website is slow. They will remove that anyway because it would no longer be considered helpful content."

How does Google measure the degree of helpfulness? Is it just the click-through rate or do they have other ways of measuring the difference between two URLs?

"It's just a vast amount of data analysis with billions of data points they're looking at. They examine all these different angles, websites, and competitors and then try to find the best possible information to show the user. That has always been the foundation of what Google has been trying to do.

Over the last few years, they have matured in their ability to do this quite significantly. We know this because you no longer often see websites that pop up using spammy backlink techniques or poor-quality content.

Occasionally, in niche areas, you will see a few things pop up. For example, in B2B and technology-based sectors, you will see some older stuff that looks a bit strange. Nonetheless, content nowadays is generally high quality. You must also keep up with Google's changes. As long as you keep improving and optimising - keeping the audience at the forefront of your strategy - Google will also recognise that."

What period is best to check your rankings? Is it years, months, or weeks?

"There are a few factors to consider there. One is how long you've been doing SEO. If you've only been doing SEO for a month, it probably doesn't even make sense to check your keyword rankings within that month, because nothing has likely changed. If you have been doing SEO for almost three years and want to measure a high purchase intent keyword, then you would want to check monthly.

On average, even checking every three months is okay, because so many changes happen within a given period. We often see projects where a page is ranked in the top 3 then, a week later, it's randomly at 80 - and it's not an indexing issue. Here, it's probably Google's doing some A/B testing, and then it moves it back up again.

Data Studio is usually helpful for this. You can create visuals for the average ranking for different keywords. That is the best way to look at it."

How many hours or days does it take before you finally conclude that you have officially lost your rankings?

"It depends on how long and how often you've been doing SEO in content production. Are you producing two pieces of content per month or are you creating 30? If it is the latter, then you can check them more often.

It would also depend on the industry competition. If you have a lot of competitors in your industry, volatility is a must because you have people competing for those top spots all the time. They are constantly optimising, and some have bigger budgets for that.

On average, looking at it from one to three months will give you a good amount of information on whether something strange has happened, like a Google algorithm update. You just need to wait and see the impact."

Suppose you have actually been knocked out from the rankings. What initial steps would you take to assess the problem and recover from there?

"Firstly, you would want to look at how far that average has dropped. Is it just a little bit or is it extreme? If it's extreme, then check if your page is still indexed. You must ensure you have all of the technical bits while checking your competitors and seeing any changes they have made. Perhaps they now have a new page that ranks above yours because it is better.

Furthermore, you can look at the technical elements of your website. Has your website become slow, and why? For example, if you are using WordPress, when you have to do a plugin update it can affect site speed.

It also helps to check Google Analytics traffic to see if the page has a high bounce rate. For instance, suppose you created some content for 2021; it performed well and had good rankings. Now, it's 2022, and people see the data is outdated, so they're not using it anymore. You would need to go and update it again. Generally, it revolves around assessing the data to identify the cause."

What shouldn't SEOs be doing in 2023? What is seductive in terms of time, but ultimately counterproductive?

"It can be tempting to think of SEO as a piecemeal approach: doing one blog here or one landing page there. With that approach, you are not really building topical authority or accumulating organic traffic like you would if you were trying to build out holistic content pillars. That is, groups of related topics and covering a topic holistically. It is a core ranking factor, especially with Google's helpful content updates.

Nowadays, it helps to cover every aspect of a topic because that is how you prove that you're a trustworthy and reliable source. Running the content piece by piece will be cheaper in terms of time and money. Yet, in the long run, you're choosing the more expensive and the less effective route because you're just elongating the time it will take for your SEO strategy to perform well."

Adriana Stein is the Founder and CEO of AS Marketing, and you can find her over at asmarketingagency.com.

Measure with what you have access to and then iterate—Jess Joyce

Jess Joyce encourages SEOs to make the most of all the data and metrics that are currently available in 2023 and measure whatever they can, to make continuous improvements based on what is already in place.

Jess says: "Measure what you can and whatever you have access to, and then iterate on that. By this I mean there are many different ways you can go about measurement and tracking and analytics, across many different platforms. The space is only getting more diverse. For most companies, you just have to work with what you have, and then get buy-in as you go to build on that and make it better, faster, stronger - as Daft Punk would say."

What are some of the most important things that you absolutely have to be measuring?

"The number one thing is revenue. Ideally, you want to track that back to whatever channel you're working on. For most of us in SEO, tracking a channel back to revenue is always the most effective option and the biggest metric that you should be looking at, in whatever way that you can.

Most of us are familiar with Google Analytics 3, or Universal Analytics, so you should be setting up goals there. However, knowing that Universal Analytics is going the way of the dinosaur in the next couple of years, I think that's going to open up the space in a lot of different ways.

That's why I like tracking it back to the metrics themselves, instead of just relying on an overall programme. You can always use a programme, just make sure that you write down the specific metrics that you want to track - whether that's pageviews, impressions, etc. Track them through your funnel and identify your revenue through that. Then you can attribute that information to whichever programme or software tool you're using once UA is gone."

Can being forced to focus solely on revenue mean that SEOs end up concentrating on bottom-of-funnel keyword phrases, and lose the opportunity or incentive to pay attention to the top of the funnel?

"Absolutely. SEOs should have secondary metrics that go along with revenue because they're all leading metrics of success. Tracking multistage attribution is not at the point that it should be in 2023. You should always have leading metrics like pageviews, impressions, click-through rates, and all those wonderful things - and then you should be setting up goals throughout your website as efficiently as you can.

GA4 is based on that. It's based on events and tracking multiple metrics. While GA3 is becoming extinct, GA4 opens up that play box, and gives you the ability to track whichever success metrics you can and set them up specifically for whichever organisation you're working with."

What's the best way of dealing with attribution at the moment? Is there a standard model that tends to work more effectively, or a software that you recommend?

"Currently, I'm using Fathom Analytics. They're a privacy-based analytics platform and they have pulled attribution through a little more than Google Analytics. I'm actually able to see if somebody's clicked on a WhatsApp chat or something else, and it brings in that direct model which is often a dark hole that SEOs struggle to measure. There are other options out there too, like Atom Analytics, where you can actually look at different variations of that dark direct traffic, which is very helpful.

As well as that, UTMs are always the go-to for any attribution model and metric, in any platform throughout the internet. Wherever you can use UTMs on any campaigns it's always a helpful thing."

Is there any kind of ideal model that you favour?

"I haven't seen anybody do this super effectively yet, especially with everything changing so quickly. Let's hope for a helpful content update in 2023.

I'm still working on a specific basis with clients for their content models depending on how much content they have, how often they're updating it, how many people they have in-house that are working on the content and how close they are to the topic, how much they've covered that content in that topic, etc.

These aren't things that you can put into Google Analytics at this point. We're doing it manually between Airtable and other places that are outside of GA. It's important to have conversations with clients about what matters to them, and what success looks like to them."

In terms of reporting, is GA4 the big thing that's happening at the moment? Is that something that all SEOs need to be completely comfortable with?

"Maybe. I think it would be good for all SEOs to at least install it on a test site and start pushing through your own events, to be able to understand how that measurement model works and how it will work in the future. If you're working on client sites, then somebody along the way will have GA4. You'll want to be able to track those models throughout the ecosystem.

On top of that, GA4 will better integrate into Data Studio. Having that connection will be fantastic because then you can pull in other third-party sources, including Search Console. I've been making some Search Console dashboards with Data Studio and then integrating some HubSpot metrics in there as well, to create as full a picture as we possibly can get to at this stage."

What are some key events that SEOs absolutely need to be tracking in their analytics?

"Definitely impressions through Search Console - and clicks. Clicks and impressions are my go-to success metrics. Besides that, look at indexing. I like to see where the sites are at as far as indexing goes.

There has been all kinds of fluctuation throughout the web, and Search Console has been updating their stuff like mad recently, so monitoring the indexing of your site, then monitoring the impressions that you're getting in search, and then monitoring your click-throughs, is definitely going to show you how everything's going.

Additionally, you should look at the keywords that Search Console is pulling through. It's not a full picture of everything (because nothing will be) but you have to measure something. My takeaway is to measure whatever you have access to, and Search Console is what we have access to. It's what Google is giving us."

What trends are you seeing in terms of indexing? Are Google less likely to index pages and what can you do to try and encourage them to index more?

"I'm seeing that Google doesn't want to index thin content. Documentation pages are wonderful, but if they're super thin and super short then you need to make them as useful as possible. Connecting those pages to other topics along the way is also helpful for getting them indexed.

Additionally, you should be linking pages better and bringing them as close to the homepage as possible. That could be with topics, categories, extra links, or placing links in multiple places throughout your pages and then linking those deeper into the site that way.

I've found that Google doesn't like pagination, and they obviously don't follow the infinite scroll all the way. Giving Google multiple routes to the same end goal is always helpful. I've even seen HTML sitemaps do it.

Bringing back the old-school internet, you can do something that dynamically pulls through an HTML sitemap of your whole site, and feed that through Google. Give them as much context and as many inroads as possible."

Should you be bringing data into other platforms besides Google Analytics, like Data Studio, to do more historical comparisons?

"100%. You should also be uploading your data to some other place. You can upload things to Amazon and their clouds, or any of the other data slicing and dicing platforms. You should definitely be doing that, especially with your GA3 data. Make sure that it's backed up somewhere before we lose it - because then you're going to have people like me coming through and wanting to know year-over-year metrics, and we're not going to have access to that.

Back that data up or make sure that you have it in a secondary location, so that somebody can have that year-over-year data, or at least quarter-over-quarter. You want a quarter that goes back to 2020, or at least 2022. There's been so much fluctuation in the past couple of years - with the pandemic and in the way people are searching, shopping, and navigating online - that data folks will want to understand.

You should be exporting monthly backups of your Google Analytics data, if your site's big enough. If it's a small site, then some of the other analytics platforms can definitely help you out, but if you're a mid-sized B2B SaaS company and you have hundreds of thousands of views, then you should definitely be backing that up at that point."

What shouldn't SEOs be doing in 2023? What's seductive in terms of time, but ultimately counterproductive?

"It's been said before but, with all the updates we've been seeing, SEOs shouldn't be focusing on search engines alone in 2023. Google doesn't focus on the search engine alone; Google focuses on the people who are using said search engine. As SEOs, we should be doing the same.

When you're making a website, you're not making a website for you - you're making it for users. You could spend a whole mountain of time looking through what search engines do and how they process things but, at the end of the day, they care about users, so you should too.

When we're talking about search engines in 2023, that's including YouTube and TikTok - even Pinterest still has a stake in all of this. All of them attribute back. I've even seen people making TikToks of how to Google these days. All of those are helping people find the information they're looking for."

How do you identify exactly what your users are doing in terms of finding and navigating through your site?

"I think it depends on the organisation. If you have a UX team, lean on them. If you have a customer support team, lean on them. Talk to support. Open up those channels and those conversations. That way, any pain points, needs, or questions that your users bring up will get fed right to the SEO team and the content team. The same goes for UX.

It's about opening up those conversations wherever you can within the organisation and making sure that all those pain points are met, so that you can address them as effectively as possible. That will make sure that the search meets the intent, and you're answering those questions for people."

Do websites still use onsite search? Do users ask many queries through onsite search, or do they go back to Google?

"I've seen users utilising onsite search a lot more in eCommerce. If humans are looking for something and the menu doesn't make sense, or the hierarchy on the website doesn't make sense, then they'll just search. If they don't see what they need on the homepage (or whatever page they land on) then they'll use the search.

This is really beneficial, and it can actually help SEOs inform their decisions about what kind of content they want to write. If somebody's looking for a 'pleated skirt in purple' 500 times, then you're going to want to write about a purple pleated skirt and ensure that answer is being met. Onsite search can be very valuable."

Jess Joyce is an SEO Consultant and you can find her at jessjoyce.com

Get comfortable with GA4—Natalie Slater

Natalie Slater advises SEOs in 2023 to stop sticking their heads in the sand and migrate over to GA4 as soon as possible. Start the transition

away from Universal Analytics, start gathering data, and start understanding the potential changes.

Natalie says: "Get comfortable with GA4. Universal Analytics is going away on the 1st of July 2023, when it will stop recording data.

The best version of this scenario would be that businesses will have migrated to GA4 already, so that they have a good amount of data to compare performance year-on-year by the time the data stops recording in Universal Analytics.

The second-best time to do it is now.

Universal Analytics will stop recording data and that impacts all kinds of things from a marketing perspective, and certainly not just SEO. You can't manage what you can't measure. Obviously, other platforms are available, but the transition from Universal Analytics to GA4 doesn't have to be as painful as some people have thought. I was very sceptical of GA4, to begin with, and I'm a new convert to the cause."

What is different about measuring things with GA4?

"The main difference is the unit of measurement. Also, the way the data is collected is different too. All other versions of Google Analytics have always been based on hits and some event tracking. However, anything that happens within Google Analytics 4 is an event.

That does mean that there are discrepancies between them. If you run GA4 alongside Universal, you're going to see some differences in the session data. If it's drastically different then that's something to look into, but there will always be some discrepancies. My advice would be to install GA4 alongside Universal for as long as you possibly can, to get acquainted with those variances in the data and figure out what's going on. For me as a practitioner, that's been invaluable in terms of learning how all of this works. Learn by doing.

It's a fairly straightforward process. If you want a basic implementation of GA4 - to just get the code on there and see what it tracks out of the box - then it's usually a five-minute job. The bigger part is when you've got a huge website with lots of manual events and goals that you're tracking. That can become quite fiddly, but take the first step and get the code up there."

How will the data change when it comes to viewing everything as events?

"GA4 does still use sessions and pageviews; those are metrics that are still in GA4. It's the step before that where the difference is; in how the data is gathered. The unit of measurement in Universal Analytics is a hit, which is then translated into sessions and pageviews data. Now the unit of measurement is an event, and all those events are untainted in GA4. There's no change in what the metric is.

I don't know a huge amount about how that works exactly, but the top line is that the unit of measurement is different, which leads to discrepancies between the two datasets. That needs to be borne in mind when making those comparisons - that some variances are to be expected."

When moving from Universal Analytics to GA4, how do SEOs take the data, make sense of the changes, and compare what they're seeing at the moment with what has happened in the past?

"The most straightforward way of doing that would be within Looker Studio and combining those two sources of data. There are plenty of templates that people have built specifically for this task.

Personally, I still run all my reports in Excel. I like to be very hands-on with the data because, that way, I don't miss anything. The manual approach is often good.

In terms of making notes within GA itself, you can still annotate with GA4. There are all kinds of custom reports using the Explore function that you can build, but I would say that Data Studio is your best bet for that direct comparison."

How far should an SEO go back to make sense of that data?

"Personally, I would go back more than a year. The only reason I'm saying that is because of how consumers have behaved so differently over the previous two years. For many campaigns I'm running, the best year-on-year comparison still tends to be against 2019, because 2020 and 2021 were so unusual.

It depends on the sector. You might be running a site where everything's just been the same all the way through, although I doubt it. For that reason,

I would say benchmarking from the start of 2019 at least can be quite helpful, as a minimum for any dataset."

Why has Google introduced GA4, and what are the benefits?

From what I can tell, it's a data protection situation. I don't spend too much time looking at Google's reasoning behind this, I mainly want to just get on with it.

It seems that the benefits are more for Google than the user. I think that's why, as an industry, people have been quite frustrated. There hasn't been as much hand-holding through this process, or as much notice as people might have liked. There are definitely flaws - or things about GA4 that are not as well put together as Universal Analytics - and that's where some of the frustration comes from, but I think they'll get there.

There have been recent changes that have made it a lot easier to do eCommerce tracking within GA4, for example, as it was quite fiddly up until a couple of months a month ago. They are ever-evolving and catching up with themselves.

It is tricky to think of the benefits because we don't like changes within Google Analytics. It takes a lot of time to get used to something. I think Universal Analytics is great and GA4 was so radically different in its measurement and its interface that it took a lot of getting used to. You do get used to it, though, and I can attest to that."

Some SEOs will be thinking of this as an opportunity to consider other tracking tools. Have you considered learning something entirely different instead?

"I'm fairly brand loyal to Google. Certainly, when there were things that GA4 couldn't do for quite some time, I understand the motivation to try out things like Matomo.

Personally, I am not doing much with any other analytics platforms, so I can't really speak to that. I totally understand the desire to, though, and it's going to make the industry a bit more exciting if there's a bit more competition.

With that being said, I hold out for GA4, and I think it's going to do what it needs to do eventually."

Would you recommend using Data Studio, or another third-party aggregator, to analyse your data and make those comparisons?

"Yes. I think you can do it without Data Studio, but the year-on-year comparison is going to be quite fiddly. Once you've got a year's worth of GA4 data, it will become much easier to do that within GA4 itself and not necessarily need to rely on something like Data Studio.

However, that is what Data Studio is for: pulling together all of the data from all of Google's platforms and all other kinds of third parties. That's what's cool about it. I don't think Data Studio is compulsory, but I think it's going to be necessary for this specific comparison exercise."

What shouldn't SEOs be doing in 2023? What's seductive in terms of time, but ultimately counterproductive?

"I would say that, especially when you're short on time, we can all be guilty of taking the view of just one expert as if it's the gospel, or definitely best practice. That's quite unwise. In an area like SEO, where so much of our job is theory, it's good to get your information about a subject matter from a range of sources.

If they back each other up, then that's great and you know you're onto a winner. Blindly following the instruction of one industry expert, however, is possibly unwise. I'm not talking about any one individual. We have an industry full of hugely talented people, and I think we can all learn a lot from collating that information and thinking about it critically, rather than just take taking one thing as read and running with it.

Someone's experience, no matter how vast, is based upon what has personally worked for them, and their situation doesn't necessarily apply to your situation."

Natalie Slater is a Freelance SEO Consultant, and you can find her by searching Natalie Slater (formerly Natalie Mott) on LinkedIn.

Is Data Studio better than GA4?—Pam Aungst Cronin

Pam Aungst Cronin believes that the future of SEO in 2023 no longer revolves around traditional SEO tactics, but rather changing how you

look at your metrics. She suggests moving to Data Studio for your reporting and relying less on GA4.

Pam says: "For this year, I'm going to go with something that is not usually thought of as SEO, but it's definitely part of it: reporting. I believe that, in 2023, you should start using Data Studio for your reporting, that is, if you are not doing so already.

Google Analytics 4 has an incredibly confusing interface. It is an entirely different measurement protocol; apples and oranges from Google Analytics 3. Plus, it's pretty overwhelming to learn. That is why I recommend that people use Data Studio for reporting in 2023 instead, because it saves you time learning the confusing Google Analytics 4 interface.

I also think it's worth your time learning how to set up reporting in Data Studio. You'll probably need it to compare prior Google Analytics 3 data to Google Analytics 4 data. Thus, it makes more sense to rely on Data Studio instead of spending time learning Google Analytics 4."

Why would the metrics vary between Google Analytics 3 and Google Analytics 4?

"It is a different measurement protocol, meaning they count the data differently. The technical differences probably arise because they are trying to improve multi-channel attribution. Basically, you'll find that there is more AI involved.

Since they are slightly different in how they count things, you will never see your Google Analytics 3 metrics for a certain timeframe exactly match the Google Analytics 4 metric in the same timeline.

Either way, you should keep comparing them and making sure they are at least similar. For instance, if Google Analytics 3 says 300 sessions for the month, you shouldn't see 3,000 on Google Analytics 4. Maybe 300 versus 400 would be okay."

There are a few other SEO platforms that already show different data. How would you compare them and know which one is right?"

"Trends and correlations are a good way to make this comparison. That is another reason why I like Data Studio for reporting. You can pull in from so many different sources, including Google Search Console. Suppose you are watching your trends with both Google Analytics 3 and Google

Analytics 4 data. Then you start to rely more on Google Analytics 4 and let go of Google Analytics 3. You can still pull data from Google Search Console and compare it with your Google Analytics data, and there should be some correlation.

Similarly, if your organic traffic is going up or down in Google Analytics. You should also see your impressions and click data going in the same direction in Search Console. If not, then that is something to dig into. What's more, whatever SEO platform you are using probably has an API you can pull into Data Studio and compare to Google Analytics and Search Console.

Overall, you would get a much bigger picture of your marketing data, including other things beyond SEO, all within Data Studio. That is great because, sometimes, there is a correlation between paid and organic. For instance, you turned off a giant ad campaign that had been getting people to Google your brand name. That can impact your organic traffic.

I can go on and on about all the great reasons to use Data Studio but one of them is precisely what you mentioned: things never quite add up on different platforms. You should see the same trends across the board for all of them, and Data studio is a good place for that."

Google started to push users to move on to Google Analytics 4 in July 2022. If you were already using Google Analytics 3 before then, will Google allow you to continue using that version?

"They didn't completely force people to transition to Google Analytics 4 yet, but they're going to as of July 2023. If you want to make year-over-year comparisons in 2023 compared to 2022, you must have set up Google Analytics 4 in time for July 2022.

If you did, I think that, during this transition, it is important to be looking at both. Data Studio is the place to do so. If you didn't do this transition before July 2022, it's not a problem. Pull your Google Analytics 3 data for 2022 and your Google Analytics 4 data for 2023 into Data Studio. And then you can do your year-over-year comparisons that way.

The issue of Google Analytics 3 stopping collecting data will happen at some point: probably July 1, 2023. Don't panic if you did not hit the July 2022 'deadline'. You can make up for it by pulling both Google Analytics 3 from 2022 and Google Analytics 4 data for 2023 into Data Studio in the same report."

Let us compare Google Analytics 3 and Google Analytics 4. Are there any metrics in Google Analytics 3 that SEOs could not use within Google Analytics 4?

"Yes. Both fortunately and unfortunately, some metrics went away with Google Analytics 4. Bounce rate is one, although people might disagree on whether that's a good thing. The bounce rate in traditional Google Analytics was inaccurate, easily manipulated, and often incorrectly recorded. Plus, it wasn't reliable. Now, they have replaced that with engagement rate, which is one of the things that I think is good. (NOTE: Since the time of writing, Google decided to reintroduce the bounce rate metric in GA4).

Another thing that went away, unfortunately, is the average session duration/time on page. However, you can create your own calculated metric in Data Studio to recreate it. Which is yet another reason for using Data Studio. It is possible to create a custom metric in Data Studio that pulls metrics from within Google Analytics 4 and calculates them to recreate that information.

Is it no longer necessary to stick with Google Analytics 4? Can you use other tracking software and bring that data into Data Studio?

"I do think you should still use Google Analytics, especially for year-over-year metrics. I don't think you should throw it out completely. However, I think it is good to start relying on other data sources for reporting other than Google Analytics.

One of the sneakiest things about Google Analytics 4 is that the data retention period has been greatly reduced. The default is only two months of data, although you can go in there and flip that over to 14 months. Still, 14 months when you are making year-over-year comparisons is nothing! They are going to offer a way for you to store more than 14 months of data, however, you must do it through BigQuery or another data warehouse you have to pay for.

We are moving towards this world where Google Analytics is more about your 'now' metrics. You are responsible for storing your own historical metrics and transitioning to Data Studio helps you find a way to retain your historical information. That is because Google Analytics can't be relied on for as much historical information going forward."

Are people moving away from GA4 and using other software instead?

"Absolutely, although I have not heard a consensus on which one they are going with. I am very curious and keeping my eyes peeled. I have not yet heard a running theme between the alternatives that people try."

I remember using alternative software before Google Analytics even existed, back in about 2004. I was using another piece of tracking software that was using a pixel which would give you a lot of information on individuals. That was before it wasn't legal to track so much information from individual users.

"Yes, that is another reason why Google made this change in the way that Google Analytics 4 measures and stores data. It is for all those privacy law purposes: GDPR, CCPA, etc. The world is moving towards a more private internet experience. Therefore, the laws concerning storing people's information are getting stricter.

I would caution anyone turning to an alternative Analytics to consider its compliance with such privacy laws. The way some software works, it easily gets into dangerous territory regarding collecting IP addresses and the like."

Should every business be using Data Studio? Is there still room for smaller companies to rely solely on Google Analytics moving forward?

"I think that smaller businesses should use Data Studio as well. The time it will take to learn the Google Analytics 4 interface just isn't worth it, in my opinion. Yes, you will also spend time learning Data Studio, however, the ROI of your time will pay off greater by spending time in 2023 learning Data Studio instead of Google Analytics 4.

For larger companies, you might already be using a different kind of dashboard reporting software, like Tableau, which is fine. I like to see businesses using some sort of data dashboard that pulls from multiple sources. I usually recommend Data Studio because it is free and therefore accessible to anyone. Really, any data dashboard tool that checks off these boxes works.

What shouldn't SEOs be doing in 2023? What is seductive in terms of time, but ultimately counterproductive?

"I'll repeat my prior statement and say it is not worth spending time learning Google Analytics 4 in 2023. You must learn how to configure it, absolutely. You should learn how to set up conversion tracking, record features, set up the data retention period, ensure that everything is accurate, etc. Beyond that, adapting to the interface and reporting system is ridiculous.

Both SEOs and small business owners are better off investing in learning either Data Studio or another similar dashboard reporting platform. It is better than learning the Google Analytics 4 interface for reporting purposes."

NOTE: Since the time of recording this contribution, Google purchased Looker and has rebranded Data Studio as Looker Studio.

Pam Aungst Cronin is President of Pam Ann Marketing and Founder of Stealth Search and Analytics, and you can find her over at pamannmarketing.com.

Preserve and utilise your web server logs— Kaspar Szymanski

Kaspar Szymanski encourages SEOs in 2023 to capitalise on an opportunity that is often overlooked by preserving and analysing your server logs so that you can understand more about what is actually happening on your site.

Kaspar says: "A great best practice that has proven to be a really phenomenal recommendation for large websites time and again is saving, preserving, and utilising raw web server logs. The vast majority of websites are not taking full advantage of this opportunity, even though they could greatly benefit from it."

Why is this important?

"The reason for utilising server logs is so that you can know rather than guess.

Typically, for a large website, a volume of landing pages are included in the sitemap, and there will be another volume of landing pages that are desirable - the cash cows and pages that we want to have indexed and crawled on a regular basis. Those two do not necessarily overlap 100%. I've been doing this for a really long time, and in my experience, there is rarely a large overlap.

You can use server logs to look at an extended period of time, and determine which pages you are telling search engines that you care about, which pages you actually care about being crawled and indexed, and which pages are being prioritised by search engines. In an ideal world, there will be a 100% overlap between those three volumes of landing pages. Frequently, however, there will be very little overlap at all.

Only by using server logs can you put yourself in a position to improve this. Crawl budget management comes in here (which is especially important for large websites) but it doesn't stop there. By having server logs that cover an extended period of time (we're talking six months to a year), you can actually evaluate your server responses. Among the most important of these are your DHCP responses. Are you getting 200 OKs? Do you have soft 404s and error pages? These are things that you can only truly understand by running a server log analysis.

Unfortunately, most websites do not take advantage of that - and that's a loss. SEO is becoming more and more technical all the time. This is something that large websites can benefit greatly from if you start saving and preserving server logs today."

Is it possible to get information on things like 200 OKs and soft 404s from online crawl tools or is that specific information only available by looking at log files?

"You can gain some insights through tools like Bing Webmaster Tools and Google Search Console. Search Console, for example, will pick up on soft 404s (which can be a sore point for large retail websites) but it's just a sample. The server logs are the only way that you can actually tell how much of the crawl budget goes towards landing pages that cannot generate revenue - because whatever used to be sold on those landing pages is sold out or unavailable.

We can gain some insights from third-party tools, and there are great tools out there, but server logs are a critical element. It is possible to have an SEO audit without server logs but, with them, the insights are so much more precise.

It is also important to identify why a website fluctuates and you can understand a lot more by using server logs. You might be able to see, for instance, that there is an increase in bot activity before a page drops in ranking because Googlebot is trying to figure out what the page is about. These kinds of correlations are highly relevant from an SEO perspective, but they are only visible if you have your server logs at hand."

Are website fluctuations a common issue?

"One of the most common questions that we encounter is: 'I've got a substantial website and a substantial brand, but it goes up and down in Google search visibility. Why is this happening?' Preferably, you want your site's position to be improving but, at the very least you want it to be relatively stable. Most of the time, this is something that can be corroborated when you look into the data. This is a very important and very common question, even for large websites.

Server logs are incredibly handy to have so that you can address these kinds of questions very specifically and precisely. Many large organisations do not record these logs, and if they have not been recorded then they can never be recovered. Either you record them, or you don't. Some organisations will only partially record server logs or retain them for a very short period of time. That's also problematic because it doesn't allow for a holistic picture."

For soft 404s, why does Google typically think that a page should be a 404 even though the server responds with a 200 OK, and how can SEOs fix that?

"I like the fact that you said 'Google thinks it's a 404', because it's often not accurate. If you happen to have a landing page that expired - perhaps a commercial item that's sold out or tickets for a concert that has ended – then the product is unavailable. In Google's mind, that should be a 404. If it returns a 200 OK then users can find that landing page, go to that landing page from SERPs, and the server response remains 200 OK, yet the landing page says that it is unavailable. That's a typical soft 404.

Google can recognise this. They are able to recognise the server response and the historic, classic content on-page but their on-page content recognition isn't flawless. There are many instances where Google says that you have soft 404s on your website, but they are just picking up on negative wording within 200 OK relevant landing pages.

Only through server logs can you tell whether those are real soft 404s. Then, you can start to determine what you are going to do about it if they are. You might want to make them into real 404s or custom 404s (which are my favourite). This is where a page still says '404', but it provides some additional added value. It provides an alternative for the user, to keep that lead and keep the user on the website in a meaningful user-relevant way. If not, you might want to noindex those pages. These alternatives are not really available without data analysis, which is always better when you have server logs at hand."

Is it possible to serve a bespoke 404 based on something like the category of the website?

"You have to stay consistent in the mind of the search engines. If you were to provide a different response to bots and users, that's something that Google might frown on. It might be considered user agent cloaking. From Google's perspective, 404s are something that should be utilised if the content is gone and it's not coming back anytime soon.

Of course, this is an ideal scenario that doesn't always happen. Publishers are sometimes of the opinion that they can retain some of their PageRank equity - which is very debatable when we are talking about sales pages that typically attract very little PageRank equity to begin with. They try to retain that equity by 301 redirecting those '404' pages to the root, or to the category, and end up creating yet more soft 404s.

This is a huge topic, but the bottom line is that 404s are there for a reason. They help the user understand that something is not available, and they help search engines to understand the same. They help us to make sure that the user experience is a good one. If Google understands (based on their data) that the user experience isn't great, then that's something that causes websites to drop in organic search. You want to prevent that from happening."

How do you preserve your log files? Where is it best to store them and what software is best for accessing them?

"That's actually something that needs to be considered on an individual basis because every website is different, and every architecture and every technological setup is different. Often, larger organisations will merge a number of websites and they will have a variety of solutions in place.

Saving and preserving should, of course, be done in a safe manner in terms of safety and data integrity. It depends on the setup and the facilities of the organisation, but it can be done on separate physical hard drives - which are pretty cheap nowadays.

I am often asked whether preserving and analysing server logs is going to cost a lot, and typically it is not expensive at all. If you're looking at generating data for SEO it's a relatively minor cost, especially for a large organisation.

The other objection that is often raised is the legal concern. I'm not providing any legal advice (I have no legal background; my background is purely focused on SEO), but there is no legal limitation on utilising and preserving raw web server logs if they're anonymized. If you're analysing raw files, you're only interested in bots. Whenever a human user has been accessing the website, that's of no consequence and can be completely dropped. The most important part of that data - the data treasure trove that can be built up over time - is verified bot entries. We're mainly talking about Googlebot and Bingbot. Once they have been isolated, that data does not pertain to any human user. That's the data that's really important.

Yes, it does touch on GDPR (or CCPA in the US), but it's not user data we're looking at. Neither legal obligations nor cost are roadblocks to saving and preserving your server logs. However, in terms of how to do this in the most efficient way, it comes down to the individual organisation and setup."

Is it useful and worthwhile to combine log file data with Search Console data?

"Absolutely. As a Google fanboy for a really long time, I also want to say that Bing Webmaster Tools is equally relevant and a great way to verify data. There are alternatives as well; Majestic is a fantastic tool, for example. The more the merrier, from my perspective.

You want to have as much relevant and fresh data as possible, but you also want to utilise a number of tools - both as data points and for analysis. Best case scenario: you're going to be able to verify the findings. If they contradict each other, you can dive a little bit deeper and drill into the code. It absolutely makes sense to combine your log data with other tools."

What shouldn't SEOs be doing in 2023? What's seductive in terms of time, but ultimately counterproductive?

"You shouldn't be building links for PageRank purposes. Yes, it can work - otherwise Google wouldn't be penalising the practice - but it's very much a double-edged sword.

You never know whether the effort and budget that you are putting in is a complete waste of your resources and money - and it can always trigger Google's wrath. Google still stands by the recommendation (and the Google Webmaster Guideline) that building links is a violation and that links should be merit-based. Hence, websites that choose to build links or do not clean up their legacy backlink issues run the risk of being penalised. Every penalty can be fixed but it's much better not to take the risk, as it is a business risk at the end of the day."

Kaspar Szymanski is a Director at SearchBrothers and you can find him over at searchbrothers.com.

Wear the data science hat more often—Begum Kaya

Begum Kaya says that SEOs need to expand their remit in 2023 and start acting more like data scientists so that you can be ready for the data revolution.

Begum says: "As SEOs, we must also be data scientists in disguise. We often take the data science and analysis steps unknowingly, one by one. As you progress as an SEO, you'll advance beyond doing work for smaller websites and have to figure out how to work on bigger datasets. As the simple tasks become more complex, you might wonder how good you are at deriving conclusions.

We tend to talk about how being data-driven is incredibly important, but are we really driven by data? If we are, how good are we at analysing and interpreting it? You might be able to dip your toes into Python, mostly for data analysis and automating some daily tasks. The biggest tip for 2023 is to get ready for the SEO data revolution and wear the data scientist hat more often."

Is there a particular process or way of working that an SEO can learn from a data scientist?

"There are five main steps to data analysis: the first being to define the questions. Let's say you have identified a problem, or tasks to analyse your current situation and ask the right questions in order to define your goals. You can do that daily - and this might even come from your clients. Then you can collect the data to be able to present something against that and do further analysis. You can gather data from Google Search Console, Google Analytics, and other third-party tools. Taking advantage of APIs and other automation tools makes this process more efficient. Then you can clean the data and, once that's done, you can start analysing it.

This part might derail some people from the conversation, but there are different models that you can use to derive analysis for the specific task at hand. Sometimes that takes the form of keyword research and sometimes it'll be internal linking, etc. However, when it comes to doing this via data science, it varies from descriptive analysis to diagnostic and predictive analysis. Lazarina Stoy is a great inspiration. She has shared many common data analysis scenarios to do with SEO analysis, and offered influence for interpreting, visualizing, and sharing results. This is the fun part of our SEO processes because whether you're using data science or not, after efficiently analysing your data you should communicate the output with stakeholders. Looker
 Studio is great and can be part of it, but you'll have to become better at it, because the data is getting better and better each day."

How do you ask the right question to define your goals?

"This is a learning curve, especially if you don't speak to developers or speak bots as Jamie Indigo does. It can be a difficult process but you should identify what your end goal is, get all of your data from Search Console and try to merge it with data from rank tracking tools.

You could use position tracking, for example. Combine multiple data points and identify what you intend to do within that process through data analysis. Everything will come together and you'll find an easier and faster way to do that without using spreadsheets or any other solutions."

In terms of collecting data, do you collect all the data available to you or do you determine specific types of data to collect?

"Getting all the data you can is one of the worst things you could do, because then you'd have to clean the data. When it comes to identifying what you want to do and how you're going to do it, keep that goal in mind and try to find the best data sets that you can get your hands on. This is a vital step.

Let's consider Google Search Console data. There are thousands of keywords there, and some of these you won't really care about. Some are just typos and others are in our reports even though we don't care about them. Excluding all of these from your data set will give you better data analysis at the end."

What are you looking to take out when you clean data?

"It depends on the irrelevant data and the data that has errors. You should remove any data with errors or that's repetitive. You can think of data analysis as a way you haven't learned yet, that's a beefed-up version of what you already do in Excel. For example, when you get your data in spreadsheets, you can just remove the duplicates and get rid of the data that's not suitable. When it comes to data analysis, there are models you can use to get rid of error data. On top of that, you can use your analysis to determine what doesn't serve you and get rid of it."

What's the best starting point for SEOs when it comes to different types of analysis?

"It depends on the analysis you're doing because, when you're doing keyword research vs crawling, things change. For example, you can crawl your website through Python and anything that you do there is going to be different from your last attempt or current keyword data. You can slice it down but it's very dependent on your task. I recommend starting with cases applicable to what you are currently working on. For example, I am learning how to deal with dictionaries at the moment to better understand working on schema with Python."

Conventionally, data science has been seen as more of an enterprise SEO thing. Should data science be approached by SEOs working in SMEs?

"Definitely. One would think it applies to enterprises more than it does to small and medium businesses since the data sets are larger in comparison. However, wearing a data science hat will help all kinds of businesses, more often than not. Frankly, in an enterprise SEO setting, the data science team would take
the burden of coding from you but it's still important to deliver your story and communicate goals clearly between teams.

The best approach is to have an understanding of what can be done with the help of data science. When it comes to working with smaller businesses, you'll mostly be doing the analysis. Data science will save you time, help you focus more on your strategy, and handle the heavy lifting so you can provide better results for your clients. Data science is something you can use regardless of the type of business you're operating in."

Can embracing data science help SEOs communicate with other departments in the business?

"When it comes to communication, it'll always be very much dependent on your communication skills. However, data science can help you derive more meaningful results from your data set. That's going to save you time that you can use to think about how to communicate things to different teams within your organisation. Paige Ford spoke about how she switches hats when talking to different teams in her day-to-day on the Opinionated SEO Opinions YouTube series. That can be a good resource on how you can present your data to different teams."

How often should this data scientist-type approach be part of regular SEO activities? Does it need to be ingrained into day-to-day activities?

"It depends on how you're going to use it. At the moment, you might think you're not going to use it that often - but you can use it to crawl XML sitemaps and get the static in bulk. This is better than typing everything into Screaming Frog. It can help you do these repetitive tasks much faster and more easily. If you are going to take that route and use it to automate some of your tasks, you can definitely use it daily. What you'll want to do is analyse the data that you have at hand and then you might end up using it less regularly."

Can this have a measurable impact on your SEO success?

"It may indirectly affect your SEO success because you'll be able to drive accurate and meaningful conclusions from your analysis based on your data set. However, for the most part, it won't affect your capabilities as an SEO, i.e. you cannot say, 'I did this analysis and it drove X% increase.' You can identify your goals and use data science to do what you were doing but in a faster and more meaningful way.

Human error is common and, when analysing big data sets, your mind can wander and it can become difficult to see the whole picture. Data analysis models are helping us to identify the gaps and where we are missing. When it comes to analysis and identifying the next steps, it can help you become a better SEO and more easily measure the effects of your work. Data analysis is useful for creating more time to spend on a strategy and executing or understanding data in new and better ways. You'll also save on projects and discover new approaches for firing up SEO in different ways.

What shouldn't SEOs be doing in 2023? What's seductive in terms of time, but ultimately counterproductive?

"Not keeping up with what's new. Also, not linking and cooperating with other channels. It's an evolving industry that's influenced by recent developments in the digital sphere. That's why it's vital to maintain curiosity.

What we're doing is exciting and the world continues to move faster and faster. Keep close contact with other marketing channels to help you retain an integrated strategy for your brands that will positively affect everyone involved."

Begum Kaya is an SEO Consultant at BK Solutions and you can find her over at begumkaya.com.

Use BigQuery (SQL) to create your own SEO tool—Omi Sido

Omi Sido believes that every website needs unique SEO in 2023, because every website is unique. He suggests that BigQuery is currently the best way to get a holistic picture of what is happening in your space online.

Omi says: "The best way to achieve provide unique SEO is by using Google BigQuery and SQL to create your own SEO tools, processes, automation, and workflows.

Why BigQuery?

"Every website and every business behind every website is unique. Every website belongs to a different niche and we know that Google treats different niches in different ways, hence the SERPs looking different in different niches. Last year, one of the best ways to do your SEO was to analyse the SERPs for your niche. This is an integral part of SEO strategy development. Every website, department, and business needs unique, boutique SEO.

This year it's going to be BigQuery. 2-3 years ago Google released a new edition called Google Analytics 4. This version of Google Analytics is a completely new way of measuring performance.

Believe it or not, GA4 comes with free access to BigQuery. You don't have to be a Google 360 user to have access to BigQuery. There are some limitations but every individual, every SEO, and every small company can use BigQuery successfully.

Why BigQuery? It's a very robust business intelligence platform database. In simple terms, it allows us to gather information from all digital platforms, including Google Analytics, Search Console, any SEO tools that use APIs, CRMs, and even offline data. When you combine all of this data you'll have a holistic view of your customers, their journeys, and why and when they buy from you. What are they buying after visiting your offline stores? How long does it take them to buy from you? What are the most profitable keywords? The possibilities are limitless. No single tool can do that for us, and there will probably never be a tool like this on the market - that can give us all the information, and a holistic view of our customers and their journey.

To summarise, every website needs unique SEO because the SERPs are different for every single niche. This is so natural and so normal for Google because, let's not forget, we are not the customers; our searcher is the customer. Google has to satisfy that person - the person who is searching for our products. They don't have to satisfy the SEOs. On one side, we require unique SEO and, on the other side, we've got access to a free tool from Google that can give us a unique angle. It can give us a holistic view of everything that's happening with our website and our customers."

In terms of SEOs getting started with BigQuery, what are the critical data sources you need to take in?

"It's best to start with Google Analytics and learn how to use Google BigQuery, because there is a bit of a learning process. Learning SQL is quite easy. You can just go and learn SQL from W3Schools.com. This will take roughly a month. Connect Google Analytics 4 to SQL and start from there. See what BigQuery can give you.

Then, you can extract data from your SEO tools and create what's called a data pool. Everybody within your business can have access to this data and you can visualise the data in Looker Studio. The benefit here is that you're going to have this holistic view that will be available to everybody. Imagine you've got access to Semrush, and now others within your company require work access too. You wouldn't be able to grant this and you wouldn't be able to teach them how to use it. However, you could easily give them access to your Looker Studio reports.

Going back to the uniqueness of SEO, every website is different. Even every product is different. The way we present the same problems on websites is different. It's important to appreciate that every product or service will be ranked differently by Google and in different scenes. Put in a unique SERP and that will be unique for your product. By embracing this, you'll know that your website needs unique SEO.

If someone asks you to rank a page for your business, the first question you should ask is what is your SERP? Don't just go to a conference and listen to what the speakers are telling you, because that might not apply to your business. You need a unique SEO approach that's exclusively tailored to your business. This will be important to your success.

For example, a client comes to you and says they've invested a lot of money into ranking a page successfully. They've invested a lot of money into search content creation, images, etc and the page is now number 1. However, they're not getting anything from this page. If they're wondering what's wrong with the meta description, copy, etc. you could simply go to the SERPs and perhaps see that Google is ranking a lot of headers and videos at the top of the page.

If you open the SERPs, you'll probably see some good advertisements and then a lot of videos that actually answer the main topic question without having to navigate elsewhere. Who's going to click through and visit a page if they can get the answer in the SERPs? If you type 'how to cook the perfect medium rare steak' and you see a video in front of you in the SERPs, you're definitely going to watch the video and probably not click through to see if the copy is amazing. In the case of the client, you'd tell them they need unique SEO and to produce a video, try to rank this video, and include it in the SERPs. That will promote the best chance at success."

It sounds like quite a manual process of checking the SERP, is it possible to automate the process of feeding what's happening in the SERP to BigQuery as well?

"In Google BigQuery - if you're good enough you can use SQL and even do the now famous machine learning - you can gather all the information from all your competitors. If you come up with a good algorithm, you'll know what you need to rank well. This algorithm will gather all the information from all your competitors, including the way they rank your competitors. You can get this data from Semrush because it's a competitor research tool. You can plug this into BigQuery, plug in the machine learning algorithm and you're good to go."

Where do you get started with this machine learning algorithm?

"It's not easy. It's best to start with GA4 and BigQuery, then think about the rest. It's a process. You have to know GA4, and you have to know how to use BigQuery - which is a new product for those who don't have Google 360 and have never worked with BigQuery before. Learn how to use the tool first, learn the basics and then start thinking about machine learning.

It's not that difficult. You could make progress with BigQuery within a year, especially if you go to W3School.com. SQL is not a difficult language and there is an excellent article from Google about how to do machine learning with SQL. It's hard to believe that they're giving us BigQuery for free now."

Is there any danger that they'll be taking it away soon, and you'll be in corporate loading all your data into that?

"That seems unlikely. They'll want to draw people in so that - when they see how it works, and how good it is - they'll start thinking about Google 360, which is relatively expensive."

Once you take your data into a tool like BigQuery, will you have more historical data to play with so you can do comparisons?

"Yes. You can make clever comparisons from different tools and even offline data. Take all the data from your offline shop and plug it into BigQuery. You just have to find a match there because you'll need something common between everything, like a product name, price, or something like that. You'll even be able to find out know what people buy from you after they buy from your offline shop. This is crazy to think.

If you see that a lot of people go to your shop and buy a product and then go online and search for a cable for this product, you can accommodate this situation. You could publish a table about the cable and a lot of people are going to buy from you because you've got the data. However, you need unique SEO because it's not the same for every single company, business, and website.

This is not just the future of SEO in 2023 but the future of SEO in general. It's going to be about bespoke SEO and the usage of big data. Practical big data, which you can now access for free."

What shouldn't SEOs be doing in 2023? What's seductive in terms of time, but ultimately counterproductive?

"In 2023 and beyond, SEO shouldn't be applying general SEO statements and advice. When building an SEO strategy, you should tailor it to the business needs. It's not only about rankings or about people coming to your website, but how you bring something to the table. Most of the time it's about revenue. How do you bring revenue to the table?

If you listen to all of Google's algorithms you'll see they have machine learning elements to them. This is the future. It's getting more and more difficult to apply general advice - that you've heard at either a conference or that you've seen somewhere on Twitter - without thinking about what's actually important to the website, and the business. SEOs need to stop copying and pasting the same strategy and applying it to different clients."

Omi Sido is a Senior Technical SEO at Canon Europe and you can find him at omisido.com.

Test more and test smarter—Emily Potter

Emily Potter encourages SEOs in 2023 to keep testing, but do so more often, with more efficiency, and working alongside your product teams to make the most of this information.

Emily says: "Building on my tip from last year, SEOs need to test smarter and with more frequency. Also, when you are testing, you should definitely still be working with your product teams - that's even more true than it was last year. Get testing with those product teams and be doing it more efficiently and more often."

What SEO testing activities should be happening that often aren't?

"The main thing is that you should be talking with your product teams. I should caveat what I'm saying with the fact that we work with enterprise companies, so we do enterprise testing and they can test at a much bigger scale than smaller websites.

Working with the product teams is so important because we're moving into the world of page experience, and user experience is impacting SEO a lot more. Even without that, product teams are often the source of a lot of frustration for SEO teams. Product teams will roll out things like JavaScript frameworks that are running client-side, and they're negatively impacting SEO.

Testing is a great way to make your business case and show them how their actions might be harming organic traffic. Show them that you're on the same team. Your product teams are also a source of great ideas and development on your website, so you should play to each other's strengths.

There are a lot of different names for these teams: product teams, CRO teams, development teams - others might just call them their engineering team. They are the people that are designing what your website actually looks like for your users and how it functions. They also tend to be doing CRO testing, which is the thing that often comes into conflict with SEO testing."

What do you mean by testing smarter?

"One aspect of that is that you can use smart technologies for fast testing, if you have the capability. That might be something like SearchPilot, which can actually change your website, or it could be trying to get set up on edge, if you have something like Cloudflare to be able to make agile changes to your website. It's using technology to bucket your pages in a way that makes them really sensitive so you can get positive results for really small incremental changes.

First, you split up your pages into statistically similar buckets. That might be taking 100 pages - 50 are control and 50 are variant - and splitting them up not just in equal traffic, but in similar traffic patterns. Then, you can detect things like 3% uplifts that come from very minor changes that you're making on your website. For enterprise customers, that can be a really big deal. That's all coming from smart bucketing and modelling.

Having things like edge or SearchPilot, or a way to change your website really quickly, means you can do lots of different tests in a short space of time. A good example is something like title tag tests. What we do with a lot of customers is we come up with 10 different title tag formats that we want to test, and we churn them out really quickly. Often, we'll land on one that's positive.

Particularly now, with Google overriding title tags, you can't easily predict what's going to work. You can't predict how Google is going to reformat your title based on the changes that you made, what parts it's going to crop out, or if it's even gonna show up at all. You should be throwing tonnes of different things at it, and you need to have the setup to do that at scale."

For smart bucketing and modelling, does SearchPilot and/or edge SEO allow you to test statistically similar pages and then implement the tests on a set number of pages?

"You need two different things. You need the technology to create the buckets and the model, and then you need a separate technology to make the change to the various pages. The meta CMS edge technology is what's going to change your variant pages. Then, you need some sort of analytic tool to help you make statistically similar buckets, and also model the impact of the change while your test is running.

At SearchPilot (with the caveat that this is for enterprise websites) we have a neural network model. We use machine learning technology to do this, which means we can create buckets based on patterns that are machine learning in real time to try and create statistically similar buckets. It's constantly changing things to figure out exactly what works best at a scale that you just can't do with humans.

Then, there's also the ability to forecast the variant sessions. With forecasting, you're measuring against the same thing, rather than measuring against control pages (which is going to introduce a lot of bias because you never perfectly split those things up)."

How could you implement this for a relatively small website, perhaps one that's a few hundred pages and WordPress-based?

"There are a lot of different tools online for doing that. There is paid software that's a bit cheaper, and there are blog posts on how to create buckets and run a causal impact analysis, for example. All of that is going to be better than what we have done historically in SEO, which is: we make a change, we see the graph go up after that date, so we call the change positive. You want to do some sort of controlled testing to get an idea of whether that traffic increase was because of an algorithm update or because of the change that you made. That's what you want to get a better answer for.

It can seem like you're losing something when you explain it in that way because people stop being able to point at graphs that go up and to the right and say, 'This is because of the change we made.' The selling point is that you are probably making changes that have positively impacted your traffic, but an algorithm update or something seasonal has happened, so it looks like your graph is negative. In reality, though, that's not because of the thing that you did and you're missing out on gains by not being able to separate all those things.

For smaller websites, it's a bigger challenge because you're working with less traffic and less data. It's still worth doing, though. Something we do with customers that have lower traffic levels is just run the tests for longer. Running these tests for just a week is probably not going to be possible at low traffic levels. You want to be looking at something like six weeks. The key is to figure out how to get a controlled testing environment as much as you can."

If you have a page that is performing reasonably well in terms of traffic, but you want to tweak the content, is it better to test those changes before implementing them?

"I think so. As an example from our own website, which is very low traffic relative to our customers, our CEO (Will Critchlow) did some basic keyword research for our Case Studies pages. He made some changes to the titles and H1s, and we could see that there was some improvement from that date, but he actually knows when he made the changes, and which pages he made them to.

Those improvements might still not be because of the change that we made but, once you at least know the best-case scenario, you can start to figure out what is possible within your website and how you can make changes to the best of your ability with the constraints that you have. That is going to work out better than just looking back and seeing if you made the correct change after the fact. Try to think ahead of time, in terms of what you can do and implementing as much as you can."

How do you look at statistical significance, and how do you know if you've actually won with your new scenario?

"Our neural network model, as we call it, generates confidence intervals for us. They are the foundation when we're talking about statistical significance. What the confidence intervals say is, 'We are 95% confident that the change will fall between this lower end and this top end.'

Something that we're all more familiar with would be the COVID vaccines, for example. For the COVID vaccine, they would have said something like, 'We're 95% confident (the scientific gold standard) that this is going to be effective from 75% to 95% efficacy rate'. They would have set a threshold that the bottom of that range needs to hit. Then we can say that, at worst, it's going to be at that threshold and, at best, it's much higher. That's what we're talking about when we're talking about statistical significance. To translate that to SEO testing, we might say something like, 'We're 95% confident, this is going to be a plus 1% increase in organic traffic to a plus 15%'. That means we are very sure that it will be positive, but the improvement could be within that range.

We generate all of that with the neural network model, but there are other tools you could use as well. CausalImpact is something you can look into. You can input the data that you have, and it will generate those confidence intervals for you. It will help you with your business case conversations as well. If you go in just saying that top-end number, your boss is going to expect the highest possible increase, even if you have a really wide confidence range."

If 95% statistical significance is the gold standard, do you stop running the test once you've achieved that?

"You want to leave it a couple of days to make sure it stays but, if it does, you can stop there. Going back to the idea of testing smarter - it's important to remember that we're doing business, not science. The 95% level was created by the scientific community, so it's technically a bit arbitrary. They have good reasons to have that standard for something like a vaccine; if it goes wrong, it could kill someone. For our cases, something like 90% confidence or 80% confidence could be fine.

We talk about using a matrix of your decision-making, for both what the result says and how strong your hypothesis is. Say you're running a test where you're adding a really high search volume keyword to the title tags - which is a pretty well-established way to improve your rankings in SEO. If that was positive at the 90% confidence interval, you might decide that the odds are good and you should roll it out, rather than miss out on those gains because you're aiming for a scientific gold standard."

Should you always be testing or is this something that you should just do every few months or so?

"Something else that Will, our CEO, has been speaking a lot about lately is what he's calling 'Moneyball SEO'. It's similar to how statistical analysis is used in professional sports. In basketball, for example, you are starting to see much fewer shots from the middle range – they are either from next to the rim or from the three-point line. From statistical analysis, they found that aiming for mid-range shots is not worth the two points that they give you, because the odds of making it are not as good as they are when you are close to the rim, and you get one less point than if you were shooting from beyond the three-point line.

Similarly with SEO, what we're finding at SearchPilot is that a lot of 'mid-range shots' that we're taking (like updating meta descriptions) are not really giving us much in return. Whereas all the things that we implement from positive tests, which are closer to the rim, are what you should be focusing on.

Focus on things that have evidence to say they will actually work, whether that's from something like SearchPilot or because you've run your own testing methodology. Something we find tends to work, regardless of whether you're testing or not, are things like new content and links. Those things do well for SEO and should always be part of your strategy.

When it comes to those mid-range things, if you can't test them or find a good reason to actually implement them and invest resources in them, you shouldn't be spending your time there. A lot of SEOs could benefit from thinking a bit more like that. If you can, you should be testing."

What shouldn't SEOs be doing in 2023? What's seductive in terms of time, but ultimately counterproductive?

"I think SEOs should stop updating templated content. We see this on enterprise websites all the time. At some point, they generated a template and they spend a lot of time trying to improve that template across the whole website. What we're seeing is that, very often, the templated content isn't any better than the previous template content that they had.

If you add new content or really good quality content, then that tends to move the needle. Often that's written by copywriters, or we've seen very advanced AI technologies that our customers work with create unique localised content. Replacing boilerplate content with new improved boilerplate content is something that doesn't move the needle very often, but it's very resource intensive for SEOs. On the other hand, just updating your title tags tends to make a big difference - though you should definitely test it because we see swings both ways."

Emily Potter is Head of Customer Success at SearchPilot and you can find her over at @e_mpotter on Twitter.

Use a test and learn approach to define your business objectives—Si Shangase

Si Shangese encourages SEOs in 2023 to get over a fear of forecasting and use a test and learn approach, utilising historic data, so that you can look to the future, confident in the knowledge of what does and doesn't work.

Si says: "My number one tip is to use a test and learn approach to define business objectives. This will help you gauge the true value of SEO activities against business outcomes.

The reason why you do a test and learn approach is that you can forecast into the future and understand what works and what doesn't work. Forecasting is one thing that SEOs detest, so there is a love-and-hate relationship between SEOs and forecasting.

Nowadays, SEO is part of a marketing remit within large organisations, and you have to treat it professionally. Conducting test and learn, and increasing conversion rates or customer satisfaction as a result of your tests, can have a massive impact on the bottom line."

Where do you recommend that SEOs get started with test and learn?

"Before you even get to the test and learn approach, the main thing that you need to do is control your data. This is for in-house SEOs and agencies as well. You need to get as much information as possible and warehouse it. As SEOs, we love to use Google Search Console, but you've only got 16 months' worth of data there unless you pipe it into an API and warehouse it in Snowflake or BigQuery - which I highly recommend that you do.

If your agency is not doing it already, please get them to do it. If you're not doing it in-house it would also be worthwhile, although I do understand that it is expensive to use large warehousing platforms.

What that will mean is that you've got a lot more control over your data, including your keyword rankings. With some large platforms, they only keep the information or data for your rank positions for up to about three years, at most. Warehouse as much of that as possible because, when you run your models and you test and learn, you want to look at historic data on any changes that you made on the website, and how that impacted performance.

There are obviously a lot of factors at play within SEO, and algorithm updates that happen. However, if you've got historic data, you can layer that in. Then, when you use these machine learning algorithms that I will recommend in a minute, you can normalize against either the changes or the algorithm updates. You can see whether a change that you made on a particular section of your website actually had an impact - negative or positive.

Control your information and control your data first. That will allow you to set the scene for any sort of testing and learning approaches that you put in play."

What's your go-to piece of software that you use to number crunch that data once you have stored it?

"Forecast Forge. I'm not affiliated with them in any way, shape, or form - and they don't pay me to say this - but Forecast Forge is really good in terms of actually helping you crunch all the data and information. You can input your variables, in terms of what you want to forecast or have a look at, and analyse it using their machine learning tools or platforms. It's also relatively cheap to purchase, so it's accessible across SEO team sizes. They also support Google Sheets, which makes it easy to share things online."

What is it about machine learning that makes it so useful for a test and learn approach?

"People make machine learning sound sexier than it actually is. Basically, it's an algorithm that can predict certain patterns, and that's all it is. When you're plugging in 2, 3, 4, or even 5 years' worth of GSC data, the model can take that span of information and it can look at seasonality, trends, monthly data, etc., and it can create something that's a lot more robust.

You can look at the things that will help you create a better forecast, for instance. If you create summer campaigns, you can put them into the model, and it can show you what that would look like if you ran the same kind of campaign next year. You can also get different bounds - so you can get upper, medium, or lower bounds. This is very surface level, in terms of the capabilities of what you can do with the information.

If you are a brand, it can give you product launch outcomes. If you've launched a product in the past and you want to launch a new one, you can use its modelling information. Machine learning is just learning what happened in the past and using that to predict what might happen in the future. It can give you modelling information about what a product launch might look like, for instance.

This can help you align your SEO activities and give you bigger picture thinking across your marketing planning, and with other activities that you might be running. You could be running a social campaign or an out-of-home campaign, and you want to know how SEO will pick that up. You can layer all the information from the past into a model, and you can start to see the outcome.

Also, when you're creating new pages, you can see how different sections of the website have impacted overall traffic. This is really great if you are a product manager or somebody that's working in-house that wants to raise a business case.

With the models that I have worked with, we normally get about an 87% confidence ratio, in terms of how accurate a model is compared to what it is trying to predict. The more information you have, and the more you teach the model or normalize anomalies for certain information or data, the better you can understand how the business might perform this year and the year after that."

Should you start by taking historical events that have happened in your business, seeing what people do with different areas of your website, and trying to improve for when that happens again in the future?

"Yes, that is a good place to start. With test and learn, you collect all the information that you have from a previous activity or anything that's happened in the past, and you're layering that into any campaigns that were running during that period. That could be Black Friday, Valentine's Day, or

Halloween, for instance. You're then able to identify how that event impacted your business.

When you run your data through something like Forecast Forge, you can use the models to essentially see the outcome for different scenarios. What would have happened if we didn't run any campaigns? What did happen when we did run the campaigns? That gives you benchmarks for the future - or starting points. For example, if there was lower search volume for a particular term in 2020, and there is a 20% increase in demand by 2023, then you can play that into your model as well. You can say that you will still see an increase of X%.

If you also gather a lot of information about your clients or competitors, you can use other third-party tools, such as Similarweb. You can plug that data in and have a look at what their traffic results have been historically - and they have an API. It is a lot more enterprise tool, for larger brands and larger organisations and agencies. You can also have a look at how they would have performed if they didn't run any campaigns during important events such as Black Friday, for instance.

When you are comparing yourself against your competitors, or against yourself and what you did or didn't do in the past, you can test out different scenarios for how things played out. Then, you can essentially see what would happen in 2023 for any campaigns that you want to run from an SEO point of view, that's integrated with the rest of your marketing plans."

How did you know that you had achieved an 87% confidence ratio with your forecasting model and what is the importance of that confidence percentage?

"That's a great question. We ran this particular model consistently with a couple of my clients at a previous agency. We would create a forecast, and run that forecast alongside the actual results. What the data was showing us was that it was about 87% close to being correct. Essentially, there was about 10% give or take - either positive or negative - in terms of its accuracy. If you predicted that you would have 100 clicks per month, the actual traffic for that specific landing page or keyword might have actually been 110 clicks or 90 clicks, for instance. When I tested it across multiple clients, that's how I knew that the confidence of that model was about 87%.

If you're an agency and you are doing something similar, with Forecast Forge perhaps, this is where you actually have scale. If you run an agency, you can implement something like Forecast Forge across all your clients, and across different verticals. Using the seasonality data and the machine learning algorithm, you will know what your specific confidence levels are within a specific industry - whether that's 70%, 80%, etc. Then, when you create those models and you pitch it to a client within that specific industry, you can say that you know (after testing the model with several different clients) that it is going to be about 70% or 80% correct. It gives you the confidence to say that you either want to take a project on, or you might give it less weight.

If you are a product manager or you work in in-house SEO, it might be a bit more costly for you. With whatever SEO tool you are using to look at your competitors' monthly traffic results (such as Semrush, Ahrefs, or Similarweb), you can take that information, take that data forward, and look at what happened in the past. You can put that into your model, put your own brand into the model as well, and you can see what the confidence is in terms of what actually happened.

Then, when you are doing a business case, you can say that you've looked at the industry, you've analysed through this learning approach, and your modelling is going to be about 70% accurate, or whatever that might be. You might have a lower confidence percentage because a particular sector or industry might not have the seasonality data, or it could be an industry that was hit by a medic update, for instance. There are a lot of black swan events that need to be factored into the model as well.

That's why it's so important to test what happened in the industry, test what's happening to your competitors, and collect all the information together. Then, when you are making those decisions on the accuracy of your model, you have that historic information."

What shouldn't SEOs be doing in 2023? What's seductive in terms of time, but ultimately counterproductive?

"The main thing to stop doing in 2023, from an SEO point of view, is overcomplicating things. I'll give you an example. When we create technical audits, there are a lot of things that we want to fix. However, some things that we want to fix within a technical audit might not actually give us the right results.

The guys at SearchPilot do this quite well because they run SEO A/B tests. If you do make a change on your website, A/B testing gives you an idea of how that change actually impacted the performance of the site, whether that's positive or negative. For certain websites, for instance, fussing about with the alt tag doesn't make any sense because the guys at SearchPilot found that it actually has a negative impact. Therefore, optimising that for an exact match keyword could hurt the site's performance.

Keep things simple. Focus on the most important things for the business; focus on good content that's specific to your market or your niche. Make sure you're using things like the Flesch-Kincaid score to understand the readability of the content for your particular topic or your niche.

Also, people think that links are dead, but speak to the guys at Majestic and they'll tell you otherwise. Focusing on good content marketing is still a really good thing to do, and I see a lot of SEOs are not really focusing on this as much. They're leaving a lot of opportunities on the table for their competitors. Your website does exist out there in the ether, but you still need to promote it, tell people about it, and create engaging content that can do that for you."

Si Shangase is an independent Digital Consultant specialising in OneSearch, measurement frameworks, and digital transformation. You can find him over at kuduhq.com.

Keep trying new things—Luis Rodriguez

Luis Rodriguez believes that the key for SEO in 2023 is to keep experimenting to keep up with Google's changes - and not give up after just a few tries. If you want to keep up, you need to be willing to take some risks.

Luis says: "My number one tip for 2023 would revolve around internationally expanding your experimentation with SEO. Over the last year, we have seen many changes in search engines. Other updates have come up and increased competition. Plus, we don't have any more pandemic distractions as well. Hence, we can all dedicate ourselves a little bit more to SEO.

That mainly increases the difficulty (as it does every year). but one of the constant principles is creating high-value, unique, and helpful content. Nevertheless, there are always new tactics and approaches coming up. Therefore, SEO experimentation is the ultimate tool over the next year.

When experimenting, there are three high-level takeaways. The first one is how to define success. Not all experiments and markets are the same. Thus, you must determine what you want to learn from specific experiments. Define whether you want to increase the click-through rate, target a new keyword, or expect incremental traffic. Defining these objectives will help you automate difficult decisions.

Secondly, you should define how you measure your success. For example, you don't want to end up scaling up something internationally that is not beneficial for your overall business or for your objectives. With specific methodologies, I recommend using causal impact analysis, which Google has repeatedly recommended in many ways. This approach identifies relationships between a test group, uses those relationships to plot the expected performance, and compares the actual results against the desired results, generally implementing causal impact analysis. However, you must have a decent amount of traffic to your pages.

Thirdly, you must persevere. We know that not all the concepts work out in different markets. Hence, you need to try out and have various iterations of the same idea in other markets and page types. Sometimes these concepts will not equate to the same benefit as well, so perseverance will become your best bet.

Lastly, it helps to try other experiments in different parts of your site while checking for what else is out there in the SERP. It always helps to identify common practices you can take and scale up internationally."

Regarding these experiments, how do you know what to change?

"You can rely on three things. First, your competitors in the SERPs. Did you try something similar but not necessarily unique? For example, the trend of adding listicles into your titles whilst trying out different numbers may actually work out. It's just a matter of observation to see what works.

Secondly, consider your historical data. What similar experiments from the past have you tried out? How can you iterate on that same concept? Looking at the SERPs can give you a lot of clues about what you can do next.

Thirdly, trust your gut and your creativity. Put yourself in the reader's position: as someone who is looking for something better than the previous version."

How many tests should an SEO expert expect to run regularly, depending on the amount of traffic to their site? How do you decide on how long it takes?

"It depends on the data itself. Sometimes, you need a longer time to understand if you made a significant impact. What truly matters is understanding if you are achieving your objective. It also requires you to build some expertise on when to say 'that's enough'. Basically, obtain a statistically significant result, and have a good way to observe that change."

Can you replicate the same tests across different country's websites? Or should you always look at the local market and design tests specifically for the local market?

"You can do both, because a lot of knowledge is transferable in different markets. It is also important to notice what people are doing in that market. For example, the type of content people deem helpful in Taiwan is not always the same content people consider valuable in the UK. Sometimes, it could be differences in the language or even the length of the information.

Thus, understanding your market and then localising known wins from other markets can help you find the best solutions."

What software do you use to go about selecting and managing your tests?

"Mostly, homebrew pro software is the go-to. Googling things and observing what is in the SERPs among competitors is also great source of information. Search Console also provides great information about what kind of keywords are providing traffic, and it allows you to experiment with concepts of keywords.

Ahrefs and Majestic also help to understand some of the competitors' tactics and which pages truly matter. Tableau is also one of the best tools because it allows you to create certain dashboards on the go and extract information from those tables. Basically, having some SEO off-the-shelf software that gives you quick insights helps out the most."

What shouldn't SEOs be doing in 2023? What is seductive in terms of time, but ultimately counterproductive?

"SEOs shouldn't hold still. The field is changing quickly, and the algorithm is becoming quite complex. Not changing your website can be counterproductive.

In experimenting and trying new concepts, you can always get more traffic and rank for new keywords. So, keep trying new things."

If you've had some content ranking for a competitive keyword phrase at number one for the last couple of years, should you keep on tweaking that and trying to gather even more traffic to that page?

"The benefits to your website are unlimited. You decide how much traffic and when you want to venture into new keywords. Even if you are ranking at number one, there are many more keywords you are not yet ranking for that you could."

Luis Rodriguez is Head of SEO at Booking.com and you can find him at booking.com.

15 EVERGREEN ADVICE

Don't forget the basics—Nik Ranger

Nik Ranger implores SEOs in 2023 to remember the basics and stop committing cardinal sins in the areas of crawlability, rendering, indexability, ranking, and conversions.

Nik says: "If you can't crawl, render or index your pages then you can forget about rankings, getting those rich snippets, and conversions. My number one tip is: don't forget the basics. When we think about how Google is evolving, if anything we're seeing the crawl capacity diminishing. It's more important than ever to consider how effective and how often crawlers are discovering and parsing content before we think about playing in the SERP personalization space.

The cardinal sin I see that plays out time and time again is that these key questions are either completely missed or glanced at without consideration, until those landing pages that they've decided to create don't get indexed or perform poorer than they could have.

These things are so important to think about. You need to think: 'How is the search engine crawling through my site and understanding the structure of my site? How can I present the information in the best way, so that it will render that content, index those pages, rank for things that I want it to rank for, and therefore have conversions that ultimately affect the bottom line?'

That should be your new mentality. So let's start there."

When you conduct an initial crawl, what are some of the things that you should focus on?

"Search engine crawlers are ambiguous, they can enter the site from a multitude of ways relatively regularly (or not, take a look at the date next to your URLs in search console or in your log files - that's the true canary in the mineshaft) with a series of guiding logic, rules which we can unpack and evaluate the signals we're presenting to those crawlers to ensure that we're able to get the most out of your crawl capacity.

One of the first things to do is open Search Console, have a look at the Pages folder, and see what is indexed and what is not indexed. Google is very good at telling you, from your pages that are not in the index, what that is attributed to. Has it been crawled and not indexed? Has it been discovered and not indexed? Are there 404s in there?

Even just going through and checking there first will give you a sense of what else might be going on with your site. I mentioned earlier that crawlers operate with a series of rules, here are some useful things to keep in mind.

There are two types of main signals you can use and it's important to keep this logic when they overlap; hints and directives. Directives are things like index, noindex, follow, nofollow, none, noarchive, indexifembedded and noimageindex. Index doesn't need to be added as it's considered default, but essentially it means that the page is indexable: all green lights, add it to the index.

The noindex tag isn't default, you have to mark it up, but it means that the page is non-indexable, so get rid of it from the index. A follow tag (which should always be the case when it comes to your internal links) parses link equity (equity is the same as authority, or what people call 'link juice') to the page respectively. Similarly, the nofollow tag doesn't parse any link equity to the page. None is a noindex and nofollow, so nuke it from the index. So they're the main directives, and you'll see these a lot. But, there are more directives that help manage your site, especially if it's quite large.

Unavailable after tag is super useful if you've got pages that have a limited shelf life on your site, like event pages. You know that, after a specific date and time, these pages aren't relevant anymore. You may want to keep them on your site if users want to look at past events, but they're not important to have crawlers re-visit them so the unavailable after tag tells crawlers after a specific date and time, not to crawl that page.

The noarchive tag is awesome if you don't want the pages to stay in Google's cache. It's especially useful if you're wanting to update content and the date is really important. Indexifembedded is a cool recent new one that is specifically for content embedded via iframes, which comes into effect only if it's accompanied by noindex. These directives are key to help police the crawlers to understand your structure and to index your key pages more efficiently, while excluding the pages you don't want to be considered. Just make sure they're added as <meta name="robots" content=""> in the <head> section, as this is the easiest way to implement it without contradicting anything.

Hints are things like a canonical tag pointing to another page. That is to say, 'This isn't the primary version of this page, please consider parsing link equity consideration there.' Your audience can view these pages and crawlers can still index these pages (a hint means it can ignore it) so if you really don't want that to happen, there may be flaws in your canonical logic somewhere else on the site. I had an instance whereby we fixed the canonical logic across thousands of pages and it started respecting where proper canonical tags had been placed. I don't know if that's 100% why, but it's a good case to at least fix the logic elsewhere if your canonicals aren't being respected.

Robots.txt is a hint, not a directive. This is helpful to know when looking at indexed, though blocked by robots.txt. This is a pesky one because the fix is counterintuitive. Even though you may disallow crawl through a subfolder of your site, Google can ignore this and index it anyway. You can't add a noindex and fix it (where I think this part is counterintuitive) because, for a noindex to be read, it can't be blocked by robots.txt. So the solution is to get rid of the disallow, place a noindex tag, wait for the crawler to re-crawl that subfolder/page path and then get it out of the index. Maddening, but that's the game of thrones of the crawl to index.

Your XML sitemap is a useful way of being able to add all of your important pages to a list that you can submit for index. It's also a super useful way of inspecting the performance of that URL list. I will say though, in the past I've pushed to have dynamic sitemaps be able to be created across multiple routing channels only to find that it didn't significantly impact the indexation of URLs. I'm now inclined to think that sitemaps are useful to debug and find index issues, but a sitemap alone cannot help index issues. It is a mere hint suggestion in the face of the internal and external link equity that crawlers pay way more attention to.

This is a perfect segway to talk about how crawlers prioritise pages that have been updated and have strong PageRank being parsed to and through them. Even though PageRank has been depreciated publically as of 2016, a version of it still exists within Google's algorithms, which we understand as the internal linking structure of the site. These internal links are so important to get right because they parse link equity between each other and highlight the relative importance of that page to the page it's being linked from.

Search engines understand this, and use that internal link structure to evaluate the importance of pages on a site. This is why pages that have had their crawl path cut, been internally nofollow linked, orphaned, etc., don't perform as well. Internal links are the unsung hero of all of this: the backbone to the muscle that's holding it all together. I pay an inordinate amount of attention to a site's internal link structure when first working with them because of this reasoning and while others call the optimisation of internal links 'link sculpting' - it'll always be a fundamental part of the strategy as I can get significantly improved results combined with understanding what motivates a user to click through.

Doing this assessment allows you to consider the site holistically, find patterns, and deploy changes to influence greater efficiency. To find patterns, you may want to take a sample of pages to see if there are clues. You can see how Google has interpreted any URL in the site by copy/pasting it to the URL inspection tool. It will show you if the URL is on Google, not on Google, or if the URL is on Google, but has issues.

Click on the page indexing drop down to find the discovery source of the URL. It'll check whether it's listed in your sitemap, the referring page (where Google has crawled to find this page via internal links), when the last crawl was, the user agent it used (for example, Googlebot smartphone), if it's been blocked by robots.txt, the page fetch, indexation status and the user-declared/Google-selected canonical. It'll also show the enhancements and experience, whether or not the page is mobile-friendly and if the schema providing context to the content on the page is correct.

Google now considers invalid errors with your structured data to diminish your chances at competitively ranking your pages, so ensuring this is fixed is even more of a priority. Something overlooked is the view crawled page option where you can see the rendered HTML, a screenshot preview of the link and more info. I've already mentioned JavaScript, but this directly shows (or doesn't show) what Google has rendered and cached in its index, if there's missing content in the HTML, or the full page with the relevant content you're hoping to index isn't in the screenshot, or critical resources couldn't be loaded - it's all going to show up here."

What are some of the common issues that you're seeing with rendering?

"Rendering is the silent killer of content. It's so insidious I took a whole chapter for SEO for 2022 just to talk about this, but it's just as relevant for 2023 as it was back then - if not, more. That's because more and more developers are utilising JavaScript to deploy complex features, content and interactive elements. The important thing to know is that JavaScript is, by default, client-side rendered, which significantly adds load time. In fact, a study conducted by Onely showed that JavaScript gets crawled 9x less than HTML because of it's lag in the render queue. So, crucial content may not get added to the index, meaning all that hard work isn't even being considered for the ranking of your pages.

To check this on a page, I'll right-click, go down to my Inspect, open up DevTools, go to Sources, and then open up the bottom tabs there with Network Conditions, or even in the Coverage tab. Essentially, I want to see what is in there that could be render-blocking. That is a good place to start. Render-blocking resources are those static files like your HTML, CSS, JavaScript, fonts, etc - the things that are vital to the actual render of the page.

Usually, when you are checking this, you will find all the resources that Google has found to be critical, and have to be rendered in order to display the page. These are the files that Google views as critical for them to process, so it puts everything else on hold.

One of the easy things to find and prioritise are these render-blocking resources. On the other hand, non-render-blocking resources don't necessarily postpone the rendering of the page (the browser can safely download them in the background after the initial page render). Not all resources that the browser deems to be render-blocking are essential, at least for the first paint. It really depends on the original characteristics of the page.

Shortening the Critical Rendering Path and reducing the page load time are good things for us to really focus on when we think about how a page loads.

A lot of people will give little screenshots from Lighthouse, and give generic advice, but it is really important that you are actually looking at these resources and understanding: are these critical or should they be non-critical? Then, making them into non-render-blocking resources, perhaps by deferring how they download.

You may want to decrease the total number of those resources using bundling, fewer HTTP requests, reducing the size of these resources, minification, etc., so that the page has fewer bytes to load up these things."

What are some common reasons why Google may choose not to index something?

"Knowing what is and what isn't being rendered is a great way to get that much more performance out of your pages if you've got development but not content resources.

In cases where you've done all the right things (you've got it in the sitemap, you've got internal links, you've got breadcrumb schema, you've got really good rich content on there, and you've optimised it the best that you can) but it's still not added to the index, Google pays attention to the Link Graph, the Social Graph, and the Knowledge Graph.

Part of why it's important to test your site's crawl to render to index efficiency is if you're adding pages (like subcategory pages or blog pages for example) and they're not getting indexed quickly. Now that could be because of a number of things, but in the case where you've done all the right things, it's probably because your site's not authoritative enough or the quality of your content doesn't meet the standard where it deserves to be indexed.

I'm not going to go into detail about content quality (one of the other contributors to the book will deep dive that way better) but, for authority - consider cross-channel alignment here. Post amplification is vital and important as it allows that post to be seen by an existing audience. I've tested this with a company that started tweeting out when they'd post content and found that it got indexed much quicker as it generated attention.

I had an old client where I was looking at the crawl and 84% of everything that Google crawled was actually a 404, which was crazy. This was a massive, multi-million-dollar site, but it was only getting a fraction of the attention it should have been. I went in there and saw that it was actually from an old migration that went horribly wrong, but Google was still picking up a tonne old pages that were missed in the 301 redirect plan.

In addition, they had an old version of their staging site from the previous version indexable, with all of their old and new ideas still indexed. That was something that we only discovered looking at the settings, going to the crawl stats and seeing the crawl request breakdown.

It was also here that we discovered the live site was 95% client-side rendered with a massive bloat of JavaScript file types lagging the load time. This resulted in a loss of millions of dollars for the business but created a new urgency to re-evaluate their platforms, third parties, and project manage a new migration after an expensive prerender solution became unviable.

This is an extreme case but working with them to identify their entities, have mapped internal link plans and structured data to their information architecture - the results are outstanding. And this all came from remembering the basic fundamentals of SEO. If you can't crawl it, render it, and index it, it won't rank and result in revenue."

Nik Ranger is a Senior Technical SEO at Dejan Marketing, and you can find her over at dejanmarketing.com.

Perfection can be the enemy of progress— Helen Pollitt

Helen Pollitt believes that, in 2023, SEOs need to stop striving for perfection and trying to tick every box. Instead, you should be paying attention to nuance and looking for ways to be more forward-thinking.

Helen says: "When we begin as SEOs, we have a checklist of things to run through for every activity we do. A list will help you be aware of all the things you need to look at and check. This type of mentality can cause you to be too reliant on the notion of 'best practice'.

When you very first start adding pages to your blog, you might look to get all the green ticks from the SEO CMS plugin you use. Alternatively, you might have a set number of characters you want to put into your page title to ensure it's not truncated in the search results. There are lots of tools at your disposal, and most of them will have some sort of traffic light system to flag errors on your website. Tools identify red or amber errors, and it'll be your responsibility to turn them green.

That's fine when you start but, as you mature and your experience widens, rigidly following checklists become problematic. You should rely on some of the context that you know about particular websites, or look closely at what worked in the past and what didn't. Put the checklist to one side and appreciate that 'best SEO practices' are becoming somewhat obsolete.

Every website, every vertical, and every industry is different. There are a few core tenants that we embrace as SEOs, i.e. 'If you do X you can reasonably expect Y.' These assumptions are less realistic than you'd think. What works well on one website isn't 100% transferable to the next. That's why most of our answers start with 'it depends', because that context and nuance are really important. When you're striving for perfection in SEO, sometimes you lose a bit of that nuance and the differences that have a big impact on a site. A lot of the things we try to fix don't need to be perfected.

For example, most websites don't have an issue with their crawl budget, but that doesn't stop people from spending time going into their website and relinking every link that points to a redirecting page. That might be good for maintenance and it's good practice for staying on top of things, but unless you've got lots of URLs that are redirecting, with lots of links pointing to these redirecting URLs, the chances are that this practice isn't going to impact how much of your website Googlebot can get through.

Doing something for the sake of ticking a box won't always drive growth. Avoid wasting time and resources that could be put to better use elsewhere."

What are some examples of other small technical issues that SEOs spend too much time on?

"The load speed of a page. There are wonderful tools like PageSpeed Insights that give you a score out of 100. However, if you score 95/100, will achieving those remaining five points really affect your growth?

Otherwise, you'd be wasting lots of goodwill from the development team making tweaks when their expertise could be leveraged elsewhere."

What causes conflict between SEOs and product teams?

"As I've already mentioned, it has a lot to do with perfectionism and the checklist attitude that can cause risks and unnecessary discussions. Product teams just want a good website - and SEOs want that too. However, when we stick to a checklist, we can get regimented in our understanding of what a good website looks like.

The fix recommended by the product or development team is often good enough. It might not be perfect in the eyes of SEO, but it's worth it if it does what it needs to, and it's not going to cause any issues from an SEO perspective. There's no point going back and forth for months on end arguing over the implementation of something. If the way something has been suggested is easiest and it's still going to work, just go with that."

What are some SEO activities that can drive growth but often get neglected?

"Technical SEO should be prioritised more because getting your technical foundation right is imperative for growth. Make sure your technical approach improves the performance of your website. From here, you can work on your content and matching user intent. It's important to get the foundation of a technically good website first and then build the rest from there."

What tools should you use to determine how Google sees your site?

"Crawl logs are great because you can look at how Googlebot is navigating around the website and see where it might be tripping up or where it's visiting pages more or less often. You can also use Search Console, that's Google's way of telling you what they're seeing on your pages.

Bing's equivalent is highly useful too, especially in the insights it can provide. Using a combination approach can help you get a good understanding of what search bots see when they visit your page."

What are some typical warning flags you see in log files and what would you do to fix them?

"Things like orphan pages. If you're not expecting a page to be an orphan, you can identify this through log files. You can see where search bots aren't visiting pages and investigate.

There could also be pages that exist on your site that you weren't aware of. Sometimes filtering systems can cause additional pages rather than taking you through to an existing page. Search bots have a way of finding those pages that you might not have been aware of. Looking at your log files can help you to see where those additional pages are being created so you can identify whether they're going to be problematic or not."

Should every website be looking at log files or is this mostly associated with bigger websites?

"Log files are often difficult to get hold of, especially if you're on the agency side. Ideally, we'd all have access to log files and be able to assess the information there. It's often not as simple as just going for it, though, because getting your hands on those log files can be a challenge. That could either be for security reasons or difficulty getting hold of the right person in your client's team.

Log files will give you lots of insight as you analyse them. Even small websites have technical issues that can create additional pages you might not be aware of. For example, the way you tag up a blog could cause additional category pages you hadn't noticed. Sometimes these aren't easily picked up through crawls. When you look at your log files you'll be surprised by the pages search bots hit that haven't been identified through a standard crawl."

What are two things that SEOs could be doing on-site to drive some quick wins?

"There isn't a one-size-fits-all answer for this because you need to know what your strategy is. Quick wins for one company are not going to be quick wins for another. Always start with a robust strategy for achieving the on-page fixes you're looking for. Assess whether you need additional pages to address particular search queries.

You might notice that users are starting to search differently and that you need to do things on-site to accommodate that. This should all become part of your SEO strategy, otherwise, you're going to deviate too far and fail to get the same results you've committed to achieving as part of your strategy."

How often should you be building and reviewing your SEO strategy?

"Your SEO strategy should be in line with how your company operates or how your client's strategies are implemented. For instance, if you have a yearly marketing strategy then you probably need a yearly SEO strategy. How in-depth that strategy goes will be dependent on the format and makeup of your company. Plan at least six months in advance, and have a rough idea for the whole 12 months.

However, with changing circumstances it's important to be flexible and willing to adjust. If you know there's something big on the horizon, you might have to be a bit more agile with your strategy. Have a loose plan and idea of where you want things to go, but nail down the specifics, the KPIs, and the actual activity that's happening to underpin that strategy. You might have to do this a little bit more in the short term."

What shouldn't SEOs be doing in 2023? What's seductive in terms of time, but ultimately counterproductive?

"Steer clear of the siloing that happens in SEO teams. We need to let go of the viewpoint that SEO is a separate channel. We often see that when teams are collaborating to come up with campaign ideas, there is a tendency to perceive SEO as risky and sitting in its own bubble. We're missing opportunities, we're missing out on insight from data, and we're missing opportunities to collaborate on ideas and create a total omnichannel approach to marketing. We need to fully integrate our teams and work together in true collaboration. We really need to see ourselves integrating more and lessening those silos between SEO and other marketing channels."

What have you done in the past to be more successful at forging greater integration with other people in the business?

"SEO can seem like a black box that's difficult to understand. No one really knows where they should and shouldn't be integrating with the SEO team. Education is a great place to start. Speak to your copywriters about how SEO and copywriting work together. Talk to your paid team about how paid search and organic search work together. Talk to your CRM team about how SEO can help keep customers within the funnel. When you're a part of training initiatives and start having those discussions, you'll open up opportunities for collaboration with others. You'll learn about the other disciplines and think about how SEO could benefit or hinder a given situation. Until you're having discussions where you're looking to educate, learn about other channels, and have them learn about yours, it'll be difficult to be successful going forward."

Helen Pollitt is Head of SEO at Car & Classic and you can find her @HelenPollitt1 on Twitter.

Look at the relationship between content and search intent—Mert Azizoğlu

Mert Azizoğlu reminds SEOs in 2023 that the main logic of SEO has always remained the same. You still need to be aware of how the content that you create is relating to the intent of the users that are searching for it.

Mert says: "In 2023 you should be looking at the relationship between content and search intent."

What is the content relationship?

"First of all, you should clarify what is happening with the algorithm updates and look at what Google is telling us with them. You will then understand the relationship between content and search intent.

The main logic of SEO has remained the same: it's to provide a crawlable platform and create useful content for the users. For example, with there being more mobile devices than ever before, mobile-first SEO has become important. Also, EAT guidelines and Core Web Vitals are centred around users being able to access the right information quickly with a good experience. There has also been an increase in AI-based content that is being addressed with Google's helpful content update.

The common point in all of this is that Google is trying to ensure that users can access the correct information with the best experience. That's why you need to pay attention to the relationship between content and search intent."

How do you know that you're creating the correct information for the right user?

"If you have a landing page that calculates something, for example, you need to host a calculation tool in your content. It would also be important for your content to mention what the calculation does and how it's used. You'd need to explain the calculation details and add a calculation widget to the landing page because users will be searching around this calculation. It's important to give the right information that people are searching for."

Should you take a keyword phrase and look at the SERP to see what's already ranking for that to determine what content to write?

"Yes, exactly. The discovery/search intent is based on great keyword research. You should execute your keyword research to perfection."

What's your process for great keyword research?

"Use it as the roadmap for finding the right search intent for your landing pages. You should start with keyword research and then group all of your keywords into categories based on intent so that you understand the purpose behind them. You can divide your keywords into transactional, informational, navigational, etc."

When determining what keywords to target at the beginning, how do you go about doing that?

"First of all, you need to know your target audience very well. Then, you need to know your direct competitors and your site competitors. You may know your direct competitors but it's important to check the SERPs to determine all of the competitors that you have, from the SEO perspective.

Your direct competitors are businesses that sell similar products and services, whereas your site competitors are people that are ranking for the keywords that you want to target. You can have different competitors for your landing pages and different competitors for your service pages.

Then, you can start your keyword research by using SEO tools like Ahrefs, Semrush, or Keyword Planner. It's all about high-quality content targeted at the right users."

In your experience, what is high-quality content and does it change depending on what country or industry you're operating in?

"High-quality content is based on a well-designed landing page. Regarding text content, you should support this with videos, podcasts, or some widgets. You should follow the old-fashioned steps to creating high-quality content.

You need to pay attention to the search intent that is driving users to the exact landing pages that you are working on if you want to secure high-quality content. AI-based content is improving daily. Google launched the helpful content algorithm update to emulate them. It will be curious to see what's coming next and what will be expected on the content creation side."

Some SEOs embrace AI content and others recommend just including it on minor pages without much traffic. What's your opinion on AI content and how we can effectively use it?

"It's not only creating the content but creating title and meta descriptions using AI as well. Let's assume that you have a big eCommerce website with lots of product pages. If you want to get indexed quickly or reduce your work time, you can use AI to create titles and meta descriptions and even product details.
Right now, it's uncertain how Google detects whether the content is AI-based or not. It would need some NLP data with the help of crawling and indexing as well. AI is a concept that's worth being open to, but not committing to wholeheartedly."

How do you produce content that puts the user experience first but at the same time ensures you have SEO in mind?

"This touches on the idea of Conversion Rate Optimisation (CRO), however, you need to pay attention to the user experience for technical SEO too. You should follow the steps to align with the Core Web Vitals guidelines. There are some really good software solutions like PageSpeed Insight and Google Search Console that will help you to improve the website experience according to those guidelines.

You can use some software like Ahrefs to measure your visitor's interactions, and use CTA buttons as part of your content and measure your user's interactions with those. You should optimise your content according to the data that tells you how your users are actually experiencing your pages."

Does improving the UX of your website result in a measurable improvement for your SEO?

"Yes. Five or six years ago, this wasn't as relevant but now it's really important from an SEO perspective because users want to access the correct information very easily. You shouldn't have lots of interstitials or pop-ups on your website, you should focus on giving the correct information to the correct search queries as directly as possible.

Your users need to have their needs met as soon as they reach your site. That's why you should pay attention to the UX while users are visiting your landing page."

What shouldn't SEOs be doing in 2023? What's seductive in terms of time, but ultimately counterproductive?

"We used to think that a long word count was good, but John Mueller made a statement about this in 2022. He said that poor content isn't about word count, it's about the relationship between search intent and landing pages. That's why we should pay attention to high-quality content.

Stop producing pages that have no obvious relationship with other things on your site. You can demonstrate what that relationship is by incorporating schema on your pages. Certainly, if you're an eCommerce site you'd be making a mistake to publish product pages without any markup data on them. Forget word counts and focus on the quality of content and support it with the right schema markups.

Schema markups didn't used to be important in the past. However, now they are really important and are improving daily. If you're an eCommerce website, schema tags are becoming more and more important, for example. It's crucial to make schema improvements to present your product pages better as well.

Otherwise, we should keep the same logic and appreciate the importance of backlinks. We should analyse our backlinks, where internal links are essential. When creating high-quality content you should combine this with other content within the site. For example, if you create a blog post you should add an internal link to important landing pages or the home page. Keep doing what has always been relevant and important, but focus on the relationship between content and intent."

Mert Azizoğlu is Senior Technical SEO at SEO Sherpa and you can find him over at mertazizoglu.com.

Roll up your sleeves and do the manual work—Kerstin Reichert

Kerstin Reichert believes SEOs in 2023 need to stop relying so heavily on tools to tell you what to aim for, roll up your sleeves, and do the manual work yourself to identify what really matters to you.

Kerstin says: "As SEOs, we all love working with tools, especially when there are new features available in our favourite tool. We love exploring new tools because they make things fast and efficient. They're great at helping us to do things at scale. However, there are risks to consider if you purely rely on what you get from tools. For example, you might get overly obsessed with a certain score, like a health or speed score. You might then spend all of your time, effort, and budget on doing that one thing very well.

Another risk is that you might see a drop in rankings. The tool could tell you there was a Google update and encourage you to take a counterintuitive action. Also, you could end up not working on content around certain topics just because the tool says there isn't much search volume around it. Imagine not covering something just because a tool says it's not a good idea! It's great to start with your tools, but then really make an effort and do manual research to look into the things that will move the needle.

Everyone uses very similar tools. If you purely stick with these it'll be difficult to get the upper hand. You need to do the extra work. Yes, it might be time-consuming, but there's no way around it. The same applies to link building. If you just look at everything the tools suggest you would only build links because your competitors have links there. Alternatively, you could proceed with something a bit more creative, find different opportunities and get some traction there. It's very important to use your tools as the foundation and then really go in and do the manual work as well."

What things are best done manually? Are you sometimes better off targeting your market rather than a particular keyword from tools?

"It's not necessarily better to do things manually, but it is a necessary step that logically follows. When it comes to technical SEO we need to rely on tools. However, it'll still be on you to focus on the right things and understand what the tools are telling you. For example, a tool might flag

X% of your pages as not being indexed. You could assume you need to change that but they might actually turn out to be PPC landing pages that are not meant to be indexed.

Don't just take what the tool says and implement something that might harm what you're doing. In terms of the technical side, some tools have the classification of what's a high priority, what's medium, and what's low. That's generally a good indicator, but it might be different for your website. It might be that there's something else that should be a priority. Use the tools for the audit, but then use your brain to look at the resources that you can work with. You can then prioritise the items on your list manually.

If you look at content, there's also a lot you can do manually. You can use your tools to come up with initial ideas, topics, and topic clusters that can be broken down into subtopics. From there, you should take it further and think about what other content ideas are relevant. Place priority on looking at what your customers are asking. What are the questions that come up frequently? You should have a rule where, if someone asks something three times, you write an article about it.

It all depends on how many resources you have and how much time. You will see lists of competitors for your content in most of the tools, but you should spend time evaluating whether those are really your competitors and then go into search results and look at what type of content they're producing. What formats are they using? Is it written? Do they have images, infographics, illustrations, videos, etc.? What can you do to deserve those top positions in search results? What can you do to become the best search result?

A big part of the process is looking at what is ranking, how you can make it better, and using this insight to interview your internal experts. You can also get stats from them and write the content before sending it back to your subject matter experts. They might then leave a comment you can integrate within the article or video. When advice comes from experts, it's even more valuable. Put the time and effort into making sure you highlight people as your own internal experts. You should also create real estate around the website to highlight them as experts, show their profiles, and find opportunities to feature them on third-party platforms, news sites, and partner sites. You can spread their expertise and build their profile so that it's more authoritative when they contribute to your content.

It starts with keyword research and looking at what topics are relevant, but it goes much further than the initial research. This applies to any part of SEO that you want to focus on."

Regarding being the best thing on the internet for your space, what does that mean in practice?

"Manual research is all about seeing what others are doing. You have to be deserving of ranking in those top positions. You can do this by seeing what you can offer that's unique and whether there is something you can do that's not just a repetition of the same topic coverage that's already out there. That's where you can do the manual work and determine how you can make something better and more comprehensive.

There might be lots of topics already covered, perhaps with complex wording that isn't very accessible. That's where you can be unique: take these topics and make them more accessible to a wider audience. You can incorporate feedback from social, or from your CEO directly, to be the best thing on the internet for that given topic."

From your experience of working with lawyers and compliance officers on getting a piece of content published, if they push back on the first piece do you push back yourself?

"It depends. If something is just misleading or factually incorrect then there's no point in convincing anyone - because you shouldn't do it. If you work with a tool like Slack, communication can be really fast, so things don't take several weeks or months. If you form a good relationship with your colleagues they'll be aware, check things, and ultimately come to you.

Sometimes there might be differences in preferences. You might want to be less out there in your marketing message or push it from a different angle, for example. Then your colleagues could say, 'hold your horses. That might be misleading.' It'll require a bit of give and take, where compromise is important. You should establish a very good way of working together where there's trust and where things aren't flagged unnecessarily. They'll know it's meant to be for readers and for marketing purposes, so they should understand that, and stick to flagging the things that really need it. Luckily that won't be too often.

If there's no direct communication between the person reviewing and the person writing, you may or may not get a review back. This can be avoided by building really good relationships, which is easier when you have direct contact with the legal team or you're not part of a huge corporation."

How do you decide who your competitors actually are and then how do you go about benchmarking your performance against your competitors?

"It can be tricky if you have a wide range of products with different sets of competitors. What you need to do is look at it from different angles. You can start by going around the business and asking your sales team who they see as the biggest competitors. You can ask your product team as well. You can then perform your manual research online by looking through the internet and seeing what else is out there.

Look at tools and see if you have a topic cluster competing with you on that. Sometimes that'll work and other times it won't. Some tools will have difficulty picking these up because there might be only so many keywords they're tracking. It'll be a combination of looking at the tools, asking around the business and then doing your manual work.

You can then take a closer look at the competition - whether they're product-related or content competitors, for example. They might not have the same offering but they might actually compete in the same content space. You can take that away and look manually at who is getting your traffic and how much of a competitor they are in terms of product and content. Then you can prioritise and benchmark them so that's set up within your tool of choice for each area. This is great if your categories are quite different and segmented."

What shouldn't SEOs be doing in 2023? What's seductive in terms of time, but ultimately counterproductive?

"We shouldn't be following a checklist approach. We all have very good checklists and everyone loves a good checklist - they're shared everywhere. There are so many checklists out there. We should step away from this approach, as we should with tools. Use these as the foundation, but always explore further. Always set your own goals and priorities and start working from there."

Kerstin Reichert is the SEO and Content Lead at SeedLegals and you can find her over at seedlegals.com.

Establish an SEO quality assurance framework—Aleyda Solis

Aleyda Solis gives SEOs in 2023 tips for creating a quality assurance framework that will prevent you from becoming part of your own SEO horror stories - including education, validation, and monitoring.

Aleyda says: "Learn and set an SEO quality assurance framework to avoid SEO f**k-ups, and it still might not be enough. Unfortunately, we have way too many errors in our SEO processes. Over the last year, I have seen very important SEO processes using well-established methods that are being held back by errors.

It's something that obviously hurts our efforts, because of the way that these challenges have been tackled. It still hasn't been properly fixed. Every single year, we see SEO horror stories, and we definitely need to make them stop."

How do you put together an SEO quality assurance framework, and what does that look like?

"There are three key areas that I want to talk about: education, validation, and monitoring.

The main problem is that, whenever we think about an SEO quality framework and avoiding errors and mistakes, we focus on catching things quickly and combatting the damage that has already occurred. If we are only looking to catch errors after they have happened, we are already behind. It is very important that we establish actions within the framework to educate and prevent SEO mistakes in the first place. Many of these mistakes, issues, errors, and bugs happen because of misunderstandings about what we want to achieve.

We also need to set a good validation workflow to avoid launching SEO errors too. Of course, if they do end up happening, we can then minimise the issues by implementing the actions we have set in place. We need to set really good monitoring systems to catch SEO incidents for us in a way that actually makes sense.

We get alerts all the time from lots of tools, and there are often so many people involved that we end up overlooking many of these alerts. It's important that your alerts are configured in a way that makes sense, and they are effectively captured by the people who are handling different parts of the process."

What do people need to be educated on? Are you talking about education for SEO teams or other departments within an organisation?

"For anybody involved in different ways. Firstly, you need to be educating stakeholders, and even decision-makers. Many of the errors that we end up seeing are a result of the boss or the director suddenly asking for something to be changed. These decision-makers ask for changes because they are not aware that there would be implications from an SEO standpoint.

It is important that we educate, and we evangelise, at different levels. Every time that I provide an SEO recommendation (when we kickstart the process and I provide the first analysis of my recommendations and actions) I will do small training sessions with the development team, the copywriting team, the product team, and then also the decision-makers - to make them aware of what is critical to keep, what is critical to change, and the 'why' behind it.

That will make it so that, whenever there's a decision involved (even one that is not to do with SEO) they keep it in mind, they are aware of it, and they know the potential implications that their actions can have. It's important that we align and that different areas of the business involving SEO are aware of what we are going to change, why we need to make a change, and what we need to keep. Then, they will take this into consideration whenever they need to do something in their own areas."

What are some typical errors that can occur if you don't employ adequate validation?

"One example is when canonical tags have been set with certain criteria, but then there is a product launch or a launch of a new section or area of the site. Things get rewritten and, all of a sudden, no canonical tags are shown, or they are shown with a different configuration or criteria. These types of mistakes happen again, and again, and again.

Many websites have a very high dynamic inventory, so we cannot expect to catch all the mistakes that are generated because of the nature of these pages. We need to set rules to prevent them and invalidate them in the first place. Whenever a facet runs out of products - and you know that they are not going to be back after a certain number of days - you can configure those pages to show that. Don't allow the page to just become a 404.

You need to identify how you can manage these pages so that you can make the most out of them, keep leveraging them, and give a good user search experience at the same time. It is necessary to do more than just set checklists and integrate and automate certain types of validation within a CMS. What is important is having alignment and an agreement between the teams involved.

You need to agree that they're actually going to use the checklist and not just have them sitting somewhere and forgotten about. You also need to agree on what is going to happen if something goes wrong. We always assume that we will never launch anything that's wrong, but it does happen from time to time. What are you going to do if something gets launched that will hurt crawlability or indexability in a very severe way? If it cannot be fixed in the first 24 hours, it probably needs to be rolled back, and you need to have an agreement on this beforehand. Don't wait for that issue or bug to occur before you sort out what needs to happen when it does.

These types of rules need to be agreed upon at the start of the process. Make it straightforward: 'Something wrong has happened in this area. Can we fix it within 24 hours? No? Then we roll back and fix it with more time.' That way, you know that you won't end up really damaging what you have been able to achieve so far.

Assumptions are the mother of all f**k-ups. That is why good validation needs to be in place. You should all agree that you will crawl and validate before launch and crawl and validate after launch - because things can happen in between. Never assume that just because there aren't any SEO releases you don't need to check. Some other kind of configuration might have changed, which could have repercussions for SEO. It's always important that you have this kind of workflow agreement or alignment for validation before and after the release, and then establish what will happen if something goes wrong."

Is there software that you can recommend for automatically checking that everything is up-and-running and in place?

"I actually love ContentKing for this, because it allows you to run it in real time. It will alert you as soon as something goes wrong or as soon as something happens. You can also configure the alerts so that they are context-aware and make sense for you.

For example, if there are certain types of pages that need to have a certain type of configuration, you can set those rules and configure the alert to go to exactly the right person that needs to be informed. That's much more helpful than getting it sent to a generic person or informing you whenever a page becomes noindexed - even when it doesn't matter to you.

Of course, there are also SEO crawlers, where you can set recurring, prescheduled crawls, and you can configure those crawls for a group that is actually necessary. You don't need to do a full crawl of everything, just crawl certain types of pages that are representative of your website – and of every type of page on the website. Then you can generate a report and easily make comparisons to the ideal configuration of each of these pages. That will allow you to confirm a before and after, as well as track whenever something happens in real time."

When it comes to monitoring things like rankings, traffic, conversion decreases, etc., do you still recommend GA4?

"Yes, of course. For traffic and when you're using Google Analytics, GA4 will directly offer the insights that you need. It's pretty straightforward to configure - but you can set this at every single level.

I mentioned ContentKing, but you also have tools like Little Warden that allow you to set real-time alerts. It's also about how you configure the tools, ultimately. A lot of rank trackers like Advanced Web Ranking will allow you to configure alerts in a way that actually makes sense for you.

You can set it so that, if you have a huge decrease in rankings (more than X for a certain group of queries that are very important head terms for you) then a specific person is alerted, or you can set it so that you are alerted when you stop showing SERP features that are very important in that context. SEO tools have become very powerful in that regard. From rankings, to crawling, to content changes, title descriptions, etc., you can configure alerts with a variety of tools in order to be informed when that happens."

What shouldn't SEOs be doing in 2023? What's seductive in terms of time, but ultimately counterproductive?

"I really dislike hearing the question: 'Is this actually a ranking factor?' At this point, you should not be chasing what you think Google might be considering a ranking factor. Google wants to provide the best user search experience for their user. Ultimately, you should do whatever you can to make, develop, or improve your content so that it is best-in-class and provides the best possible experience to your users.

You should be taking authors into consideration, if that is going to clarify for your users that this article has been written by an expert. If it's going to provide confidence and trust - and allow you to better connect and establish your authority with your users - then add it. The effort is minimal.

We know that Google wants to get there. Google wants to replicate and simulate the type of criteria that users take into consideration when assessing information. Do it. Stop thinking about whether Google is actually thinking this, not taking that, or already capable of identifying one thing or another. If you are always thinking like that, you are always going to be behind. Go and take a look at what the best-ranked players in your sector are doing, do it, and do it much better than them. Stop asking: 'Is this a ranking factor yet?'"

Aleyda Solis is SEO Consultant and Founder at Orainti and you can find her over at orainti.com.

Stand out—Fili Wiese

Fili Wiese gives SEOs in 2023 advice on how to stand out from the crowd, improve the quality of your content, and ensure that your pages are a step above the competition.

Fili says: "Stand out – it is super important. You need to make your websites stand out from your competition, improve content quality, and have a Unique Sales Proposition that helps you to get the user to come to your website."

Is it the SEO's job to have a Unique Sales Proposition?

"It's not the SEO's job as such, it's actually businesses' job. The CEO and everyone else in the company should know what the company or organisation's Unique Sales Proposition is. It doesn't need to be a business - it could be a non-profit or just an individual - but you need to stand out.

If you don't have a USP, you have a bigger problem. You need to go higher up in the chain of your organisation and figure that out before you tackle

SEO. Once you do have it, it will automatically fill in the blanks for your SEO.

You need to make sure that every indexable page (every page that ranks in the search engines) has a USP. You need to convince users so that they click on the search result, and those pages actually deliver for that user's intent."

How can each individual page on a website have a USP? What are the key elements on pages that can make them unique?

"First, you need to start at the level where the user first encounters the page, assuming they don't know the brand yet and don't know the page itself. This is often from a search engine source like Google, so I'll focus on that for now.

When we're talking about first exposure, we're generally talking about Google search results. At this point, when a user types in a query they come across, say 10 links. Some might be enriched, there might be a Q&A, etc., but they will see 10 organic search results. Of those 10 organic search results, they're going to pick one. Which one are they going to pick? This is where you need to start standing out, and where you need to have a Unique Sales Proposition.

You can do this by optimising the page title and meta description. Make sure that both of these elements contain the right messaging. What makes this particular search result better than the other main search results? Is it a call to action? On top of that, the benefit for the user is very important. What is in it for them? Why should they click on your link instead of one of the other nine?

Of course, the meta description and the page title also need to be descriptive of the actual content on the page. It can't just be a call to action, like 'Hey, click me!', it really needs to be descriptive of the content. Once the user clicks, you also need to deliver - so you actually need to have the content and match the user's expectation that you created in the search results. This is where you start to show a USP, and it has to be on an individual page level."

How can you ensure that you do stand out?

"It's twofold. First, it is good to have a general sense of what the competition is doing on the SERP, but that's not a big source of information on how to improve your overall USP. Again, the USP has to come from higher up. You already need to ask yourself, as a business, 'How am I better than my competitor?' Forget SEO for a second, you need to solve that first.

Then, you can go down to the individual SEO pages and try to communicate this to the user. 'We have free deliveries' is a benefit for the user, as is 'We have the best items as reviewed by X number of users'. 'We are a market leader' is a way of communicating authority and thereby standing out. These are all types of messaging that you can use within the SERP to stand out. That's where you start.

Then, you look at the user intent of people who come to your page. If you have a query that you are ranking for, but no one is clicking, you can definitely improve that. It's a quick and easy win to experiment with and see where you can improve that page with different snippets. The problem is that some of these things take time, especially in SEO.

One of the big caveats in SEO is time. You make a change, hopefully it gets implemented and you get developer resources, then it gets launched, then Google has to crawl it, then Google has to test it and see if it actually benefits the user or if their automated solutions like automated snippet generation are performing better. All of this needs to happen, and it takes time.

What you could do, as a quick experiment to find areas for improvements, is take a query that you're currently ranking highly for in Google Search Console, where you are getting a lot of exposure. Look in those stats for places where you perform well when it comes to impressions, but your click-through rates are non-existent. Maybe you have 100,000 impressions but 20 clicks in total. This is something that can be improved.

Assuming that your niche allows for it, you can take a very limited budget, go through something like AdWords, and experiment with a couple of different variations of ad tags and ad titles - the length of which are similar to what we see with meta descriptions and page titles. With that, you can quickly test what works and what doesn't. The cost can be extremely low, especially if it's a query that is a bit more long-tail where you have less competition from other advertisers. You can still test what will work better in that case, and then you can try to implement that across the website.

I often hear the question of whether or not you can use templates to make your meta descriptions stand out. The word 'templates' is a misunderstood word. Yes, you can template how you make your meta description but that's an action, not an item that is being used. You can template it, as an action, and thereby improve things. Your overall business USP can be templated through every single representation in the SERP."

How many SERP results nowadays are actually using the meta description versus text that has been selected by Google from the webpage?

"I don't know the exact percentage, but I don't think we need to worry about that too much right now. From what I've seen, it's still more than 50% that are displaying the original meta description. Whenever possible, Google will try to use that - although there are caveats, of course, with Google automating more and more around this.

The one thing we have control over as webmasters is what goes into those algorithms. Part of that is the meta description. This is something that we do have control of.

You should use your salespeople to help out with defining some of these meta descriptions. Ask them what helps convert when they're talking to a customer. Does reminding them about free delivery often close the sale? If yes, why is that not in the meta description? You can replace this with any other benefit, of course, but the idea is there and that's something you absolutely can use.

It's also very important, if you are active in any kind of advertising, that you talk to people within the ad team. They often already know what converts and what doesn't convert. They already know how to manage expectations, especially when they're active with things like AdWords.

For anyone who doesn't know, AdWords is paid search - which basically means paid advertising on top of the organic search results. This is something that you do not need to spend a lot of money on for SEO purposes. It is another acquisition channel. It's not SEO, but that doesn't mean that you can't use it as a tool for SEO - to run short-term, limited-budget experiments. Depending on the keyword (and depending on the long-tail part of the target query) you could potentially run a successful experiment for less than 100 bucks, and significantly improve your overall SEO over time.

There's one other element that we haven't discussed as much and that is the delivery on the page. You want to make sure that, when you experiment like this, you also measure success. One way to measure that success is within Google Search Console. You can see the CTR going up, and the clicks coming through, and you can potentially even see the clicks coming through within your log files or within your analytics programmes. However, that doesn't mean that you actually had a conversion.

Anyone can make any page rank - if it's related to certain topics. If you're targeting sensitive areas (like adult-themed or copyright infringement-related topics) it's relatively easy to rank and get absolutely no conversion out of it. People can drive traffic to your website - they can have botnets, etc., working on these things - but that doesn't mean that traffic will actually convert. In the end, our business runs on conversions and even SEO is a tool to drive conversions. This could be a direct conversion, or it could be an indirect conversion, like brand recognition, rather than an actual sale. At the end of the day, SEO supports the business, not the other way around.

You do need to track conversions as well. When you run these experiments, did your conversions actually go up? Did your conversion rate improve? Sometimes you may end up with less traffic, but higher conversions, and that's perfectly fine. If you show up 70 times for a search query instead of 1,000 times, but you have a 20% conversion rate rather than 1% - I would rather have the 270 than the 1,000, because that drives more conversions."

What shouldn't SEOs be doing in 2023? What's seductive in terms of time, but ultimately counterproductive?

"Don't postpone SEO audits. It's important to keep on regularly auditing your website - even if it's just for defensive purposes - to know what is wrong and what you can improve. Google is pushing out updates all the time, even daily. Most of them are unannounced, so you need to keep an eye on what's going on.

If you don't audit your website, you will lose out, and you set yourself up for failure in the future. Even though you need to be careful about where you spend your efforts and your time, you need to make sure that you audit your websites regularly. It should be at least an annual cycle, if not more frequently for some other sites, just to figure out what needs to be improved.

So much changes in SEO and in the industry. Even the title of this series already tells you that things change yearly and, because of that, you need to audit. You need to check and double-check because, without it, you don't have enough information to make business-critical decisions.

When you're looking at what to cut to save time, I would definitely look at the pages within your website. This may sound like a technical issue, but the fewer pages you have to focus on means fewer pages that you have to improve and fewer resources that need to be put in.

There are a lot of things that you can do to improve your website. You can add data to each individual indexable page that you collected from your own users. You can just focus on the pages that really convert and make you stand out. Just because you can have 100,000 pages on the Google SERP doesn't mean that you should. It's better to have a few really high-performing pages (and we're talking maybe 100, 500, or 1,000) versus having 100,000 or 1,000,000 pages that don't perform - even if you have the data.

Just because it's long-tail doesn't mean that everyone's going to look for it. If it shows up only once or twice in a search result, that doesn't mean it's actually going to be ranking or people are going to click on it. In the meantime, you're wasting crawl budget, you're wasting effort, and you're spending money on content writing and other things like that. Refocus on the pages that actually do matter. Prune the pages that don't need to exist on your website. It comes back to standing out. Don't have rubbish content."

Fili Wiese is an SEO Expert and you can find him over at seo.services.

Tailor your CV to every job—Orit Mutznik

Orit Mutznik has advice for SEOs looking to stand out in the job market in 2023, and suggests that you should highlight all your previous SEO wins and avoid sending generic CVs if you want to land your dream role.

Orit says: "Look at your CV and think about everything mentioned in the job description to nail your dream role in SEO."

What are common mistakes that you see in the CVs of SEOs?

"Spending extra time on that CV is important, especially when you are agency side and want to move in-house. It's easy to send hundreds of CVs that are the same, yet you can make slight necessary tweaks and adapt them to the job description if you want to stand out.

One of the biggest mistakes happens when recruiting for international roles for non-English speakers. Often, people send CVs that are not in English. When you apply to a global company, you will want to use English because not everybody understands your language.

Also, English is a critical workplace skill, regardless of where you come from. You can never go wrong with an English CV. Even in multinational companies, their HR department could sometimes be in an English-speaking country. Having both versions would go a long way."

Are there any distinctive features that US recruiters look for in a CV/resume rather than a more European version?

"It's not a case of the European versus American version. Rather, every role is looking for particular things, and it's important to be clear on those.

For example, suppose you are agency-based and want to apply for an in-house role in Europe or America. In the agency, you probably worked with a lot of brands, usually in a very short timeframe. With some, it was brief, and with others, more in-depth. It helps to mention all the relevant brands you have worked with, as well as some details of your involvement, what you did, and the results you achieved.

Since people are looking for relevant experience, no matter where you are coming from. You need to spend some time and work on including those details. Anything that indicates growth (like percentages and statistics) will get you on top of the CV pile. Better still, you can have a general template that you customise for every application."

Would you recommend removing experience that's not as relevant for the job and just focusing on what is most relevant?

"It depends on the amount of information you already have on your CV. You probably would not want to trim anything, because the more experience you have, the better. However, it does still help to pick and choose the experience that is relevant to the role.

If your experience is relatively thin for the role you are applying for, you should highlight other aspects of your experience. Review the job description and look at the day-to-day expectations for that role. If you haven't worked in a relevant company, then make sure that you highlight that part of your experience that is relevant to the day-to-day activities of the new role."

What key things do you need to do before the interview to make it more likely that you'll get that SEO job?

"Firstly, don't say goodbye to the job description. It comes in handy if you are interviewing and helps you to prepare for it. Craft your narrative and think about the questions you'll probably be asked about your experience. Keep referring back to the day-to-day activities required and tailor your speech accordingly. You'll need to show how your experience links with what they are looking for.

Then, if you haven't matched your CV or your experience to this specific role, you can use the interview to do that. The interview allows you to connect the experience back to the current job for companies you have listed that they don't know much about. You can then explain your roles and responsibilities at that company in detail.

Also, it's important to listen to the recruiting manager. Usually, they'll give background and some context on the role in addition to the job description. Using that information, adapt your experience to what they have said and convince them that you are a perfect match based on your experience.

That's also your chance to show that you know your role and your importance because the CVs can be pretty limited. Talk about your projects, how important you were to the business, and the results that you have achieved."

What soft skills are recruiters looking for in SEOs, nowadays?

"You've got to spend those few minutes before the interview to hype yourself up and build some confidence because that is what most recruiters are looking for. On top of that, they are also mainly looking for proactiveness and enthusiasm. That applies at every level, whether it is a managerial position or a junior SEO.

At the end of the day, recruiters are looking for the best people for the role. Those are usually people who are keen and able to hit the ground running as soon as possible. Sometimes, you may be a bit shy. The recruiter might offer some icebreakers in most cases and you must act confident and at least try to fake the enthusiasm because it goes a long way in showing how you will work when hired. Make sure that you don't speak too quickly, either.

For video interviews, deal with all the technicalities beforehand. Find good lighting and ensure you have good internet speed. All these are important and could cost you good opportunities because there are many other qualified candidates."

Are recruiters specifically looking for SEOs who can also work with other departments?

"There are always many departments to work with, from the junior side to the more senior SEO manager roles. All of these roles will require you to work with different people. SEOs have to be influential and communicative enough to work with other departments, which is definitely a skill that recruiters are looking for.

That is why enthusiasm is a critical part of the role - to motivate people that you depend on to do their job well. Remember, SEOs are not independent. They rely on product teams, writers, content people, designers, technical developers, and others.

The main task is always keeping it simple, adapting your narrative to the different departments, and encouraging others. Knowing how to leverage their wins is important because it creates a positive feedback loop, where they produce things for you knowing that you will shine and share that accomplishment with everybody. That way, they will be more motivated to help and work with you because they'll also see you as an advocate for their achievements."

What shouldn't SEOs be doing in 2023 when finding their dream job? What is seductive in terms of time, but ultimately counterproductive?

"Usually, it is seductive for SEOs to mass-produce their CV and send hundreds of them to different businesses. That will not be productive because every role has its peculiarities. You might want to have that balance between time, productivity, and trying to reach as many employers as you can.

When you find a handful of jobs you really want, ensure that your CVs are all adapted to the specific job descriptions. Don't just send a blank, generic CV to a job you really want because you will probably just crash and burn.

It's not worth it losing an opportunity you wanted because you were trying to save some time."

Orit Mutznik is the International SEO Director at Forbes, and you can find her by searching 'Orit Mutznik' on LinkedIn.

CLOSING THOUGHTS

If you've managed to read every single piece of advice in SEOin2023 thus far, congratulations! You've absorbed many SEO tips that will hold you in good stead throughout 2023 and beyond.

Which tips are right for you?

But, what's next? You need to decide on which tips are right for you, which tips you should run with, and which tips aren't the best use of your time at the moment.

How do you decide? It's a combination between your personal passions and abilities, where you see your career going, what industry you're working in at the moment, the current strengths and weaknesses of your company's SEO, and where your current knowledge gaps are.

My advice is to take a few of the tips in the book and run with them – don't attempt to try to implement everything, or you won't do a great job at anything.

Why not get started by selecting a single tip from each chapter of the book and run with that? After you select the tips, learn more about them and then implement them in your ongoing SEO strategy, before reviewing their ongoing value.

Of course, the tips that are right for you are unlikely to be the same tips chosen by another SEO – and that's the way that it should be. Nobody's circumstance is exactly the same.

For example, the following are the tips from each chapter that I might gravitate towards personally: (N.B. I'm not necessarily suggesting that you should select these tips for yourself – you should choose the advice that's best for you)

Chapter 1: Martin MacDonald – Move from SEO'ing for "information retrieval" to SEO'ing for "information suggestion"

Chapter 2: Charlie Williams – Review your content quality (or lack thereof) through content inventories

Chapter 3: Jake Gauntley – Focus on building out your expertise, authoritativeness, and trustworthiness (E-A-T) as a brand

Chapter 4: Mark Williams-Cook – Include zero-volume keywords in your SEO strategy

Chapter 5: Paige Hobart – Map out what you're creating and why across the entire business

Chapter 6: Lily Ray – Expand your content strategy into other formats

Chapter 7: Jason Barnard – Google is a child that is thirsty for knowledge and you need to learn to educate it

Chapter 8: Sara Moccand-Sayegh – Check the SERP and build your personal brand entity online

Chapter 9: Maria White – Focus your SEO strategy on users

Chapter 10: Jan-Willem Bobbink – Optimize your Internal Links

Chapter 11: Greg Gifford – Optimize the heck out of your Google Business Profile

Chapter 12: Joseph Khan – Harmonize all channels and ranking signals into one repeatable formula

Chapter 13: Bastian Grimm – SEOs need to get their heads around the wide-ranging nature of AI

Chapter 14: Luis Rodriguez – Keep trying new things

Chapter 15: Helen Pollitt – Perfection can be the enemy of progress

After selecting these tips, I would then research each topic more and, for each tip, decide if it's something that I should incorporate into my SEO strategy for the coming year.

Now it's your turn to select the tips that resonated most with you!

Thank you

However you decide to use the knowledge contained in their book, thank you so much for being part of SEOin2023.

Remember, if you haven't done so already, we'd love for you to join in the discussion. Why not share what resonated with you most using the hashtag #SEOin2023 @ Majestic on Twitter?

Of course, SEOin2023 was produced as a free video and podcast series as well as a book, so check out the links to the video and audio episodes at SEOin2023.com if you haven't done so already.

Maybe we can even include you as a contributor in a similar, future series? Here's hoping! Don't be a stranger… let's keep the conversation going!

David Bain
Author, *SEOin2023*
Founder, *CastingCred.com*

Printed in Great Britain
by Amazon